Praise for
Class Matters

"Asians aren't 'diverse' enough, poor whites' 'underrepresentation' is irrelevant, admitting Black corporate executives' children is 'leveling the playing field.' In university admissions, the buzzwords are as frayed as their rationales. *Class Matters* shows where we have gone wrong so far, and how we will get to justice, equality, and even diversity for real."

—John McWhorter, professor of linguistics, Columbia University, and newsletter writer, *New York Times*

"How the promise of the civil rights revolution was betrayed for half a century by a system of cosmetic racial preferences that mask growing economic inequality is a tragic and fascinating story. No one is better qualified to tell it than Richard Kahlenberg, who has devoted his career as a thinker and activist to the dream of a color-blind, egalitarian America."

—Michael Lind, author of *The New Class War*

"Exceptionally strategic in a Supreme Court case that ended racial affirmative action in college and university admissions, Kahlenberg joined a pantheon of legends—Robert Kennedy, Martin Luther King Jr., and Bayard Rustin—and found common ground with conservatives to create social and economic class admissions."

—John C. Brittain, UDC School of Law, and former chief counsel, Lawyers' Committee for Civil Rights

"For several decades, Kahlenberg has been one of America's most widely respected, original, and consequential thinkers on education, housing, workers' rights, and affirmative action. *Class Matters* is his semi-autobiographical magnum opus. This engagingly written book is the definitive insider's account of how elite colleges' race-based affirmative action policies camouflaged extreme rates of rich-kid admissions, clashed with public opinion, and crashed in the Supreme Court. Even better, Kahlenberg offers an authoritative, evidence-based roadmap for turning top universities into genuinely diverse communities in which low-income and working-class students of every demographic description are truly well-represented and respected. This magnificent book is not only a must-read; it's the text of the debate on the past, present, and future of affirmative action in America."

—John J. DiIulio Jr., Frederic Fox Leadership Professor, University of Pennsylvania

"Kahlenberg has been manning the lonely ramparts of class-based affirmative action for decades. The world has finally caught up with him now that race-based affirmative action has been struck down by the Supreme Court. In his indispensable new book, Kahlenberg lucidly surveys the history of the race-based approach and explains how class-based affirmative action can and must take its place. Liberals and conservatives alike should read this book as a guide to what might come next."

—Ruy Teixeira, coauthor of *The Emerging Democratic Majority*, and senior fellow, American Enterprise Institute

"For decades, Kahlenberg has been the country's leading proponent of 'class not race' in debates over college admissions. The latest iteration of his argument, *Class Matters*, is characteristically forthright, accessible, and informative. Anyone deeply interested in ongoing struggles over the selection of candidates for seats in the nation's most selective colleges and universities must come to grips with Kahlenberg."

—Randall Kennedy, Michael R. Klein Professor, Harvard Law School

"*Class Matters* is a must-read for anyone who believes diversity should be more than skin deep. With the Supreme Court's decision ending race-based admissions programs, Kahlenberg suggests that social and economic class can be barriers to equal opportunity—regardless of race. His book details ways universities can alleviate the barriers to success they cause."

—Linda Chavez, chair, Center for Equal Opportunity

"Kahlenberg has eloquently argued for decades for socioeconomic preferences in college admissions to ensure equity, diversity, a more interesting education for all enrolled, and more informed and inclusive leaders for the country and beyond. Now that the Supreme Court has ruled against race-based preferences, we really must attend to Kahlenberg's thesis, so powerfully and persuasively argued here. This is essential reading for all who care about our future society and the future of justice."

—Anthony Marx, president, New York Public Library, and former president, Amherst College

Class
Matters

Class
Matters

THE FIGHT TO GET BEYOND RACE PREFERENCES,

REDUCE INEQUALITY, AND BUILD

REAL DIVERSITY AT AMERICA'S COLLEGES

RICHARD D. KAHLENBERG

PUBLICAFFAIRS
New York

PublicAffairs
Hachette Book Group
1290 Avenue of the Americas, New York, NY 10104
www.publicaffairsbooks.com
@Public_Affairs

Printed in the United States of America

First Edition: March 2025

Published by PublicAffairs, an imprint of Hachette Book Group, Inc. The PublicAffairs
name and logo is a registered trademark of the Hachette Book Group.

The Hachette Speakers Bureau provides a wide range of authors for
speaking events. To find out more, go to hachettespeakersbureau.com or
email HachetteSpeakers@hbgusa.com.

PublicAffairs books may be purchased in bulk for business, educational, or
promotional use. For more information, please contact your local bookseller or the
Hachette Book Group Special Markets Department at special.markets@hbgusa.com.

The publisher is not responsible for websites (or their content) that are
not owned by the publisher.

Print book interior design by Bart Dawson.

Library of Congress Control Number: 2024037449

ISBNs: 9781541704237 (hardcover), 9781541704251 (ebook)

LSC-C

Printing 1, 2025

To Bennett

Contents

Contents

My Front-Row Seat in the Battles over Affirmative Action

I N NOVEMBER 2020, WITH THE COVID-19 PANDEMIC RAGING, I carefully took off my mask and sat down nervously in the witness stand at the federal district courthouse in Winston-Salem, North Carolina.

I was in Judge Loretta Biggs's courtroom to testify as an expert witness for Students for Fair Admissions (SFFA), a conservative group challenging racial preferences at the University of North Carolina (UNC). (SFFA and I were also involved in a parallel suit against Harvard University.) I would be testifying that racial student body diversity is very important to achieve on college campuses, but that, according to my research, UNC–Chapel Hill could create an integrated campus without using race if it jettisoned its preferences for privileged children of alumni and faculty and also gave a meaningful admissions boost to economically disadvantaged students of all races who had overcome odds.

Class Matters

I was nervous in part because I was soon to be cross-examined by UNC's star lawyer, Patrick Fitzgerald, a highly regarded former federal prosecutor who knew his way around a courtroom well enough to put powerful figures such as Illinois governor Rod Blagojevich behind bars. But what made me even more uncomfortable was eyeing my friend, David Hinojosa of the Lawyers' Committee for Civil Rights, an organization that was representing UNC students. That group would have the chance to cross-examine me after Fitzgerald was done.

This was a very unusual position for me to be in. Over the years, I'd almost always allied myself with civil rights groups and leading Black officials on issues of schooling, housing, and employment. I had worked closely with civil rights leader Maya Wiley to integrate public schools in New York City and with President Barack Obama's education secretary John King to desegregate schools across the country. I had strategized with members of Congress such as Keith Ellison (D-MN) and the late John Lewis (D-GA) on legislation to make labor organizing a civil right. I had allied with former Lawyers' Committee for Civil Rights chief counsel John Brittain to curtail legacy preferences in college admissions, which is a form of affirmative action for the rich. I had teamed up with former Washington, D.C., school superintendent Clifford Janey to improve civics education and reduce the possibility of electing another authoritarian figure like President Donald Trump. And I would soon be working with Missouri Democratic congressman Emanuel Cleaver to reduce exclusionary housing practices that segregate neighborhoods and schools.[1]

But on the issue of whether preferences at elite colleges should be based on race or class, I was on the opposite side from many of my friends and had allied myself with an unlikely group. The attorneys at Consovoy McCarthy with whom I was working were deeply conservative. A few had clerked for Justice Clarence Thomas, and one was representing Trump to keep his tax returns private. Students for Fair Admissions was the brainchild of conservative activist Edward Blum, who had challenged a key section of the Voting Rights Act—litigation with which I strongly disagreed. Many of my friends—liberals like me—were mystified, even appalled, that I decided to help Students for Fair Admissions.

I had long been convinced, however, that there was a better way to achieve the valid goals of racial affirmative action. I agreed with my liberal friends that campuses needed to be racially integrated. It is crucial that in a multicultural democracy, students learn to appreciate and value individuals of all backgrounds. And I agreed that the nation had to take steps to remedy a terrible history of racial oppression. But giving a break to economically disadvantaged students, the evidence showed, could help universities do both. The UNC case data vividly showed that precisely because of the legacy of discrimination, Black and Hispanic students would benefit disproportionately from an approach based on socioeconomic class. And poor white and Asian students would benefit, too, as in my view they should. The policy would also have a powerful effect on politics. Whereas racial preferences divided working-class white and Black people in a way that advanced conservative interests, economic preferences would remind the groups of their common challenges.

The media depicted UNC as championing social justice by teaming up with civil rights groups. But the dirty little secret of higher education in the United States is that the admissions system mostly benefited the wealthy, and racial preferences for Black, Hispanic, and Native American college students provided cover at places like UNC and Harvard. The framework of race-based preferences disproportionately aided upper-middle-class students of color and sustained a system of favoritism for children of alumni, wealthy donors, and the offspring of faculty. This is because the racial diversity affirmative action produced gave the impression that the larger system was fair. In fact, the University of North Carolina, which prided itself on its politically progressive values and called itself the "university of the people," had sixteen times as many wealthy students as it did students from low-income backgrounds.

Class Matters

Major public and private universities clung to racial preferences because it was cheaper than creating a fairer admissions system that rewarded economically disadvantaged students who had overcome obstacles and would need financial aid to get them through. Colleges acted as if racial preferences were the only way to promote racial diversity, but that simply wasn't true. It was just better for them.

Some worried that if racial preferences went down, universities would just give up on diversity altogether and conservatives would win. The good news, however, was that the evidence suggested that universities valued racial diversity, which had become part of their identity. When barred from using race, they adopted new policies that created both racially and economically diverse student bodies.

My interest in creating a fairer system of affirmative action based on economic disadvantage was sparked about forty years earlier. As an undergraduate at Harvard in the 1980s, I wrote my senior thesis under presidential historian Richard Neustadt about Robert Kennedy's 1968 campaign for president. Kennedy fought hard to dismantle racial discrimination through passage of landmark civil rights legislation, but he came to believe that the next fight would be economic in nature. Kennedy told journalist Jack Newfield, "You know, I've come to the conclusion that poverty is closer to the root of the problem than color."[2] Kennedy was tapping into a vein of thought also championed by Dr. Martin Luther King Jr., who said the best way to address the nation's legacy of racism was not to create a narrow Bill of Rights for Black People, but instead to institute a more inclusive Bill of Rights for the Disadvantaged.

Justice William O. Douglas, another one of my heroes, championed affirmative action based on class rather than race when the issue first came before the U.S. Supreme Court in the 1970s. As a student at Harvard Law School in the late 1980s, I was excited by Douglas's ideas and wrote a long research paper about them. I suggested that affirmative action based on class disadvantage would be fairer and more legally sustainable, given the direction of the courts in the era of President Ronald Reagan.

4

My Front-Row Seat

I became even more convinced of this approach in the early 1990s, while working for Virginia Democratic U.S. senator Chuck Robb, President Lyndon Johnson's son-in-law. Johnson had outlined the need for affirmative action, but, like King, had preferred economic rather than racial means, and now Robb seemed intrigued by this idea. We met with Clarence Thomas, a Black Republican, after President George H. W. Bush nominated him to the Supreme Court. During the meeting, Robb asked Thomas his position on affirmative action. Thomas responded with a question of his own: Why should his own son receive preference in college admissions over a poor white applicant from Appalachia? It was an interesting moment for me. Not only was a Black judge telling a white senator that Black people did not need a preference, but a Republican was telling a Democrat that class disadvantage matters.[3] Robb was struck by the judge's position and cited it in his speech supporting Thomas's nomination.

In the mid-1990s, I thought President Bill Clinton might move the federal government toward a system of affirmative action for the economically disadvantaged. Following the 1994 midterm elections, the House of Representatives was delivered to Republicans for the first time in forty years. Clinton, who had grown up in a working-class family, said he was exploring the idea of shifting from race-based to economic-based affirmative action. After I wrote a cover story in the *New Republic* about the idea, Joel Klein, a Clinton aide and future chancellor of New York City schools, immediately called me to find out more. It was a false start, though. Jesse Jackson threatened to run for president in 1996 if Clinton didn't "stand firm" on affirmative action, and Clinton quickly backed down.

In early 2002, I thought I had another shot when the Supreme Court—which now included Thomas—decided to take up challenges to racial preferences at the University of Michigan. I traveled with conservative activist Linda Chavez to the White House to meet with President George W. Bush's staff to support a third way on affirmative action. Chavez provided the conservative bona fides; I provided the compassion. Bush filed a good amicus brief in favor of finding new paths to diversity, but the higher education establishment prevailed with five justices supporting racial preferences.

After that Supreme Court ruling, I needed to adjust strategies. In 2004, I worked with Harvard University president Larry Summers and Amherst College president Tony Marx to push the idea of *supplementing* racial affirmative action with economic affirmative action. I was excited about this idea for a time, but I grew disappointed as the movement largely fizzled. While elite colleges were passionate about racial diversity, it turned out they didn't want to spend much on the financial aid required to promote economic diversity.

When Barack Obama ran for president in 2007, my hopes were raised again when he said his own daughters did not deserve a racial preference and that working-class students of all colors did. But after his election, I followed up with one of his top aides, Cassandra Butts, who was also Obama's law school classmate. She investigated and reported back that because of interest group politics, Obama could only implement the shift "if the courts forced him to."

In the end, that's what led me to my unusual alliance with Edward Blum and my testimony in the Harvard and UNC cases. In 2014, I became part of a team that dove into a treasure trove of documents that showed the seedy underside of admissions—the emails about preferences for donors and the internal studies that found athletic status, legacy, and race counted a lot in admissions, while universities mostly gave lip service to boosting the odds of economically disadvantaged students in the process. A Duke economist and I simulated—using actual past applicants—what would happen if Harvard and UNC stopped using race in admissions and instead provided preferences for the economically disadvantaged. We found that universities could produce both racial and economic diversity and maintain high academic standards if they invested in this new approach.

Students for Fair Admissions lost in the lower courts, but it was a heady moment for me in October 2022 when the Supreme Court justices, in their oral arguments in the case, debated simulations about class-based affirmative action that I had helped create. After decades of ups and downs, it looked like colleges might move toward economic rather than racial affirmative action. In March 2023, while awaiting the Supreme Court ruling, the *New York Times* ran a front-page profile about me as a "liberal maverick" pushing affirmative action based on class. The article emphasized how my ideas were moving to center stage, but also how anathema they had become to the elite left.

In June 2023, the Supreme Court struck down racial preferences in a decisive 6–3 vote. It appeared that an idea I'd picked up from giants like King, Kennedy, and Douglas would finally see its day. President Joe Biden, who installed busts of Kennedy and King in the Oval Office, announced to the nation that colleges should adopt a "new standard" to reward students who had overcome "adversity."

Universities began announcing that they would adopt new reforms because they could no longer use race in admissions. Some said they would discontinue legacy preferences, early admissions, and other policies that tilt toward the rich. Some said they would give an admissions boost to students who had overcome economic obstacles. Others announced initiatives to increase financial aid, create recruitment programs, and automatically admit students with top grades from high schools throughout the state, including the very poorest.

Almost forty years after I began studying Robert Kennedy's remarkable 1968 campaign for president, it appeared, paradoxically, that a conservative Supreme Court decision striking down the use of race in admissions could lead to a progressive policy outcome. It finally became realistic to ask, Would selective universities soon open their doors to meaningful numbers of low-income and working-class students?

Richard D. Kahlenberg
Rockville, Maryland

Who Enters the "River of Power"?

WHEN EDMUND KENNEDY, A LOW-INCOME BLACK STUDENT from Ohio, arrived at Amherst College's leafy campus in the spring of 2020, he immediately felt out of place. Virtually everyone was from upper-middle-class or wealthy families, it seemed, including most of the other Black students. When COVID-19 hit campus, he recalls, "The other students are saying, 'We're going to go to our house in LA or we're going to take our plane to Cabo until this blows over.'" The few other low-income and working-class students at Amherst, meanwhile, were scrambling. "We can ask our cousin in Boise who's got an extra basement or whatever," Kennedy recalls. He concluded that at Amherst, "the divide is between rich and poor. It's the starkest divide I've ever seen in my life. Far more classist than racial."[1]

Kennedy's story is replicated again and again at elite colleges. Universities, which take great pains to signal their virtue on issues of race, turn a blind eye to class. Ironically, research suggests that in the larger society, class has become increasingly salient in allocating opportunity in America. Since 1970, racial residential segregation has declined 30 percent while class segregation has doubled.[2] The academic achievement gap between rich and poor is now twice as large as the achievement gap between Black and white students.[3] As Robert Putnam has observed, "The power of race, class, and gender to shape life chances in America has been substantially reconfigured."[4]

This book lays out a different vision for the future of affirmative action. The media has been reporting widespread alarm that the Supreme Court's historic decision, upending a half century of precedent that had allowed racial preferences in admissions, will inevitably cause racial diversity to plummet. But it doesn't have to be that way. If elite universities think creatively and invest in new approaches, they can produce economic and racial diversity alike.

The Stakes

Why should it matter who gets to spend four years at a relatively small number of colleges in the United States that have employed racial affirmative action programs? Most Americans don't have a bachelor's degree, and only 11 percent of college students attend the most selective schools where affirmative action has been practiced most extensively.[5] So why should we care?

To begin with, like it or not, selective colleges provide much of the leadership class in America. Joe Biden, himself a graduate of a less selective state college, was amazed when he came to Washington, D.C., and discovered he was something of an anomaly. In a book about the 1988 presidential campaign, journalist Richard Ben Cramer tells the story of Senator Biden sitting in his backyard in Wilmington, Delaware, with friends. Biden asked one, "Where's your kid going to college?" His friend replied, "Christ, Joe! He's eight years old!" According to Cramer, Biden responded, "Lemme tell you something. There's a river of power that flows through this country. Some people—most people—don't even know the river is there. But it's there. Some people know about the river, but they can't get in . . . they only stand at the edge. And some people, a few, get to swim in the river. All the time. They get to swim their whole lives . . . in the river of power. And that river flows from the Ivy League."[6]

Data back Biden up. One writer noted, "Harvard and Yale educate eight hundredths of one percent of American undergraduates and gave us 89 percent of the current Supreme Court."[7] As of 2024, five of the last six presidents had been Ivy League graduates.[8] Although Biden graduated from the University of Delaware, *Politico* found that 41 percent of his high- and mid-level White House staff had Ivy League degrees.[9] More broadly, research shows that 50 percent of America's top government leaders and 49 percent of corporate leaders are graduates of just twelve wealthy colleges and universities, even though the undergraduates at those institutions represent just 0.7 percent of the national total.[10] These institutions provide powerful social connections and shower students with enormous resources, spending more than seven times as much as nonselective colleges.[11] Harvard spends about $120,000 per student, while City University of New York spends $15,000.[12] And elite universities can transform lives. Attending a selective college can put low-income and minority students on an entirely different trajectory in life.[13] "You're talking about one of the best tickets to upward mobility in human history," says a former chancellor of the University of North Carolina. "So there's a lot of debate about who deserves that ticket and who doesn't."[14]

Outside the narrower confines of higher education, the larger issue of when, if ever, it is appropriate to count race in allocating opportunity raises a series of profound and challenging moral questions that help define what kind of society we want to be.

On the one hand, how does a society compensate for one of the world's great horrors? White Americans, backed by the force of law, enslaved Black Americans for centuries and treated them with unspeakable cruelty. White enslavers raped Black women and divided families for sale. When the U.S. Civil War finally brought an end to slavery, white people instituted decades of de jure segregation. This forced Black children to attend separate schools, and Black people of all ages to use separate bathrooms and drinking fountains. To enforce racial hierarchy, white mobs lynched Black people, and it took decades before Congress could muster the votes to outlaw the practice. When the federal government created programs to bring homeownership to Americans, it simultaneously instituted a cruel system of redlining that robbed most Black families of the chance to build wealth. Employers explicitly barred Black applicants from good-paying jobs, and union locals were often racially segregated. Shouldn't a fair and just society take affirmative steps to remedy this horrific history, or risk replicating the legacy of inequality for generations to come? In addition, because Americans come from all corners of the earth, isn't it imperative that our educational institutions bring students of all backgrounds together to learn from their differences and see what they have in common as Americans?

On the other hand, what are the costs of a regime of racial preferences in favor of subjugated groups? After building a powerful moral consensus, the nation concluded that race should not be counted when deciding who gets ahead in society. We should be judged based on individual worth rather than on one's racial group. Is it okay to turn on a dime and suspend that principle, perhaps for a long time to come? In a country wracked by a history of racism, is it prudent to stir resentment among the white majority? And can we really claim that racism is the only source of unfairness in society? How will economically disadvantaged white people react when white elites, who have never experienced discrimination *or* economic hardship, tell them they are bigoted unless they support racial preferences? How will average people feel when they are told color blindness is now considered a form of racism? And what are the special challenges faced when one tries to create a well-meaning set of progressive racial preferences in a country made up of what Heather McGhee calls "ancestral strangers"?[15] Isn't this nation a place that must do everything it can to create the glue necessary for social cohesion? Finally, if some of what motivates advocates of racial preferences is the idea that any racial disparity in outcomes is the result of racism, does that give rise to the dangerous notion that when groups—such as Asian and Jewish Americans—are *overrepresented* in certain academic contexts, they are engaging in some sort of nefarious behavior?[16]

These are challenging issues, and there are more. How should we weigh the benefits of promoting racial integration and directly addressing historical wrongs against the costs of dividing working-class people in a society where economic inequality is skyrocketing and bringing about change requires people to work across racial lines? And how should a society navigate an issue where elites hold such a different set of views from the broader public? Should it give leaders pause that despite more than fifty years of trying to convince the public that racial preferences were the best way to remedy past discrimination, roughly three-quarters of Americans continued to reject that approach? If the majority think that affirmative action allows people of color to "cut in line," as one sociologist found, does tolerating this practice threaten to undermine democratic norms and values altogether because it allows demagogues to ride the backlash and exploit these frustrations?[17]

For more than half a century, courts, presidents, legislators, interest groups, and the public have struggled with these difficult issues. The fundamental question posed by this book is whether providing a leg up to economically disadvantaged people can honor the best arguments from both sides of a very divisive debate.

Chapter Outline

As laid out in Chapter 1, the idea of affirmative action for disadvantaged students of all races first surfaced in the 1960s and 1970s. Passing civil rights laws to prohibit future discrimination was not enough to correct for an egregious history of racial oppression, and liberals debated passionately about whether new efforts to level the playing field should focus narrowly on racial preferences, as civil rights advocates like Whitney Young and James Farmer suggested, or be constructed more broadly to advance low-income and working-class people of all races, as other civil rights leaders like Dr. Martin Luther King Jr. and Bayard Rustin advocated.[18]

Liberals on the Supreme Court were also divided. Justice Thurgood Marshall, the first Black member of the Supreme Court, championed class-blind racial preferences as a temporary remedy to address our nation's historical wrongs, while William O. Douglas, one of the most liberal justices on the Court, supported affirmative action for economically disadvantaged students of all races.

But neither theory won the day. Instead, in a 1978 decision, *Regents of the University of California v. Bakke*, Justice Lewis Powell Jr., an appointee of President Richard Nixon, advocated a different theory championed by elite universities such as Harvard. By boosting the number of Black and Hispanic students on campus through racial preferences, the learning environment at predominantly white institutions would be enriched. Powell said that underrepresented minority students add novel perspectives to campus discussions in the same way that farm boys do on a campus dominated by students from large metropolitan areas.[19] In this vision, admissions deans act less as objective evaluators of talent and more like casting directors trying to advance the interests of the university. This approach can include admitting minority and rural students who will contribute different views, as well as legacy students whose parents will make financial donations.[20] As a result, selective universities have created the type of situation that Edmund Kennedy found at Amherst—a racially diverse class that also has thirteen times as many rich students as poor students.[21]

As detailed in Chapter 2, the Powell-Harvard idea of how admissions should work has never sat well with the public. Polls have consistently found that about three-quarters of Americans oppose racial preferences and about the same proportion oppose legacy preferences.[22] Many Americans learned from the civil rights movement that race and ancestry shouldn't be used to decide who gets ahead. They also believed that disadvantaged students who overcame odds should receive favorable consideration.

Who Enters the "River of Power"?

Starting in the mid-1990s, voters across the country supported referenda that would ban the use of race in admissions at public universities. These citizens voted to end racial preference in red states such as Nebraska, Oklahoma, and Idaho and in blue states such as California, Washington, and Michigan.[23]

What happened next in these states was fascinating. If racial preferences were unpopular, so, it turned out, was the resegregation of higher education by race. When voters forced universities to stop considering race in admissions, they didn't give up on diversity. Instead, in state after state, they adopted the essence of the King-Douglas approach. Public universities in these states gave a meaningful admissions boost to economically disadvantaged students of all races. Financial aid budgets were increased. Schools such as the University of Texas and the University of Florida accepted top-ranking students from high schools across the state, including those in poor communities. Some universities dropped the use of legacy preferences and increased the number of transfer students from community colleges.[24]

Even so, as Chapter 3 describes, universities struck back in the early 2000s. When conservatives challenged the University of Michigan Law School's use of racial preferences, the higher education establishment, military, business elites, and civil rights organizations mobilized. They believed that the new approach in some states to help disadvantaged students wouldn't work and required too much financial aid. They flooded the Court with amicus briefs claiming that the King-Douglas approach employed in several states did not produce sufficient levels of racial diversity, despite emerging evidence to the contrary.[25] The gambit worked. Just as Nixon appointee Lewis Powell saved racial preferences in 1978, Reagan appointee Sandra Day O'Connor provided the swing vote to sustain their use in 2003. Like Powell, O'Connor gave tremendous deference to the claims of elite universities. She said that she took Michigan Law at its word that it would stop using racial preferences as soon as alternative paths to diversity became available. In her opinion, O'Connor blessed racial preferences for a twenty-five-year period.[26]

With this major victory on race in their pocket, in 2004, a few inspiring higher education leaders asked whether Douglas's class-based affirmative action idea could serve not as a substitute but as a supplement to racial affirmative action. As explained in Chapter 4, one major impetus for the reform was data showing that elite universities provided big preferences for athletes, legacies, and Black and Hispanic students, but no break whatsoever to low-income students, despite rhetoric to the contrary.[27] The presidents of Harvard and Amherst, appalled by data showing that rich students outnumbered poor students by twenty-five to one at elite colleges, announced new programs to boost admissions to economically disadvantaged students and expand financial aid programs to enable them to enroll. A few institutions also pledged to end programs that provided a special channel that increased the odds of being admitted if a student applied earlier in the process rather than through the regular admissions cycle. (This change was backed by research showing that low-income students were less likely to know about this trick.)[28]

The momentum seemed real, but the movement soon collapsed. A few years later, top schools reinstated early admissions. Despite receiving lots of positive press about providing a free ride to low-income and working-class families, elite universities did not actually admit many of them. One researcher said that it was "as misleading as those television commercials from Shell and other energy giants that advertise their commitment to developing clean energy alternatives—not a lie, exactly, but fundamentally misleading."[29]

In the coming years, the economic skew at elite universities would remain largely unchanged. One study found that thirty-eight highly selective institutions had more students from the top 1 percent of the income distribution than the bottom 60 percent.[30] Universities had little incentive to adopt economic affirmative action as long as they could use racial preferences to recruit upper-middle-class students of color to achieve the racial diversity they wanted. The idea of considering both race and class in admissions sounded good in theory, but it wasn't going to happen in practice.

Who Enters the "River of Power"?

In the coming period, however, new political and legal pressures mounted on racial preference programs. As discussed in Chapter 5, the University of Michigan's victory in the Supreme Court was short-lived, as Michigan residents voted overwhelmingly to enact a ban on racial preferences in the state in 2006. In 2008, Barack Obama, an exciting Black candidate for president, raised questions about whether economically privileged students of color, like his own daughters, deserved a racial preference in college admissions.

Moreover, the Supreme Court was becoming more conservative as Justice Sandra Day O'Connor retired and was replaced by Justice Samuel Alito. Alito joined other conservative justices in striking down racial school integration policies at the K–12 level in Louisville and Seattle. Many thought affirmative action in higher education might be next.

The test came in 2012 when the Supreme Court heard the case of *Fisher v. Texas*. The litigation squarely raised the question of whether the University of Texas (UT) at Austin could achieve racial diversity without using race. Whereas Justice O'Connor had said she would take universities at their word that alternatives—such as class-based affirmative action—wouldn't work, that deference was unlikely to survive.

Some nine years after the Michigan Supreme Court decision, strong evidence was emerging that race-neutral strategies—such as those that gave a leg up to economically disadvantaged students or automatically admitted top students from different high schools— could produce racial and economic diversity. Texas state legislators had devised the "Top 10 Percent" plan, which automatically admitted students with the top grades at any high school to UT Austin. The resulting Black and Hispanic populations were slightly *larger* than they had been when UT used racial preferences. Research also found that seven of ten flagship universities using socioeconomic preferences and other nonracial means—including the University of Florida and the University of Washington—were able to maintain or increase Black and Hispanic representation without relying on racial preferences.[31]

Class Matters

In 2013, the Supreme Court issued an opinion that jettisoned O'Connor's deference and instead held that universities had to demonstrate that race-neutral strategies were unworkable. The High Court remanded the case to the lower courts so that they could apply the new rule to the facts in Texas. Most observers thought this was the death knell for racial preferences and that universities would have to find new ways to achieve racial diversity going forward.

As noted in Chapter 6, given the 2013 ruling, researchers doubled down on exploring what new types of programs might work. Using national data, scholars at Georgetown University found that if universities eliminated legacy preferences and adopted meaningful boosts to socioeconomically disadvantaged students, the most selective public and private universities could maintain racially diverse classes and remain academically excellent. A researcher at Tel Aviv University came to the same conclusion.[32]

But UT Austin had never liked the Top 10 Percent plan, which state legislators had imposed on it, because it reduced the college's discretion over whom it would admit. So, UT came up with new arguments against the plan. Surprisingly, the lower courts concluded that UT Austin had no viable options for producing racial diversity short of racial preferences. They faulted the Top 10 Percent plan in part for often helping working-class Black and Hispanic students instead of more affluent ones. When the Supreme Court took up the case again—presumably to overturn the decision of the lower courts—Justice Alito was incredulous about UT's argument. Alito suggested that the Top 10 Percent plan's ability to reach working-class students who had overcome odds should be seen as a virtue, not a deficit. "The reason for adopting affirmative action in the first place," he said, was "because there are people who have been severely disadvantaged through discrimination and—and lack of wealth, and they should be given a benefit in admission."[33]

Justice Anthony Kennedy, the swing vote on the Court, was surprisingly quiet during the oral arguments. In 2016, Kennedy shocked the higher education world when he sided with UT Austin. Among other things, he argued that giving a preference to low-income students was not a viable option because they would not be as well prepared academically as their wealthier peers. He wrote, "The Equal Protection Clause does not force universities to choose between a diverse student body and a reputation for academic excellence."[34] Kennedy ignored extensive evidence showing that Top 10 Percent students did quite well at UT Austin. Elites had won again.

But Kennedy's would not be the last word from the Supreme Court on affirmative action. As I describe in Chapter 7, even as Kennedy was ruling, opponents of racial preferences were developing a new lawsuit against America's oldest undergraduate institution, Harvard College, which had been Justice Powell's model for the "correct" way to implement affirmative action back in the 1970s. This chapter, which capitalizes on my role as an expert witness in the case, focuses on the unique opportunity the litigation provided to lift the veil on an admissions process that is normally shrouded in secrecy. Because Harvard was forced to turn over documents and data on admissions, it was possible to reveal previously unknown details about the school's system of rewarding donors and faculty members with special preferences for their children, and its practice of routinely awarding low scores to Asian American applicants for a subjective rating meant to capture factors such as "integrity."

It was also possible to examine the relative weight Harvard provided to different factors in the admissions process. It turned out that Harvard provided Black students more than twice the admissions boost that economically disadvantaged students received. Additionally, the boost for legacy students was also much larger than for first-generation college students. Nearly 75 percent of Black and Hispanic students came from the top socioeconomic 20 percent of the Black and Hispanic populations nationally, according to the data. The result at Harvard was racial diversity but economic segregation. A majority of the class consisted of students of color, but wealthy students outnumbered low-income students fifteen to one.[35] In short, Harvard "looked like

America" when one focused on skin color, but in no way did it reflect the country's economic diversity. The university had in essence created a multiracial aristocracy, which was better than an all-white aristocracy but was still an aristocracy.

Was this the only way to achieve racial diversity? In the past, researchers had simulated what would happen if elite institutions stopped using race in admissions and shifted to a system of class-based affirmative action using student indicators such as grades and test scores to gauge the strength of applicants. But the litigation allowed for a more nuanced approach, considering ratings for factors such as extracurricular activities and letters of recommendation. The evidence confirmed my suspicions that Harvard could create an academically superb, racially diverse, and more socioeconomically integrated class by eliminating its racial and legacy preferences and giving a more robust boost to low-income and working-class students. This approach would open the doors to talented students of modest means who lack connections.

Harvard is a private college, but would things be different at the University of North Carolina at Chapel Hill, a public institution? The school had a reputation as progressive, and its financial aid program had received national attention. But as I note in Chapter 8, the documents and data painted much the same picture as in the Harvard case. UNC also had a system that provided large legacy preferences to out-of-state applicants, where the competition is much stiffer than in-state. Additionally, it provided preference to Black students of any socioeconomic group that was twice as large as the preference for economically disadvantaged students. As a result, in the class of 2013, 60 percent of students came from the richest 20 percent of the population, and just 3.8 percent came from the poorest 20 percent.[36]

As in the Harvard case, the modeling showed that UNC could maintain high levels of academic excellence, increase socioeconomic diversity, and achieve high racial diversity levels without providing preferences for Black and Hispanic students if it eliminated legacy preferences and provided a meaningful boost to economically disadvantaged students.

UNC had another viable option: to adopt a version of the Texas Top 10 Percent plan, which would admit students with the highest grades from high schools across the state. Unlike Harvard, which has a national pool of applicants, UNC admits about 80 percent of its students from North Carolina. The simulation showed that UNC could produce a trifecta of academic excellence, racial diversity, and socioeconomic diversity if it jettisoned racial and legacy preferences and employed a percentage plan. UNC could take one of these alternative approaches, although it would be more expensive due to the need for more financial aid for a more economically diverse class.

Courts were supposed to decide the UNC and Harvard cases on the specific facts involved, but a judge's thinking about affirmative action would inevitably be shaped by the larger societal discussions about race that engulfed America during the years of the litigation. And so, in Chapter 9, I examine the broader debates around racial justice that played a central role during the presidencies of Donald Trump and Joe Biden.

The rise of Trump was deeply alarming to me, as I viewed him as the most openly racist presidential candidate since Alabama governor George Wallace. So, too, were the march of neo-Nazis in Charlottesville, Virginia, and the horrific, high-profile police killings of Breonna Taylor, George Floyd, and many other unarmed Black people. In response to Floyd's murder, in particular, a multiracial coalition of tens of millions of Americans participated in mostly peaceful protests. In a welcome and overdue development, some white Americans, for the first time, acknowledged the reality of anti-Black racism.

But some social justice activists overreached and adopted dubious and politically toxic ideas—such as "defund the police," and "abolish ICE" (the U.S. Immigration and Customs Enforcement agency). Some embraced the ideas of Ibram X. Kendi, who championed a system of racial preferences that could reach endlessly into the future.[37]

Class Matters

Most Americans, including many Democrats, disagreed. In deep-blue California, in November 2020, voters opposed an effort to reinstate racial preferences in admissions at public colleges and in government contracting by fourteen percentage points, even as they supported Joe Biden over Donald Trump by twenty-nine points. In an April 2022 Pew Research Center poll, 74 percent of respondents said race should not be used as even a minor factor in college admissions. This view was shared by majorities of all racial groups, including Black and Hispanic participants.[38]

On issues of race generally, and issues of affirmative action specifically, many Americans were searching for a middle ground. They rejected Trump's racist worldview, which said an Indiana-born judge's Mexican American heritage would inevitably lead him to rule against Trump. And they also rejected race essentialism on the left, which said racial oppression was America's defining feature and that the importation of enslaved people in 1619, rather than the Declaration of Independence in 1776, represented the country's true founding. On affirmative action, the public supported preferences for economically disadvantaged students by almost two to one.

It is against this backdrop that I outline, in Chapter 10, the deliberations of the Supreme Court in the Harvard and UNC litigation. Would the justices seize a third way? In the run-up to oral arguments in October 2022, the higher education establishment continued to claim that socioeconomic preferences and other strategies would not produce sufficient racial diversity. The press seemed particularly taken by an amicus brief filed by the University of California (UC) system claiming that despite the expenditure of "hundreds of millions of dollars," race-neutral strategies to produce racial diversity "have fallen abysmally short."[39]

It was a bizarre claim, and one contradicted by the admissions offices of the most competitive institutions within the UC system. In 2020, UC Berkeley boasted that it assembled "the most ethnically diverse freshman admitted class in more than 30 years."[40] And in

2021, UCLA announced that it had admitted the highest proportion of underrepresented minority students "in over 30 years."[41] About 70 percent of students at both institutions were Asian, Hispanic, Black, or Native American. And UCLA and UC Berkeley routinely rank as the most socioeconomically diverse of America's selective colleges. University opposition to race-neutral strategies seemed centered less around the racial results, and more around the "hundreds of millions of dollars" it cost to get there.

The Supreme Court's five hours of oral arguments in the Harvard and UNC cases were fascinating to watch. The conservative justices questioned Harvard's concern for racial diversity, citing preferences that tended to benefit wealthy white people, such as those for legacies and boutique sports like fencing. Others asked when racial preferences would end. The most riveting moment came when the lawyer representing Harvard declared that race counts in admissions the same way that being a good oboe player counts. This line of thinking was likely to sound peculiar to average Americans, who know there is a fundamental difference between Harvard treating students differently based on musical ability that can be honed through hard work and treating them differently based on an immutable factor like race. Chief Justice John Roberts saw an opening. He declared, "We did not fight a Civil War about oboe players. We did fight a Civil War to eliminate racial discrimination."[42]

In June 2023, the Court issued a definitive 6–3 ruling in the UNC case and 6–2 ruling in the Harvard case that ended racial preferences. Roberts, writing for the majority, declared, "Eliminating racial discrimination means eliminating all of it."[43] At the same time, all nine justices—the dissenters and majority alike—wrote positively about race-neutral strategies, including class-based affirmative action. The Supreme Court decision was a bombshell. The higher education establishment had narrowly dodged bullets in 1978, 2003, and 2016. But in 2023, some fifty-five years after the advent of racial preferences in higher education, the Court brought the practice to an end.

Class Matters

The end of racial preferences did not inevitably mean the end of racial diversity or our nation's reckoning on race, as some critics claimed. As I outline in Chapter 11, instead, it meant that to achieve racial diversity, universities would have to return to the King-Douglas vision of affirmative action for the disadvantaged of all races. It would be more expensive to go down this path, and universities must balance their books. But the evidence suggested that a combination of private and public resources could make the new system viable.

Old ideologies don't die easily, and there was resistance on both the far left and the far right. On the left, historian Richard Rothstein argued that colleges should "defy" the Supreme Court. Some colleges appeared willing to exploit the consideration of student essays about race in a way not intended by the Supreme Court. On the far right, some activists sought to strike down class-based affirmative action as "proxy" discrimination. This effort seemed unlikely to prevail, given that conservative justices had been *urging* colleges to consider factors like class instead of race for decades.

But most schools seemed to come around to the view that it was time to find new paths to diversity, centered around addressing America's great class divide. A number of colleges announced their plans to end legacy preferences, boost financial aid, and adopt other strategies. Two Republican-leaning southern states, for example, adopted percentage plans like the one used by UT Austin. These were all steps that should have been taken years earlier, but it took the Supreme Court's decision on race to prompt the reforms.

As I note in the epilogue, the move from race- to class-based affirmative action has a number of broader implications that portend a more hopeful future. For one thing, the Supreme Court's decision on affirmative action in higher education has important consequences for the use of race in government contracting and employment. In the future, policies that have caused racial division and resentment could be reinvented along class lines, which will put them on sounder legal and political footing.

Who Enters the "River of Power"?

The shift from race to class in affirmative action policies also has significant and exciting ramifications for American politics. A big part of the reason Dr. King proposed a Bill of Rights for the Disadvantaged rather than a Bill of Rights for Black People sixty years ago was that he believed in "solidarity liberalism"—an alliance of working people across racial lines. That approach contrasts with the current model of "charity liberalism," in which working-class people of color have to hope that upper-middle-class white liberals will consistently set aside their self-interest in order to advance racial and economic justice.[44]

For six decades, racial preference policies have frustrated the possibilities of solidarity liberalism by pitting working-class Black and white people against one another. The shift in affirmative action policies from race to class could support the opposite dynamic, where working-class people reach across racial lines to promote policies that will benefit their children mutually. We have already seen it happen in Texas, where legislators representing working-class white, Black, and Hispanic constituencies have formed an unusual alliance to ensure their children have access to UT Austin. This same sort of thing could happen time and time again in the coming years.

Civil rights leader Bayard Rustin recognized that moving from racial to class preferences could also create more democratic unity. Rustin, who organized the 1963 March on Washington for Jobs and Freedom, a high-water mark of cross-racial harmony, argued in 1987, "Any preferential approach postulated along racial, ethnic, religious, or sexual lines will only disrupt a multicultural society and lead to a backlash." By contrast, he argued, "special treatment can be provided to those who have been exploited or denied opportunities if solutions are predicated along class lines, precisely because all religious, ethnic, and racial groups have a depressed class who would benefit."[45]

Finally, in the college setting itself, the movement from racial to economic affirmative action could transform the lives of large numbers of impressive economically disadvantaged students who have been left out. The small number of low-income students like Edmund Kennedy who make it into elite universities represent a tiny slice of the highly motivated, highly intelligent students of modest means in America. Researchers have found that tens of thousands of high-achieving low-income students never even apply to selective colleges.[46] Just as higher education widened the circle to include women and students of color in previous generations, it can do so again.[47]

CHAPTER 1

Kennedy, King, and the Corporate Lawyer Who Diverted the Dream

W HEN I ATTENDED HARVARD COLLEGE IN THE EARLY 1980S, affirmative action admissions programs—a recent innovation— were a big subject of debate on campus. During my first year, I took a constitutional law class taught by law professor Archibald Cox. The Supreme Court's 1978 decision in the *Bakke* case—in which Justice Powell struck down racial quotas but supported the use of race as a factor in admissions—was a central text.

A symbol of Yankee rectitude, Cox was a hero of mine from his days as a special prosecutor during the Watergate scandal. The former Kennedy administration solicitor general was chosen by the University of California to defend racial quotas in the Supreme Court's oral argument in *Bakke*. He argued that Black students deserved a leg up in college admissions after a terrible history of discrimination, and that all students benefit from having diversity on campus. Just as having students from rural areas would enliven discussions, so would having meaningful numbers of students of color enrich life on campus.[1]

Cox's worldview was familiar and attractive to me at the time. I was raised in a family of politically active, socially conscious idealists. My father—a liberal, Harvard-educated Presbyterian minister who wrote his thesis in graduate school under Reinhold Niebuhr—later got in trouble for his sermons criticizing Richard Nixon. He left the ministry to become a classics teacher, focusing on the contributions of Greeks and Romans to the foundations of liberal democracy. My mother, a Wellesley-educated feminist, was a citizen activist and school board member in my upper-middle-class St. Paul, Minnesota, suburb called White Bear Lake—a name that neatly captured the town's racial demographics. Our family's heroes were liberal senators like Minnesota's Hubert Humphrey and Walter Mondale.

We were not rich, but we had a cushion. My maternal grandfather had been a successful patent attorney in Chicago, and his wealth helped ease a life of public-spiritedness for my parents and for me. His earnings (passed through my parents) paid my full tuition at Harvard and, a generation later, the college tuitions of my four children. They also helped my parents buy a summer home in Chautauqua Institution in upstate New York, a resort where mostly liberal, civic-minded individuals gathered in the morning to hear lectures about history, policy, and literature and in the evening to listen to the resident symphony orchestra.

In retrospect, I recognize that I had an exceedingly fortunate childhood. I was raised by loving parents who nurtured me intellectually, emotionally, and morally. Like many kids, I assumed that my experience was somehow typical, so I took it for granted. With this background, I fit in with the other students at Harvard, most of whom were at least as affluent and liberal as I was. My impression—later documented—was that many of the Black and Hispanic students were economically advantaged too.[2] White working-class people were mostly an abstraction to me. They were filtered through the lens of the 1970s television sitcom

Kennedy, King, and the Corporate Lawyer

All in the Family, whose protagonist Archie Bunker was an ignorant bigot who was the butt of jokes. I was pro–civil rights and supported the underdog, which meant that, like Cox, I favored racial preferences in college admissions. As I saw it, the controversy pitted the interests of less privileged Black people against those of more privileged white people. As a liberal raised with a strong sense of fairness, I instinctively knew which side I was on.

Outside the walls of Harvard Yard, however, liberals in the age of Ronald Reagan were getting crushed politically. As a government major, I thought it was important to understand why. Particularly upsetting to me was the movement of blue-collar white voters, who had been the bedrock of the Democratic Party, into the Republican fold. The phenomenon was new enough that they were called Reagan Democrats; today, they are the Republican base. I became obsessed with why these voters were defecting and how they could be won back without abandoning core values. Why was my political party so out of touch with these working Americans?

I learned that affirmative action was a key part of the story. Racial preferences were deeply unpopular, especially with working-class white voters. In a famous study of blue-collar white voters in Macomb County, Michigan, in the 1980s, pollster Stanley Greenberg found a massive shift in political orientation over time—from 74 percent support for Lyndon Johnson to 67 percent support for Ronald Reagan. A lot of factors explained the change, but a big piece was due to Democrats' endorsement of racial preferences. Greenberg concluded from focus groups of working-class white voters that "discrimination against whites has become a well assimilated and ready explanation for their status, vulnerability and failures."[3]

This was a deeply foreign way of thinking for me. White Americans had treated Black people in such unspeakable ways for centuries that racial preferences seemed the least that society could provide. But during my college years, I broadened my view of who deserved extra consideration.

Class Matters

The seed had been planted my senior year in high school when I saw a paperback book at a garage sale for thirty cents that intrigued me. *Robert Kennedy: A Memoir*, by *Village Voice* journalist Jack Newfield, chronicled Senator Bobby Kennedy's 1968 campaign for president. Newfield provided a deeply moving portrait of a politics quite different from what either party was articulating in the 1980s. After John F. Kennedy's 1963 assassination, RFK had developed a deep empathy for disadvantaged people. He championed Mexican American farmworkers in the campaigns led by Cesar Chavez for better treatment, visited poor Black families in the Mississippi Delta, and took a profound interest in the struggles of Native American people. And when he ran for president in 1968, Black, Hispanic, and Native American voters turned out for him in droves. But what was truly extraordinary, Newfield wrote, was Kennedy's ability to appeal to disaffected blue-collar white voters who were increasingly alienated from the Democratic Party over issues like the Vietnam War and urban rioting. Indeed, Kennedy—this tribune of disadvantaged people of color—even managed to win support from some working-class white people who had previously voted for segregationist George Wallace in earlier presidential primaries, by communicating that he understood their struggles too.[4]

In college, a classmate, a graduate student, and a professor helped me rethink my ungenerous embrace of Hollywood's Archie Bunker stereotype of working-class white people. I had five roommates during my first year. Three had attended prestigious prep schools, and one, like me, was a legacy student from an affluent public high school. By contrast, my fifth roommate came from Waltham, Massachusetts, a white working-class suburb of Boston. One of the rare Republicans on campus, he was keenly aware that working-class people of all races faced obstacles, and we got into heated discussions about affirmative action. He asked why only Black and Hispanic students received affirmative action preferences, especially since many of our Black and Hispanic classmates were from well-off families.

Kennedy, King, and the Corporate Lawyer

John DiIulio, a PhD student who taught my sophomore tutorial seminar in the Department of Government, also challenged my thinking. DiIulio—who later taught at the University of Pennsylvania and headed George W. Bush's Office of Faith-Based and Community Initiatives—grew up in a white working-class community in South Philadelphia, in a row house across from a Catholic church where the fictional Rocky Balboa got married. His father worked in a General Electric plant that was in the process of shutting down, and his mother worked in a textile sweatshop and in a department store.[5] A Democrat for life, DiIulio helped educate me about the worldview of people from his community who struggled to make ends meet. They did not appreciate being told by Boston Brahmins like Archibald Cox (a graduate of St. Paul's School, Harvard, and Harvard Law) that racial quotas were necessary to make up for past discrimination. In his seminar, DiIulio assigned a paper on the *Bakke* case and pushed me to defend my assumptions about affirmative action.

A third powerful influence was Professor Robert Coles, a child psychiatrist.[6] He taught one of my favorite classes, The Literature of Social Reflection, dubbed "Guilt 101," in which we talked about race and class inequality through the novels of Charles Dickens, Ralph Ellison, George Orwell, and Flannery O'Connor.

One of Coles's most memorable lectures recalled his early 1960s experience as a doctor in the South. During this time, he witnessed Ruby Bridges, a courageous six-year-old Black girl, help integrate the New Orleans schools in the face of virulent white hostility. Coles, who came to know Ruby and counsel her, was particularly struck by her silent prayers directed toward the white parents who tormented her with hateful chants.[7] Ruby Bridges's story, immortalized in Norman Rockwell's painting *The Problem We All Live With*, resonated powerfully with me and other Harvard students as a story of pure good and evil.

But more challenging to Harvard students like me was Coles's take on another school desegregation fight—in nearby Boston during the mid-1970s. He recounted that when the city was aflame over court-ordered busing to desegregate its public schools, most of the Harvard community was understandably aghast as white working-class people threw bricks at buses carrying Black students to white schools. Coles condemned the violence but caused an enormous stir when he said he understood white working-class resentment of compulsory busing policies that left out wealthier surrounding communities such as Wellesley, Newton, and Cambridge.

"I think the busing is a scandal," Coles told the *Boston Globe* at the time. "I don't think it should be imposed like this on working-class people exclusively. It should cross these lines and people in the suburbs should share in it." Coles argued that the "ultimate reality is the reality of class. . . . That's the real struggle here." Working-class people, both white and Black, he said, have "gotten a raw deal. . . . Both groups have been ignored. Both of them are looked down upon by the well-to-do white people."[8]

Coles didn't romanticize blue-collar white people in Boston, acknowledging that they were known to hurl racial epithets not used in polite society. But he added, "I don't think that all these experts . . . these various social scientists and those in favor of integration like myself should be in a position to deliver sermons to the people of Boston . . . until we have been made a part of all of this." Of people living in wealthy suburbs, he said, "Their lives are clean and their minds are clean. And they can afford this long, charitable, calm view. And if people don't know that this is a class privilege, then, by golly, they don't know anything."[9]

Studying Bobby Kennedy's Views on Race and Class

The education I was receiving about paying attention to the challenges faced by working-class white Americans as well as communities of color was front of mind during my junior year at Harvard as I thought about senior thesis topics. With Reagan running for his second term on the theme of "Morning in America" and the polls showing his strong support among working-class white voters, I thought back to Jack Newfield's book about a more exciting political time, when Bobby Kennedy had drawn the enthusiastic support of working-class Black, Hispanic, and white voters. I had three big questions.

First, was it possible to build a coalition of working people across racial lines? Had Kennedy really done it? Newfield thought so, as did other hard-bitten journalists at the time, such as David Halberstam, David Broder, and Theodore White. But a set of debunkers had argued that RFK's coalition was an exaggeration.[10] Who was right? Second, if RFK had built the coalition, how did he do it? Why was he able to succeed where other Democrats could not? And third, would it be more or less desirable for the country if Democrats were to win with a political coalition consisting of people of color and educated liberal white voters, as opposed to a multiracial working-class coalition?

Presidential historian Richard Neustadt agreed to supervise the thesis. He had worked for President John Kennedy and introduced me to many Robert Kennedy campaign staffers. I spoke with historian Arthur Schlesinger Jr., economist John Kenneth Galbraith, speechwriters Ted Sorensen, Peter Edelman, and Jeff Greenfield, and novelist and Kennedy friend Carlos Fuentes. I also spent time with Robert Coles, who was close with RFK and wrote the final speech he gave. In all, I interviewed more than thirty people involved in the campaign, including one of Kennedy's bitter rivals for the 1968 nomination, former senator Eugene McCarthy.

My thesis—written as Reagan was cruising to a landslide victory over Walter Mondale (525–13 in the electoral college)—became my passion. I took numerous trips on the Boston T to the John F. Kennedy Library, which housed a vast collection of Robert Kennedy campaign materials, including oral histories, papers, polls, and television ads. I tracked down precinct results in primary states, particularly in Indiana, where the evidence of Kennedy's coalition was most contested.

Class Matters

On my three big questions, I concluded that (1) Kennedy had, in fact, built a powerful multiracial coalition of working-class voters (i.e., the debunkers deserved to be debunked); (2) he had done so both by recognizing that passage of civil rights laws had made class a more pressing problem than color and by communicating his concern for working people across racial lines; and (3) his coalition was highly desirable for bringing about social change, preserving social peace, and warding off right-wing populism.[11] I did not know it at the time, but my thesis findings would have a profound impact on my thinking about a range of issues—especially affirmative action—for decades to come.

Putting together a multiracial alliance of working-class people was not easy for Kennedy, who ran in the 1968 Democratic presidential primaries against two opponents—Eugene McCarthy and Hubert Humphrey. (The incumbent president, Lyndon Johnson, dropped out of the race shortly after Kennedy began campaigning.) By 1968, as Halberstam noted, "The easy old coalition between labor and Negroes was no longer so easy; it barely existed. The two were among the American forces most in conflict."[12] The groups were particularly divided over social issues and foreign policy.

Kennedy was clearly identified as sympathetic to civil rights for Black people. In a 1968 Harris Poll, Kennedy was the national candidate (Republican or Democrat) most closely identified with speeding up racial progress—more so than either Humphrey or McCarthy. And he had staked out a more dovish position than Humphrey on Vietnam.

The most natural step as a pro–civil rights, anti-Vietnam politician would have been to build a political coalition of Black and Hispanic voters, college students, and upper-middle-class educated white liberals. But McCarthy had entered the race before Kennedy and had wrapped up most of the educated white voters, so Kennedy tried to do the difficult work of piecing back together the "Black and blue" (African American and blue-collar white) coalition that had served Democrats well in President Franklin Roosevelt's New Deal era.

Kennedy, King, and the Corporate Lawyer

The key test case was Kennedy's first primary, in Indiana. Northern Indiana had been the site of tremendous racial strife. The mayoral election a year earlier had sharply divided the city of Gary. Although 90 percent of the white population in Gary were registered Democrats, they had voted five to one for the white Republican, Joseph Radigan, over the Black Democratic candidate, Richard Hatcher.

But Kennedy wanted the support of both groups, and in May 1968, he began an extraordinary motorcade through Gary and nearby towns. Mayor Hatcher sat on one side; on the other was Tony Zale, a white boxer who was a hero to blue-collar white citizens. "It was hard to escape the meaning of that kind of symbol," Kennedy speechwriter Jeff Greenfield recalled. Kennedy told journalist Jack Newfield, "I think there has to be a new kind of coalition to keep the Democratic party going, and to keep the country together. . . . Negroes, blue-collar whites, and the kids. . . . We have to convince the Negroes and the poor whites that they have common interests."[13]

The research for my thesis showed that Kennedy's strategy worked in Indiana. He won 85 percent of the Black vote and did well enough with working-class white voters to win the seven largest Indiana counties where George Wallace ran strongest during the 1964 presidential primaries. A May 1968 analysis by pollster Stanley Greenberg found that RFK ran well among most European ethnic groups in Indiana. And a May 1968 Harris Poll found that statewide Kennedy beat McCarthy and Humphrey's stand-in candidate, the popular governor Roger Branigin, two to one among Catholics and industrial workers across the state. Harris concluded that Kennedy's victory "went a long way toward establishing his claim as perhaps the likeliest Democrat in 1968 who can deliver both the Negro and the lower-income white urban vote." Statewide, the *New York Times* noted, Kennedy assembled "an unusual coalition of Negroes and lower income whites," and that he did well "with blue-collar workers in the industrial areas and with rural whites."[14]

Reflecting on the results, my professor, Robert Coles, told me he had remarked to Kennedy, "There is something going on here that has to do with real class politics." Kennedy appealed to lower-middle-income white voters, Coles told me, because they thought, "This guy isn't going to use us to show those rich Harvard-types what a great guy he is [by labeling us as backward]. He may be for them [African Americans], but he's for us, too."[15]

There were many reasons Kennedy was successful with blue-collar white populations—he was the brother of a revered martyred president, had a strong history as a cold warrior, and was known for his toughness. But he also was able to communicate to working-class white voters that he recognized their struggles as deserving of attention, just like those of Black voters. Kennedy became increasingly convinced, he told Halberstam, that "it was pointless to talk about the real problem in America being black and white, it was really rich and poor, which was a much more complex subject."[16]

During the campaign, RFK continually emphasized the ability of rich people to escape taxes by exploiting loopholes. He offered "A Program for a Sound Economy," which the *Wall Street Journal* denounced in an editorial titled "Soak the Rich."[17] Recognizing that tax reform was a complicated issue, he tried to cut through the fog by calling for a minimum 20 percent income tax for those who earned over $50,000 annually (about $450,000 today) "to prevent the wealthy from continuing to escape taxation completely."[18] RFK speechwriter Jeff Greenfield recalled that Kennedy was not afraid to name names on the stump. "He would constantly cite" oil tycoon H. L. Hunt. Kennedy "would use statistics of two hundred people who made $200,000 a year or more and paid no taxes.... He kept coming back to those two hundred people ... and then he'd say, 'One year Hunt paid $102. I guess he was feeling generous.' If you think about it, there is no better populist issue than that issue."[19]

He also communicated class anger about the Vietnam War. In language likely to resonate with working-class people of all races who disproportionately sent their offspring to Vietnam, Kennedy actively confronted college students who received draft deferments. Although the student draft deferments were supported by the public by a margin of 54 percent to 31 percent, Kennedy attacked them as unfair. At Notre Dame University, Kennedy was booed for saying that college draft deferments should be abolished. "You're getting the unfair advantage while poor people are being drafted," Kennedy said.[20]

Kennedy also ran a strong "law and order" campaign. Because of his record on civil rights, the phrase did not have the same racially charged connotation as it did when used by someone like George Wallace. Kennedy's stance was criticized by upper-middle-class white liberals who lived in safe neighborhoods; but he knew that low-income and working-class people of all races were the biggest victims of crime, and believed that taking a tough stance would resonate. While some viewed support for the police among blue-collar people as racist, it turned out these voters also supported law and order in dealing with white college students protesting the Vietnam War.[21]

In Indiana, Kennedy took the advice of campaign officials and spoke of himself not as the former attorney general, but told audiences, "I was the chief law-enforcement officer of the United States. I promise if elected, I will do all in my power to bring an end to this violence. We needn't have to expect this violence summer after summer." RFK aide Gerard Doherty recalled, "I said if he was going to win, he has to conduct a campaign for sheriff of Indiana. And he did." The message got through. At one point during the presidential campaign, Richard Nixon remarked to Theodore White, "Do you know a lot of these people think Bobby is more a law-and-order man than I am!"[22]

During the Indiana campaign, Kennedy also communicated his deep respect for people engaged in manual labor. In one television commercial, Kennedy was shown speaking to an audience of factory workers while a narrator said, "There's one thing Robert Kennedy knows for sure. When he talks to men who do the real work in this country, he's talking with people who aren't afraid of a new challenge."[23]

In my research, I also discovered that RFK took a very different position from my own on the issue of racial preferences. As the question emerged in the 1960s about how to compensate for America's history of racial oppression, some argued that Black people should receive preferential treatment, at least for a limited time. For example, James Farmer from the Congress of Racial Equality championed a system of racial quotas in employment and organized boycotts of corporations in cities like Philadelphia to pressure companies to agree. Likewise, Whitney Young from the National Urban League called for "a decade of discrimination" in favor of Black people.[24]

Kennedy rejected that approach. He spoke of a "special obligation" owed to Black Americans in light of American history, but thought racially inclusive social mobility programs were the right answer. In 1963, for example, in testimony before the Senate Judiciary Committee he rejected even a mild form of race consciousness. During questioning, he was asked about a directive issued by the U.S. Army Corps of Engineers requiring that if a Black applicant ranked among the top three candidates for a job, any decision not to select them had to be explained in writing. Kennedy replied, "I would not issue those regulations. I don't think that they are wise regulations." RFK said he supported outreach—"a major effort to try to find Negroes who are eligible"—but not a change in eligibility standards themselves.[25]

As attorney general, Kennedy saw a dearth of Black lawyers at the Justice Department and wanted to address the issue. But the affirmative action program he advocated was limited to improving outreach to law schools. RFK wrote to law school officials, "We're not seeking to give Negroes preferences. But we're not getting any applications, and we want these young people to know that they will not be excluded because of their race."[26]

This position seemed consistent with Kennedy's larger worldview. If the core issue of inequality was more closely related to class than color, and if it was critical to encourage working people of different races to see their common interests, then providing preferences based on race made little sense. As with issues like law and order and the Vietnam draft deferment, Kennedy had no problem bucking what educated white liberals considered to be the most virtuous position.

My third conclusion was that the coalition assembled by Kennedy was not only possible, but it was also highly preferable to a coalition composed solely of upper-middle-class white citizens and people of color, for a variety of reasons. To begin with, a multiracial working-class coalition was more likely to yield broad progress on the fundamental fight for economic fairness, because it did not rely on the noblesse oblige of wealthier white liberals, who might sometimes be unreliable allies. The great dream of people like labor and civil rights leader A. Philip Randolph was to create a cross-racial, class-based coalition rather than a race-focused, cross-class coalition because the former did not rely on charity but self-interest.[27] On the issue of housing, for example, upper-middle-class white liberals might vote for Democrats but often defend exclusionary zoning policies that build walls around their communities, to the detriment of working people.[28]

In addition, I concluded that to promote social peace, it was crucial to find ways for highly frustrated working-class people to work together. While an alliance of affluent white liberals and Black people was sometimes easier to build, Arthur Schlesinger told me that "the more important thing to do, obviously, is to try to bring the low-income whites and low-income blacks together . . . to preserve social cohesion."[29]

Relatedly, the Kennedy campaign was a reminder that if Democrats didn't make strong and energetic appeals to working-class white voters, other, sometimes deeply nefarious figures could fill the vacuum. After RFK was assassinated in June 1968, Paul Cowan, a reporter for the *Village Voice*, found that in Massachusetts, Governor George Wallace's rallies and speeches—almost all in white working-class neighborhoods—were attended by many former Robert Kennedy supporters. "The clear majority of Wallace's audiences, day or night, are white working-class men," Cowan wrote. "Many of them planned to vote for Robert Kennedy this year. 'He wasn't like the other politicians,' said a television repairman from Framingham. 'I had the feeling he really cared about people like us.'" Cowan concluded that Robert Kennedy was "the last liberal politician who could communicate with white working class America."[30] There were voters, said Halberstam, "who thought the choice in American politics narrowed to George Wallace or Bobby Kennedy."[31] Failing to appeal to working-class white voters could open the door to authoritarian candidates like Wallace (a prospect that would become all too real a half century later).

Martin Luther King Jr., Bayard Rustin, and Lyndon Johnson's Economic Approach to Affirmative Action

Kennedy's position on class, race, and affirmative action mirrored in many ways the thinking of my other great hero from the 1960s, Dr. Martin Luther King Jr. Like Kennedy, King believed something had to be done about the nation's racial history. However, he disagreed with Farmer and Young's stance that racial preferences were the right answer, both substantively and politically.

King clearly saw the need to take affirmative steps. In his 1963 book *Why We Can't Wait*, he made the moral case for compensation for slavery and segregation. "The ancient common law has always provided a remedy for the appropriation of the labor of one human being by another. This law should be made to apply for American Negroes," King wrote. "The nation must not only radically readjust its attitude toward the Negro in the compelling present, but must incorporate some compensatory consideration for the handicaps he has inherited from the past." While some friends "recoil in horror" at the notion of compensatory treatment, King said, "it is obvious that if a man is entered at the starting line in a race three hundred years after another man, the first would have to perform some impossible feat in order to catch up with his fellow runner." He wrote, "It is impossible to create a formula for the future which does not take into account that our society has been doing something special against the Negro for hundreds of years."[32]

All of this sounded like the predicate for a Whitney Young–type proposal for racial preferences—at least for some period of time. Instead, King argued in favor of a racially inclusive Bill of Rights for the Disadvantaged.[33] He offered three valuable insights.

First, precisely because of America's terrible history of slavery and segregation, a Bill of Rights for the Disadvantaged would disproportionately benefit Black people and thereby serve as a remedy for past discrimination. Second, King saw that while racial discrimination was a central source of inequality in American society, it was not the only one. Deprivation mattered too. Accordingly, King wrote, "It is a simple matter of justice that America, in dealing creatively with the task of raising the Negro from backwardness, should also be rescuing a large stratum of the forgotten white poor."[34] Third, like Kennedy, King knew that class-based programs had the potential to unite working-class people across racial lines, whereas race-based programs would divide the very political constituencies of civil rights and labor that constituted the 1963 March on Washington for Jobs and Freedom coalition. King was well aware that wealthy white interests had used race to divide working people throughout history. King told the AFL-CIO in 1961, "The forces that are anti-Negro are by and large anti-labor." He noted, "The labor-hater and the labor-baiter is virtually always a twin-headed creature spewing anti-Negro epithets from one mouth and anti-labor propaganda from the other mouth."[35] The opponents of civil rights were antilabor because they knew that the unification of working-class white and Black workers through unions could upend the politics of the South, leading to the loss of control for the powers that be.[36]

Divide and conquer was as old as American history. As Heather McGhee has noted, white servants and enslaved Black people joined together in the late seventeenth-century Bacon's Rebellion in Virginia, but soon after—to prevent such cross-racial alliances—"colonial governments began to separate the servant class based on skin color."[37] Back in 1848, Senator John Calhoun, a white supremacist, sought to rally white people around racial rather than class identity. He declared, "The two great divisions of society are not the rich and poor, but white and black."[38] Biracial coalitions of working people began to emerge in Virginia and elsewhere during the Reconstruction Era, Jamelle Bouie writes, but wealthy interests responded with a system of Jim Crow.[39] The tactic worked as intended. W. E. B. Du Bois noted in his 1935 study of Reconstruction and the relationship between Black and white workers in the South, "There probably are not today in the world two groups of workers with practically identical interests who hate and fear each other so deeply and persistently and who are kept so far apart that neither sees anything of common interest."[40]

Although it was difficult to pull off a cross-racial economic coalition, King believed it was necessary to try. Toward the end of his life, he dedicated himself to a Poor People's Campaign that would draw poor and working-class people of all races together. King told his staff, "We're going into the Southwest after the Indians, into the West after the Chicanos, into Appalachia after the poor whites, and into the ghettoes after the Negroes and Puerto Ricans." He continued, "And we're going to bring them together and enlarge this campaign into something bigger than just a civil rights movement for Negroes."[41]

Mindful of the long history of privileged white communities trying to divide disadvantaged people along racial lines, King demurred about backing new programs of racial preference, no matter how well intended they might be. Setting off a zero-sum competition between races would backfire. He wrote to an editor of *Why We Can't Wait*, "It is my opinion that many white workers whose economic condition is not too far removed from the economic condition of his black brother, will find it difficult to accept a 'Negro Bill of Rights,' which seeks to give special consideration to the Negro in the context of unemployment, joblessness, etc. and does not take into sufficient account their plight."[42] King viewed the Black and blue-collar white coalition as essential. He wrote,

Kennedy, King, and the Corporate Lawyer

"In the case of organized labor, an alliance with the Negro civil-rights movement is not a matter of choice but of necessity."[43]

The ideas articulated in *Why We Can't Wait* became increasingly important to King. In 1966, he argued, "We are now in the most difficult phase of the civil rights struggle [involving] the basic class issues between privileged and underprivileged."[44] In 1967 testimony before the Kerner Commission tasked with investigating the origins of civil unrest, King reaffirmed his class-based argument for affirmative action. He even drew language verbatim from *Why We Can't Wait*.[45] And in 1968, a week before he would be assassinated in Memphis, Tennessee, King said in an interview, "You could say we are engaged in a class struggle," though not simply for materialistic reasons. "I feel that this movement in behalf of the poor is the most moral thing—it is saying that every man is heir to a legacy of dignity and worth."[46]

King's decision to pivot from race to class was deeply controversial with his fellow civil rights leaders and his own staff. Why did he take a different path? Perhaps it was related to his economically comfortable childhood. A recent biography found that King harbored substantial guilt due to his upbringing in a relatively privileged Black family.[47] He was also surely influenced by his role as a Christian minister. Like all the great faith traditions, Christianity had a special place for poor people of all races, which was reflected in King's approach. In addition, King's thinking on a number of issues—including affirmative action—was enormously influenced by his lieutenant, Bayard Rustin.

A gay man who had to stay behind the scenes in an era of blatant homophobia, Rustin was most famous for brilliantly organizing the 1963 March on Washington for Jobs and Freedom that showcased King's "I Have a Dream" speech. Rustin also helped convince King that Gandhian nonviolence was the best path to reform. When Rustin first met King during the 1950s Montgomery, Alabama, Bus Boycott, in fact, there were guns lying around King's home for self-protection. According to civil rights leader Vernon Jordan, Rustin, who studied history deeply, was "our intellectual bank, our Brookings Institution."[48]

Class Matters

As the civil rights movement gained success in combatting legalized racism with passage of the Civil Rights and Voting Rights Act, says historian David Garrow, "Rustin had been telling King that the most serious issues facing the movement were economic problems of class, rather than race."[49] In an important 1965 article in *Commentary*, "From Protest to Politics," Rustin argued that because passage of civil rights laws had destroyed "the legal foundations of racism," it was time to address the economic legacy of racism.[50] As King would memorably put it, "What does it profit a man to be able to eat at an integrated lunch counter if he doesn't earn enough money to buy a hamburger and a cup of coffee?"[51]

Rustin argued that the second phase of the civil rights movement would be much more expensive and therefore required additional allies. With Black people constituting just one in ten Americans, Rustin said, it was necessary to build on the March on Washington for Jobs and Freedom's coalition of "Negroes, trade unionists, liberals, and religious groups."[52] Rustin would later write, "There can be no such thing as an exclusive Negro economic program, for that would counterpose the interests of a little more than ten percent of the society to those of the overwhelming majority."[53] Rustin feared that racial preferences would sever the coalition necessary for change. In the years to come, he rooted his opposition to racial preference policies in this concern.

Kennedy, King, and Rustin's economic approach was mirrored by President Lyndon B. Johnson as well. LBJ argued that compensation was due in response to a terrible history of oppression. In a famous 1965 speech at Howard University, Johnson employed King's metaphor of a sprint, suggesting, "You do not take a person who, for years, has been hobbled by chains and liberate him, bring him up to the starting line of a race and then say, 'you are free to compete with all the others,' and still justly believe that you have been completely fair."[54]

Contemporary news accounts, however, noted that he did not believe that racial preferences were the appropriate remedy. Instead,

Kennedy, King, and the Corporate Lawyer

LBJ called for a number of programs to promote social mobility more broadly, as well as targeted efforts to let Black people know about opportunities. At a subsequent White House conference, when the issue of racial preferences in decision-making was introduced, Johnson officials made sure it was killed.[55] And when Johnson's labor secretary Willard Wirtz designed a plan for implementing racial quotas in the Philadelphia construction industry, it received little backing and was rescinded before the president left office.[56]

Indeed, Johnson's Executive Order 11246 called for corporations doing business with the federal government to take "affirmative action to ensure that applicants are employed, and that employees are treated during employment, *without* regard to their race, creed, color, or national origin."[57]

Affirmative Action in the Courts:
William O. Douglas Versus Lewis Powell

If King, Rustin, Kennedy, and Johnson advocated making special efforts to help the disadvantaged, colleges and universities preferred the path suggested by Farmer and Young, which entailed outright racial preferences. Universities wanted to signal that they cared about racial equality, but in the least expensive way possible. They were not interested in satisfying the public's desire for fairness in the admissions process. Nor did schools care about which policies would support a larger multiracial coalition seeking to effect change in the country. And so, they adopted explicit racial preferences in admissions, regardless of whether the students benefiting were economically disadvantaged. If universities could bring together upper-middle-class students across racial lines, that would achieve their stated goal of racial diversity without the need for substantial financial aid for working-class students. Selective universities across the country implemented racial preference programs and, in some cases, explicit racial quotas in their admissions processes.

Class Matters

Many Americans were outraged by these university policies. They thought the whole point of the civil rights movement was that race should *not* count in things like college admissions. And so before long, racial preferences were challenged in the courts. In the 1970s, two cases would make it to the Supreme Court: *DeFunis v. Odegaard* (1974) and *University of California Regents v. Bakke* (1978). And just as the civil rights community split over racial preferences, between King and Rustin's economic approach and Farmer and Young's racial approach, the liberal justices would also be divided. On the one hand, Justice William O. Douglas backed preferences for the economically disadvantaged as a matter of fairness. On the other, Justice Thurgood Marshall favored class-blind racial preferences as a remedy for past discrimination. A third justice, Lewis Powell Jr., would win the day and shape racial preference policies with a conservative twist.

The litigation began in 1971 when a white applicant, Marco DeFunis, sued the University of Washington (UW) Law School for denying him admission under a system of racial preferences. DeFunis was a sympathetic figure: a low-income Sephardic Jew who had worked his way through college. UW Law School had set up a separate admissions procedure for white and minority students, and thirty-six of thirty-seven minority students admitted had test scores lower than DeFunis's.[58] The trial court ruled in favor of DeFunis, finding that his constitutional rights were violated, and ordered his admission to the law school. The case was reversed by the Washington Supreme Court and later appealed to the U.S. Supreme Court, where it was argued in 1974.

Many liberal organizations supported DeFunis, among them the AFL-CIO. Organized labor had been a strong supporter of the 1964 Civil Rights Act. Indeed, former Missouri Democratic congressman Richard Bolling argued, "We would never have passed the Civil Rights Act without labor. They had the muscle; the other civil rights groups did not."[59] Labor supported the law in part because discrimination and segregation inspire racial hostility, which inhibits worker solidarity.

Kennedy, King, and the Corporate Lawyer

For precisely the same reason, the AFL-CIO filed an amicus brief supporting DeFunis in the Supreme Court case to challenge the use of racial preferences. While such preferences were well-intentioned, they unwittingly made it easier for latter-day John Calhouns to use race to divide and conquer. Moreover, as observed by Albert Shanker, president of the American Federation of Teachers, racial preference programs ignored fundamental questions of economic fairness that animated organized labor: "The particular woman or black who gets the job may have come from an affluent, advantaged background and may have pushed out an economically poor, disadvantaged white male." He argued that advantaged white communities protected their own position, while accusing working-class voters of being bigoted for opposing affirmative action. "What if you said give 20 percent of Time Inc. or U.S. Steel" to Black people, Shanker asked. "Who would be narrow then?" He saw the larger political impact as well, arguing that racial quotas were part of what had "impelled millions of white working-class 'ethnics,' as well as middle-class whites, to move over to the Republican side" in Richard Nixon's 1972 landslide victory over George McGovern.[60]

Bayard Rustin also weighed in with a column on the *DeFunis* case, outlining how racial preferences were dividing the liberal coalition.[61] In a 1974 letter to the *Wall Street Journal*, Rustin, carrying King's flame, wrote, "To transform the demand for Negro rights into a call for the displacement of whites would inevitably elicit instantaneous and widespread resistance from a society otherwise disposed to view the civil-rights agenda favorably." Rustin knew that lower-middle-class white populations were a swing vote in America, and that "the question is not whether this group is conservative or liberal, for it is both, and how it acts will depend upon the way issues are defined." Racial preferences encouraged white working-class voters to vote their race, not their class, which was exactly what conservatives wanted.[62]

Labor would find a willing champion on the Supreme Court in Justice William O. Douglas. Considered the Court's most liberal justice,

Douglas, raised by a struggling single mother, was appointed to his seat in 1939 by Franklin Roosevelt. Douglas saw the importance of class inequality in virtually all his jurisprudence. He joined in decisions striking down California's "anti-Okie" law that made it a crime to transport a poor individual into the state, providing the right of counsel to indigent criminal defendants, and invalidating poll taxes that required people to pay to exercise their right to vote.[63]

In the *DeFunis* case, Douglas suggested that class was a better basis of affirmative action than race. He wrote that while race per se should not be considered, class disadvantage could be: "A black applicant who pulled himself out of the ghetto into a junior college may thereby demonstrate a level of motivation, perseverance, and ability that would lead a fair-minded admissions committee to conclude that he shows more promise for law study than the son of a rich alumnus who achieved better grades at Harvard. That applicant would be offered admissions not because he is black, but because as an individual he has shown he has the potential, while the Harvard man may have taken less advantage of the vastly superior opportunities offered him." Douglas continued: such an applicant "may not realize his full potential in the first year of law school, or in the full three years, but in the long pull of a legal career his achievements may far outstrip those of his classmates whose earlier records appeared superior by conventional criteria."[64]

Douglas did not prevail. A majority of the justices in the *DeFunis* case ruled that the point was moot because DeFunis had already graduated from law school. But the larger issue did not go away. In 1978, Allan Bakke, a white son of a milkman, filed a lawsuit after being denied admission to the University of California at Davis Medical School, despite having stronger academic credentials than many of the minority students admitted through a racial quota that set aside sixteen out of one hundred seats.[65] Civil rights groups and universities mostly sided with the University of California, while the Leadership Conference on Civil Rights, a group comprising civil rights, Jewish, and labor organizations, was divided and did not take a stance.[66]

Kennedy, King, and the Corporate Lawyer

The American Federation of Teachers and Shanker again weighed in, arguing that special consideration should be provided to disadvantaged individuals of all races. Meanwhile, Rustin again raised concerns about what racial preferences were doing to the liberal coalition.[67] But Douglas had retired from the Supreme Court, so labor lost its champion.

In *Bakke*, four liberals on the Court, led by Thurgood Marshall and William Brennan, argued that UC Davis's quota system was a legitimate response to the brutal history of oppressions in America. There was a powerful moral force to Marshall's argument. To support his case, he cited reams of socioeconomic statistics showing that Black people were disproportionately poor because of discrimination. For example, Marshall noted that Black people were four times more likely to live in poverty, and their median family income was only 60 percent of white people's.[68]

Interestingly, Marshall emphatically rejected the notion that racial preferences should be focused on disadvantaged Black applicants, an idea that Justice Brennan included in an early draft of the opinion. According to an account in the *New York Times*, Brennan "asked Marshall whether he thought his own son, applying to college, should benefit from affirmative action. 'Damn right,' Marshall answered, according to Brennan's account. 'They owe us.'"[69]

The four conservatives argued that UC Davis's plan was a violation of the 1964 Civil Rights Act, which was written to be universal in character, forbidding discrimination on the basis of race, full stop. When the issue of quotas and reverse discrimination came up during congressional deliberations on the Civil Rights Act, they noted, "the proponents of the legislation gave repeated assurances that the Act would be 'colorblind' in its application." The conservatives pointed to Senator Hubert Humphrey's remark that racial discrimination arose when there was any "distinction in treatment" based on color, even if it benefited people of color. It would be discrimination, Humphrey said, if the Internal Revenue Service ruled that people of color "can pay their taxes

6 months later than everyone else."[70] UC Davis had clearly violated the law against racial discrimination, they argued.

Justice Douglas's middle ground, which aimed to compensate for history in a racially neutral way by providing a leg up to the economically disadvantaged, found no champions. To the contrary, Justice Harry Blackmun claimed alternative programs, such as economic preferences, wouldn't work to produce racial diversity: "I suspect that it would be impossible to arrange an affirmative action program in a racially neutral way and have it successful. To ask that this be so is to demand the impossible. In order to get beyond racism, we must first take account of race. There is no other way."[71] Blackmun offered no empirical evidence for his pessimistic views about the ability of low-income Black students to qualify for admissions under an affirmative action system based on class rather than race. But the idea appears to have been drawn from an article by former Harvard dean McGeorge Bundy, whose language Blackmun incorporated into the opinion. In a November 1977 article in *The Atlantic*, Bundy asserted— without any statistical evidence—that "to get past racism, we must take race into account. There is no other present way."[72] Blackmun did not explain why he took at face value the word of Bundy, an architect of the disastrous war in Vietnam and a representative of a college that would benefit financially from a race-based, rather than class-based, preference system.

And Harvard would have an even more powerful influence on another key justice in the *Bakke* case, the deeply conservative Lewis F. Powell Jr. A Richard Nixon appointee who worked closely with the U.S. Chamber of Commerce and served as a lawyer for Philip Morris, Powell was as far as one could get from the prolabor Douglas.[73] But he was the deciding vote in *Bakke* and would take Harvard's advice on two critical issues that would reverberate for decades.

First, whereas the Court's liberals argued for racial preferences as a morally appropriate response to racial oppression, and the conservatives said racial preferences represented an abrupt upending of the moral consensus around nondiscrimination, Powell said that affirmative action was not really an issue of fairness. Powell's view, which echoed Harvard's brief, represented a major departure from the way most people thought about affirmative action. Because an elite education could put someone on a different trajectory in life, many Americans believed that opportunity should be allocated in a way that rewards hard work and merit. But the higher education establishment, along with Justice Powell, did not see it that way. Indeed, they suggested it was naive to view the admissions process as a university decision about who *deserves* admission. Racial and geographic preferences were necessary so that universities could structure a particular educational environment that included both Black and rural students and helped educate the mostly white and metropolitan student body on campus.[74] Black people and farm boys were not treated as ends in themselves, but rather as a means of enlightening others.

This line of thinking rendered objections based on fairness as both unsophisticated and irrelevant. When thorny questions were asked about whether the son of a Black doctor deserved a leg up, the answer was that admissions should not be guided by considerations of what is fair to applicants, but rather by who will add the most value to the college. This could be due to the accident of a student's race or the accident of their being a legacy whose parents will add to the institution's coffers. As the philosopher Michael Sandel notes, honest rejection letters under this way of thinking would read, "Dear (Unsuccessful) Applicant, We regret to inform you that your application for admission has been rejected. . . . Those admitted instead of you were not themselves deserving of a place, nor worthy of praise for factors that led to their admission. We are in any case only using them—and you—as instruments for a wider social purpose."[75]

Second, Powell said that while explicitly setting aside sixteen seats was unconstitutional, a university could use race as a "plus factor," and again pointed to Harvard's approach. His reasoning had some appeal because a fixed number of slots seemed arbitrary, but the turn was a troubling one. Whereas university quotas would make transparent the degree to which they used race in admissions and subject them to scrutiny and public debate, race as a vague "plus factor" of unknown magnitude allowed institutions to keep the system opaque. It enabled college officials to claim that under a system of "holistic admissions" they weighed an infinite number of factors, and it was really none of the public's business to know how the sausage was made. Many liberals, who normally believed that sunshine served as a disinfectant and agreed with the idea that "democracy dies in darkness," went along with Powell to support the cause of racial preferences.[76]

As a practical matter, "race as a factor" could be calibrated to achieve remarkably consistent results year in and year out, akin to a covert quota. Therefore, it remains unclear whether Powell succeeded in avoiding the same concerns he had with the UC Davis system. Over the years, for example, Harvard's "holistic review" in which race was used as a "plus factor" yielded little variation in the share of Black, Hispanic, and Asian students enrolled each year.[77]

After *Bakke*, Powell's vision of affirmative action with race as "one factor" became the new "compromise position" among liberal elites (though not rank-and-file Democrats). It replaced the old middle-ground policy of economic affirmative action advocated by King and Douglas. In a remarkable transformation, James Farmer's support for racial preferences moved to the mainstream among leaders on the left. The social critic Michael Lind wrote, "If today's establishment were honest, Martin Luther King Day would be James Farmer Day."[78]

The Reagan Justices on Affirmative Action

Powell's endorsement of racial preferences under Harvard's logic did not sit well with average voters, and was part of a much larger set of issues (including the economy and foreign policy) that propelled Ronald Reagan's victories in 1980 and 1984. Affirmative action was especially unpopular among blue-collar white "Reagan Democrats," who were sometimes less economically advantaged than Black beneficiaries of affirmative action.

Once in office, Reagan appointed Supreme Court justices who opposed racial preferences. One appointee, Antonin Scalia, criticized the unfairness of racial preferences from a class perspective. In one law review article, Scalia, then a professor at the University of Chicago, argued, "I am entirely in favor of according the poor inner-city child, who happens to be black, advantages and preferences not given to my own children because they don't need them. But I am not willing to prefer the son of a prosperous and well-educated black doctor or lawyer—solely because of his race—to the son of a recent refugee from Eastern Europe who is working as a manual laborer to get his family ahead."[79] Reagan's other appointees—Justice Sandra Day O'Connor and Justice Anthony Kennedy—also expressed strong reservations about racial preferences, especially during their early years on the Court.

The impact of the three Reagan appointees became clear in January 1989, when the Supreme Court delivered a major blow to the use of racial preferences in government contracting through the case of *City of Richmond v. Croson*.[80] By a 6–3 vote, the Supreme Court struck down Richmond's practice of reserving 30 percent of construction contracts for minority-owned companies, and encouraged cities to provide a more general boost to economically disadvantaged firms instead.[81]

While conservative justices were making this case, a few left-of-center leaders were also still championing the Douglas approach. During his tenure as New York City mayor from 1978 to 1989, Democrat Edward Koch implemented a class-based affirmative action program for government contracting. He established a 10 percent subcontracting set-aside for small firms located in New York that did at least 25 percent of their business in depressed areas or employed economically disadvantaged workers as at least 25 percent of their workforce.[82]

And King's lieutenant Bayard Rustin continued to back such programs. In 1987, he gave a speech at the Memorial Church of Harvard University to honor King's birthday, during which Rustin backed preferences "along class lines." He warned that using race as a proxy for disadvantage was dangerous because it helped foster a new form of racism based not on biology but on "observed sociological data." Rustin said, "The new racist equates the pathology of the poor with race, ignoring the fact that family dissolution, teenage pregnancy, illegitimacy, alcohol and drug abuse, street crime, and idleness are universal problems of the poor. They exist wherever there is economic dislocation . . . among the white jobless of Liverpool as well as among unemployed blacks in New York."[83] Research found, for example, that young Black men were more likely to commit violent crimes than white men. But when one compared Black and white men who were employed, "differences in violent behavior vanished."[84]

Rustin, who died later that year, paid a terrible price for his apostasy. Some Black leaders ridiculed him with scorn. In Rustin's *New York Times* obituary, James Farmer claimed, "Bayard has no credibility in the black community." He alleged that Rustin's "commitment is to labor, not to the black man," which to Farmer constituted a form of racial betrayal.[85]

Finding a Better Way?

During the time of Rustin's speech and the Supreme Court's Richmond set-aside decision, I was a student at Harvard Law School. After the first year of law school, I married my college sweetheart, Rebecca Rozen, a student at the Kennedy School of Government; and after the second year of law school, we had our first child. Although my life at home was wonderful, I found myself bored in most of my law school classes, ranging from contracts to civil procedure.

One exception was constitutional law. I became fascinated by the unusual convergence between the line of reasoning advanced by conservative justices in the *Croson* case and the ideals of Douglas, MLK, RFK, and Rustin. I was cognizant that the conservatives might be using class-based affirmative action as a talking point against racial preferences. But I wondered whether their jurisprudence on race would ultimately lead to the adoption of class-based programs advanced by my liberal heroes.

In 1989, in the second semester of my third year, I approached one of my law professors, Alan Dershowitz, to supervise an independent research paper on economic affirmative action programs. Dershowitz was a well-known and controversial character on campus. He was known as a strong supporter of civil liberties and wasn't afraid to take on challenging public policy issues. I was intrigued by an article he wrote with a student that raised important questions about affirmative action. Dershowitz and his coauthor argued that Harvard's "diversity" model, which Justice Powell so admired, had originally been designed to cap the number of Jews on campus. I'd always been concerned about anti-Semitism, but my marriage to Rebecca, who had attended yeshiva, raised my antennae further. Dershowitz also objected that racial preferences were "classically overinclusive (including advantaged blacks) and underinclusive (not including disadvantaged whites)."[86]

Dershowitz readily agreed to supervise the paper, and I got to work. I argued that transitioning to class-based affirmative action presented a rare opportunity where a commitment to fairness, the desire to build a powerful political coalition, and legal imperatives all lined up nicely. The policy would combine the idealism and political logic of RFK, MLK, and Rustin and the legal rationale of Douglas, Scalia, and O'Connor.

The issue would resurface for me soon enough. After graduating from law school, I went to work for the newly elected Democratic U.S. senator Chuck Robb. The son-in-law of Lyndon Johnson, Robb was a former marine who had served in Vietnam. In the early 1980s, he was a highly popular governor of Virginia. Robb was strongly supportive of civil rights, but he was also a leading New Democrat and chaired the Democratic Leadership Council, which questioned some liberal pieties. The group emphasized that the party should be for equal opportunity, but not equal group result and racial quotas, which drew the ire of civil rights leader Jesse Jackson.[87]

I encouraged Robb to support the Civil Rights Act of 1991, to strengthen legal protections against discrimination, which he did. I also encouraged him to vote against Supreme Court nominee Clarence Thomas that year, but that proved a tougher sell. Along the way, however, I took part in a fascinating conversation between Robb and Thomas on affirmative action. As outlined in the prologue, Thomas went after the Achilles' heel of racial preferences when he asked why his son should receive a preference in college admission over a poor white student. Later, in the confirmation hearings, Thomas also raised his support for affirmative action based on economic disadvantage rather than race. "The kids could come from any background of disadvantage," he suggested. "The kid could be a white kid from Appalachia, could be a Cajun from Louisiana, or could be a black kid or Hispanic kid from the inner cities or from the barrios, but I defended that sort of a program [in the 1970s] and I would defend it today."[88] Thomas's phrasing had a canny resemblance to that used by King when he discussed assembling a Poor People's Campaign.

From today's vantage point, many liberals assume that supporting racial preferences is the default position for idealistic, forward-thinking people. But the early history suggests a different story. In the 1960s and 1970s, liberals like King, Kennedy, Johnson, Douglas, Rustin, and Shanker advocated a different path based on economic disadvantage. They believed that providing support for those who are economically disadvantaged would help remedy the nation's history of racial oppression, which left a powerful economic legacy. Additionally, they recognized that poor or working-class white citizens also deserve a leg up. This approach would promote social cohesion and help support a multiracial working-class coalition, something that racial preferences could never achieve. During this era, racial preferences were supported by civil rights groups, but this approach survived only because it was backed by elites at Harvard University and their champion on the Supreme Court, the corporate-friendly Justice Lewis Powell.

It was a stunning turn of history when Powell, the corporate lawyer, diverted King and Kennedy's dream. The public, however, never supported racial preferences, and that opposition contributed to the rise of Republican presidents whose appointments to the Supreme Court posed new legal threats to the racial approach.

CHAPTER 2

The Blue State Populist
Revolt Against
Racial Preferences

W HILE STILL WORKING FOR SENATOR CHARLES ROBB, I HAD
become excited about the presidential candidacy of Robb's fellow southern Democrat, Arkansas governor Bill Clinton. Like Robb,
Clinton was part of the New Democrats movement. After three consecutive Democratic presidential losses—those of Jimmy Carter in 1980,
Walter Mondale in 1984, and Michael Dukakis in 1988—it was clearly
time to try another approach.

Clinton, Robb, and others had founded the Democratic Leadership
Council to move the Democratic Party toward the political center on a
variety of issues, including affirmative action. Prior to the 1992 election,
one of Clinton's pollsters, Stanley Greenberg, explained to journalist
Peter Brown that among the public "there is no debate on affirmative
action. Everyone is against it. There is a very small share of the [white]
electorate—zero—that believes they have personal responsibility for

this. That they ought to be paying for the injustice. . . . They can't even begin to understand the logic on it. It does not even reach the level of common sense for the majority of Americans. . . . It is a political problem of historic proportions."[1]

When Clinton ran for the 1992 Democratic presidential nomination, he was an advocate of civil rights but at best a lukewarm supporter of racial affirmative action programs. In the 1992 New York Democratic primary debate, he fudged when a reporter raised a question about racial preferences. When asked about racial set-aside programs in contracting, Clinton's rival, California governor Jerry Brown, said, "Sure, I support that," but Clinton hedged. He said that while he supported affirmative action goals, public contracts should not go to minority firms that bid above the lowest offer. One reporter noted that he backtracked "from the actual practice in many set-aside programs."[2]

Clinton badly needed to win back some Reagan Democrats. His campaign aide George Stephanopoulos later wrote that Clinton was uniquely positioned to draw "black and white workers together in common cause. Just like Bobby Kennedy had tried to do before an assassin's bullet struck him down." Stephanopoulos noted that in the intervening years, Republicans had used issues like crime and racial quotas to gain the support of blue-collar white voters: "By 1991, RFK's 'black and blue' coalition was a distant memory. Maybe Clinton could put it back together. That was his dream and mine."[3]

Others saw promise in Clinton's approach. In March 1992, after the Super Tuesday primaries, the *New York Times* editorial board drew parallels to RFK. The *Times* said Clinton's showings "give healthy evidence, probably for the first time since Robert Kennedy's Indiana primary campaign in 1968, that it is politically possible to bring poor blacks and blue-collar whites together."[4] Harvard professor William Julius Wilson was similarly impressed by Clinton's "remarkable biracial coalition" of lower-middle-class white and Black voters.[5]

During the general election campaign against the patrician president George H. W. Bush, Clinton and his running mate Al Gore published a populist campaign book called *Putting People First.* The book never used the term "affirmative action" but firmly declared the pair's opposition to racial quotas.[6]

After Clinton was elected president in 1992, his language shifted. The Bubba who understood working-class sensibilities was also a graduate of Georgetown, Oxford, and Yale Law and knew how to speak the language of race employed on those campuses. He also wanted to reward constituency groups that helped him take the White House.

In his first signal to voters while assembling his presidential cabinet, he leaned heavily on the rhetoric of elite universities about the importance of diversity and popularized the concept that a cabinet should "look like America."[7] It was a telling phrase. The emphasis on "looking" like America was different from a commitment that the cabinet would "reflect" America in all its dimensions. There was no expressed desire to include people from all walks of life, including those who had experienced economic hardship. Instead, Clinton stocked his cabinet with corporate lawyers from a variety of races, which led one commentator to quip that the administration, which had promised a new covenant with the people of America, resembled "Covenant and Burling"—a reference to the prominent corporate D.C. law firm.[8]

Early in his administration, Clinton also advocated racial preference policies to promote diversity. In 1994, when a Hispanic student challenged a University of Maryland scholarship that was reserved for Black students only, the Justice Department backed the racially exclusive award. Even more controversially, in 1994, Clinton's Justice Department reversed the Bush administration's position and backed the Piscataway, New Jersey, school board's decision to lay off a white teacher who had equal seniority with a Black teacher in order to preserve racial diversity among the faculty. Instead of the typical coin flip to decide who would lose her job, Clinton supported using race in such decisions, a move that teacher union leader Albert Shanker strongly opposed.[9] (The Third Circuit later struck down the school board's practice, and civil rights groups encouraged the board to withdraw the case on appeal to the Supreme Court because an unfavorable ruling against affirmative action was expected.)[10]

In November 1994, Democrats suffered a stunning defeat in the midterm congressional elections, as voters put Republicans in control of the House of Representatives for the first time in forty years. Pundits dubbed it the year of the "angry white male." In 1992, white men had split evenly in congressional races, favoring Republicans 51 percent of the time; but in 1994, white men went for Republican candidates 62 percent of the time. And it was a certain type of white male who was most likely to turn against Clinton. One Democratic pollster said, "The big story of the election is the hostility among blue collar men who haven't gone to college."[11]

Although the 1994 election had been about many issues—including an ill-fated effort to promote a complicated health care system, engineered by First Lady Hillary Clinton—Republicans were quick to tie the results directly to affirmative action. In early February 1995, Senate Majority Leader Bob Dole announced he was considering a repeal of affirmative action programs and asked, "Why did 62 percent of white males vote Republican in 1994? I think it's because of things like this, where sometimes the best qualified person does not get the job because he or she may be one color."[12]

Clinton knew he was politically vulnerable on the question of affirmative action and recognized that the issue wasn't going away. Potential attacks were coming from both the judiciary and a voter initiative in California slated for November 1996, which would both keep affirmative action in the news and require a response from the president.

In early 1995, shortly after the election, the Supreme Court heard oral arguments in a challenge to racial preferences in government contracting in *Adarand v. Peña*. In the 1990 *Metro Broadcasting v. FCC* decision, the Court had narrowly supported racial preferences in federal contracting. But with changes in the Court, the justices were being asked to overrule that case. The most significant shift was Clarence

Thomas's replacement of Thurgood Marshall. Later in the year, the Court would indeed overturn *Metro Broadcasting*.[13]

Even worse for Clinton, conservatives planned to highlight the affirmative action issue by placing an anti–racial preference referendum on the 1996 ballot in California, coinciding with the president's reelection campaign. Some within the administration thought Clinton should endorse the ballot referendum to neutralize the issue (a tactic he would later employ in signing welfare reform legislation). Assistant Attorney General for Civil Rights Deval Patrick was asked to analyze the effect of Clinton's endorsement.[14]

Bill Clinton's Flirtation with Class-Based Affirmative Action

With the Republicans and the Supreme Court reconsidering affirmative action, Clinton declared at a February 24, 1995, press conference that he had ordered a "review" of all such federal programs. One journalist noted that no president since Lyndon Johnson had evaluated these programs—"even those Republican presidents who had campaigned against affirmative action."[15]

In a subsequent press conference on March 3, 1995, Clinton went further and said he was considering shifting the basis of affirmative action from race and gender to economic need: "I want to emphasize need-based programs where we can because they work better and have a bigger impact and generate broader public support." The *Washington Post* front-page headline read, "In Shift, President Supports Affirmative Action Based on Needs."[16] Would Clinton really embrace the logic of Martin Luther King Jr., Robert F. Kennedy, and William O. Douglas?

A few days later, my phone rang around 6:00 a.m. at home, and I assumed there was an emergency. But it was Marty Peretz, editor in chief of the *New Republic*, who knew about my work on class-based affirmative action. He was calling to see if I'd be willing to write an article explaining why Clinton should follow through on his trial balloon and endorse need-based, rather than race-based, affirmative action.

I had known and liked Peretz since my sophomore year at Harvard, when I took his social studies seminar on nationalism. On the first day of class, he asked each of us, "If a Martian arrived on Earth, how would you describe yourself?" Somewhat embarrassingly (in retrospect), many of us saw our status as Harvard students as central to our identities. Others talked about their religious, ethnic, or racial background. Peretz observed that none of us described ourselves as American, a point that has always stuck with me.

He took a genuine interest in his students, and in later years, he invited my wife, Rebecca, and me to several of the legendary Cambridge dinners he and his wife, Anne, hosted. The gatherings included a mix of professors and students, along with at least one luminary, such as Jerry Brown or the Irish politician and writer Conor Cruise O'Brien. Peretz advised us about how to handle the challenges of an interfaith marriage and attended our wedding at West Point. He provided a generous blurb for a memoir I wrote about Harvard Law School, *Broken Contract*, and facilitated my introduction to Chuck Robb for a job interview.

Peretz remains a controversial figure who has his blind spots. In October 1994, he made space in the prestigious pages of the *New Republic* for a racist article by Charles Murray positing the genetic inferiority of Black people. Much of the staff was appropriately outraged, and the magazine published several rebuttals.[17] Years later, Peretz would humiliate himself by making disparaging comments about Arabs, for which he later apologized.[18]

The *New Republic*'s editor at the time, Andrew Sullivan, liked my draft and featured the story on the cover. The headline read in all caps, "Class, Not Race: A Liberal Case for Junking Old-Style Affirmative Action in Favor of Something That Works."[19] The title accurately described the *means* I advocated for shaping preferences, but I took pains to explain why the *outcome* of such a policy would be diversity across both racial and class lines.

Invoking research from my thesis on Robert Kennedy, I wrote that politically, switching from race-based to class-based preferences would help Clinton "turn a glaring liability for his party into an advantage—without betraying basic Democratic principles" that champion the underdog. People understood that class was the primary predictor of opportunity in America, I argued. For that reason, programs that gave a leg up to economically disadvantaged people who overcame odds were popular.

Because class-based affirmative action was at that point more of a vague idea than an actual policy, the article tried to put meat on the bones about how the program would work, particularly in college admissions. There were plenty of skeptics, including at the *New Republic* itself. *TNR*'s Michael Kinsley, for example, asked, "Does Clarence Thomas, the sharecropper's kid, get more or fewer preference points than the unemployed miner's son from Appalachia?"[20] I thought problems like this were solvable and pointed out that admissions officers frequently deal with these types of comparisons between students who had similar academic records but different life experiences.

In my article, I noted that research had shown that many socioeconomic factors were associated with academic achievement, including family income, parental education, family structure, family wealth (net worth), neighborhood poverty levels, and K–12 school poverty levels, so students who did well despite these obstacles were special. The same could be said for a student who overcame racial discrimination. Moreover, I noted, college admissions officers have unusual access to socioeconomic data through student applications and financial aid forms.

Skeptics worried that a class-based program would mostly end up helping poor white individuals. I pointed out, however, that using a complete set of socioeconomic indicators—rather than just income—would do a better job of capturing the nation's history and ongoing struggles with racial discrimination and therefore disproportionately benefit Black and Hispanic students. "Even among similar income groups, blacks are more likely than whites to live in concentrated poverty, go to bad schools, and live in single-parent homes," I noted.[21] I ended by calling for a return to King's concept of a Bill of Rights for the Disadvantaged of all races.

I had been mulling these ideas for some time, but the *New Republic* article provided my first opportunity to bring them to a broader public. In the mid-1990s, *TNR* was a great launching pad. The article received a tremendous amount of play. As a thirty-one-year-old whose career had mostly been spent as a Hill staffer, receiving attention from senior public figures was a pretty heady experience. More intriguing, though, was that the response did not fall along predictable ideological lines.

Some conservative intellectuals opposed the class-based approach. Harvard professor Nathan Glazer wrote a response in the *Wall Street Journal* titled "Race, Not Class." He suggested that shifting to need-based affirmative action would be inefficient (because it would help many poor white and Asian students) and expensive (because it would require more financial aid for economically disadvantaged students).[22] Likewise, Abigail Thernstrom, a senior fellow at the Manhattan Institute, wrote an article in the *Washington Post* titled "A Class-Backwards Idea: Why Affirmative Action for the Needy Won't Work," which argued that "adopting an economic needs test would, more than likely, simply exacerbate the already serious problem of victim status creep."[23]

Meanwhile, some within the Clinton White House were interested and wanted to know more. Joel Klein, a lawyer in the White House Office of the General Counsel at the time (and later chancellor of New York City Public Schools), contacted me. He was part of a group of center-left New Democrats in the administration, along with Bill Galston, arguing for cutting back on racial affirmative action. Other Clinton insiders—such as Christopher Edley and Deval Patrick—were staunch supporters of such programs.[24] The fight within the administration would play out in the coming months.

Caving In to Democratic Interest Groups

The political dilemma was clear for Clinton. On the one hand, the president would have the public on his side if he shifted to a policy of class-based affirmative action. A 1995 *Washington Post* poll found that 60 percent of white people and 44 percent of Black people agreed that "affirmative action should be for low-income people, not for persons of a specific race or sex."[25] On the other hand, virtually all the organized interest groups within the Democratic Party were adamantly in favor of racial and gender preferences.

Clinton aide George Stephanopoulos later wrote that Clinton's suggestion that affirmative action programs "should move to an 'alternative' based on economic need rather than race" sent "a shock wave through affirmative action supporters." Jesse Jackson, who ran for president in 1984 and 1988, threatened to challenge Clinton for the Democratic nomination in 1996 if he didn't "stand firm" on affirmative action. The threat was taken very seriously. "Remembering the rule that primary challenges almost always cripple incumbent presidents," Stephanopoulos wrote, "I was convinced we'd lose if Jackson ran."[26]

Later, Stephanopoulos met with Jackson to discuss Clinton's policy on affirmative action. Stephanopoulos recalled that Jackson sat behind a large map marked with state-filing deadlines and "rehearsed speech rifts" such as "If we can use goals, targets, and timetables to get fair trade with Japan, we can use goals, targets, and timetables to get a fair shake for our own folks. That's what affirmative action is all about."[27]

There was a certain irony in Jackson's opposition to class as a basis for affirmative action because he had long argued for a cross-racial populist politics. He spoke of the need to "leave the racial battle ground and come to the economic common ground." He told Black and white audiences, "When a baby cries at midnight because it has no supper, that baby doesn't cry black or white or brown or male or female. That baby cries in pain."[28] But now Jackson told Stephanopoulos, "I'm not moving one inch on set-asides" and was ready to call Black business leaders to finance his presidential run if Clinton opened up affirmative action to disadvantaged people of all races.[29]

Organized interest groups in Washington, D.C., including the higher education lobby and their allies in big business, as well as civil rights and women's groups, all benefited in some way from maintaining the status quo. Race- and gender-based programs tended to benefit upper-middle-class minority students and business contractors, catering to their interests.[30] For civil rights and feminist groups, whose primary constituencies were politically active middle- and upper-middle-class people of color and women, the switch to class-based advocacy only had downsides. And universities hated the idea of having to spend more on financial aid for economically disadvantaged students.

In the past, politically powerful labor unions had championed the class approach because even well-intentioned policies that divided people by race inhibited the possibility of multiracial solidarity. But a lot had changed for labor in the two decades since the AFL-CIO had opposed racial preferences in the *DeFunis* case. Labor membership had been in free fall, resulting in a significant loss of power. As a result, labor increasingly had to rely on its allies in the civil rights and feminist communities. Remarkably, when Clinton voiced his support for need-based affirmative action, the AFL-CIO sent him a letter in support of *maintaining* racial preferences.[31] When I met with American Federation of Teachers president Albert Shanker in 1995, he told me, "I may be the only person in labor circles today" to oppose racial preferences publicly. "That doesn't mean others are for it, it just means that everybody shut up, because it's politically incorrect."[32] Just as Rustin's position in favor of economic affirmative action to promote cross-racial alliances was marginalized within the civil rights community, so was Shanker's within the labor movement. (I would later write about Shanker and Rustin's friendship in a biography I wrote on Shanker.)[33]

In the spring of 1995, Clinton remained torn between satisfying the broader public or the narrow interest groups that drive policy. In April, he gave a speech to the California Democratic convention, which was divided between pro– and anti–affirmative action camps, and gave rhetorical support to both sides. "We don't have to retreat from these affirmative-action programs that have done great things for the American people and haven't hurt other people," he said. "We don't. But we have to ask ourselves, are they all working? Are they all fair? Has there been any kind of reverse discrimination?" As one journalist noted, both sides were heartened by Clinton's remarks. Stephanopoulos thought, "Good, he stayed on script."[34]

But Clinton ultimately had to make a decision, and he announced the results of his affirmative action review in July. In an address at the National Archives, he argued that affirmative action programs should be "mended" rather than "ended." He announced four core principles by which affirmative action programs should be judged and directed all federal agencies to comply with them. "The policy principles," he said, "are that any program must be eliminated or reformed if it: a) creates a quota; b) creates preferences for unqualified individuals; c) creates reverse discrimination; or d) continues even after its equal opportunity purposes have been achieved."[35]

The policy involved little, if any, affirmative action mending. The first principle, "no quotas," simply codified existing law under which quotas were illegal. The second principle, "no preferences for the unqualified," also lacked bite because even the biggest advocates of racial preferences did not support advancing genuinely unqualified candidates who would likely fail. At a competitive college, there may be thousands of applicants who could graduate if admitted, but only a much smaller number of spaces available. The tough issue was whether, within this large pool of minimally qualified students who could graduate, racial preferences should benefit the relatively less qualified over the more qualified, which the Clinton principles still allowed. The third limiting principle, no "reverse discrimination," was also insignificant. For most people, using racial preferences in college admissions constituted reverse discrimination against white and Asian applicants. But Clinton used a much narrower definition of "reverse discrimination" as that which was "illegal." Under *Bakke*, the use of racial preferences was perfectly legal. As a result, Clinton's limitation on reverse discrimination had no real-world impact. The final principle, that preferences should be "retired when the job is done," was also without practical impact because Clinton said preferences should end when discrimination was eradicated. The president did not give a single example of a program that violated any of his four principles.[36]

Nevertheless, the speech was a political success. Clinton's pollsters found that "over three-quarters of blacks and three-quarters of whites felt that Clinton did not favor one race over another."[37] Clinton's formula was one Democrats would employ in years to come: signal concerns about racial preferences to the broader public, which disliked them, and yet hold fast on actual implementation, which would please interest groups that are important to the party.

The experience taught me a sobering lesson about the realities of interest group power. The labor movement's steep decline in membership meant that the political primacy of class issues was submerged, while the dramatic expansion in the number of people of color in the broader American public gave rising political salience to issues of race and ethnicity.

Meanwhile, realities on the ground were moving in the opposite direction of the politics. As William Julius Wilson's groundbreaking book *The Declining Significance of Race* documented, after passage of the 1968 Fair Housing Act, middle-class Black people began moving out of high-poverty neighborhoods and racial residential segregation declined. White support for interracial marriage increased significantly, from 4 percent in the late 1950s to 64 percent in the mid-1990s. At the same time, beginning in the early 1970s, economic inequality between rich and poor began to grow. Income gaps widened, as did residential segregation by income level. Beginning in the mid-twentieth century, marriages across class lines began to decline.[38]

To the American public, which was experiencing these conflicting trends of race and class, it seemed obvious that affirmative action programs should be based on economic disadvantage. But to Democratic politicians, who needed to listen to interest groups, the imperative to stick by racial preferences had grown—and would continue to grow in coming years.

The tragic irony was that most Black people could not take advantage of the positive trends on race. Stuck in the downward pull on working-class people, hastened by the labor movement's declining power, low-income and working-class Black Americans faced stagnating wages. As Robert Putnam observed, the slow rise in Black life prospects decelerated because most Black people belonged to the working class and suffered economic stagnation like other working-class Americans.[39] The varying life experiences of higher-income and lower-income Black people led them to view the world very differently. While 60 percent of middle-class Black people identified more closely by their race than their class—a worldview civil rights groups embraced—only 5 percent of poor and working-class Black people felt the same way.[40] For poor and working-class Black people, who often live in heavily Black neighborhoods and whose interactions with white people are more limited, the daily struggle to make ends meet takes precedence over issues of race.

I was deeply disappointed in Clinton. For a moment, it had seemed that the political and legal stars had been aligned for the president to be a transformative figure on racial preferences—to revive the King and Douglas approach and universalize affirmative action for the economically disadvantaged of all races. Instead, he chose to obfuscate how racial preference programs worked in practice under heavy pressure from narrow interest groups.

Republican politicians, of course, were not bound by the same contradictions between public opinion and the politics of Democratic interest groups. Even as some conservative intellectuals like Glazer and Thernstrom opposed class-based affirmative action, conservative politicians were smart enough to take up the mantle. Congressman Newt Gingrich said race-based programs should be replaced with special help for people "who come out of poor neighborhoods, who come out of poor backgrounds, who go to school in poor counties." Senator Bob Dole declared, "The real focus should be on helping citizens who are economically disadvantaged, to provide assistance based on need and not on skin color—in other words, needs-based preferences, not race-based preferences."[41] And Congressman Jack Kemp said, "Affirmative action should be predicated on need.... We're not divided by race so much as economics."[42]

The Revolt in the States Against the Interest Groups

Clinton's support for racial preferences was not the end of the story. Opponents had two primary ways to outmaneuver D.C. interest groups. One was the courts, our least democratic institution. The other was the initiative and referenda process, our most democratic of institutions. Both came into play in 1996.

Although the *Bakke* 5–4 decision in 1978 had affirmed the ability of universities to use race in admissions, the rightward tilt of the U.S. Supreme Court in affirmative action contracting cases like *Croson* (1989) and *Adarand* (1995) did not go unnoticed by litigants or the lower courts. In September 1992, Cheryl Hopwood, a white plaintiff, had brought a suit against the University of Texas Law School after she was denied admission. She alleged that UT's use of race in the admissions process was discriminatory. Hopwood cut a sympathetic profile. She had a stronger academic record than many of the minority applicants who were accepted, even though she was raised by a widow and worked her way through high school, community college, and California State University.[43] One judge noted that when she applied, she was the "wife of a member of the Armed Forces stationed in San Antonio and, more significantly, [was] raising a severely handicapped child."[44] She lost in the district court, but in March 1996, she prevailed in the Fifth Circuit Court of Appeals. In light of Supreme Court rulings on affirmative action since *Bakke*, the Circuit Court ruled that the law school could not "continue to elevate some races over others, even for the wholesome purpose of correcting perceived racial imbalance in the student body."[45] In July 1996, the Supreme Court declined to take the case on appeal, leaving the result undisturbed. Because race could not be used in admissions in Texas, advocates of racial diversity turned to class disadvantage as a way of indirectly promoting racial diversity. The state higher education commissioner said, "We'll be looking at diversity more in terms of haves and have-nots."[46]

On a parallel track, activists proposed the California Civil Rights Initiative, a ballot referendum to bar racial preferences in public universities and government contracting statewide. The language of what became known as Prop 209 was simple: the state "shall not discriminate against or grant preferential treatment to, any individual or group on the basis of race, sex, color, ethnicity or national origin in the operation of public employment, public education, or public contracting."[47]

Early polling showed the referendum might pass, prompting opponents to paint the measure as racist and show film footage of Ku Klux Klan leader David Duke expressing his support. But Ward Connerly, a University of California regent and Black businessman who backed Prop 209, strongly rebutted the claim. He had encountered a great deal of racism growing up in Louisiana and California in the 1940s and 1950s. His grown uncle was called "boy" by a gas station attendant. His gym teacher told him Black people couldn't be good swimmers. And when he moved into a white neighborhood, he was greeted with a sign using the N-word. But Connerly expressed his belief that racial preferences violated King's vision of a color-blind society. Instead, he supported efforts to improve educational opportunities for disadvantaged students.[48] Connerly's critics were unrelenting. State Senator Diane Watson said of Connerly, "He probably feels this makes him more white than black, and that's what he wanted to be. He married a white woman."[49]

Although Clinton had stood by racial preferences in his affirmative action review, he was lukewarm in his opposition to Prop 209. In a late

October 1996 speech to a largely Black audience in Oakland, the president said that while he opposed the initiative, it was also time to move beyond racial grievance: "We've got to get to the point in this country where we can let some of this stuff go and say, 'You know, if you believe in the Constitution and the Declaration of Independence and the Bill of Rights, if you show up for work every day or you show up for school every day and you do what you're supposed to do, and you're doing the best you can, we don't need to know anything else about you.'"[50] The language suggested that while Clinton opposed Prop 209, he recognized that in the not too distant future, it would be time to end racial preferences.

In November 1996, Clinton easily won his reelection campaign against Senator Bob Dole. He also won California by a convincing thirteen points (51 percent, compared with Dole's 38 percent and Ross Perot's 7 percent). Even so, Prop 209 passed by ten points, 55 percent to 45 percent.[51] It was a wake-up call for supporters of racial preferences.

Connerly knew he had the public on his side and worked to build on his victory in California with similar ballot initiatives in other states. In November 1998, Washington State followed California's lead and easily passed an anti–affirmative action initiative, despite strong opposition from the business and political establishment. A liberal electorate, which overwhelmingly supported an initiative to raise the minimum wage the same year, rejected racial preferences by an even larger margin than in California.[52]

With successes in California and Washington under his belt, Connerly's next goal was to place an antipreference initiative on the Florida ballot in 2000, a presidential election year. Republican governor Jeb Bush, however, had concerns that putting affirmative action on the ballot might boost Black turnout and hurt the chances of his brother, Texas governor George W. Bush, in a tight presidential contest (a prescient concern in an election that would be decided by a small number of hanging chads).[53] In November 1999, Jeb Bush preempted Connerly's initiative by outlawing racial preferences through an executive order, making Florida the third state to act on the issue. Counting Texas, which was barred from using race by the *Hopwood* decision, there were now four sizeable states that no longer allowed public universities to employ race as a factor in admissions.

Reinventing or Junking Merit?
Derrick Bell Versus Lani Guinier

In the late 1990s, with the future of affirmative action up for grabs, I was invited to participate in several panel discussions on university campuses. One of the most memorable took place at Columbia University where I shared the stage with two civil rights luminaries, Lani Guinier and Derrick Bell, to discuss "Reinventing Merit: The Future of Affirmative Action on Campus."[54] Guinier had been Bill Clinton's choice for assistant attorney general for civil rights, but she lost support and withdrew after a *Wall Street Journal* op-ed labeled her a "quota queen," a phrase that one law professor noted "resonates mellifluously with welfare queen."[55] When I met Guinier, however, she was nothing like the right's caricature of her.

Guinier believed, like I did, that while the Enlightenment principle of using merit in deciding who advances in education and employment was valuable, it needed to be reinvented to recognize the lack of genuine equal opportunity in America. We both believed that merit should be understood as qualifications in light of what obstacles an individual had overcome in life (i.e., the distance they have traveled). And we both thought ideas of merit should be broadened to consider not just test scores, but also what sort of contributions a student would make to improve the world.[56]

Far from endorsing racial quotas, Guinier suggested that affirmative action was a poor substitute for rethinking our admissions process from top to bottom. She later argued in a book that affirmative action "has failed because it has not gone far enough to address the unfairness of both our current merit system and its wealth-driven definition of merit." Like me, she was critical of the fact that universities tended to admit "the children of upper-middle-class parents of color who have been sent to fine prep schools just like the upper-middle-class white students." She complained that universities often sought "cosmetic diversity" of wealthy Black students, many of whom were recent immigrants. One study, she noted, found that "more than 90 percent of parents of Harvard's African students had advanced degrees."[57]

Derrick Bell, a father of critical race theory (CRT), was also an intellectually provocative thinker, but he fell into a very different camp from Guinier or me. Like many CRT advocates, Bell questioned critical elements of the Enlightenment. On the panel at Columbia, Bell called merit a "smokescreen" for power. The idea wasn't—as Guinier and I argued—that merit should be properly understood. Bell instead believed that racism in America was "an integral, permanent, and indestructible component of this society."[58] As a result, any system of merit would inevitably be tainted by racism. In place of merit, he believed in a regime of explicit group rights in which positions of power were allocated to different racial and ethnic groups.[59]

Bell was also famous for his "interest convergence theory," which said that every advance for Black people in the civil rights movement did not result from a moral awakening among white people, but rather from their self-interest in supporting civil rights initiatives. The quintessential example was the Court's decision in *Brown v. Board of Education* (1954), which Bell said desegregated schools mostly to help Americans prevail in the Cold War against the Soviet Union. America's policy of apartheid in the South made it difficult to win allies in developing countries.[60]

Bell overstated the case. In my assessment, white Americans were motivated not simply by the self-interested reasons Bell articulated, but also by a mix of moral arguments advanced by Dr. King and others. But it seemed to me that the logic of Bell's thinking, which placed white self-interest at the center of decision-making, made his solution of allocating positions of power to racial groups politically impractical. If anything, taking the interest convergence theory seriously was a strong argument for shifting to class-based preferences, as it would result in both white and Black people benefiting from the program.

I found Bell intellectually interesting and provocative. And his personal demeanor was always friendly and open, despite his deep pessimism about white people as a group. In later years, Bell and I were on a number of panels together on the issue of racial school integration at the K–12 level (I favored it, he opposed it). But even as we tangled over the issue, our exchanges were always cordial.[61]

Although he died in 2011, Bell's impact on intellectual elites remains significant, as evidenced by the fact that nearly all students in a class I teach at George Washington University advocate his approach. But in the larger world, the path taken by Guinier, who died in 2022, continues to win the day in the court of public opinion. Most Americans want to come up with better realizations of merit, rather than junking it entirely, because there is no real alternative to a merit-based system.

New Paths to Diversity in the States: Back to Class

In the 1990s, as states began to ban racial preferences, there was an open question as to whether they would just give up on diversity or find substitutes. The ballot referenda, after all, ended the use of race without mandating the creation of new class-based affirmative action programs. Due to the absence of a positive replacement program, I would have reluctantly voted against California and Washington initiatives had I been a voter in those states. For all the faults of racial preferences, I believed something had to be done to address our nation's history, and I didn't want universities to forego racial diversity altogether. Although I disagreed with Derrick Bell and his view that votes against racial preferences were just a thinly disguised way of telling Black people they should stay in their place, I couldn't be sure that class-based alternatives would be adopted.

It turned out to be a wasted worry. Not only did the American public oppose racial preferences, but it also opposed the resegregation of higher education. In each of the states where racial preferences were discontinued, new programs sprung up in their place. It turned out that giving a leg up to economically disadvantaged people of all races was a bipartisan goal in Texas, California, Washington, and Florida.

In 1997, after the Texas lower courts banned racial preferences in the *Hopwood* case, an unusual coalition of Black and Hispanic liberal legislators from urban areas allied with conservative white legislators representing rural areas to pass the Top 10 Percent plan. This initiative automatically admitted students at the top of their high school classes to any public institution, including the University of Texas at Austin, irrespective of SAT scores. Although race and ethnicity were powerful fault lines in Texas politics, the old Bobby Kennedy coalition of working-class white, Hispanic, and Black voters supported the plan.

The reason was clear. UT Austin's student body had for years been dominated by students from rich and mostly white suburbs. That changed under the Top 10 Percent plan. Black, Hispanic, and white students from low-income and working-class high schools that had rarely sent anyone to the flagship university suddenly had access—and proved they could successfully do the work. (Years later, in 2009, when UT Austin tried to significantly curtail the number of seats that would be awarded through the Top 10 Percent plan, the same working-class coalition came together to block the effort.)[62] In addition to aiding students from poor schools, the University of Texas system also began providing a leg up to socioeconomically disadvantaged students in the remaining seats, and Texas A&M dropped its use of preferences for the children of alumni.

In California, likewise, after an initial plunge in minority admissions at top institutions such as UCLA and UC Berkeley, the University of California implemented a series of changes. The system boosted its preference for economically disadvantaged students, increased financial aid budgets, admitted top-ranking students from high schools in poor communities, and dropped the use of legacy preferences. It also pledged to increase by 50 percent the admission of students transferring from community colleges, which educate large numbers of individuals who are poor, working-class, and of color. A decade later, more than a quarter of new students enrolling in the UC system were transfers from California community colleges.[63]

Particularly heartening was the reaction of UCLA Law School. Richard Sander, a law professor and economics PhD, was motivated and equipped to create a sophisticated system of class-based admissions of the type I'd recommended. Sander, who would become a close friend and collaborator, began his career as an organizer on the South Side of Chicago. Upon becoming a law professor, he cut his teeth on housing segregation issues.[64] As an economist, he knew the academic literature about how Black and Hispanic students of the same income group as white students typically lived in poorer neighborhoods, attended higher-poverty schools, and came from families with much less wealth—all of which imposed independent disadvantages. In the system he helped design, UCLA Law asked applicants to provide details about seven socioeconomic factors, which would be weighed by admissions officers. Applicants gave information about family income, parents' education level, and family wealth. In addition, UCLA used a student's address to calculate the proportion of single-parent households, families receiving welfare, and adults who did not graduate from high school in their neighborhood.[65]

The University of Washington didn't give up either. After Washington State banned racial preferences, racial minority representation initially dropped. But administrators at the University of Washington swung into action. They created a new "student ambassador" program to recruit students at predominantly minority high schools to apply, expanded financial aid programs, and created a new set of admissions factors based on personal adversity and economic disadvantage.[66]

Finally, after Florida's ban on the use of race in admissions was enacted, Governor Jeb Bush and the University of Florida instituted a number of changes. The state created the Talented 20, a percentage plan for admitting top high school students into state colleges, and a new "Profile Assessment" admissions path that considered the socioeconomic disadvantages a student had overcome. Administrators boosted financial aid through the statewide Florida Student Assistance Grant and a special Florida Opportunity Scholar Fund at the University of Florida. And the university instituted a major, highly successful push to increase recruitment of underrepresented minority students to apply.[67]

In the coming years, a central point of contention would be whether socioeconomic preferences and geographic plans could produce sufficient levels of racial diversity while maintaining high academic standards. By definition, the most efficient and direct method of producing racial diversity was to consider race. But if universities cared about both racial and socioeconomic diversity—as they claim to—which system would work best? The evidence would be at the heart of Supreme Court litigation in the years to come.

———————

The mid- to late 1990s was a period of dramatic ups and downs for class-based affirmative action. At the federal level, an innovative president who had brought Democrats out of a political wilderness tried to move the party from race- to class-based preferences, but failed after special interests balked. At the state level, opponents of racial preferences found ways to work around interest groups. They successfully challenged racial preferences in Texas and launched victorious voter initiatives in major states, including California and Washington, and forced an antipreference executive order in Florida. The good news was that in all four states, new class-based programs emerged. Elite interests could kill class-based affirmative action where they held power, but the idea kept seeping through and finding success where it could.

CHAPTER 3

The Establishment
Strikes Back

O'Connor's "Victory for de Tocqueville"

W HILE CALIFORNIA, TEXAS, FLORIDA, AND WASHINGTON
were developing exciting, robust class-based and geographic
affirmative action programs that drew broad public support in the late
1990s, three sets of actors were set in motion. Opponents of racial preferences were launching a new set of legal cases challenging the practice
at the University of Michigan. Universities and other establishment
groups fiercely opposed any efforts to change the system of racial preferences for upper-middle-class minority students and legacy preferences
for the wealthy and began a concerted effort to fight back. And a small,
innovative group of researchers started testing whether a third-way
alternative—affirmative action based on class—would produce racial
diversity while maintaining high standards at selective universities
nationwide.

Class Matters

The Strivers Experiment

The most exciting research was being conducted by the Education Testing Service (ETS), which administered the SAT. The project was meant to identify "strivers"—economically disadvantaged students who scored higher on the SAT than expected, given the socioeconomic obstacles they had to overcome. The research was led by an ETS vice president named Anthony Carnevale, who would over time become a close friend and collaborator of mine. Carnevale later told me he undertook the Strivers research at the urging of Clinton administration staffers, who feared that racial affirmative action would be struck down in the courts and wanted to have a plan B ready.[1]

In August 1999, the *Wall Street Journal* revealed certain details about ETS's Strivers project. The effort sought to quantify how various economic indicators affected a student's likely SAT score. The model examined fourteen variables—including parents' education, income, and occupation; the language spoken at home; the quality of the high school attended; and the socioeconomic status of both the neighborhood and the school—to generate an expected SAT score. When students scored two hundred points higher than predicted, colleges would be notified that they were strivers. The model allowed colleges to look at race as a distinct disadvantaged factor or keep the process race-blind, which was required in California, Washington, Texas, and Florida. The measure, Carnevale said, was designed to look at "not just where students are, but how far they've come"—precisely as Lani Guinier and I had suggested.[2]

Carnevale was just the right person to lead the research. A brilliant thinker with a gift for translating complicated concepts into clear and memorable phrases, he developed his outrage about class inequality as a child. Carnevale grew up poor in a town called Hodgdon in the wilderness of northern Maine, and he and his two brothers (who both went into labor organizing) earned what he called a "very strong sense of injustice and a supposition that it's all around us." During Carnevale's childhood, his father, a schoolteacher, contracted multiple sclerosis, and was only able to teach part-time. He spent much of his life bedridden starting at the age of twenty-eight. Carnevale's mother devoted her life to taking care of her husband and their three sons. The family got by living off the land; they canned fruits, and neighbors would shoot animals and share the meat with them. As a boy, Carnevale said, he and his brothers were "the kind of kids you would not want your kids to play with," as they skipped school for "months at a time." He says his anti-elitism was "bred in the bone." Looking back, he says, "It gave me a career."[3]

Two teachers believed in Carnevale and encouraged him to apply to and attend Colby College on a full scholarship. When he arrived on campus, Carnevale immediately recognized that Colby was an extraordinarily wealthy school. He says of his classmates, "Those kids were not like me." In college, a government professor said he should get a PhD in public finance economics from Syracuse University, which Carnevale did. But even after joining the rarefied circles of the very highly educated, his concern about inequality did not dissipate. As a graduate student, he did research to support an affidavit in the federal lawsuit *San Antonio v. Rodriguez* (1973), which sought to equalize K–12 public school funding for poor kids.[4] (The suit lost by a 5–4 vote in the U.S. Supreme Court.)

Carnevale worked for Democratic senator Edmund Muskie of Maine on the Committee on the Budget, gaining political savvy, before becoming a top aide to Jerry Wurf, head of the American Federation of State, County, and Municipal Employees, where Carnevale sharpened his anti-elitist instincts.[5] When he arrived at ETS in 1996, as racial affirmative action was coming under attack, Carnevale hoped the Strivers program would help colleges ensure fair college admissions in a new political environment. He personally supported race-based affirmative action, but he also knew the obstacles faced by working-class kids of all races and understood the political realities. Carnevale told the *Wall Street Journal*, "Our polls show that people don't want to give the rich African-American daughter of an African-American lawyer special treatment. But the poor African American woman from the wrong part of town and bad school is a different story."[6] Carnevale said ETS had a strong incentive to create a Strivers program. If racial affirmative action went down, civil rights lawyers were telling him they would go after the SAT as discriminatory on the basis of race.[7]

I didn't know Carnevale at the time, but I was elated to read about the program. These were precisely the types of students I was hoping would benefit from class-based affirmative action. But unlike me, the ETS researchers could quantify the number of low-income, high-achieving students and identify their racial backgrounds. With that information, ETS could calculate how much racial diversity a class-based affirmative action program would produce.

Not long after the *Journal* article was published, the College Board, which represents colleges and contracts with ETS to produce the SAT, moved to kill the Strivers program. The organization claimed that most higher education institutions already rewarded low-income students in admissions, an assertion that research showed was patently untrue. A University of North Carolina scholar, for example, found that law schools "are not currently placing special consideration or weight on SES [socioeconomic status] factors in the admissions process," and subsequent research would confirm that the same was true for colleges.[8]

I wrote an op-ed in the *Washington Post* defending the Strivers program. One underlying reason colleges did not like the program, I charged, is that if some good actors started publicizing the number of strivers they had admitted, it would pressure other colleges to follow suit. I concluded the piece by writing, "The Strivers program would help restore the truly meritocratic promise of the SAT and put pressure on colleges to uncover America's diamonds in the rough. ETS should stand firm against university leaders who would strangle this promising program in its cradle."[9]

I didn't know it at the time, but Carnevale later revealed in an interview with the *Chronicle of Higher Education* that there was a second reason the Strivers research was killed: its impact on the racial affirmative action debate. Carnevale's internal research found that by looking at socioeconomic factors, including wealth (as defined by how much the families had saved for college), "black and Hispanic enrollments would be actually higher than they had been under affirmative action."[10] After being privately briefed on the research, higher education and civil rights leaders were livid. If the courts found out that race-neutral alternatives were available, racial preferences would likely be struck down. These groups saw class-based affirmative action as a "nefarious distraction" that could undermine a policy of racial preferences.[11] Universities—which are supposed to be dedicated to scholarship and the pursuit of the truth—wanted the research squelched.

Carnevale later said that College Board president Gaston Caperton had little choice but to shut down the Strivers project. Selected members of his board, which included leading college officials, threatened to resign unless he acted. "The world was working in a way that was okay for higher ed, and they did not want anything that would upset the apple cart. They used affirmative action in many ways as a shield," Carnevale said.[12]

In 2000, ETS hired Kurt Landgraf as its new CEO, a former executive at DuPont chemical company, whom Carnevale characterizes as someone who "had the morals of a guy who came from a chemical company." Carnevale says Landgraf ordered him to stop working on Strivers and "told me that I needed to shred all the documents." In a clear message that his work was out of favor, Carnevale was moved from a prime space in a beautiful D.C. office building that housed Henry Kissinger's firm to a windowless office elsewhere in the building.[13]

The Challenge to Racial Preferences at the University of Michigan

One reason universities were so worried about the Strivers research was the challenges to racial preferences in higher education that were actively in the works. A conservative shift among the justices appointed by Reagan and Bush made it likely that these challenges would prevail. None of the five justices who had supported racial preferences in *Bakke* was still on the court. Given the 1989 *Croson* case and the 1995 *Adarand* decision striking down racial preferences in government contracting, the question loomed: Would education be next?

In the late 1990s, lawsuits opposing racial preferences were filed at both the college and law school of the University of Michigan. By the early 2000s, they were making their way through the court system and becoming a big topic of discussion.

In March 2002, I served on a panel at a Harvard Law School conference on affirmative action in higher education. University of Michigan philosopher Carl Cohen, a member of the liberal ACLU and one of the driving forces behind the litigation, was also on the panel. He was deeply disturbed by Michigan's admissions system, which provided a specific set of points to students based on their race.[14] My panel also included Harvard Law professor Christopher Edley, a key architect of President Clinton's decision to retain racial affirmative action programs, as well as Harvard Education School's Gary Orfield, who argued that racial preferences were necessary. Orfield pointed to evidence that Black and Hispanic students were more likely than white students from the same income group to attend schools with concentrated poverty and to come from families with lower wealth. He said those were predictors of opportunity in America. Arguing for a third way between Cohen, Edley, and Orfield, I responded by saying I agreed with Orfield's empirical data. Precisely for those reasons, I believed colleges should consider wealth and concentrated poverty in addition to income in a class-based affirmative action system. I thought I had the better of the argument, but the moderator, Harvard Law professor Elena Kagan, didn't tip her hand as to where she stood. She would have plenty of time to do that eight years later, once she was appointed and confirmed as a U.S. Supreme Court justice.

In December 2002, civil rights and higher education communities were horrified when the Supreme Court agreed to hear the two

The Establishment Strikes Back

Michigan lawsuits: *Grutter v. Bollinger*, which involved the law school; and *Gratz v. Bollinger*, which involved the college. Both suits featured sympathetic plaintiffs. Jennifer Gratz, a white working-class student, thought it was unfair that Black and Hispanic students, even those with much more economic privilege than her, automatically received twenty bonus points toward the one hundred necessary for admission to the University of Michigan. When her application was rejected, she sued.[15] At the law school, Barbara Grutter, a white student who also came from a challenging background, sued as well after she was rejected. The law school did not employ a point system as explicit as the undergraduate program, but it did proudly count race as a factor in admission decisions. This was done to achieve what it called a "critical mass" of minority students, which Grutter argued sounded an awful lot like a quota.[16]

The Establishment's Dubious Claims About Class-Based Affirmative Action

In 2003, a series of polls found Americans preferred a system of preferences based on class rather than race. This approach would have benefited many Black and Hispanic students while recognizing that Jennifer Gratz and Barbara Grutter faced obstacles too.[17] But America's establishment—the military generals, the *Fortune* 500 CEOs, and the Ivy League presidents—had a very different view. In February 2003, a front-page *Washington Post* article noted, "As the Supreme Court faces its biggest showdown over racial issues in 25 years, America's business, education and labor leaders are throwing their weight behind the University of Michigan's bid to preserve race-conscious college and university admissions."[18]

Many of these leaders had good intentions. They recognized (as I did) that it was enormously important to have racially integrated college campuses to produce a diverse leadership class in America. These wholly legitimate interests were widely discussed in the press. But the media rarely reported the fact that the establishment also had less selfless reasons to use racial preferences as the *exclusive* means of achieving racial diversity: namely, they provided an inexpensive way to produce integration. Achieving racial diversity through providing financial aid to working-class Black and Hispanic students, as well as working-class white students like Jennifer Gratz or Barbara Grutter, was more costly for colleges compared to admitting upper-middle-class students of color using racial preferences. The same was true for the military, which, if barred from using racial admissions preferences, would have to find new paths to diversity, such as spending extra funds on outreach to high schools to encourage more talented minority students to apply to the military colleges at West Point and the United States Naval Academy. Big business and law firms liked the existing system used by elite colleges, which produced a diverse pool of graduates from polished, upper-middle-class backgrounds. More working-class students, even after four years at an elite college, might not fit in as easily with a corporate culture. Research has found that firms typically preferred employees from advantaged backgrounds, all other qualifications being equal.[19]

For that reason, universities had strong incentives to highlight—and in some cases exaggerate—potential drawbacks to race-neutral strategies. In the Michigan cases, university amicus briefs made three questionable—and sometimes contradictory—claims: (a) that the schools were already giving a significant boost in admissions to economically disadvantaged students; (b) that economically disadvantaged students were not academically qualified to do the work; and (c) that economic affirmative action wouldn't produce racial diversity because it would mostly help white students.

In one amicus brief, for example, eight elite universities, including six from the Ivy League, claimed that alongside race, they already were giving "significant favorable consideration" to students who overcame socioeconomic obstacles.[20] In seeming contradiction to that claim, heads of elite institutions also alleged that low-income students were mostly unqualified. University officials relied heavily on *The Shape of the River*, an influential book by William G. Bowen and Derek Bok, the former presidents of Princeton and Harvard, respectively, who had produced a scholarly study of forty-five thousand students at twenty-eight elite universities from the entering classes of 1976 and 1989.

Most of Bowen and Bok's book consisted of a defense of racial preferences. Their data showed that race was a significant factor in admissions. If race were dropped and universities offered no alternatives, Black matriculation would fall by almost half, from 7.1 percent at the twenty-eight institutions to 3.6 percent. (In a telling omission, the book's data focused on Black and white students, while excluding data on Hispanic and Asian students.) Bowen and Bok found that once admitted, Black students, despite receiving substantial preferences, performed well and graduated at higher rates than they would have had they attended less well-resourced schools. In other words, there was some wiggle room in the strict academic criteria universities employed.[21]

And yet, the authors also claimed to worry that economically disadvantaged students of all races would not succeed if they were given similar preferences: "The problem is not that poor but qualified candidates go undiscovered, but that there are simply too few of these candidates in the first place."[22] They asserted, "It usually requires more than a single generation to move up to the highest rungs of the socioeconomic ladder," as if this were an immutable fact of life. It seemed that brilliant Harvard professors like William Julius Wilson and Daniel Patrick Moynihan, both of whom grew up in very difficult circumstances, were unreliable freaks of nature.

Because elite universities alleged that economically disadvantaged students were academically incapable, they admitted very few of them. Only 3 percent of the entering classes of 1989 at the elite institutions came from lower-socioeconomic-status families (the bottom 28 percent of families with college-age children nationally). On the other hand, 41 percent came from the top 9 percent of the socioeconomic distribution. Even the Black students were disproportionately wealthy. Bowen and Bok's data showed that 86 percent of Black students enrolled at the twenty-eight institutions came from middle- or upper-middle-class families.[23] To Bowen and Bok, the enormous socioeconomic stratification found at elite universities was not a bug but a feature that reflected the hard realities of who was capable of doing the work at academically rigorous institutions.

In a telling interview with a student publication, Bok argued, "I am not very keen on viewing preferential admissions as some way to atone for the injuries of the past. . . . I am not sure that [minority] students we admit are the ones who most need atonement." He then recounted the story of a student of color he'd spoken to who had recently celebrated her birthday in Italy. "I don't think any reparations are due to her," he said, but "I'm glad she's here."[24]

This reality was at odds with the common perception—and moral power—of affirmative action as portrayed in the popular press. Rob Rogers of the *Pittsburgh Post-Gazette*, for example, drew a cartoon supportive of affirmative action in which an African American girl states, "I survived life on welfare and food stamps . . . in a poor, crime-ridden neighborhood with crumbling schools filled with guns and violence . . . in a world that rewards rich, white men. So now, affirmative action will help me into college." Her white male colleague retorts, "That's so unfair."[25]

It was not always the case that elite colleges focused so heavily on socioeconomically advantaged students in their affirmative action programs. In 1972, just 29 percent of Black students at elite colleges came from the top socioeconomic quarter of the population. But by 1992, as the Black middle and upper-middle class grew, universities gravitated toward more privileged Black students, and the proportion from the top socioeconomic quarter rose to 67 percent.[26]

Bowen and Bok claimed that another problem with class-based affirmative action was that it would end up helping too many poor white and Asian students. They pointed to research by Harvard professor Thomas Kane, who concluded that "the problem is one of numbers." Kane argued that although income-based preferences would disproportionately benefit minority students, a majority of those who would benefit would be white and Asian.[27]

Pushing Back Against the Establishment with New Data

There were enormous problems with each of the higher education establishment's three claims—that it already provided a preference to economically disadvantaged students; that additional low-income and working-class students could not do the academic work; and that socioeconomic preferences could not produce much racial diversity. In advance of the *Grutter* and *Gratz* oral arguments in the Supreme Court, I joined forces with two partners—one liberal and one conservative—to push back. Neither group I worked with had a quarrel with the *goal* of racial diversity, which we valued. But we questioned the idea that racial preferences were the only way to get there.

In the first effort, I teamed up with Anthony Carnevale of ETS. I approached him and his ETS colleague Stephen Rose to see if they would publish a research paper in a book I was editing that would analyze some of the big questions surrounding class-based affirmative action. They readily agreed and, to my surprise, received permission from ETS to do the work. The findings of their study, which examined socioeconomic and racial data at the nation's most selective 146 institutions, were fascinating. We published them in March 2003, prior to the oral arguments in *Grutter* and *Gratz*, and they received a great deal of attention.

Carnevale and Rose found that contrary to the claims of some universities, selective colleges did not already offer an advantage in admissions to economically disadvantaged students. Race-based preferences on average tripled the representation of Black and Hispanic students (to 12 percent) compared to an admissions regimen based on grades and test scores (which would yield a representation of 4 percent), but universities did nothing to boost socioeconomic representation.[28] In fact, the researchers found that the share of poor and working-class students was slightly *lower* at selective colleges than it would have been if grades and test scores were the sole basis for admissions.[29]

As a result, these selective colleges had very little socioeconomic diversity. The key finding—which would be repeated hundreds of times by news accounts—was that 74 percent of students at the most selective 146 colleges and universities came from the top socioeconomic quartile and only 3 percent from the bottom quartile. In other words, you were twenty-five times as likely to run into a rich student as a poor student on the nation's selective campuses. Just 10 percent of students came from the bottom socioeconomic half of the American population.[30] Other research found that Carnevale's broad findings about the socioeconomic tilt of selective colleges were borne out at the college that was the subject of the litigation, the University of Michigan. In 2003, Michigan's freshman class included more students from families earning over $200,000 ($340,000 in 2024 dollars) than from the bottom half of the income distribution.[31]

Carnevale and Rose also rebutted Bowen and Bok's claim that selective colleges would love to have more economically disadvantaged students on campus, but knew these students were simply not cut out to succeed academically. Carnevale and Rose found that "there are large numbers of students from families with low-income and low levels of parental education who are academically prepared for bachelor's degree attainment even in the most selective colleges." Only 44 percent of low-income students who scored in the top academic quartile attended a four-year college, and this group constituted "low-hanging fruit" for selective colleges—a finding confirmed by subsequent research.[32] Indeed, Carnevale and Rose found that the top 146 institutions could greatly expand seats devoted to students from the bottom socioeconomic half while maintaining high standards. The representation of the bottom economic half could rise from 10 percent to 38 percent at these colleges, and graduation rates would actually increase slightly.[33]

Finally, contrary to the research by Thomas Kane claiming that socioeconomic preferences would mostly benefit white and Asian students, Carnevale and Rose found that significant racial diversity could be achieved under two conditions: (a) socioeconomic slots were expanded to accommodate more academically capable disadvantaged students than currently attend selective colleges; and (b) universities defined socioeconomic disadvantage by considering a more robust set of economic factors beyond family income.

Each of these points was important. To begin with, one way for a class-based affirmative action program to avoid squeezing out Black and Hispanic students in favor of white and Asian students was to expand the number of seats provided for economic affirmative action. If one assumed a fixed number of affirmative action seats—the same for all economically disadvantaged students as those used for racial minorities (say, 20 percent of the class)—then working-class Black, Hispanic, and white students would have to duke it out for those limited spots. As a matter of simple math, Black and Hispanic students would lose out compared with the old system where race was the only affirmative factor. But Carnevale and Rose's research found it was possible to almost quadruple the number of seats for the bottom economic half while also maintaining high academic standards, and thereby avoid the crowding-out effect on Black and Hispanic students. This would not require expanding the total number of slots a university offered, though it would require fewer seats currently set aside for privileged students, such as legacies and those involved with boutique sports like fencing and squash.

Second, Carnevale and Rose's research confirmed statistically my hypothesis that the racial dividend of class-based affirmative action differs a great deal depending on what socioeconomic factors a university employs to define economic disadvantage. Kane's study found that white and Asian students would be the main beneficiaries if class-based affirmative action were limited to family income.[34] But that was the wrong approach, I argued. As a matter of fairness, because students of any income level faced extra disadvantages if they also lived in high-poverty neighborhoods and attended high-poverty high schools, it was important for colleges to examine those types of factors as well. Research has long found that living in high-poverty neighborhoods and attending high-poverty schools results in less opportunity and more exposure to violence.[35]

Importantly, because of racial discrimination and segregation in the housing market, Black and Hispanic students of any income level were on average more likely to face those extra socioeconomic obstacles associated with neighborhood and schools than white students, and therefore would disproportionately benefit from a program that considered those hurdles. In fact, Black middle-income families typically lived in more disadvantaged neighborhoods than low-income white families.[36] A 2003 study found that Black families with income in excess of $60,000 lived in neighborhoods with *higher* poverty rates than white families earning less than $30,000 a year.[37] (Of course, these preferences would also benefit some white and Asian students living in disadvantaged neighborhoods and attending disadvantaged schools, as they should.)

Carnevale and Rose's approach—modeling a broader set of socioeconomic factors and a larger proportion of the student body—yielded higher racial diversity results than Kane's.[38] With racial preferences, underrepresented minorities had a 12 percent share (6 percent Black students and 6 percent Hispanic) in the first-year class at selective colleges. If colleges relied strictly on academic preparedness, those shares would drop to 4 percent (1.6 percent Black and 2.4 percent Hispanic). With class-based preferences, underrepresented minority shares rose to 10 percent (4 percent Black and 6 percent Hispanic). Meanwhile, the bottom socioeconomic half would see its share increase from 10 percent to 38 percent.[39]

In sum, as I wrote in an op-ed in the *Washington Post* at the time, selective colleges would see "a 2-percentage-point decline in racial diversity and a 28-percentage-point increase in socioeconomic diversity." I argued, "If diversity is defined broadly, to value differences in both economic and racial backgrounds—kids from trailer homes and ghettoes and barrios as well as suburban minorities—economic affirmative action would provide a large net gain in the total student body diversity at elite colleges."[40] These students would also be well prepared academically, and overall graduation rates would increase from 86 percent to almost 90 percent.[41]

Carnevale and Rose's results were impressive, even though their study lacked one factor I had long argued would boost racial diversity further: family wealth. Wealth (net worth) is an important predictor of opportunity in America. Moreover, because of slavery, segregation, and redlining, Black median income was 62 percent of white income, while Black median net worth was just 12 percent of white median net worth.[42] Using wealth in admissions would boost Black representation, but the dataset Carnevale and Rose used did not include family wealth.

I did not realize it at the time, but Carnevale's internal research from ETS—which he was not at liberty to disclose—confirmed that including family wealth yielded favorable racial results. At the time the 2003 study was released, Carnevale and Rose said that to avoid a small drop in Black shares, race and class should be used in conjunction with each other. But a reporter from the *Chronicle of Higher Education* noted, "Carnevale knew he was not giving the world the whole story, that by tweaking the formula he and Rose were describing—and taking accumulated family wealth into account—colleges could in fact use class-based affirmative action to maintain their current levels of racial and ethnic diversity. But he could not discuss such tweaks without bringing up the suppressed findings of his striver research, which would cause him to run afoul of his bosses at ETS."[43] (Carnevale left ETS in 2004, so he and I would have a chance to revisit this issue later, but not before the Supreme Court oral arguments in the Michigan cases.)[44]

Working with the Compassionate Conservatives

While Carnevale and I were critiquing the higher education establishment from the left, I also worked with conservatives in the George W.

Bush administration in advance of the Supreme Court's oral arguments. Bush, who had run as a "compassionate conservative," was a nuanced critic of racial preferences. Unlike some on the right, he strongly endorsed the idea that universities were better and stronger when they were racially diverse.

On one level, because he was normally allied with corporate America, Bush might have been expected to support racial preferences as the cheapest way to produce racial diversity. But as governor of Texas when the *Hopwood* decision had barred racial preferences, he gained firsthand experience in developing a set of race-neutral strategies, such as supporting socioeconomically disadvantaged students and implementing the Texas Top 10 Percent plan. He knew these had been effective in producing racial diversity and maintaining high academic standards.

It was a bit awkward for me to align myself with the Bush administration. I had strongly supported Al Gore in the 2000 presidential election and was a vocal critic of Bush's educational efforts. I opposed his efforts to expand private school vouchers and impose accountability on schools without providing them with necessary resources.[45]

But I was impressed with Bush's efforts to employ race-neutral strategies in Texas. As the administration considered its position on the Michigan cases, I joined two conservative activists—Linda Chavez and Roger Clegg of the Center for Equal Opportunity—to meet with Jay Lefkowitz, a member of Bush's domestic policy council. When we entered the White House, there were awkward hellos for Chavez, who had been appointed by Bush to be secretary of labor, but had to withdraw over concerns that she had not paid Social Security taxes for a friend who had provided childcare. When we met with Lefkowitz, I joked that Chavez and Clegg were the conservatives, and I was there to throw in the compassion.

The administration's amicus brief took what I viewed to be just the right path: endorsing the goal of racial diversity, but showing that it could be achieved through race-neutral means. Members of the U.S. Department of Education asked me to help with a report cataloging what states had done to achieve racial diversity in the face of bans on racial preferences. I agreed to do so, and in March 2003, the department published a well-documented analysis, shortly in advance of the oral arguments in *Grutter* and *Gratz*.

The report showed that at the University of Texas at Austin, the number of Black students in the first-year class was higher (272) in 2002 than it had been with affirmative action in 1996 (232). Likewise, Hispanic enrollment increased from 932 in 1996 to 1,137 in 2002. At the University of Florida at Gainesville, likewise, the percentage and number of Black students rose between 1999 (when racial preferences were employed) and 2002 (when race-neutral strategies were used). Hispanic and Asian American numbers also rose. Florida's special focus on recruitment efforts was particularly successful.[46]

UC Berkeley's Black and Hispanic numbers dropped significantly in 1998, the year after the ban on racial preferences was adopted. However, enrollment had partially rebounded with the adoption of race-neutral strategies.[47] UCLA Law School was also showing success. According to law professor Richard Sander's calculations, if UCLA had used LSAT scores as the only criterion for admissions, Black, Hispanic, and Native American students would have represented just 2.3 percent of the student body. With socioeconomic affirmative action, that representation grew to 13.1 percent. According to Sander, while the socioeconomic approach produced racial diversity levels lower than racial preferences, UCLA faced an unfair disadvantage as it was trying to recruit talented underrepresented minority students in an environment where virtually all its competitors could still use race. In the fall 2002 entering class, Black students were 11.4 times as likely to be admitted using wealth and income and other socioeconomic criteria as through other admissions programs, and Hispanic students were 5.6 times as likely to be admitted.[48]

Importantly, these plans also produced more socioeconomic diversity than racial preference plans had, which helped create a better learning environment for students (an issue discussed in further detail below). For example, before the percentage plan was adopted, students from just 10 percent of Texas's 1,500 high schools, mostly in wealthy areas, accounted for 75 percent of the students at UT Austin. After the percentage plan was adopted, the number of high schools represented at UT Austin grew by 135. At UCLA Law, more than a third of students came from the bottom half of the socioeconomic distribution and did well academically, achieving the highest bar passage rate in the school's history.[49]

Justice O'Connor's Elitist Ruling

On April 1, 2003, the U.S. Supreme Court heard oral arguments in the *Grutter* and *Gratz* cases, with all eyes on Justice Sandra Day O'Connor, who often served as a swing vote. O'Connor, the lead author of the 1995 *Adarand* decision striking down racial preferences in government contracting, had been a longtime critic of racial preferences because they violated the principle that people should not be treated differently based on their race. She had always been especially concerned about whether preferences had been in place for too long; Whitney Young's "decade of discrimination" in favor of Black people had long since expired.[50] At the oral argument, O'Connor asked Michigan's lawyer, "In all programs which this Court has upheld in the area of—you want to label it affirmative, there's been a fixed time period within which it would operate. You could see at the end—an end to it, there is none in this, is there? How do we deal with that aspect?"[51]

But O'Connor also seemed willing to support Justice Powell's position in favor of racial preferences, if administered subtly. When the plaintiffs' attorney said race should not be a factor in admissions, O'Connor noted that precedent had allowed a nuanced use of race. "You are speaking in absolutes, and it isn't quite that," she said. The justices also pressed the plaintiffs and the Bush administration about an amicus brief in which military generals expressed their support of racial preferences—another sign that the Court might find a way to support the status quo.[52]

Sure enough, when the decision was handed down in June, O'Connor, citing the briefs of the military brass and business establishment, supported racial preferences. She argued that racial diversity on campus was important for two key reasons. First, a racially diverse class sparked deeper discussions and deeper learning. Second, because America's leadership class is disproportionately derived from elite colleges, having racial diversity would instill a sense of legitimacy in the eyes of citizens. I thought both points were valid. But then O'Connor took what I viewed as several wrong turns.

To begin with, she drew a sharp distinction between the University of Michigan undergraduate program's automatic point system (which she declared unlawful because it was too mechanical) and the University of Michigan Law School's use of race as a discretionary "plus factor" to achieve a "critical mass" of underrepresented minority students (which she sustained because it took a more individualized approach). I found this distinction to be problematic. It made little sense to say a university could set a quantifiable goal of how much diversity it needed (a "critical mass") but couldn't use a point system to get there.[53]

Ironically, statistical research found that racial preferences at the law school were even *larger* than those used by the undergraduate program—the equivalent of scoring more than one grade point higher in college.[54] Among students with a certain set of grades and LSAT scores, Michigan's law school "was admitting virtually every black applicant while white and Asian American applicants had less than a 1 in 40 chance of getting in."[55] The bottom line was that the law school's use of race boosted the underrepresented minority population from 4 percent to 14.4 percent.[56]

Moreover, the distinction was not merely illogical but fundamentally antidemocratic. A public institution should be accountable for its actions, and it is much easier for citizens to judge whether they support a public policy if a university is explicit about the weight it affords to race. Justice David Souter, dissenting in the *Gratz* case, pointed out that "it seems especially unfair to treat the candor of the admissions plan as an Achilles' heel. . . . I would be tempted to give Michigan an extra point of its own for its frankness. Equal protection cannot be an exercise in which the winners are the ones who hide the ball."[57]

For me, the biggest failing was O'Connor's rejection of the growing research literature suggesting that it was possible to achieve racial diversity without racial preferences. O'Connor had long been a champion of using race-neutral alternatives to achieve diversity goals in contracting, so it was surprising she gave such little consideration to the issue in the *Grutter* decision. In a stunning omission, she did not even discuss economic affirmative action as a possible solution. She dismissed two other ideas—lottery admissions, which compromise academic standards; and percentage plans, which are more difficult to apply to private institutions and professional schools. But she neglected the class-based program that answered both of those criticisms.

O'Connor gave universities a free pass, declaring, "We take the Law School at its word that it would 'like nothing better than to find a race-neutral admissions formula' and will terminate its race-conscious admissions program as soon as practicable."[58] This show of deference ignored the extraordinary financial interest universities had in using racial preferences as a less expensive alternative to class-based admissions. Because economic affirmative action would require shifting resources to student financial aid from other institutional priorities, such as boosting faculty salaries, it was naive to think universities would "like nothing better" than to find alternative means for achieving racial diversity.[59] O'Connor's position also ignored Carnevale's research, and studies by the U.S. Department of Education, that race-neutral alternatives were viable.

In addition, O'Connor's decision also ignored the educational benefits of socioeconomic diversity, which race-neutral strategies did a *better* job of achieving than racial preferences. O'Connor was right to say that racial diversity improved the learning environment of colleges and instilled legitimacy in the eyes of the citizenry. But the same rationale applied to socioeconomic diversity as well. Including students who have faced disadvantages would make for more interesting discussions and add to the legitimacy of the institutions (a point we return to in Chapter 6).

In an opinion that was strange and deficient in many respects, O'Connor offered one bone to the vast majority of Americans who opposed racial preferences. To address her long-standing concern that racial preferences should not last forever, she said she hoped that in twenty-five years they would no longer be necessary.

University officials, business leaders, military generals, and civil rights advocates all hailed the decision as a victory for liberal values. I saw it differently. In fall 2003, I participated in a seminar with several academics, including Derrick Bell. My piece was titled "The Conservative Victory in *Grutter* and *Gratz*." I argued that while the liberal justices prevailed over the conservative ones, the real-world impact was precisely the reverse. Sustaining racial preferences meant that universities could continue to avoid addressing larger issues of class inequality and instead pursue, as one observer later put it, "racial justice on the cheap."[60] The Court's elevation of secrecy in university admissions also undercut liberal values of candor, openness, and democratic sunshine.

More broadly, *Grutter* was a victory for elites over the public. As Charles Lane wrote in the *Washington Post*, there was an enormous gulf between the views of big business, elite colleges, and the military generals on the one hand and the general citizenry on the other.[61] Several polls taken in 2003 found that the public consistently opposed racial preferences by two to one and supported economic preferences by the same margin, but O'Connor had not even discussed that option.[62] Instead, she deferred to the received wisdom found in the amicus briefs from 3M, General Motors, and the U.S. Armed Forces. The liberal journalist Nat Hentoff wrote in the *Village Voice* that hers was an "elitist decision."[63]

In particular, the ruling was a victory for wealthy white people, who benefited from legacy preferences for the advantaged children of alumni. In his dissent, Justice Clarence Thomas recognized that the two issues were joined at the hip. Supporters and beneficiaries of legacy preferences liked that racial preferences gave college admissions an appearance of fairness, thereby propping up their own form of affirmative action for the wealthy. Thomas wrote, "Were this Court to have the courage to forbid the use of racial discrimination in admissions, legacy preferences (and similar practices) might quickly become less popular—a possibility not lost, I am certain, on the elites (both individual and institutional) supporting the Law School in this case."[64] Lani Guinier, who did not often agree with Thomas, also detected an "elitism" in O'Connor's decision, and pointed out how diversity provided "a fig leaf to camouflage privilege."[65]

Some higher education leaders recognized that because *Grutter* was a victory for elites, it might prove unstable in the long run. After the decision was handed down, Anthony Carnevale attended a private conference at Harvard with about fifty civil rights and higher education leaders who all supported racial preferences. He said it was meant to be a celebration, but Harvard president Larry Summers had a warning for the group. He told those assembled, "This was not a victory for the American people; this was a victory for de Tocqueville." The nineteenth-century French political theorist Alexis de Tocqueville was famously worried about the "tyranny of the majority" and very much appreciated, as one observer noted, that American government succeeded "because it didn't empower the people too much."[66] Carnevale believed that Summers was signaling that "American elites just won. The public is opposed to affirmative action. The military, corporate America, intellectual America, they just won."[67]

I was deeply disappointed. I had become, as one higher education journal at the time put it, "arguably the nation's chief proponent of class-based affirmative action in higher education admissions."[68] But now, those possibilities seemed dashed once again. My hopes had been raised and then deflated by Bill Clinton in 1995. Now, eight years later, I had thought the Supreme Court might force universities to do the hard work of creating racial diversity in new ways, but Justice O'Connor had balked.

———————

Overall, the late 1990s and early 2000s was a disappointing period in the quest to create a fairer system of affirmative action based on class. States that had banned racial preferences had been making good progress in finding new paths to diversity, and powerful new evidence from ETS researchers suggested that selective universities could create racial and economic diversity and maintain high standards by looking at class disadvantage. But rather than recognize these realities, the U.S. Supreme Court had taken on faith the self-serving testimony of elite universities, corporate executives, and military brass that racial preferences were the only viable path forward. In the fight for working-class and low-income students, I needed to rethink my strategy.

CHAPTER 4

Fits and Starts

The Failed Effort to Address a Piece of America's "Most Serious Domestic Problem"

ONCE THE U.S. SUPREME COURT ISSUED ITS RULING IN *Grutter*—which appeared to provide smooth sailing for race-based affirmative action for the next twenty-five years—the dynamics around class-based affirmative action shifted in important ways. Most of the interest in class-based preferences up until then had come in states like California, Texas, Florida, and Washington, where race preferences had been banned in admissions. The motivation for using class in those states was not primarily to promote economic diversity per se, but to find a new way to promote racial diversity indirectly. As Richard Sander of UCLA told me, "Only one out of every 20 people I've talked to in the legal academy attach value to the idea of economic diversity."[1]

At the same time, economic affirmative action had suddenly become less threatening to supporters of racial preferences. So long as class threatened to substitute for race in admissions, the higher education establishment believed it was necessary to fight against it tooth and nail. But with racial affirmative action now apparently on safe ground, would it become acceptable for elite educators to take on socioeconomic diversity as a cause?

The Trio

I was leery because university leaders had not shown much interest in the past. However, something interesting began to happen in 2004. Anthony Carnevale's study showing there were twenty-five times as many rich students as poor students on selective campuses hit a nerve, leading a trio of important leaders of higher education—the presidents of Harvard and Amherst and the former president of Princeton—to take up the mantle of socioeconomic diversity. I was intrigued. Would university leaders be willing to add class-based affirmative action on top of their existing race-based programs?

The first to address the issue was Harvard president Larry Summers. A brilliant and at times controversial economist who had served as treasury secretary in the Clinton administration, Summers had enormous stature, so I was thrilled when he spoke up publicly. In February 2004, Summers declared at an American Council on Education (ACE) meeting in Miami that the growing gap between rich and poor children in America was "the most serious domestic problem in the United States today."[2] Citing Carnevale's research on the economic divide at selective colleges, Summers said higher education had to do its part in addressing the issue.

It was a stunning reversal of the position taken by Summers's predecessor at Harvard, Derek Bok. It was just six years earlier that Bok had expressed in *The Shape of the River* such little confidence that low-income students could do the work at a place like Harvard. Now, Summers declared in his ACE speech that the gross underrepresentation of low-income students at elite colleges was not just a reflection of "native ability or academic preparation." Leading universities needed to change their ways.[3]

Fits and Starts

In the speech, Summers announced a new Harvard Financial Aid Initiative, a policy under which any student from a family making less than $40,000 a year would receive a free ride. Summers also said Harvard was "intensifying" outreach to get low-income students to apply and "reemphasizing" a policy of considering economic obstacles a student had overcome in making admissions decisions. I would have preferred something more aggressive, like a commitment to tripling the number of students from the bottom economic half. But it was a powerful statement coming from the leader of an institution that had previously lacked faith in boosting socioeconomic diversity.[4]

An even more dramatic reversal came in April 2004 when Bok's *Shape of the River* coauthor William Bowen, former president of Princeton and now president of the Mellon Foundation, delivered a series of lectures at the University of Virginia (UVA) that called on universities to put a thumb on the scale in favor of socioeconomically disadvantaged students.[5] In the lectures, Bowen revealed an extensive project he had undertaken to study what factors counted in admissions at elite universities. Among the institutions that shared detailed admissions data were thirteen elite colleges: Barnard, Bowdoin, Columbia, Harvard, Macalester, Middlebury, Oberlin, Princeton, Smith, the University of Pennsylvania, the University of Virginia, Williams, and Yale. The research debunked several critical claims that universities had made during the *Grutter* litigation. (Bowen later acknowledged that he withheld the release of the research until the Supreme Court had announced its decision in the affirmative action litigation.)[6]

The study, which Bowen coauthored with two colleagues, found that elite universities did not provide *any* admissions boost to low-income students. Being a recruited athlete increased the chances of admission by thirty percentage points for a student with a given academic profile at the thirteen elite colleges. Being an underrepresented minority increased one's chances by twenty-eight percentage points; a legacy, twenty percentage points; a first-generation college student, four percentage points; and being in the bottom income quartile (relative to the middle quartiles), not at all. For instance, if an applicant had a 40 percent chance of admissions based on their merits, being African American, Hispanic, or Native American increased their chances to 68 percent, while low-income status did not provide any advantage. Low-income students, Bowen and his colleagues wrote, receive "essentially no break in the admission process; they fare neither better nor worse than other applicants."[7]

In addition, whereas Bowen and Bok had in 1998 claimed "the problem is not that poor but qualified students go undiscovered, but that there are simply very few of these candidates in the first place," Bowen now revealed that universities could easily boost the percentage of low-income students by 55 percent (from 11 percent to 17 percent) without compromising academic quality. Moreover, Bowen and colleagues did not claim that 17 percent representation for low-income students was a ceiling beyond which students would be academically incapable. Instead, their rationale for the 11 percent to 17 percent increase was that it could be achieved by providing a boost similar to that given to legacy applicants. The authors wrote, "The idea of a 'legacy thumb' appeals to us in part because there is a nice symbolic symmetry associated with it." I found the logic strained: legacy preferences were for students who had been given much in life. Didn't low-income students deserve a much more substantial admissions boost, so long as they could do the work?[8]

Importantly, Bowen and colleagues also found that low-income students who were admitted to selective colleges performed well academically. Black students at elite colleges graduated with a class rank sixteen percentile points below their white colleagues who had the same entering SAT scores and high school grades.[9] But low-income students, by contrast, did just as well in college as their SAT scores and high school credentials predicted.[10]

I was stunned by Bowen's new findings and gave him enormous credit for reexamining his earlier position, running the data, and reversing himself. It was an astounding admission, coming from the very heart of the educational establishment. Within months of the *Grutter* decision, Summers and Bowen had delivered an enormous blow to two key strategies universities had offered in defense of racial preferences: that they already provided socioeconomic preferences, and that there were simply too few low-income students to do the work.

The third major establishment voice to emerge in support of class-based affirmative action was Amherst College president Anthony Marx. Within a month of taking office in July 2003, he asked me to speak to a class about boosting socioeconomic diversity in education.[11] We also met at the president's home and discussed the steps he was interested in taking to establish Amherst, considered among the best liberal arts colleges in the nation, as a leader in the area of recruiting low-income students.

In May 2004, Marx went public with his ideas at Amherst's 183rd commencement. Citing Carnevale's data, he declared that "the passive approach to letting talent rise is not working," and said that selective colleges "must embrace economic diversity." He called for colleges to "make public the measures of our economic diversity and be held accountable for them." Top colleges competed on a number of measures, he said, but now "let the world's greatest higher education system compete" on the "noble grounds of opportunity, not on the flash of brand-name obsession. Let our competition drive us to meet social needs, knowing that today this is also how we strengthen our institutions."[12]

Marx's implementation of a socioeconomic diversity plan at Amherst benefited Anthony Jack, a Black student from a working-class family who had a comparatively low SAT score of 1200. Without the plan, he would not have been admitted to Amherst. The school said that Jack was admitted as a matter of fairness—and getting meritocracy right. As Amherst dean of admissions Tom Parker later noted, "Tony Jack with his pure intelligence—had he been raised in Greenwich, he would have been a 1500 kid." A student like Jack also strengthened the learning experience of everyone else at Amherst. In a seminar on pov-erty, populated by economically comfortable students, he could share what it was like to live on food stamps.[13]

With strong interest from three heavy hitters in elite higher edu-cation, I sought to sustain the momentum by assembling a three-hour meeting of top education leaders to discuss a path forward. Summers, Bowen, and Marx agreed to serve as the anchors of a June 2004 pri-vate gathering in New York. As word spread about the event, it became something of a hot ticket. Lee Bollinger, the named defendant in the *Grutter* and *Gratz* cases for his role as Michigan president and now the president of Columbia, attended, as did Princeton president Shir-ley Tilghman and Cornell president Jeffrey Lehman. Strong civil rights advocates and defenders of racial affirmative action—including law professor Lani Guinier, journalist Nicholas Lemann, and economist Thomas Kane—also came to discuss this "new frontier" for affirmative action based on socioeconomic status.

It was an exciting day. I introduced myself to Summers, and he said he greatly appreciated the work I'd been doing. He seemed particu-larly interested in the Strivers hypothesis—that investing in students who overcame odds would have a big payoff for society. It was fair, but was it efficient? The discussion that followed gave me key insights into the thoughts and concerns of those who had the actual power to make change.

Summers, who had the biggest personality of the group and spoke with admirable candor, opened the meeting and said that when he first started as president of Harvard, he attended an admissions meeting as a "fly on the wall." He observed that when a student was a legacy, an underrepresented minority, or an athlete, it seemed like a metaphor-ical light switch went on in the room and everyone paid close atten-tion. However, this was not the case when the candidate came from a low-income background. Bowen's data had confirmed that impres-sion quantitatively for several elite universities. Summers said the problem stemmed from institutional constituency groups. The development office pushed for legacies, the coaches for athletes, and constituencies of color for underrepresented minority students, leaving the run-of-the-mill high-achieving low-income student without any advocates.[14]

Summers raised a number of research questions that, depending on how they were answered, might make the case for change within institutions of higher education. Did students who received financial aid at elite colleges and went on to be economically successful donate more money to their alma maters out of a sense of gratitude? If Bowen's findings are accurate that SATs overpredict college grades for minority students and athletes, but accurately predict grades for low-income students, how do low-income graduates perform over time, when the initial effects of family disadvantages will have presumably dissipated? In the long haul of their careers—as Justice Douglas had suggested—as low-income students are able to take advantage of new opportunities provided, would the drive and determination that helped them beat the odds in the first place lead them to overperform in life? One study of Harvard students in the 1950s, 1960s, and 1970s found that blue-collar students with more modest SAT scores were the most successful adults as measured by income, personal satisfaction, and community involvement.[15] What new research could be done along these lines?

Marx talked about his own efforts at Amherst, where he asked big donors, Can we raise $100 million to expand socioeconomic diversity so that Amherst would have more Pell students than legacies on campus? The response was enthusiastic. To put the pressure on other institutions to do the right thing, however, universities should disclose annually how many students came from families that were rich, poor, or middle class, he suggested.

Bowen said that because poor students were much less likely to score 1400 on the SAT as compared to wealthier students, those who beat the odds have done "astonishingly well" and it was inexcusable that they received no boost in admissions. Lani Guinier sought to broaden the conversation beyond traditional notions of merit based on test scores. She emphasized the need to study how different types of applicants could contribute in the long run to addressing society's most challenging social problems.

A few weeks after the meeting, Carnevale and I had a discussion with Clayton Spencer (a former staffer to Senator Ted Kennedy who later became president of Bates College) and Anthony Broh, director of research for the Consortium on Financing Higher Education (COFHE), a collective comprising over thirty highly selective private colleges and universities, to talk about the next steps. COFHE had a treasure trove of information, and with a membership that included the top elite privates, it had the power to encourage collective decisions, such as the publication of socioeconomic data.[16] COFHE presidents were set to meet in November, Broh said, and the topic of socioeconomic diversity would be a big item of interest.[17]

There were other follow-ups to the June 2004 meeting. One of the attendees, Sandy Baum from the College Board, reached out to suggest a meeting with Carnevale and College Board president Gaston Caperton, to discuss ways to promote socioeconomic diversity in selective colleges. It was a fascinating request. In 1999, Caperton had shut down Carnevale's ETS Strivers research. Now, five years later, socioeconomic diversity was hot and Caperton was eager to help. When we met, Caperton seemed friendly and engaged, but I noticed that his jaw clenched when the Strivers project was mentioned. Nevertheless, Caperton said the College Board was making socioeconomic diversity a major theme at its upcoming conference in Chicago.

Caperton was true to his word. In early November 2004, I attended that College Board conference, where Summers gave a keynote address on Harvard's new initiative for socioeconomic diversity. I asked a question from the audience about whether he would support legislation requiring disclosure of socioeconomic diversity at colleges. He demurred, but said Harvard would voluntarily disclose more data.

Fits and Starts

Later that day, I served on a panel with University of North Carolina at Chapel Hill chancellor James Moeser on the "National Imperative for Educating Low-Income Students." Moeser spoke of UNC's new financial aid program—the Carolina Covenant—to cover tuition for low-income students. I congratulated Moeser and said UNC was part of the "second wave" of socioeconomic efforts. Institutions such as the University of California, the University of Washington, and the University of Florida were part of the first wave that replaced racial preferences with increased admissions of low-income students and the financial aid to support them. Now, we were seeing promising new financial initiatives that serve as a supplement to racial preferences.[18]

Over the next few years, momentum continued to build. In September 2006, Moeser, Caperton, Bowen, and former North Carolina governor James Hunt Jr. all spoke at a national conference at UNC–Chapel Hill, "The Politics of Inclusion: Higher Education at a Crossroads," which cataloged the growing movement for socioeconomic diversity at selective colleges across the country. I spoke on a panel at the conference with Ted Fiske, a former *New York Times* reporter and editor of the *Fiske Guide to Colleges* book series, about efforts being made at different institutions. The conference organizers said that a total of twenty-four institutions had adopted new financial aid initiatives to boost socioeconomic diversity.[19]

The following month, in October 2006, I spoke at a conference at Yale titled "A Seat at the Table: Socioeconomic Diversity and Access to Selective Colleges and Universities." Bowen, Marx, and Yale president Richard Levin were in attendance. Over meals, I got to know Yale dean of admissions Jeff Brenzel, who came from a working-class background and seemed committed to promoting socioeconomic diversity on campuses traditionally marked by privilege.

At the conference, I also got to know Harvard admissions dean Bill Fitzsimmons. He had signed my admissions letter to Harvard back in 1981, but I'd never met him. Fitzsimmons, a first-generation college student whose father ran a gas station and convenience store, attended

Harvard on a full scholarship. In our conversations, he appeared committed to boosting socioeconomic diversity. In September, in fact, Harvard had made headlines for ending its early admissions process, in which students received an advantage for applying ahead of the regular schedule. The discontinuation was due to concerns of bias against low-income students. Fitzsimmons explained the rationale: "An early admission program that is less accessible to students from modest economic backgrounds operates at cross-purposes with our goal of finding and admitting the most talented students from across the economic spectrum." Princeton and the University of Virginia made similar commitments soon thereafter.[20]

It had been a deeply exciting couple of years. I was no longer sniping from the sidelines about the need for socioeconomic diversity. The leaders of some of the oldest institutions of higher education in America seemed to be on board. I had gone from battling and criticizing former Princeton president Bill Bowen to speaking with him at conferences on the importance of socioeconomic diversity. We became friendly and corresponded, and he publicly expressed that he appreciated my work to narrow economic disparities.[21]

It was also nice to be working with my friends in the civil rights community again. At the K–12 level, I worked closely with civil rights leaders while writing books and articles in support of school integration. But my advocacy for using class preferences as a *substitute* for racial preferences in the higher education arena from 1995 to 2003 had been highly controversial with those allies. The *Grutter* ruling created a different dynamic. Maybe it *was* possible to realistically champion both racial- and class-based affirmative action?

However, there was one false note at the Yale conference. Everyone was abuzz about Harvard, Princeton, and UVA having abandoned early admissions. When would Yale announce too? And would the rest of the Ivy League and all the other selective private and public colleges follow suit? I asked Yale's Jeff Brenzel at dinner about the question, and he was noncommittal. It was an early sign that something was amiss.

Fits and Starts

The Movement Fizzles

Looking back, 2004–2006 turned out to be yet another false start, as the movement for socioeconomic diversity would fizzle over time. To begin with, Yale chose not to abandon early admissions, even though the practice was deeply unfair to low-income students, who don't have counselors advising them that applying early can provide an advantage equivalent to scoring one hundred points higher on the SAT.[22] Nor did other universities go along. Instead, despite their public announcements about how regressive the policy was, Harvard, Princeton, and UVA would all later *restore* early admissions.[23]

Likewise, so long as race-based affirmative action was available, subsequent efforts to reform other unfair practices, such as legacy preferences, failed in the coming years. To my mind, while there were powerful arguments on both sides of the affirmative action debate, legacy preferences, which further benefit an already privileged group of students, were indefensible. It would be absurd in most other areas of life. It's hard to imagine giving students a head start in a track meet just because their parents ran track years ago. Yet the research found that legacy preferences were used at about three-quarters of *U.S. News & World Report*'s top one hundred universities. Research found these preferences, purportedly used only as a "tie-breaker," in fact added the equivalent of 160 SAT points for a typical applicant.[24]

During the Obama administration, I edited the first book-length treatment of legacy preferences and recruited a number of authors who argued for the practice's elimination. I thought our case was morally forceful, though one of the authors, Daniel Golden, wasn't sure it would win the day. He told me that after he wrote a Pulitzer Prize–winning series in the *Wall Street Journal* exposing how prestigious universities were essentially selling admissions spots—a practice he considered outrageous—he received several inquiries from readers wanting to know precisely how much they would need to donate to get their kids into particular institutions.

Nevertheless, I thought it was worth a shot to reform the legacy admissions racket, either by pressuring universities to change their practices or by enacting policies to force them to do so. I believed this would be a good issue for the Obama administration to take on, and while planning an event at the National Press Club to publicize the book's release, I knew I wanted my friend Michael Dannenberg to speak. He was a senior policy adviser to Obama's point person on higher education issues, Martha Kanter. Dannenberg, who had worked as an aide to Senator Ted Kennedy in the early 2000s, was a prominent critic of legacy preferences and was involved in drafting legislation aimed at curbing their use.

Dannenberg knew in his bones the unfairness of legacy preferences. He was raised in Westchester County, New York, by his single mother, who was disabled by childhood polio and worked for the state Department of Motor Vehicles, and his grandparents, all of whom lacked a college degree. His grandfather worked as a clothing salesman.[25] When he left for Boston University (BU) in the late 1980s, he told me, "It was tough culturally being a maximum Pell Grant student. I'd say no more than one in ten of my friends even knew what a Pell Grant was, much less had one." His peers all seemed to have Mac computers, but he told me that in his senior year of college in 1991, "I was still writing papers on a typewriter that my family got me just before college."[26]

When Dannenberg attended Yale Law School in the 1990s, he felt even more out of place. BU was "populated by new money," he said. "Yale Law School's old money." According to Dannenberg, Yale used a fifteen-point scale to grade applicants, with those who earned a score of fifteen being admitted, while those who earned a fourteen were often admitted, and those who earned a thirteen were usually wait-listed. Underrepresented minorities and legacies got an extra point. Dannenberg supported the preference for racial minorities but found the legacy preference outrageous.

In 2001, Dannenberg joined the staff of Senator Kennedy and proposed the idea of federal legislation to combat legacy preferences.

Dannenberg recalls that some senior staffers "thought I was crazy" because "big donors" in politics "are often legacies or have children they would like to see advantaged," and Kennedy himself was a legacy. But the senator viewed legacy preferences as "an anachronism" and saw the question as a "civil rights issue" because of its disproportionately negative impact on racial minorities. The higher education establishment lined up against the idea, though, and Dannenberg and Kennedy had to back down. When Dannenberg left Kennedy's office, the senator, a Harvard graduate, joked that his eighty-five nephews and nieces would not be sorry to see the young staffer go.[27]

But at the forum, it was very clear that Dannenberg was on a tight leash. He spoke not as an Obama official, but as a former aide to Ted Kennedy.[28] This was not going to be an issue that Obama would champion.

I thought the outside game might work better, and asked my good friend, civil rights lawyer John Brittain, who had coauthored a chapter in the legacy book, to convene a group of activists to put legal and political pressure on universities to end legacy preferences. Brittain's book chapter found that even though affirmative action programs had been in place for decades, Black and Hispanic students were still significantly underrepresented among the legacy pool. At Harvard, for example, only 7.6 percent of legacy admits were underrepresented minorities, compared with 17.8 percent of all students; at the University of Virginia, 91 percent of early decision legacy admits were white, 1.6 percent were Black, and 0.5 percent Hispanic.[29]

I had met Brittain while working together on school integration, and I'd been impressed by his commitment to both racial and economic justice in the great tradition of Dr. King. Brittain's parents worked for the family of Samuel Candler Dobbs, a former president of the Coca-Cola Company. Brittain's father served as Dobbs's chauffeur, yacht captain, and antique vehicles manager. His mother served as a maid, chef, and nanny. As a baby and young child, Brittain lived with his parents in the Dobbs mansion in Saugatuck, a section of Westport,

Connecticut, located on the Long Island Sound. Later, Dobbs's daughter helped the Brittains purchase an affordable home in an all-white neighborhood in Norwalk, Connecticut, where young John was the only Black student in his elementary school. Brittain had seen economic and racial inequality up close, and he remembered both as he pursued his career.[30]

Brittain went to college and law school, subsequently becoming the first Black tenured professor at the University of Connecticut Law School. There, he led an effort to desegregate the public schools in Hartford, Connecticut, and the surrounding suburbs by both race and class. In 1994, he told *Harper's Magazine*, "The most signal fact about Hartford is not that it's 92 percent nonwhite but that it's 63 percent poor."[31] If most upper-middle-class civil rights lawyers focused singularly on race, Brittain held firm that addressing class inequality should also be part of the fight.

On the legacy preference issue, Brittain spearheaded two meetings with leaders of the top civil rights groups.[32] But I was deeply disappointed, as these leaders passed. As accomplished professionals who had worked hard to win their degrees, many said they wanted legacy preferences to benefit both their children and the children of other Black and Hispanic professionals. Because affirmative action had not begun until the late 1960s, the children of those Black professionals did not start receiving the advantage of alumni preferences until the late 1990s. Why pull the rug out just a decade after Black and Hispanic students were beginning to benefit?

I found this line of argument—a version of trickle-down economics—troubling. Rather than helping working-class Black students who had overcome obstacles, the civil rights leaders wanted to replicate an unfair system for the benefit of their own children. And even on racial grounds alone, Brittain's data showed that the biggest beneficiaries of legacy preferences were wealthy white students.

Perhaps more important, these civil rights leaders did not want to attack their allies in elite higher education. It turned out there was an unwritten agreement between the civil rights groups and the universities: as long as universities provided racial preferences, civil rights groups would not challenge their legacy practices. In some ways, supporters of racial affirmative action appreciated the existence of legacy preferences, as it rebutted the claim that without racial preferences, college admissions would be a pure meritocracy. Racial preference advocates would return to this theme time and again.[33] And supporters (and beneficiaries) of legacy preferences liked racial affirmative action because the diversity it produced gave the appearance that the system was fair and open to all, thereby reducing pressure to end programs like legacy preferences.[34] Justice Thomas had been right when he observed that the legacy and racial preference issues had a symbiotic relationship—and that a victory for racial affirmative action was a victory for legacy preferences.[35]

More generally, for all the talk of adopting robust class-based affirmative action programs on top of racial programs, subsequent research studies—published in 2009, 2015, 2017, and 2018—found that universities continued to give a much smaller boost in admissions based on socioeconomic status compared to race.[36] In other words, your chances of being admitted were much better if you were an affluent Black applicant than a poor white applicant with the same record. One of the studies found that at highly selective private colleges, less advantaged white students were only a third as likely to be admitted as upper-middle-class white students who were *similarly* qualified.[37]

Reports in the coming decades would conclude that despite the rhetoric, socioeconomic diversity remained flat at elite universities on the whole.[38] A 2011 analysis by the *Chronicle of Higher Education*, for example, found that the percentage of students receiving Pell Grants at the wealthiest fifty institutions did not change much between 2004–2005 and 2008–2009. Thirty-one colleges actually saw declines in the proportion of Pell recipients.[39] A 2016 analysis found that between 2000 and 2013, the percentage of students eligible for Pell Grants at the most selective institutions had barely budged, rising from

16 percent to 17 percent, while during the same period, the share of Pell recipients at noncompetitive colleges had risen from 42 percent to 51 percent.[40] And in 2022, an initiative supported by Bloomberg Philanthropies concluded that high-profile pledges to boost the enrollment of low-income students had fallen short.[41] Tony Marx said he was disappointed that others hadn't followed Amherst in pursuing socioeconomic diversity. He told me that while Amherst had made some strides to boost socioeconomic diversity, "I hoped our peers would follow, but their numbers never moved as significantly."[42]

To be fair, the proportion of students eligible for Pell Grants did increase at a few elite institutions over time, which looked like a positive step.[43] But even here, there was less progress than met the eye. For one thing, eligibility rules about who could qualify for Pell Grants became much more generous over time, eventually covering the bottom half of the income distribution; thus, increases in Pell percentages didn't necessarily mean an actual change in socioeconomic diversity.[44] Moreover, there was evidence that institutions gamed their admissions process to make their Pell data look good. They would admit substantial numbers of the wealthiest Pell-eligible students and then reject most of those who came from the same basic economic background but just missed eligibility for Pell Grants. One study found that students who were barely eligible for Pell Grants had ten times the chance of admissions compared to those who were slightly wealthier and did not qualify for Pell. Taking these factors together, data showed that Princeton, for example, doubled its Pell representation from 2004 to 2013 "while only barely increasing the number of actual low-income students on its campus."[45]

Colleges never adopted Marx's idea of requiring annual disclosure of the full range of low-income, middle-class, and wealthy students, which would have given a much more accurate picture of the state of play and encouraged economic diversity. But individual research studies did report such data on an episodic basis in subsequent years, and the picture was not pretty. A 2011 study of the top twenty law schools found that just 2 percent of students came from the bottom socioeconomic quarter of the population, while more than three-quarters came from the richest socioeconomic quarter of society.[46] The study's author, Richard Sander of UCLA Law School, noted that the underrepresentation of low-income students at selective law schools was "comparable to racial representation fifty years ago, before the civil rights revolution."[47]

Subsequently, a blockbuster 2017 study by Harvard researcher Raj Chetty and his colleagues released a detailed breakdown of the income representation at virtually every college in the country. Chetty was given special access to IRS tax returns (with names removed), belonging to tens of millions of Americans. Because families often take tax deductions for tuition paid, Chetty was able to link data on more than thirty million students to the colleges they attended. The results were breathtaking. The data indicated that at prestigious colleges, if you took a casual stroll around campus, you would be twenty times as likely to bump into a wealthy student as a student from a low-income background. The über-rich—students from families in the top 1 percent of income nationally—often took up more seats than students from the bottom 60 percent by income combined.[48] While racial diversity improved over time at places like Yale, socioeconomic diversity actually worsened. Between 1927 to today, the share of students coming from the richest fifth of the population increased by twenty-six percentage points, from 47 percent to 73 percent.[49]

Despite the genuine commitment shown by Summers, Marx, and Bowen, Chetty found that the institutions they once led—Harvard, Amherst, and Princeton—were still severely lacking in socioeconomic diversity. Walking around Harvard's campus, in the class of 2013, one was fifteen times as likely to bump into a rich student as a low-income student; at Princeton, the odds were thirty-three to one; at Amherst, thirteen to one.[50]

In the end, the flurry of activity around socioeconomic diversity from 2004 to 2006—and the positive publicity that came from it—was misleading. The "race plus class" approach to admissions preferences proved to be a chimera. Universities continued to provide much larger preferences based on race than class, and racial diversity coincided with economic segregation.

How did universities and students deal with that reality? In the coming years, they would double down on social justice rhetoric, moving further and further to the left on cultural issues, to compensate for remaining bastions of privilege. As David Brooks noted, "Elite institutions have become so politically progressive in part because the people in them want to feel good about themselves as they take part in systems that exclude and reject."[51] Privileged students at schools like Yale would adopt what one critic called "luxury beliefs"—such as defunding the police and the idea that marriage is outdated—which "confer status on the upper class but often inflict real costs on the lower classes."[52]

Structural Impediments

The effort to add considerations of socioeconomic diversity on top of racial diversity—an idea supported by many of my liberal friends—failed mostly because it did not grapple with the fundamental forces that drive university behavior. Universities deserve credit for recognizing that racial diversity is part of what makes them excellent, and they have woven a commitment to it into their DNA. But why did all the statistical analyses of admissions—including from strong supporters of racial affirmative action—find that universities pay so much less attention to class diversity for its own sake? Four explanations stand out.

First, because achieving class diversity is more expensive than racial diversity (which can be accomplished by recruiting upper-middle-class students of color), attention to class cuts against all the other interests universities are trying to advance. Nonprofit colleges compete for prestige, which requires attracting the best students and faculty. Schools need to spend a lot on faculty salaries and campus amenities to recruit high-achieving students.[53] Enrolling high-achieving low-income students doesn't help—indeed, it hurts—because the financial assistance they require "diverts" resources. As the former president of Reed College explained, why spend $50,000 in aid on a promising low-income student when you can instead give five $10,000 grants in non-need-based merit aid to recruit students with high SAT scores who will boost the college's standing?[54]

A big part of university prestige today is associated with rankings in a guide put out by *U.S. News & World Report*. Students follow it, boards of trustees pay attention to it, and college presidents' compensation can even be tied to schools' *U.S. News* ranking.[55] "Think about the incentives," said former Vassar president Catharine Hill. "Every dollar you use for financial aid could have been used otherwise to improve your ranking. Spending on every other thing ups your score."[56]

Another big reason that college presidents have avoided using class preferences (at least while racial preferences were available) is that it poses a risk to dip into endowments to pay for financial aid. After consulting with multiple college presidents, Georgetown University's Anthony Carnevale said that presidents fear "they will get fired" if they are seen as allocating a significant portion of the endowment's earnings to financial aid.[57]

All of this means colleges have a self-interest in limiting economic inequality concerns to those associated with race, which are more manageable to address. As social critic Walter Benn Michaels argues, focusing on race rather than class tells the wealthy "what they want to hear—that the only poverty they need worry about is the poverty that's the effect of racism." It renders white poverty "invisible."[58] Colleges then double down on this approach by admitting Black and Hispanic students from upper-middle-class backgrounds rather than those from poor communities, saving even more money.

Second, as a practical matter, universities focus more on race than class because it is easier for selective institutions to mask a lack of socioeconomic diversity on campus than a lack of racial diversity. Race is far more visible to the naked eye than class. And while the federal government requires universities to detail the racial makeup of student bodies every year, it does not require those same universities to provide a socioeconomic breakdown by income quartile or quintile.

Third, as Larry Summers pointed out, elite universities are subject to strong bureaucratic forces pushing for racial diversity, legacy preferences, and athletic preferences, but comparatively few institutional forces promoting socioeconomic diversity. Professors may be Black, Hispanic, or female, but because they are often graduates of elite colleges, few come from working-class backgrounds. Indeed, faculty members are twenty-five times more likely than the general population to have a parent with a PhD.[59] It is telling that even with strong support for socioeconomic diversity at the presidential level at Amherst and Harvard, the Chetty data reveal that overall socioeconomic profiles of their student bodies remained enormously skewed toward the wealthy.

Fourth, it appears that America's selective colleges may reflect ugly cultural attitudes that flow from an excessive embrace of a meritocratic ideology. As the Harvard philosopher Michael Sandel has noted, American meritocracy gives rise to what he calls "the last acceptable prejudice": a disdain for families with less formal education. Social scientists have found that highly educated elites "may denounce racism and sexism but are unapologetic about their negative attitudes toward the less educated." A study conducted by five psychologists concluded that well-educated elites in the United States exhibit no less bias than those who are less educated; "it is rather that [their] targets of prejudice are different."[60] Given this milieu, it is not surprising that legacy applicants receive more plus points in admissions than students from families without college-educated parents.[61]

As a result of these four forces, the culture on America's elite college campuses has become disconnected from that of everyday Americans. Most people experience a daily reality marked by rising economic inequality and a slow decline in racial inequality. And yet on campus, race utterly dominates discussions. Although it is commonly said that "we don't like to talk about race," Walter Benn Michaels argues, "in fact, we love to talk about race. And, in the university, not only do we talk about it; we write books and articles about it, we teach and take classes about it, and we arrange our admissions policies in order to take it into account." He contended that we do so to avoid talking about class, discussion of which remains largely off-limits.[62]

Michaels captured the mindset in the story about a Harvard student who felt discouraged by his classmates' lack of interest in supporting the efforts of custodians and food workers to win higher wages. But then the student used a racial angle and began to get traction. "The only way I can get them at all interested in this thing is by saying, 'Most of these people are black,'" the student said. Michaels concluded, "Harvard students can't see underpaid workers as a problem unless they can see the problem as racism."[63]

Heather Berg, a student at the University of Virginia from 2011 to 2015, noticed the same dynamic. "We talk about race, gender, politics, but we never talk about class," she said in a 2013 interview. Berg, who is white and grew up in Florida, understood issues of class very clearly. When she was in seventh grade, her mother got divorced and began working a variety of minimum-wage office jobs. The family at times relied on food stamps, got clothes from Goodwill, and lived in a "tiny two-bedroom apartment with multiple pets running around." Berg said that she started working as a restaurant hostess and server in the tenth grade. Her high school was socioeconomically and racially diverse, with about half the students speaking Spanish in the hallways. But Berg was one of the few students to go out of state for college. Among her high school classmates, she said, "there was a lot of untapped potential." According to her, many students did not attend selective colleges out of "a lack of awareness" rather than "a lack of ability or potential."[64]

Berg was one of the exceptions. She saw an advertisement for a program called QuestBridge, which matches talented low-income students with selective colleges that provide full scholarships. She was admitted to UVA, and upon arrival, she was astonished by the wealth of the students on campus, signified by what she wryly referred to as the "UVA dress code." Women wore Barbour jackets and Lululemon leggings, and men wore button-down shirts and Sperry shoes. Classmates spoke casually about foreign travel and their parents' work as C-suite executives, doctors, or lawyers.

Berg took a number of social justice–oriented classes and recalls that "so many of the discussions were centered around other identity issues" such as race, gender, and sexual orientation, while "class was something that just wasn't explicitly mentioned in the conversation." Discussions of class, she said, seemed to make "people feel uncomfortable." There was a "fragility" and "delicacy" around the issue.[65]

Similarly, Chase Sackett, a student at Washington University in St. Louis, said that while students were used to talking about race, class always seemed to be "something that was under the rug."[66] Sackett, who grew up in an upper-middle-class family and received a merit scholarship, said his sense of injustice was stirred when he heard friends tell stories about how uncomfortable they were on a campus where everyone seemed to have enough to pay for things. Some students were extraordinarily wealthy. When Sackett was at Washington University, he knew of two fellow students whose families owned different professional baseball teams.[67] When Sackett went on to Yale Law School, he observed the same socioeconomic imbalance and insufficient attention to issues of class inequality. He helped organize a survey that found that only 8 percent of those at Yale Law were first-generation college students (in a country where two-thirds of adults lacked a college degree) and 77 percent had parents with graduate degrees (in a country where 12 percent of adults fell into that category).[68]

The Exception

Given the powerful financial, bureaucratic, and cultural forces pushing against admitting more low-income students, what hope did I have that universities would ever adopt class-based affirmative action? One, and only one, lever appeared to work: taking away the ability of universities to use race. Experience suggested that when race-preference bans were implemented, universities turned to economic preferences to achieve racial diversity—not out of a newfound interest in class, but because it became their sole avenue for attaining something they truly value.

In California, for example, Richard Sander reported that "one of the most striking effects of formal race-neutrality across the UC system was a jump in the interest of administrators and many faculty members in the use of socioeconomic status (SES) metrics as an alternative to race in pursuing campus diversity."[69] Research found that students from economically disadvantaged backgrounds were significantly more likely to be admitted to universities in California after the state banned racial preferences.[70] Likewise, when UCLA Law School adopted a socioeconomic affirmative action program, the proportion of students who were the first in their families to attend college roughly tripled.[71]

In later years, it hardly seemed like an accident that the University of California dominated the list of schools "doing the most for low-income students" in the *New York Times* "College Access Index." A *Times* reporter marveled at "California's upward mobility machine." Of the top seven institutions for social mobility, six were from the UC system, and the seventh, the University of Florida, had also implemented race-neutral strategies in the face of a racial preference ban.[72] The *Chronicle of Higher Education* likewise found that five of the eight most socioeconomically diverse well-resourced institutions it identified were UCLA, UT Austin, Michigan State University, the University of Washington, and Texas A&M—all of which had adopted race-neutral alternatives to racial preferences.[73]

The experience of trying to add class preferences on top of race preferences in the mid-2000s solidified for me the impossibility of doing so in the real world. Over the years, well-meaning liberal friends have repeatedly told me that because race and class both independently shape opportunity in America, both should count in admissions. I respond that I agree with the first half of the statement, but not the second. The hard reality, born of decades of experience, was that universities will never address class disadvantage unless racial preferences are removed. There are too many powerful forces preventing their considering class in a meaningful way. "Race plus class" in theory ended up meaning "just race" in practice. And in a society where class disadvantage has become a bigger impediment to opportunity than race, the race-only approach made no sense to me.[74] If one wanted race and class diversity on college campuses, it would be necessary to shape class preferences in a way that fully reflected the country's terrible history on race.

CHAPTER 5

Obama's Daughters and Other Challenges to Racial Preferences

A S I WAS SOURING ON THE POSSIBILITIES OF A "RACE PLUS class" preference approach to opening up universities to more working-class and minority students, the political and legal momentum appeared to shift again. Just three years after the victory for racial preferences in the *Grutter* case, new political and legal challenges to the use of race emerged.

Following the Supreme Court's *Grutter* ruling, Ward Connerly and other opponents of racial preferences decided it was time to head back to the voters. In a choice whose symbolism was hard to miss, they went straight to Michigan and placed the question of racial preferences before voters on the November 2006 ballot.

Supporters of racial affirmative action had a lot going for them. Democrats were riding high in Michigan at the time, and voters would reelect Governor Jennifer Granholm and U.S. senator Debbie Stabenow by comfortable margins in the 2006 election. Virtually the entire state establishment lined up in favor of racial preferences: business interests, labor unions, colleges, civil rights organizations, religious organizations, and both the Republican and Democratic candidates for governor. These groups helped supporters of using race in admissions outspend opponents by a three-to-one ratio.

But whereas Justice O'Connor had been persuaded by elites that the Michigan Law School's use of racial preferences was compelling, average voters begged to differ. In a direct repudiation of O'Connor, the electorate that supported Democrats for major offices also passed the referendum banning racial preferences by a whopping sixteen-point margin (58 percent to 42 percent). Taken together with the earlier votes in California and Washington, and Governor Bush's executive order in Florida, nearly one-quarter of the U.S. population now lived in states where racial preferences were banned at public institutions.[1] (In subsequent years, voters in Nebraska, Arizona, Oklahoma, and Idaho would pass similar bans, as would the New Hampshire state legislature.)[2]

Barack Obama's Ambivalence on Affirmative Action

Following the 2006 elections, all eyes turned to the big presidential race in 2008 as George W. Bush would be stepping down. No one excited me more than Illinois's electric new senator, Barack Obama. The son of a Black father and a white mother, he spoke about America in a way that was deeply inspiring. Additionally, on the topic of affirmative action, he had very interesting things to say.

A few years earlier, Obama had rocked the Democratic National Convention when he gave a powerful speech that appealed to Dr. King's emphasis on universalism and *e pluribus unum*. I was swept away by his mantra that while some tried to slice and dice America, Obama believed "there's not a Black America and white America and Latino America and Asian America; there's the United States of America. . . . We are one people, all of us pledging allegiance to the stars and stripes, all of us defending the United States of America."[3] His larger message was one of "hope and change," not grievance.[4]

Obama knew well the history of right-wing efforts to divide working people by race. As a young Harvard Law student in the early 1990s, Obama was deeply influenced by the writings of Bayard Rustin about the importance of building a multiracial, working-class alliance. He was also intrigued by Rustin's class-based approach to affirmative action. In an unpublished book manuscript, Obama and his classmate Robert Fisher observed, "If it has been working-class whites who have been most vociferous in their opposition to affirmative action, this at least in part arises out of an accurate assessment [that] they are the most likely to lose in any redistributionist game." Obama and Fisher called for universal economic policies that would "use class as a proxy for race." This was the most politically sustainable path, they argued, because "we cannot realistically expect white America to make special concessions toward blacks over the long haul."[5] Interestingly, when Obama applied to become a member of the *Harvard Law Review*, he did not check a box indicating his race because he wanted to avoid the stigma of receiving a racial preference.[6]

Fast-forward a decade and a half, and as Obama began his presidential campaign in 2007, I was thrilled to hear shades of Rustin's class-based approach to affirmative action resurface in the candidate's response to a question about racial preferences. He had generally supported racial affirmative action programs as a state legislator, but when asked in a May 2007 interview whether his own daughters deserved a preference in college admissions, Obama said, "I think that my daughters should be treated by any admissions officer as folks who are pretty advantaged." Then, he went further: "I think that we should take into account white kids who have been disadvantaged and grown up in poverty and shown themselves to have what it takes to succeed."[7]

It was not a one-off comment. In March 2008, Obama came under attack following a series of articles about his highly controversial minister, Rev. Jeremiah Wright, who appeared to be Rustin's opposite, viewing the world almost exclusively through a racial lens. In response,

Obama delivered a remarkable and widely acclaimed speech on race in Philadelphia. Like King, he built a powerful case for the nation engaging in some kind of affirmative action to address a terrible history of discrimination, including redlining and segregation. But he also acknowledged an important downside to racial preferences. "Most working- and middle-class white Americans don't feel they have been particularly privileged by their race," Obama said. "As far as they're concerned, no one handed them anything." Resentment builds, Obama continued, "when they hear that an African American is getting an advantage in landing a good job or a spot in a good college because of an injustice that they themselves never committed." These resentments, he said, are not "misguided or even racist," but rather are "grounded in legitimate concerns."[8]

During this time, I wrote a number of articles for outlets such as *Slate*, *The Guardian*, and *The Atlantic* about Obama's unique potential to transition the nation to a fairer, less divisive, and more popular form of affirmative action based on class. To begin with, I argued that it would be the right thing to do on the merits. If class-based affirmative action gave a leg up to low-wealth families and those living in high-poverty neighborhoods, it would directly address the legacy of discriminatory redlining that Obama cited in his Philadelphia speech. And because some disadvantaged white individuals would benefit from a preference based on wealth and neighborhood, class preferences could accomplish the repair without arousing the white working-class resentments Obama had acknowledged as legitimate. The approach would be color-blind, but not blind to history. It would also align with Obama's stance of rejecting the idea of a separate Black America and white America. Moreover, the shift would remove a political albatross that had hurt Democrats for decades. Citing Bobby Kennedy's belief that "poverty is closer to the root of the problem than color," I suggested that, "as the first serious African-American candidate for president, Obama has a chance to resurrect this lost thread of tough liberalism."[9]

Obama's Daughters and Other Challenges to Racial Preferences

Although Obama's Philadelphia speech was considered a master-stroke, the issue of affirmative action kept resurfacing. In an April 2008 debate, Obama was again asked about affirmative action policies; he said his daughters Malia and Sasha "had a pretty good deal in life" and should not benefit from racial preferences.[10] In July 2008, Obama told a convention of minority journalists, "We have to think about affirmative action and craft it in such a way where some of our children who are advantaged aren't getting more favorable treatment than a poor white kid who has struggled more."[11] The same month, Obama spoke to the NAACP and emphasized the types of programs one might expect to hear about in an address to the AFL-CIO. He made no mention of affirmative action, and instead called for more police on the street and the need to address poverty, whether people "live in Anacostia or Appalachia."[12]

Not everyone in higher education agreed with Obama's approach to affirmative action. The University of Chicago's admissions director said he would in fact give Obama's children a "break" in admissions because "those children, for all their privileges, will have interesting things to say about American society." It highlighted once again the gulf between the academy and the general public. If Obama had endorsed the idea that his kids should receive a preference because they could say "interesting things" or claimed that "yes, my daughters have it worse than poor white kids in Appalachia," it would have posed an enormous political risk, as it should have.[13]

I was thrilled when Obama was elected president in November 2008. It was a long overdue moment for the country. After centuries of oppression, millions of Americans now collectively decided to entrust the most powerful position in the world to a Black man. On Election Day, Children's Defense Fund president Marian Wright Edelman wrote in *Politico*, "This morning, as I stood in line to vote, I was moved by the realization that finally this is the day on which my fellow Americans are willing to do what Dr. King envisioned: vote for a President based on the content of his character rather than the color of his skin."[14]

I was excited for Obama's election because of his support for health care reform and measures to smooth some of the rougher edges of capitalism, and for his intriguing statements about affirmative action. As the first Black president, I thought Obama might have the political capital Bill Clinton lacked to ease a transition back to the King-Douglas approach to affirmative action.

I talked with Cassandra Butts, a senior vice president at the Center for American Progress (CAP), who had been a close friend of Obama's since their days as Harvard Law School students. She was part of a small group of female advisers to Barack and Michelle Obama, alongside Valerie Jarrett and Susan Rice, described as the "Sisterhood."[15] I'd become friendly with Butts because the organization I worked for shared space with CAP. She and I both tended to arrive earlier at the office than most other people, and we started having conversations in the coffee room.

I told Butts how excited I was about the president-elect's support for class-based affirmative action and said I wanted to help. Butts, who had worked for the NAACP Legal Defense Fund, disagreed with me on the issue of racial preferences. But she promised to bring up my interest with high-level officials on the transition team and report back on what they said. A few days later, she relayed to me that following through on Obama's campaign comments about affirmative action would be a nonstarter. There was no way the president-elect was going to go against civil rights and other organized interests in the Democratic Party, she said. He would have to toe the line, as Bill Clinton had. The only way Obama could make the transition to affirmative action based on class, she said, was "if the courts forced him to."

I watched with disappointment in the coming years how, whenever the issue of affirmative action arose, the president would ignore his earlier statements about the importance of emphasizing economic disadvantage.[16] It was a sign of the hardening line within the Democratic Party in favor of racial preferences. Unlike Bill Clinton, Barack Obama engaged in no sort of affirmative action review process to reconcile his campaign statements with his governing. There was no "Mend It, Don't

End It" speech. There were no serious debates within the administration. Something had changed within the Democratic Party between 1995 and 2009. Part of the shift may have been demographic change. As the Hispanic population grew along with the percentage of white people with a college education and more liberal views on race, the Democratic Party began to view working-class white voters who were strongly opposed to affirmative action as less significant. Whatever the reason, the process of jettisoning Obama's campaign comments in support of class-based affirmative action was completed before his presidency even began.

What did Obama think in his heart of hearts? It was hard to know. Perhaps he was just cynically catering to working-class white voters by raising questions about affirmative action during the 2008 campaign. Maybe he had only pushed the class approach to get elected. On the other hand, it was possible that deep down, Obama wanted to follow Rustin's class-based approach but couldn't because of interest group politics within the Democratic Party.

After all, Obama did follow Rustin's thinking on health care. The passage of the Affordable Care Act (ACA), the biggest legislative accomplishment of the progressive movement since the administration of Lyndon Johnson, was essentially a form of class-based affirmative action applied to medical care. The ACA was not designed to provide favorable treatment, as college affirmative action programs did, mostly to well-off people of color, nor did it exclude low-income white and Asian people from the policy's benefits. Instead, Obamacare provided its largest subsidies to low-income and working-class people of all races—a framing that explained its long-term political potency.[17]

In fact, when radio commentator Rush Limbaugh tried to paint Obamacare as "reparations" for Black people—a shamefully racist attack—the gambit fell flat, because the program clearly benefited working people of all races.[18] By the same token, Obamacare *did* disproportionately benefit Black people by narrowing racial and ethnic gaps in accessing health care, which was a positive outcome for the country.[19]

The ACA could have been a model for how Obama approached affirmative action, but he chose otherwise.

Finally, it was possible that in answering the question of how his daughters should be treated by admissions officers, Obama's response was not just a bow to political realities but a poignant and wholly appropriate reflection of Black pride. Michelle and Barack Obama had worked hard to become enormously accomplished professionals. When white people mistook Barack Obama for a valet on one occasion or a waiter on another, the conflation of race and class rankled.[20] Perhaps the president rejected the idea that Sasha and Malia needed a special preference in admissions because the benefit was coupled with a demeaning insult.[21]

Legal Clouds: Supreme Court Strikes Down
Racial Integration in Seattle and Louisville

Whatever Obama truly felt, the bottom line was clear: if change were going to happen, it would have to be forced by the courts. Although the 2003 *Grutter v. Bollinger* ruling appeared to clear the way for racial preferences for a quarter of a century, it came in a narrowly divided 5–4 ruling, and George W. Bush had since moved the Court to the right. Bush had appointed the reliably conservative Samuel Alito to replace the more moderate O'Connor and, in an even swap on issues of race, had appointed Chief Justice John Roberts to replace the conservative William Rehnquist.

The importance of the changes in Supreme Court personnel became clear in June 2007, when the Court, by a 5–4 vote, struck down the use of race in K–12 school integration programs in Seattle, Washington, and Louisville, Kentucky. In *Parents Involved in Community Schools v. Seattle*, the Court held that using race as a factor in student assignment policies—even for the benign purpose of promoting racial integration—was a violation of the Equal Protection Clause of the Fourteenth Amendment. Writing for four conservative justices,

Chief Justice Roberts declared, "The way to stop discrimination on the basis of race is to stop discriminating on the basis of race."[22] The *Parents Involved* decision, coming just four years after *Grutter*, led Justice Stephen Breyer to note in his oral remarks announcing his dissent, "It is not often in law that so few have so quickly changed so much."[23]

The fifth vote to strike down the voluntary school integration plans came from Justice Anthony Kennedy, who took a more nuanced position. He wrote that integrating schools by race was a "compelling" purpose, but school districts should only use race after exhausting "race-neutral alternatives," such as integrating schools by socioeconomic factors. Race had to be a last resort.[24]

Employing socioeconomic factors in K–12 student integration plans was an approach I had advocated in a book called *All Together Now: Creating Middle-Class Schools Through Public School Choice*. The research evidence had long suggested that to raise academic achievement, it is more important to have a healthy socioeconomic mix of students in a school than a specific racial mix. Black achievement tended to rise in racially desegregated schools not because of the pigmentation of the classmates but because low-income students of all races benefit from being in economically mixed schools where parents are actively involved in school affairs and classmates expect to go on to college. This was not a race issue: middle-class Black parents volunteered in the classroom just as often as middle-class white parents, for example, but low-income parents of all races, dealing with the stress of poverty, were less likely to do so. Racial integration was crucial for other reasons. It was found to reduce white racism and increase cross-racial understanding, for example. But because of the relationship between race and class in America, socioeconomic integration typically yielded racial integration as well.[25]

The Supreme Court decision in the *Parents Involved* case dramatically accelerated the interest of school districts in promoting socioeconomic integration as a way of achieving both racial and economic diversity at the K–12 level. When I started researching the issue in 1996, there were only two school districts in the country, educating about thirty thousand students, that employed socioeconomic factors in student assignment policies, such as admissions to magnet schools or the drawing of school boundary lines. But the numbers soon grew. By 2020, there would be 171 school districts and charter school chains (educating more than four million students) that employed socioeconomic factors. I was personally involved with those efforts in various communities, including Chicago, New York, Charlotte, and Los Angeles.[26]

College leaders immediately saw the implications of the *Parents Involved* decision for higher education. Justice Kennedy, the swing vote, had raised the salience of educational institutions proving that race-neutral alternatives wouldn't work before resorting to race. This was a far cry from Justice O'Connor's view in *Grutter* that she trusted universities to transition to race-neutral alternatives at the earliest opportunity.

It looked as though class-based affirmative action might have another shot, and strong supporters of racial preferences began inviting me to conferences to discuss my research. In January 2008, John Brooks Slaughter, former president of Occidental College and chancellor of the University of Maryland, asked me to speak at a meeting of the National Action Council for Minorities in Education about the meaning of *Parents Involved* for higher education.[27] Given the changing legal environment, I argued, universities should begin exploring need-based affirmative action programs. A few months later, the Ford Foundation, which had a long history of supporting racial preferences, asked me to speak at a conference about socioeconomic alternatives to racial affirmative action in higher education. Ford had assembled a group that almost universally supported the continued use of race in college admissions, but the organizers knew they needed to hedge their bets in case the logic of the Seattle case was applied to colleges.[28]

The Challenge to Affirmative Action in *Fisher v. Texas*

The higher education challenge came quickly. In April 2008, a white plaintiff, Abigail Fisher, filed a lawsuit challenging the University of

Texas at Austin's use of racial preferences in admissions.[29] Focusing on Justice Kennedy's concern in the Seattle case, opponents of racial preference believed the University of Texas at Austin was the perfect illustration of the viability of race-neutral alternatives. UT Austin had undergone three different admissions systems in the previous few years.

- Prior to 1996, UT employed racial preferences.
- For a period in the late 1990s and early 2000s, UT stopped using race in admissions. In the years after the 1996 Fifth Circuit *Hopwood* decision struck down the use of racial preferences in Texas, but before the Supreme Court gave the go-ahead to use race nationally in the 2003 *Grutter* decision, UT Austin suspended the use of race and adopted two race-neutral alternatives. The university employed the Top 10 Percent plan to automatically admit students with top GPAs from every state high school (public and private); and for the remaining seats, UT used an admissions system that considered a series of "special circumstances," including "socio-economic status, whether the applicant is from a single-parent home, language spoken at home, family responsibilities, socio-economic status of school attended, and average SAT or ACT score of the school attended in relation to the student's score."[30]
- Following the 2003 *Grutter* decision giving the green light for racial preferences, in 2005, UT Austin reinstated the use of race in admissions for some seats, but also retained the Top 10 Percent plan. Over time, the hybrid system would fill three-quarters of the class through the percentage plan, and for the remaining quarter, UT used a variety of admissions factors, including race.[31]

The lower courts, applying the *Grutter* decision, sided with UT, but in February 2012, the U.S. Supreme Court agreed to take up an appeal in *Fisher v. Texas*. The move seemed to signal a dissatisfaction with the lower court result. If the Supreme Court were pleased with what the lower court had done, it could have refused to take the case, as it does in most appeal requests.[32]

The unusual history of UT Austin's use of race over time allowed the Supreme Court to examine race-neutral alternatives in a fashion not possible at most universities. First, the Supreme Court could compare the 1996 level of racial diversity using racial preferences with the 2004 level of diversity using race-neutral alternatives. And, thanks to the subsequent hybrid system, the Court could compare the racial and economic diversity of the 75 percent of students admitted through the Top 10 Percent plan with the 25 percent who were admitted through discretionary admissions, which included racial preferences.

In the clean comparison between racial preferences and race-neutral alternatives, the data showed that UT Austin achieved *higher* levels of Black and Hispanic representation using race-neutral approaches than it had in the past using racial preferences. In 2004, race-neutral programs produced a class with 4.5 percent African American and 16.9 percent Hispanic representation, while in 1996, using race, the class had 4.1 percent African American and 14.5 percent Hispanic shares. Geographic and socioeconomic diversity also increased under the race-neutral alternatives. The findings appeared to powerfully vindicate race-neutral strategies like percentage plans and socioeconomic preferences.[33]

The Texas experiment also revealed a fascinating comparison that distinguished the population that benefited from the Top 10 Percent plan from those who benefited from the discretionary admissions plan that included racial affirmative action. In public debates, UT Austin leaders had positioned themselves as champions of diversity. UT Austin president Bill Powers waxed eloquent, arguing, "In my 38 years in the classroom, I often have seen how a diverse classroom enriches discussion, provides valuable insights and offers a deeper learning experience." Powers had claimed that capping the share of students admitted through the percentage plan at 40 percent or 50 percent of the freshman class would enable UT to use its larger discretionary pool of slots more efficiently for enhancing racial diversity through the provision of targeted racial preferences. This approach, according to Powers, would outperform the Top 10 Percent plan, which helped some white and Asian students as well.[34]

Civil rights groups didn't buy UT's argument for discretion because they couldn't be sure whether UT would use its freedom to benefit Black and Hispanic students. An official with the Mexican American Legal Defense and Education Fund opposed the limit, saying, "There's no better merit system than the Top 10 percent plan."[35] The civil rights groups were right. Although Powers claimed UT would use discretionary admissions and racial preferences to boost racial diversity, data from 2011 revealed that UT used its discretion mostly to benefit wealthy white students. Conversely, the percentage plan provided a much better path to diversity.[36]

Nine out of ten Latino and Black students admitted to UT in the previous two years had come from the percentage plan rather than the racial preference plan.[37] According to UT data, 29 percent of those admitted under the percentage plan were Hispanic, compared with just 14 percent under the discretionary plan. Black students represented 6 percent admitted through the percentage plan, but 5 percent under the discretionary plan. Asian American students also did better under the percentage plan. White students, meanwhile, accounted for 58 percent of discretionary admits, compared with 41 percent under the percentage plan.[38]

The percentage plan also tended to benefit low-income and working-class students, while UT Austin's discretionary admissions program tended to benefit rich kids. Of the students admitted through the percentage plan, 9 percent were from poor families with annual household incomes below $20,000, compared with just 3 percent of the discretionary admits. Students from working-class families (making between $20,000 and just under $40,000) constituted 14 percent of those admitted through the percentage plan, compared to just 7 percent of those admitted through the discretionary program. Meanwhile, at the other end of the scale, students from wealthy families (making more than $200,000 per year) were far more likely to be represented among discretionary admits (29 percent) than among percentage plan admits (13 percent). And those admitted under the percentage plan were three times as likely to be first-generation college students (33 percent) compared with discretionary admits (11 percent). On the flip side, 34 percent of percentage plan admits had a parent with a graduate degree, compared with 54 percent of discretionary admits.

The Debate over Race-Neutral Strategies Moves to Center Stage

UT and others couldn't deny the clear data showing that race-neutral alternatives produced more diversity. So instead, they made three arguments that the Top 10 Percent plan was deficient.

The first argument was that the Top 10 Percent plan did not produce sufficient socioeconomic diversity *within* the student body's Black and Hispanic populations. This reasoning called for "diversity within diversity." Texas argued that those admitted through the Top 10 Percent plan were more likely "to be the first in their families to attend college," for example, than those admitted through racial preferences. Having wealthier Black and Latino students in the mix, UT argued, was critical for the process of "breaking down racial stereotypes" that other students might have about racial and ethnic minorities. Racial preferences, UT argued in its brief, were needed for admitting students such as "the African-American or Hispanic child of successful professionals in Dallas," who would play against stereotypes.[39]

Second, critics complained that the success of the Top 10 Percent plan in achieving Hispanic representation compared to racial preferences could be attributed to the growth of Texas's Hispanic population. The Top 10 Percent plan did not reach anything like proportional representation for Hispanics, opponents argued. Third, skeptics said that the percentage plan might work to produce diversity in Texas, but it would not work everywhere, particularly at private universities that draw on a national rather than state-level pool of applicants.

In advance of the Supreme Court's oral argument in the *Fisher* case, I wrote a report that addressed these issues and others. To begin with, I found the "diversity within diversity" argument doubly wrong. As an empirical matter, selective American universities had no dearth of privileged students of color—and never would. The research studies were virtually unanimous in concluding that Black and Hispanic students on campus came mostly from economically well-off families. Bowen and Bok had found almost nine out of ten Black students at selective colleges came from the middle or upper classes. At the top twenty law schools, another study found that 89 percent of Black students came from the top half of the socioeconomic distribution, and 66 percent from the top quarter.[40] Research has found that even without a system of racial preferences, about one-third of the Black students currently on campus would still be admitted based on a system of grades and test scores. And because well-off students of all racial groups tended to have more educational opportunities than disadvantaged students, it was often the case that those Black and Hispanic students admitted without a preference were also the wealthiest.[41]

At a more basic level, the argument that the Texas Top 10 Percent plan admitted "too many" working-class students of color stood the issue of fairness in admissions on its head. To most Americans, the case of the privileged Black or Hispanic applicant benefiting from racial preferences was the Achilles' heel of affirmative action. That is precisely why President Obama said his own daughters did not deserve a racial preference.[42]

As a matter of fairness, for a truly meritocratic system of admissions that considered academic accomplishments in light of obstacles overcome, research suggested that working-class Black and Hispanic students should be given a much *bigger* leg up than their more privileged counterparts. In 2010, I teamed up with Tony Carnevale and his colleague Jeff Strohl to publish a book that included research documenting how much of an academic disadvantage growing up in a low-socioeconomic-status family imposes on students. Carnevale and Strohl examined a large dataset to measure the extent to which a series of socioeconomic disadvantages—such as low family income and parental education, a poor neighborhood environment, and low family wealth—affects SAT scores. They found that the most economically advantaged and most economically disadvantaged students are separated by 399 points out of a possible total SAT score of 1600. Race (i.e., the residual difference between Black and white students) accounted for a much smaller, fifty-six-point disadvantage.[43] Carnevale noted that the measure of wealth in the study (student-reported college savings) was "limited" and "does not capture the full racial effects of a more robust wealth factor."[44] Therefore, a better measure might further reduce the effect of race in the prediction. The bottom line was that socioeconomic disadvantage had an enormous impact on achievement.

The point of Carnevale and Strohl's study was not that racism had little effect on the academic achievement of Black students. After all, racism helped put Black families into lower socioeconomic groups to begin with. Rather, the study suggested that most of the effects of discrimination are captured by socioeconomic disadvantage.[45] Given all this evidence, UT's concern that an affirmative action program did not help enough privileged Black and Hispanic students showed how far universities had strayed from basic considerations of fairness.

Carnevale and Strohl's research was consistent with a growing body of scholarship showing that class disadvantage had eclipsed race as the primary impediment to opportunity. For example, in a 2011 comprehensive analysis of the test score gap among groups of students, a Stanford researcher examined nineteen nationally representative studies going back more than fifty years. The study found a dramatic shift in the size of achievement gaps by race and socioeconomic status. Whereas the average gap in standardized test scores between Black and white students used to be about twice as large as the gap between rich and poor students, by 2011, the income gap (between those in the ninetieth percentile of income and the tenth percentile) was nearly twice as large as the gap in test scores between white and Black students.[46]

The growing academic gap between rich and poor and the declining gap by race mirrored trends in the larger society. Although racial residential segregation was declining, income segregation was rising; and while the Black–white income gap remained steady, the income gap between rich and poor was exploding. Deindustrialization, the decline in organized labor, and the devastation of factory towns had left working-class people—Black, white, Hispanic, and Asian—much worse off. In addition, researchers found that as the economic payoff to education rose, wealthy families began investing more money in the cultivation of their children's skills than they had in the past. Between 1983 and 2007, parents in the top tenth by income increased their spending by 75 percent per child in real dollars, the middle fifth spent 6 percent more, while spending on children by the bottom tenth dropped by 22 percent. The wealthiest parents now invested nine times more than low-income parents to enriching their children.[47]

Even such a widely discussed racial phenomenon as the mass incarceration of Black men, according to New York magazine, turned out to be "primarily a function" of Black people's "overrepresentation among the poor and working class."[48] Racial discrimination was real, as evidenced by research finding that résumés submitted by applicants with "Black-sounding names" were less likely to be recruited by employers. But research also found that job applicants who gave clues to having lower-class social backgrounds (such as an interest in country music) were thirteen times less likely to be interviewed by prestigious law firms than those with clues of higher-class backgrounds (such as an interest in classical music).[49] In sum, on the heels of growing economic inequality, the Great Recession, and the Occupy Wall Street movement against the wealthy, Texas's argument that the Texas Top 10 Percent plan was helping too many working-class Black and Hispanic students was shockingly tone-deaf.

As to the second concern raised by critics of the Texas plan—that rising Hispanic representation had not kept up with the expansion in the statewide Hispanic numbers—I pointed out that UT was on weak legal ground. The argument for racial preferences in *Grutter* was that a college needed a "critical mass" of students to encourage a healthy and robust discussion. Proportional representation had never been a permissible goal, because some groups outperform others academically, which may have nothing to do with discrimination. For example, few would argue that the overrepresentation of Asian Americans and Jewish Americans in elite higher education was due to discrimination against white Christians. It was also unfair to hold the Top 10 Percent plan to a goal of proportional representation because even racial preference programs rarely met those aggressive standards.[50]

With respect to the higher education establishment's third concern—that percentage plans were hard to apply in certain circumstances, such as at private universities with national pools of applicants—I responded that there were myriad other ways that public and private universities could pursue diversity. The old hypothesis from Justice Blackmun in the 1978 *Bakke* case—that "in order to get beyond racism, we must first take account of race. There is no other way"[51]—had been disproved repeatedly. Universities had found other methods. By 2012, seven states, representing more than one-quarter of American high school students, had abandoned racial and ethnic preferences at state colleges and universities, and two additional leading institutions had dropped the use of race in admissions. Despite this change, most of these colleges and universities had found viable new paths to diversity.[52] In October 2012, I teamed up with another researcher to examine in detail the experiences of these universities.

The good news was that states and universities almost never just gave up on racial diversity. Instead, they created a number of new plans—and percentage programs were just one approach of many. Seven of nine states provided new admissions preferences for low-income and working-class students of all races. Eight expanded financial aid budgets to support the needs of economically disadvantaged students. Six states spent money to create new partnerships with disadvantaged schools to improve the pipeline of low-income and minority students. In three states, individual universities dropped legacy preferences for children of alumni, who were generally more privileged and disproportionately white. In three states, colleges created percentage plans.[53]

Moreover, seven of ten universities had been successful in using these race-neutral strategies to sustain racial diversity levels. At Texas A&M, the University of Arizona, the University of Florida, the University of Georgia, the University of Nebraska, the University of Texas, and the University of Washington, the proportion of African American and Latino students met or exceeded the proportion achieved in the past using racial preferences.[54]

Many of these colleges had initially been adamant that race-neutral alternatives could never succeed. For example, in 1998, the University of Washington (UW) was forced to abandon racial preferences because of a ballot initiative. At the time, University of Washington president Richard McCormick spoke out against the referendum and made dire predictions about its effect on racial diversity. But the university ultimately crafted new approaches to achieve diversity. It recruited more students from predominantly minority high schools to apply, expanded financial aid, and considered such factors as "personal adversity" and "economic disadvantage" in its admissions decisions. By 2004, McCormick said, "the racial and ethnic diversity of the UW's first-year class had returned to its pre-1999 levels," when race was still considered in admissions, and the new admissions policy also increased economic diversity among the student body.[55]

Similarly, in 2000, the University of Georgia adopted a number of race-neutral strategies after a federal court struck down the university's use of race in admissions.[56] In particular, the university began using a number of socioeconomic factors in its admissions process, including parental education and high school environment. It also began admitting the valedictorian and salutatorian from every high school class and stopped giving preference to children of alumni. Although alumni opposed the end of legacy admissions, the university reported that it had "not encountered noticeable fundraising challenges as a result of the change."[57] Although minority enrollment initially dropped after the ban on using race in admissions, it subsequently rebounded to higher levels than before the ban on using race took effect.[58]

The three exceptions in the study were the University of California's Berkeley and Los Angeles campuses and the University of Michigan at Ann Arbor. But each drew more heavily on a national pool of applicants, and thus had to compete on an unfair playing field against competitors free to provide racial preference in admissions. A talented Black student who applied to Berkeley and was admitted without a preference, for example, might also be admitted to Stanford with a preference and choose to attend the more highly ranked institution.[59] (In subsequent years, these three outliers would make substantial progress as well.)[60]

Because race-neutral alternatives were now front and center in the *Fisher* case, my public role was much larger than it had been in the 2003 *Grutter* case. On the morning of the oral argument, I wrote an op-ed in the *Wall Street Journal* outlining "A Liberal Critique of Racial Preferences." I argued that by backing the percentage plan and socioeconomic rather than racial preferences, liberals could "reclaim the moral high ground from university officials who seem more interested in assembling multiracial classes of affluent students than they are in educating less-privileged students."[61] That evening, I was asked to appear on *PBS NewsHour* opposite Debo Adegbile, acting president and director-counsel of the NAACP Legal Defense and Education Fund. I told the *NewsHour* producer that if the program wanted a red meat conservative opponent of racial preferences, I was not the right person. My objections were more subtle. The producer said that's exactly what they wanted, and Adegbile and I were interviewed cordially by Ray Suarez about the morning's Supreme Court oral argument in *Fisher*.[62]

Obama's Daughters and Other Challenges to Racial Preferences

The arguments, which I attended in person, had been fascinating. Justice Samuel Alito Jr., George W. Bush's replacement for Justice Sandra Day O'Connor, showed none of O'Connor's reluctance to criticize racial preferences. I was no fan of Alito generally, because he usually sided with corporations against workers, but he was brilliant in zeroing in on UT's astonishing "diversity within diversity" argument. Alito asked the lawyer representing UT, Gregory G. Garre, about the school's claim that it needed to use race to admit "the African-American or Hispanic child of successful professionals in Dallas." Justice Alito began, "I thought that the whole purpose of affirmative action was to help students who come from underprivileged backgrounds, but you make a very different argument that I don't think I've ever seen before."[63]

Justice Alito noted that Texas was able to admit "lots of Hispanics and a fair number of African-Americans" through race-neutral alternatives. He pressed hard on Texas's argument that the race-neutral alternative approach was nevertheless "faulty because it doesn't admit enough African-Americans and Hispanics who come from privileged backgrounds." Alito asked whether a minority applicant whose parents are successful lawyers and in the "top 1 percent of earners in the country" deserves an admissions preference over white and Asian applicants from less affluent families. Garre's eventual response—"We want minorities from different backgrounds"—spurred Justice Kennedy to comment, "So what you're saying is that what counts is race above all." Kennedy continued, "The reason you're reaching for the privileged is so that members of that race who are privileged can be representative, and that's race."[64] With Alito and Kennedy deeply skeptical, it looked like the Court might well be ready to strike down racial preferences.

Awaiting the Decision

After the October 2012 oral arguments, as I eagerly waited for the Court's ruling, I sensed the wind blowing in my direction. The first sign came in November 2012, when I arrived to speak on the campus of Middlebury College in Vermont, a highly selective institution with a wealthy student population.[65] I'd spoken about socioeconomic inequality on dozens of college campuses over the years, but never before had I witnessed what I saw on my visit to Middlebury. Students from the sponsoring organization, Money at Midd, began the forum by publicly announcing their names and how much they and their families paid each year in tuition and fees. The first student, Samuel Koplinka-Loehr, said his family paid about $18,000, and he added $3,000 from his job. He passed the microphone to the next student, who said his family paid the full $56,000 comprehensive fee. A young woman said her family could not afford to pay anything, but she worked to pay $1,200 toward college costs. I was dumbstruck, then elated, by the frank nature of the exchange. At Middlebury, at least, economic class was coming out of the closet.[66]

My student host, Koplinka-Loehr, told me that working-class students often felt out of place amid the wealth on campus, ashamed that they didn't understand the cultural references commonly employed by classmates. Students of modest means felt alone and resented the failure of classmates to acknowledge that the immense wealth found on campus was worlds away from the lives of most Americans. A Middlebury administrator who grew up in a low-income family that had to ration food and drink told me that she still felt out of place amid the luxurious surroundings on campus. "I still can't pour myself more than half a cup of orange juice," she said.[67] I wondered if the Supreme Court justices would have these isolated Middlebury students in mind as they weighed the future of affirmative action.

The second development came in March 2013, when Stanford's Caroline Hoxby and Harvard's Christopher Avery published a fascinating study revealing that America had an untapped reservoir of high-achieving low-income students who could do well at selective colleges. The study, which was featured on the front page of the *New York Times* under the headline "Better Colleges Failing to Lure Talented Poor," undermined the claim of elite universities that they would love to admit more low-income students if only they were academically prepared.[68]

Looking at students whose grades and test scores put them in the top 4 percent of the high school class of 2008, Hoxby and Avery found that 34 percent of those from the lowest income quartile of households attended one of the nation's most selective 238 colleges, compared with 78 percent of those from the richest quartile. *Times* reporter David Leonhardt wrote, "The findings underscore that elite public and private colleges, despite a stated desire to recruit an economically diverse group of students, have largely failed to do so."[69]

One big question was whether doing a better job of recruiting these students would also promote racial diversity on selective campuses. The study found that 69.4 percent of low-income high achievers were white, 15.2 percent Asian, 5.7 percent Black, and 7.6 percent Hispanic. But if the measure of disadvantage were wealth or neighborhood (as opposed to family income), an even higher share of high-achieving students were likely to be Black and Hispanic. Moreover, even if race were barred from admissions, there was nothing to stop colleges from making special efforts to get high-achieving low-income Black and Hispanic students to *apply*.

In a private email exchange a friend shared with me, Hoxby said that universities could achieve as much racial diversity as they currently were using racial preferences by specifically targeting high-achieving low-income underrepresented minority students. She wrote, "Our numbers suggest that there are [a] sufficient number of low-income high-achieving, underrepresented minority students out there to keep selective institutions as racially diverse as they now are—without affirmative action in admissions" if universities did a much better job of recruiting and specifically targeted high-achieving low-income students from underrepresented minority groups.[70]

Despite mounting evidence that my fight for class-based affirmative action might prevail, I was feeling more and more isolated from elites in my political tribe. In March 2013, as the Supreme Court justices were preparing their opinions in *Fisher*, the *New York Times* identified me as "perhaps the most prominent self-described progressive with doubts about the current version of affirmative action."[71] It was an astonishing statement, given the fact that earlier liberal heroes like William O. Douglas, Bayard Rustin, Martin Luther King Jr., and Lyndon Johnson had supported class-based rather than racial preferential programs. Enormous skepticism about racial preferences still prevailed among rank-and-file Democrats. But among thought leaders, the giants supporting class-based affirmative action were gone, and a researcher and writer like me was among the few carrying the flag for affirmative action based on economic disadvantage.

My isolation increasingly made me a pariah among the liberal establishment. That March, for example, I spoke at a conference at the University of Richmond Law School in favor of school desegregation efforts. During the event, I saw UCLA Civil Rights Project leader Gary Orfield, whom I'd known and admired since the mid-1990s.[72] I'd often cited Orfield's research on the importance of finding ways to avoid concentrations of school poverty. He recognized the significance of class, writing that "educational research suggests that the basic damage inflicted by segregated education comes not from racial concentration but the concentration of children from poor families."[73]

Over the years, Orfield and I had a cordial and respectful dialogue over issues of race and poverty. But now that the Supreme Court appeared to be poised to clamp down on racial preferences in admissions, Orfield took on a harder edge with me. In the hallway at the Richmond conference, he cornered me in front of several friends and began shouting that I was doing enormous damage to the civil rights movement by talking about the viability of employing class preferences. I asked him how he could be satisfied with a system of elite higher education that left out poor and working-class Black and Hispanic students, along with poor and working-class white and Asian students. Orfield, with his self-righteousness and voice rising, declared me an enemy of civil rights. I left the conference feeling shaken. My friend, the civil rights lawyer John Brittain, later told me that a colleague of his from the civil rights community who had witnessed the exchange told him, "Your boy took a whupping from Orfield." The left's position was hardening. The idea that class-based affirmative action might be a fairer approach, which President Obama had entertained just five years earlier, had moved beyond the pale for some liberal elites.

The Surprising 7–1 Decision in *Fisher v. Texas*

In June 2013, the *Fisher v. University of Texas* decision came down in a very unexpected fashion. While most people had believed the court would issue a decision with a clear liberal–conservative split, the justices instead ruled in a 7–1 vote neither to sustain racial preferences nor to end them, but instead to impose stricter guidelines on when such preferences could be justified. The issue of race-neutral alternatives—like socioeconomic preferences and percentage plans—would remain center stage. Under the new standard, the justices held that colleges could not employ racial preferences unless "the reviewing court [is] satisfied that no workable race-neutral alternatives would produce the educational benefits of diversity." Moreover, in pursuing the goal of diversity, universities would bear "the ultimate burden of demonstrating, before turning to racial classifications, that available workable race-neutral alternatives do not suffice."[74]

The opinion was a paradox: a victory for racial diversity, but a defeat for racial preferences. On the one hand, the Court upheld earlier precedents finding that the educational benefits of diversity are compelling. On the other hand, the Court put enormous new pressure on universities to find workable alternatives. Kennedy had essentially turned his dissent in the *Grutter* case into the law of the land. He had replaced Justice O'Connor's more lenient standard—which took universities at their word that race-neutral strategies were unavailable—and required that they prove it.[75]

Rather than issuing a final decision on whether UT had violated the law, the justices remanded the case to the lower courts to apply the new, stricter standard on when racial preferences could be used and to resolve any remaining unanswered questions. What precisely did it mean that the race-neutral alternatives were "workable"? And what was "sufficient" diversity? The Court said that race-neutral strategies had to work "about as well" at getting the educational benefits of diversity.[76] That was also hard to determine. Legal scholars such as Harvard's James Ryan and his colleague Thomas Kane said it was unclear whether a plan "that produced, for example, 60 percent as many minority students would be sufficient."[77] Overall, though some questions remained, the decision looked like a big victory for class-based affirmative action and other alternatives like the Top 10 Percent plan. This interpretation was underlined by the lone dissenter in the case, the liberal icon Justice Ruth Bader Ginsburg.

She claimed that race-neutral alternatives were really no different from racial preference programs. "Only an ostrich could regard the supposedly neutral alternatives as race unconscious," she argued. Texas's plan capitalized on the racial segregation of high schools, she noted: "It is race consciousness, not blindness to race, that drives such plans."[78] Ginsburg believed that if universities wanted to achieve racial diversity, they should be frank about using racial preferences to do so.

I normally agreed with Ginsburg's view of the world, but I thought her opinion in *Fisher* was poorly reasoned. There were enormous, on-the-ground differences between overt racial preferences and race-neutral alternatives, even those partly aimed at creating racial diversity. While racial diversity was a goal of both the Top 10 Percent plan and Texas's plan to prefer socioeconomically disadvantaged students of all races, it wasn't the only rationale—or the only outcome.

To begin with, percentage plans and class-based preferences may have produced similar levels of racial diversity as racial preferences, but the Black and Hispanic beneficiaries constituted a different *subset* of students. As I noted above, students admitted through the percentage plan were much more likely to have overcome the odds associated with growing up in low-income or working-class families and living in segregated neighborhoods. Only by viewing racial groups as a monolith could one conclude that the Top 10 Percent plan's effect was identical to that of racial preferences.[79] And by broadening the number of feeder schools that served UT Austin, the percentage plan also brought a more geographic diversity compared to racial-preference plans.

Moreover, getting in based on ranking in the top 10 percent of one's high school class avoided any stigma linked to admission because of one's race. As Glenn Loury, a Black economist at Brown University, tartly observed, "Knowing that I'm being judged by standards that are different and less rigorous by virtue of the fact that my ancestors suffered some indignity is itself undignified."[80] Even supporters of affirmative action acknowledged that racial preferences can be demeaning to recipients. Anna Holmes, an accomplished writer who is Black, noted, "When I was starting out in magazines, I was told by a colleague that my hiring was part of the company's diversity push, and that my boss had received a significant bonus as a result of recruiting me. Whether or not it was true, it colored the next few years I spent there, making me wonder whether I was simply some sort of symbol to make the higher-ups feel better about themselves."[81] By contrast, the Top 10 Percent plan did not hold any racial group to a lower standard; instead, it rewarded students of any race who worked hard to achieve the highest GPAs in their high school.[82]

Additionally, the Top 10 Percent plan avoided the racial animosity that research has found can arise from the use of racial preferences. In one study, political scientists Paul M. Sniderman and Edward G. Carmines asked half of a group of white respondents what they thought about Black people and subsequently asked a question about affirmative action. For the other half of respondents, the order of the questions was reversed: they were asked first about affirmative action and then what they thought of Black people. The two groups were matched by education, levels of prejudice, social background, and political outlook. The researchers found that positioning the affirmative action question at the beginning of the survey resulted in an increase in the percentage of white respondents agreeing with negative stereotypes of Black people. The share of people who embraced the slur that "most blacks are lazy" increased from 20 percent to 31 percent, and the proportion who agreed with the libel that "most blacks are irresponsible" increased from 26 percent to 43 percent. The experiment involved varying the order of only one question in a survey of more than one hundred, yet it triggered a statistically significant jump in white hostility.[83]

The Top 10 Percent plan had the opposite effect. It didn't divide by race. To the contrary, when a cross-racial, working-class political coalition arose in support of the Top 10 Percent plan, it allowed legislators who were often antagonists to work in common cause, reducing discord between working-class communities across the color line.[84]

Finally, Ginsburg and other critics faulted the Top 10 Percent plan for relying on a social ill—the racial segregation of high schools—to produce racial diversity at UT Austin.[85] But while segregation was certainly regrettable, a program that provided *relief* to victims of the social ill was something to be celebrated.

A Victory for Class-Based Affirmative Action?

Even though the justices did not offer a final decision on UT's policies, and instead remanded the case to the lower courts, most people interpreted the *Fisher* decision as a victory for race-neutral strategies like class-based affirmative action and percentage plans. One journalist said that what had been seen as a Quixote-like campaign by a policy wonk without an organized interest group was poised for a breakthrough.[86]

The civil rights activists with whom I'd worked on K–12 school integration, but crossed swords with on affirmative action in college admissions, now showed a new openness to class-based affirmative action as the best plan B. Several participated in a two-day seminar I organized with the Lumina Foundation in August 2013 on new paths to diversity.[87]

There were other signals that people were coalescing around an economic approach to affirmative action. In the spring of 2014, Sheryll Cashin—a longtime civil rights advocate, Georgetown law professor, and former clerk to Justice Thurgood Marshall—published a stunning book rejecting racial preferences, titled *Place, Not Race: A New Vision of Opportunity in America*. Cashin acknowledged that "what I am writing is sacrilegious to the civil rights community." But she thought it was time for a new strategy.

I'd known Cashin for years. She was a classmate of mine at Harvard Law School, and we worked together on promoting K–12 school integration. Through this partnership, I had come to appreciate her powerful insights. As an upper-middle-class African American woman, she had questions about whether her own children deserved a racial preference in admissions. And like me, she was particularly concerned about the low-income and working-class Black and Hispanic students, as well as white and Asian students, who were being left behind.

In the book, Cashin criticized racial preferences as a crude, legally unsustainable instrument that tended to benefit wealthy students of color and alienated working-class white Americans who should be part of the progressive alliance. She argued for a new, stronger form of affirmative action based on actual disadvantage rooted in the neighborhoods where students grew up. While many proponents of affirmative action, including Cashin's old boss Justice Marshall, cited high poverty rates among minority students to paint a sympathetic picture of applicants who have overcome obstacles, in practice, Cashin charged, universities "create optical blackness but little socioeconomic diversity."[88]

She proposed giving a leg up in college admissions to students of any race from economically disadvantaged neighborhoods and high-poverty schools. While most would be students of color, not all would be. As Cashin noted, "Whites who do live in impoverished environs or attend high-poverty schools are no less deserving of special consideration." She said, "Place, although highly racialized, now better captures who is disadvantaged than skin color." The place-based approaches, she concluded, would benefit individuals living in segregated environments who are in need, rather than enabling "high-income, advantaged blacks to claim the legacy of American apartheid."[89]

In August 2014, I helped organize a meeting of leading college presidents to discuss race-neutral strategies for producing racial and economic diversity.[90] The establishment was coming around. It looked like the tide had turned, and universities were finally going to embrace the King-Douglas approach to affirmative action.

The period spanning from the late Bush administration to most of the Obama administration saw a rise in new political and legal attacks on racial preferences, upending the era of tranquility that the *Grutter* decision was intended to initiate. While President Obama did not implement the class-based affirmative action idea he'd outlined during his presidential campaign, it seemed that the courts and voter referenda were pushing colleges in that direction. With new research evidence showing the rising significance of class disadvantage in society, and the economic and geography-based admissions plans proving effective in creating racial diversity without the toxic side effects of racial preferences, pragmatists in the university and civil rights communities appeared to show a new openness to shifting the basis of preferences from race to class.

CHAPTER 6

A Justice Flips
and Elites Prevail

W HILE COLLEGE PRESIDENTS GATHERED IN 2014 TO DISCUSS alternatives to racial preferences, there remained some unfinished business in the courts. Litigation was ongoing since the Supreme Court had remanded the *Fisher* case to the lower courts with instructions to apply the new, more exacting standard for using race-neutral strategies. I knew from years of experience that the higher education establishment was unlikely to give up without a fight.

The Establishment Fights Back in *Fisher II*

UT Austin continued to defend its use of racial preferences. To my astonishment, the district court judge in the *Fisher* case once again sided with UT by arguing that there were no "workable" alternatives available, despite the Supreme Court's new, tougher standard. In 2014, even more surprisingly, the Fifth Circuit agreed.[1] On June 29, 2015, however, the Supreme Court granted certiorari to hear the case again. It seemed to me a hopeful sign. Had the justices been happy with the lower court decisions siding with UT, there would have been little reason to take the case. It looked like the University of Texas was likely to lose in the High Court.

In September 2015, I submitted an amicus brief to the U.S. Supreme Court, responding point by point to the Fifth Circuit decision. Drawing heavily on new research from a book I edited for the Lumina Foundation, *The Future of Affirmative Action*, I outlined some of the important new data showing that race-neutral strategies can work well.[2]

In discussing socioeconomic preferences, the Fifth Circuit pointed to Thomas Kane's 1998 study, which found that using *income-based* affirmative action would result in a decrease in racial diversity.[3] In response, I noted that was true enough, but focusing only on income made little sense because it ignored the extra burdens Black and Hispanic students typically faced coming from high-poverty neighborhoods and families with little wealth. Indeed, recent research in the Lumina volume found a much bigger racial dividend when universities considered those additional factors alongside income.[4]

My old friends Anthony Carnevale, Stephen Rose, and Jeff Strohl of Georgetown looked at what would happen if top colleges considered not only family income, but also such factors as family savings and the poverty level of the schools applicants attended. Under that scenario, the combined Black and Hispanic representation would actually *rise* from 11 percent to 13 percent.[5] The schools would also have a richer socioeconomic mix of students.[6] And the students admitted under the simulations would be well prepared academically, with a mean SAT score higher than that of the students currently admitted to these colleges.[7]

Astonishingly, the Fifth Circuit grappled with none of the powerful new research showing that socioeconomic affirmative action could provide racial diversity and maintain high academic standards. Instead, it relied on a single study from the 1990s that looked at income alone. Why didn't it dig into the research? The judges appeared to make a classic ideologically driven mistake by claiming that socioeconomic affirmative action programs were flawed because they "conclude that skin color is no longer an index of prejudice."[8] This argument drove me nuts. It was *precisely* because of redlining, housing discrimination, and segregation that middle-income Black families tended to live in higher poverty neighborhoods and have less accumulated savings. That's exactly why Carnevale's research had shown that Black and Hispanic students benefit when universities look at a broader set of socioeconomic factors that capture the economic manifestations of racial discrimination.

The Independent Educational Value of Socioeconomic Diversity

I was deeply troubled by another aspect of the Fifth Circuit decision. In evaluating whether the Top 10 Percent plan was "workable" for achieving the educational benefits of diversity, the judges ignored the value of the plan's ability to enhance socioeconomic diversity. The Supreme Court had long recognized that the educational value of diversity comes not only from bringing together students of different races, but also students from different geographic regions and economic backgrounds. In *Grutter*, for example, the Court noted that Justice Powell's *Bakke* opinion was "careful to emphasize that in his view race 'is only one element in a range of factors a university properly may consider in attaining the goal of a heterogeneous student body.'"[9] The *Grutter* decision found that having a diverse student body enhanced discussions and demonstrated that pathways to leadership are open to all in a democratic society. Racial and ethnic diversity contributed to both goals, I argued in my amicus brief, but so too did socioeconomic diversity.

"The nation's future," the Court observed in *Grutter*, "depends upon leaders trained through wide exposure to the ideas and mores of students as diverse as this Nation of many peoples," noting that "'classroom discussion is livelier, more spirited, and simply more enlightened and interesting' when the students have 'the greatest possible variety of backgrounds.'"[10] But if one were looking for a lively discussion among students with different backgrounds, including a poor white student from a trailer park might add at least as much diversity as a wealthy Black graduate of a prep school. As one University of Pennsylvania Law professor noted, his racially diverse class had "very few students who come from . . . the blue-collar working class. What that means is that no one has any idea what life is like on the other side of the tracks. That leads to a very sterile discussion when it comes to labor law."[11]

The *Grutter* Court suggested that diversity was also necessary "in order to cultivate a set of leaders with legitimacy in the eyes of the citizenry." The Court continued, "All members of our heterogeneous society must have confidence in the openness and integrity of the educational institutions that provide this training."[12] Socioeconomic diversity was surely relevant on this score. A racially diverse class that effectively excluded students from families in the bottom half of the socioeconomic spectrum was unlikely to instill legitimacy. Social mobility had always been a core American value; if elite universities were seen as perpetuating inequality, they would lose credibility.

The paucity of working-class white students, in particular, helped feed an ideological slant on elite campuses. A wide body of research found that elite colleges had faculty and student bodies that leaned much further left than the country as a whole.[13] The ideological bubble created by the exclusion of working-class white students undermined the interests cited by the *Grutter* Court. It resulted in less viewpoint diversity, which made for less interesting classroom discussions, and undermined political support for elite institutions among members of the Republican Party. The Top 10 Percent plan, by guaranteeing admissions to students from rural high schools, was likely to remedy these problems. Yet the Fifth Circuit expressed no interest in this dimension of diversity and focused solely on race.

Likewise, the Fifth Circuit undervalued the importance of promoting cross-class understanding in a society riven politically by a diploma divide. In the context of race relations, Harvard professor Gordon Allport's well-known "contact hypothesis" suggested that racial prejudice diminished when people of different racial groups interacted on a basis of equal status. But the logic of Allport's thinking also applied to class. Exposing professors and fellow students to bright young individuals of working-class backgrounds had the potential to deepen empathy and mitigate the problem highlighted in Chapter 4: that highly educated elites "are unapologetic about their negative attitudes toward the less educated."[14]

The Supreme Court Oral Argument in *Fisher II*: Scalia and Alito

In December 2015, I attended the oral arguments in the U.S. Supreme Court in *Fisher II*, in which the justice's questions ranged from scandalous to brilliant. Much of the press attention to the oral argument centered around an offensive comment that Justice Antonin Scalia made, suggesting that Black students would be better off if they went "to a less advanced . . . a slower-track school where they do well." He continued, "I'm just not impressed by the fact that the University of Texas may have fewer [Black students if the admissions policy changes]. Maybe it ought to have fewer. And maybe, when you take more, the number of blacks, really competent blacks, admitted to lesser schools, turns out to be less." He added, "I don't think it stands to reason that it's a good thing for the University of Texas to admit as many blacks as possible."[15]

I strongly disagreed with Justice Scalia's highly insulting comments, given that most Black students at selective colleges did well. But I cheered a different set of comments made by Justice Samuel Alito, which went in the opposite direction of Scalia's. Alito picked up a thread from the *Fisher I* case, where he had questioned UT's insulting view that the Top 10 Percent plan was flawed because so many of the Black and Hispanic students it admitted were from working-class, rather than affluent, families. In the *Fisher II* argument, Alito again pounced on this line of reasoning.

The Obama administration's solicitor general argued that the U.S. military needed the affluent Black and Hispanic students admitted through a discretionary racial preference program, rather than the minorities from working-class backgrounds admitted through a percentage plan approach. Alito disagreed: "One of the things I find troubling about your argument is the suggestion that there is something deficient about the African-American students and the Hispanic students who are admitted under the Top 10 Percent plan. They're not dynamic. They're not leaders. They're not change agents. And I don't know what the basis for that is." He pressed on: "Do you think that the African-American and Hispanic students who were admitted under the Top 10 Percent plan make inferior officers when compared to those who were admitted under holistic review?"[16]

Alito suggested the Top 10 Percent plan's ability to reach working-class students who had overcome odds should be seen as a virtue, not a drawback. "The reason for adopting affirmative action in the first place," he said, was "because there are people who have been severely disadvantaged through discrimination and—and lack of wealth, and they should be given a benefit in admission." It was a brilliant set of questions that turned the tables. If Scalia made statements that appeared to be borderline racist, Alito challenged UT and the Obama administration for making classist assumptions about the working-class Black and Latino students admitted to UT under a race-neutral policy.

Rising Hopes While Waiting for the Decision

If Scalia and Alito made the most news, Justice Kennedy—who was usually the swing vote on the Court—was relatively quiet, and it would be some time before his opinions would become known.[17] Blockbuster decisions tend to come from the Supreme Court at the end of June. In the intervening six months, I became increasingly excited that the Supreme Court could help push universities toward a new and better form of affirmative action.

In February 2016, I was enormously inspired about possibilities in a post–*Fisher II* world when I spoke at the inter–Ivy League

First-Generation College Students Conference at Harvard.[18] When I was an undergraduate at Harvard, there were student organizations dedicated to supporting identity groups based on race and ethnicity, but none for students who were economically disadvantaged. However, a Harvard College First-Generation Student Union had been established and was hosting a conference of 350 students and administrators, mostly from Ivy League institutions. The organization aimed to boost the presence of disadvantaged students on elite campuses and reduce their sense of alienation. It was a stunning development, one speaker noted, quoting the Black feminist writer bell hooks, who declared, "Class is rarely talked about in the United States; nowhere is there a more intense silence about the reality of class differences than in educational settings."[19]

Students organized not around being poor, which they wanted to escape, but rather around being "first-generation" college students. Ana Barros, a Harvard student who grew up in a home built by Habitat for Humanity and whose father worked as a janitor, told me that while organizing around poverty made some people uncomfortable, celebrating advancement—being the first in one's family to attend college—had a much broader constituency.[20]

When Barros, then a senior, arrived at Harvard as a freshman, she felt marginalized and out of place in a sea of wealth—a theme repeated time and again at the conference. Students told me they were shocked to find that even many of the Black and Latino students came from prominent families with highly educated parents. Speaking to the assembled group, Barros teared up when she said that she had entered Harvard a few years earlier with feelings of shame and isolation because of how different she was from her classmates. Now, surrounded by a few hundred working-class students from several elite colleges, she said that it was time to claim first-generation status as "a badge we can wear proudly." She concluded, "Thank you for giving me a community," as the crowd rose in a standing ovation.[21]

It was a stunning moment for me. In the Science Center classroom where I once took classes as a Harvard student, I saw a beautiful manifestation of both Martin Luther King Jr.'s vision and Robert F. Kennedy's political coalition. Because race continued to shape opportunity, there were substantial numbers of Black and Hispanic students at the gathering. But because class disadvantage crosses racial lines, low-income and working-class white and Asian students were present as well. And instead of fighting over the validity of racial preferences, this multiracial audience of impressive first-generation college students, all of whom had overcome odds, were fully allied and fighting for a common cause—to increase the representation of economically disadvantaged students at top colleges.[22] If the Supreme Court were to strike down racial preferences, I thought to myself, I could see in this room what the next generation of affirmative action might produce.

Kennedy's Shockingly Elitist *Fisher II* Decision

In May and June, I checked in frequently on the *SCOTUSblog* website, which provided live announcements of Supreme Court decisions. During the oral arguments in December, the justices had seemed to be lining up 5–3 against racial preferences (with Justice Kagan recused). In the intervening period, however, Justice Antonin Scalia's unexpected death in February led to a major fight in the Senate over whether to confirm President Obama's nominated replacement, Merrick Garland. In an unprecedented move, Republicans refused to confirm any new appointee until after the November 2016 presidential election. Still, even without Scalia, *Fisher II* looked to be a 4–3 decision against the University of Texas.[23]

On June 23, 2016, the Supreme Court announced its ruling in *Fisher II*. But instead of ruling against racial preferences, Justice Kennedy dramatically flipped his position. He wrote an opinion, joined by Justices Ginsburg, Breyer, and Sotomayor, declaring that those preferences should survive. Justices Alito, Thomas, and Roberts dissented.[24] "Affirmative Action Advocates Shocked," read the *Washington Post* headline for an article that noted supporters were both surprised and elated by the decision.[25] Thirty-eight years after *Bakke* and thirteen years after *Grutter*, racial preferences once again lived to see another day.

Justice Alito's dissent in the case began with these words: "Something strange has happened since our prior decision in this case."[26] And that was the big question: What happened to Kennedy? Why did he mysteriously switch sides? According to Supreme Court reporter Joan Biskupic, the Court had been poised to end racial preferences in *Fisher I.* However, Justice Sotomayor was preparing a scathing dissent, which caused Kennedy to back off and remand the case.[27] Surely some of that early hesitation explained Kennedy's decision in *Fisher II* to retreat even further.

Fisher I's holding—that universities bear "the ultimate burden of demonstrating, before turning to racial classifications, that available, workable race-neutral alternatives do not suffice"—had left open a few important questions. First, what was "sufficient" racial diversity? That is, what constituted a "critical mass" of underrepresented students? And second, what made a race-neutral strategy "workable" or "unworkable"?[28] In *Fisher II*, Kennedy gave the answers, intellectually unsatisfying though they were.

The term "critical mass" by its nature suggests a numerical measure. Given that the Top 10 Percent plan provided *higher* levels of Black and Hispanic representation than Texas's previous use of race had, it would seem to have been satisfied. But now, Kennedy said, "The compelling interest that justifies consideration of race in college admissions is not an interest in enrolling a certain number of minority students." So how would colleges know when a critical mass has been achieved? Kennedy's majority opinion referenced the goal of providing an academic environment that offers a "robust exchange of ideas, exposure to differing cultures, preparation for the challenges of an increasingly diverse workforce, and acquisition of competencies required of future leaders"—all laudable goals—but did not say what level of diversity was required to achieve these outcomes.[29]

And why were the Top 10 Percent plan, and other strategies like socioeconomic preferences, not "workable" alternatives in Kennedy's eyes? In a highly revealing passage, he said that enhanced consideration of socioeconomic disadvantage was not a viable alternative because "the Equal Protection Clause does not force universities to choose between a diverse student body and a reputation for academic excellence."[30] The elitist subtext of this passage was that programs that relied on recruiting economically disadvantaged students to achieve racial and economic diversity inherently conflicted with high academic standards.

The Court provided no evidence for its position, presumably because there was plenty of evidence contradicting it. Researchers at Princeton University found that students admitted through the Top 10 Percent plan had done well. "Top 10% black and Hispanic enrollees arrive with lower average test scores yet consistently perform as well or better in grades, first-year persistence, and four-year graduation likelihood" as many white students, they found.[31] Moreover, in 2000, when the Top 10 Percent plan was in effect, but racial preferences were not, UT's president noted that "minority students earned higher grade point averages last year than in 1996 and have higher retention rates."[32] Overall, by 2017, UT's graduation rates had increased to record levels.[33] After UCLA Law School adopted a socioeconomic preferences program, the school's California bar exam passage rate rose to an all-time high.[34] National simulations showed that top universities could nearly quadruple the proportion of students from the bottom socioeconomic half and maintain high graduation rates.[35] And extensive research found that universities could tap into a wellspring of talent among high-achieving, economically disadvantaged students, thousands of whom were Black and Hispanic, by doing a better job of recruiting.[36]

In his dissent in *Fisher II*, Justice Alito noted that Top 10 Percent plan students didn't struggle academically; in fact, they received "higher college grades than the African-American and Hispanic students admitted under the race-conscious program."[37] And while UT fancied itself as a champion of racial justice, Alito noted that the university had been embroiled in a scandal over providing admissions preferences for influential alumni. Using a "secret process," he noted, "university officials regularly overrode normal holistic review to allow politically connected individuals—such as donors, alumni, legislators, members of the Board of Regents, and UT officials and faculty—to get family members and other friends admitted to UT, despite having grades and standardized test scores substantially below the median for admitted students."[38] A report compiled by an independent consulting firm found that UT president Bill Powers insisted on certain "must have" applicants. In one case, the admissions director told Powers's chief of staff that there was "no way I can admit this student" given the applicant's record, but she replied, "Well, I speak for the president and he wants it done." The applicant was admitted.[39]

And yet, astonishingly, Justice Kennedy had declared the Top 10 Percent plan—which produced racial diversity, social mobility, and academic excellence—an "unworkable" alternative. By preserving the status quo, Kennedy ensured that Ana Barros and her friends—and many other working-class students at elite colleges—would remain isolated. A *New Republic* article published after the *Fisher I* decision crediting me as an "affirmative action prophet" turned out to be grossly wrong in light of *Fisher II*. Wealthy students of all races had won, and low-income students of all races had lost. Maybe this result should not have been so surprising after all.

A Frightening and Even More Shocking Populist Revolt in 2016

The *Fisher II* decision in the summer of 2016 represented a major victory for the higher education establishment's long-standing system of racial and legacy preferences. But that same establishment would suffer a stunning comeuppance in the fall of 2016, when its favored presidential candidate lost to a right-wing populist who ran on the theme that the deck was stacked against average Americans.

Class Matters

Affirmative action was not a voting issue in the 2016 presidential campaign, but Justice Kennedy's worldview in the *Fisher II* decision had powerful parallels in the view expressed by Democratic candidate Hillary Clinton. Kennedy's dim view of the abilities of working-class students echoed Clinton's disdain for the working-class white supporters of her Republican opponent, Donald Trump—a condescending attitude that Trump, a deeply dangerous and authoritarian figure, exploited to the fullest. Philosopher Michael Sandel says that Trump was "keenly alive to the politics of humiliation" and knew how to exploit it.[40] Likewise, Kennedy's endorsement of a discretionary admissions system of racial preferences not only buttressed but also provided cover for preferences for the well-connected and elite, thereby reinforcing Trump's charge that elites skewed the rules in their own favor. Some liberals suggested that racism was the driving force behind the frustration of Trump voters, but that didn't explain why another populist candidate, the aging socialist Bernie Sanders, also did surprisingly well against Clinton in the Democratic presidential primaries.

The election of Donald Trump in November 2016 would have significant consequences on the narrower issue of affirmative action itself. In the years to come, Trump would have three chances to appoint justices to the Court—and they would have much more to say about affirmative action after Trump left the White House.

In 2015 and the first half of 2016, I had been fully expecting that *Fisher II* would usher in a new, better form of affirmative action based on disadvantage. The evidence had grown even stronger since *Fisher I* that race-neutral alternatives could work to produce racial and socioeconomic diversity while maintaining high academic standards. I had become even more excited when I spoke to Harvard's assembly of impressive and diverse first-generation college students, thinking their moment had arrived. Justice Kennedy's *Fisher II* decision, which sided with higher education elites and presumed, without evidence, that working-class students were incapable of excelling at selective colleges, was both astonishing and enormously discouraging. Kennedy's condescending attitude was part of a much larger elite mindset that helped fuel an antiestablishment revolt in 2016 that was at once terrifying and completely understandable.

CHAPTER 7

Peeking Behind the Admissions Curtain

How Harvard Creates a Multiracial Aristocracy

THOUGH I WAS OUTRAGED BY THE *FISHER II* DECISION, WHICH ignored powerful evidence about the effectiveness of race-neutral strategies, I took solace in knowing that the UT Austin case might not be the last word on the issue. Edward Blum, the conservative activist behind the *Fisher* litigation, had approached me about participating in a case challenging Harvard University's racial preference policy brought by Students for Fair Admissions (SFFA), an organization he created. (He also asked me to be involved in a parallel lawsuit against the University of North Carolina, discussed in Chapter 8.)

An attack on Harvard's policy would go straight to the heart of racial preferences in America. Harvard had been Justice Powell's model in the *Bakke* case for how to implement affirmative action policies in the "right way." But Harvard's use of race in admissions had never been subject to a thorough examination. Moreover, some suspicious evidence suggested that Harvard's vaunted system used race to discriminate against Asian American students, who have higher achievement levels on average than students in other racial groups and were already represented in greater numbers on campus than in the general high school population.

SFFA lawyers Will Consovoy and Tom McCarthy asked me to be an expert witness in the case, analyzing whether Harvard could achieve racial diversity without racial preferences. They were deeply conservative: Consovoy had clerked for Justice Clarence Thomas, and McCarthy had worked for conservative jurist David B. Sentelle of the D.C. Circuit Court of Appeals. But I liked that they did not show undue reverence for the Ivy League. Both had graduated from George Mason Law School, which ranked far outside the top twenty schools, and knew that talent was found in lots of places.[1]

Walking across the aisle and joining the Students for Fair Admissions team would be a big step for me personally, and I had to weigh the risks and benefits. I knew signing on as an expert would alienate most of my liberal friends with whom I had worked closely on many issues: Darren Walker from the Ford Foundation, who was an ally on improving community college funding; John King from the Obama administration, who was a partner on school integration at the K–12 level; American Federation of Teachers president Randi Weingarten, with whom I'd worked to oppose private school vouchers; and members of Congress Keith Ellison and John Lewis, who had championed an idea I'd advocated to make labor organizing a civil right.[2] These were my people—and they all favored racial preferences. Civil rights allies had tolerated my writing books and articles suggesting that class-based affirmative action was a better way of promoting racial and economic diversity, but testifying in federal court as part of a lawsuit was likely to annoy and possibly infuriate them. The fact that I wanted colleges to use socioeconomic factors that captured the legacy of racism was beside the point; in American politics, you were supposed to choose sides and stick close to your allies.

Peeking Behind the Admissions Curtain

Moreover, I knew that people in my circles deeply disliked Edward Blum. He had been a driving force behind the *Shelby County* litigation in which a majority of justices (including Justice Kennedy) gutted a key section of the Voting Rights Act, requiring some jurisdictions (mostly in the South) to clear any changes to voting rules with the Justice Department in advance. Members of the press put the challenge to racial preferences in the same bucket. TV reporter Soledad O'Brien told me Blum was "anti–civil rights."[3] A reporter for the *Washington Post*, whom I knew from my work on school integration, told me she thought that Blum and Students for Fair Admissions were "racists." One friend at the *New York Times* said some of his colleagues wondered why, when I was so good on housing issues, I could be part of an "evil" effort to go after racial preferences.

I saw Blum differently. He was raised in a politically liberal, pro–civil rights family and frequently spoke about his Jewish values. He told the *New York Times* that growing up, "the idea of treating people equally, not being a racist, not being a bigot, was a conversation at my dinner table. My father and mother knew antisemitism."[4] To be sure, we were odd bedfellows, and I disagreed with his *Shelby County* litigation because I viewed preclearance as an important antidiscriminatory tool to ensure voting access. But Blum's opposition to racial preferences in college admissions wasn't racist in my view. Instead, it aligned with the original universalistic vision of the civil rights movement that many commentators, including civil rights champion Cornel West, recognized as a source of strength.[5] If Blum were racist for opposing racial preferences, then so were three-quarters of Americans, including a majority of Black people, according to polling by Pew.[6]

Moreover, being an expert witness in the case would allow for— indeed require—some measure of distance between me and the litigation team's positions. Blum and the Consovoy McCarthy lawyers believed the Constitution barred the use of race to advance diversity in colleges, full stop. I would be free to testify to my own belief that racial diversity was indeed highly desirable and achievable through class-based affirmative action and other race-neutral strategies in most cases. However, if these strategies failed, I supported the use of race as a last resort. (My endorsement of the benefits of racial diversity would later be cited by lawyers defending racial preferences in the U.S. Supreme Court.)[7] My task would be to test whether race-neutral approaches would work at Harvard, given its applicant pool.

In addition, my growing frustration with the lack of progress on class-based affirmative action cut in favor of testifying. My attempts to work with left-of-center leaders to promote class-based affirmative action—including the Clinton and Obama administrations, as well as college presidents like Larry Summers and Tony Marx—had led to a string of disappointments. Given the power of special interests in the Democratic Party and college communities, the courts provided the clearest path for change. It would take the judiciary, as Obama staffer Cassandra Butts had told me, to "force" Democrats to act.

Finally, being an expert witness would place me in the position to provide a detailed blueprint for possible reforms. I would have the chance to join a team that would examine Harvard's internal files and dig inside its admissions process to determine whether any policy changes could produce racial diversity without relying on racial preferences.

In the end, I decided I couldn't sit this one out. While I appreciated and agreed with my friends in the civil rights community on the goal of integrating elite colleges, I thought higher education had hijacked a good impulse and employed the most inexpensive, divisive, and unpopular path to get there. Involvement in the case provided a once-in-a-lifetime opportunity to open the doors of selective colleges for the first time to meaningful numbers of working-class students. I decided to become, as Teddy Roosevelt put it, "the man who is actually in the arena," even if it meant burning some bridges with my liberal colleagues in the process.[8]

Peeking Behind the Admissions Curtain

The New Urgency to Understand Trump Voters

Signing on with Blum and Students for Fair Admissions as an expert in late 2014 may have been politically awkward, but as the litigation proceeded and Donald Trump began his ascent to power, the situation became even more uncomfortable. I was horrified by the election of Trump, whom I viewed as the twenty-first-century equivalent of George Wallace. With his open attacks on Muslims and Mexican immigrants in the 2016 campaign, he helped poison race relations and further polarize politics. A few days after the election, I coauthored an article in *The Atlantic* with Clifford Janey, former superintendent of D.C. public schools, in which we denounced Trump as an authoritarian, demagogue, and racist. We argued that his election was a Sputnik moment for civics education to prevent the rise of a demagogue ever again.[9]

During Trump's first year, I cringed when a front-page story in the *New York Times* reported that his administration was devoting resources to combat racial preferences in colleges.[10] Civil rights advocates saw this move as part of Trump's larger pattern of racial hostility, but I believed Trump was laying a trap for Democrats because he knew the public was on his side in opposing racial preferences.[11] I told a *Washington Post* reporter, "It will be tempting for progressives like me to say that a challenge to affirmative action at elite universities is another example of Donald Trump beating up on minorities, like the Muslim ban or the transgender bar in the military or voter suppression." But racial preferences were different in kind and opposed by many people who generally disagreed with Trump on issues of race.[12]

While my involvement in the case became more awkward in the age of Donald Trump, the paradox was that Trump's ascent underlined precisely why I believed Democrats needed to shift from race-based to class-based affirmative action. The movement of working-class white voters to the Republican Party had been a long time coming, but Trump added a new dimension. As one historian noted, under Lyndon Johnson, "Democrats had lost their grip on the Deep South; under Obama,

Appalachia slipped away; in 2016, it was the Rust Belt."[13] At a time of rising inequality, when working people might have been expected to move closer to the Democratic Party, the opposite was happening.

After Trump's stunning election, Democrats engaged in a brief period of introspection. Critics such as Columbia University's Mark Lilla noted the problem inherent with Hillary Clinton's embrace of identity politics. On the campaign trail, Lilla noted, Clinton called out her commitment "to African-American, Latino, L.G.B.T. and women voters at every stop." The issue, he said, is that "if you are going to mention groups in America, you had better mention all of them. If you don't, those left out will notice and feel excluded."[14]

But rather than embrace the wisdom of this observation, the left reacted with fury against Lilla. Because Trump himself was so odious, many Democrats resisted looking in the mirror to see if their policies or elitism contributed to white working-class anger. Instead, a conventional wisdom quickly congealed that the problem was with the voters themselves, who were fundamentally racist.

Some jumped on research finding that "racial resentment" strongly predicted support for Trump. The theory's flaw was that the measure used to detect high levels of racial animus against Black people was inaccurate. Researchers assumed that voters were anti-Black if they agreed with statements like the following: "Irish, Italian, Jewish, and many other minorities overcame prejudice and worked their way up. Blacks should do the same without any special favors." But voters expressed roughly *similar* levels of opposition to "special favors" for those who were "Nepalese" or "Lithuanians."[15] What was showing up as racial resentment might more accurately be described as belief in self-reliance and opposition to special favors for *anyone*.

More broadly, a Barnard political scientist noted that the widely touted explanation that Trump and other right-wing populists gained traction because of increasing levels of racism "has obvious empirical problems: racism has been declining in the United States and Western Europe for decades."[16] Approval of interracial marriage, for example, increased from 4 percent in 1958 to 94 percent in 2021, according to Gallup.[17] In fact, researchers at Stanford and the University of Pennsylvania found that supporters of Mitt Romney in 2012 had higher levels of racial animus on average than Trump voters: "In 2016 Trump's largest gains in support, compared to Mitt Romney in 2012, came from whites with moderate racial resentment."[18]

Nevertheless, Hillary Clinton had herself disastrously argued that many Trump voters were bigoted. Rather than focusing her attacks on Trump, she went after his voters, most of whom were white Americans without college degrees. During fundraisers in the Hamptons, Martha's Vineyard, and Beverly Hills, before groups of donors she described as "successful people," Clinton declared, to laughter from the audiences, that half of Trump's sixty million supporters fell into "the basket of deplorables."[19] The language was telling. Clinton did not say that the attitudes or beliefs of some Trump voters were deplorable. She switched from adjective to noun: racism was what defined them as people. More than two-thirds of Americans thought Clinton's charge was unfair.[20]

For white working-class people who were accustomed to being held in contempt by their wealthier, college-educated white counterparts, the language was political dynamite and confirmed their worst suspicions about the Democratic Party. Not only had these voters lost out in the meritocratic competition economically; they were also beneath respect culturally. White working-class voters may have noticed, as one liberal journalist noted, that while Clinton used the term "deplorables" to describe Trump supporters, many of whom were working-class people, she never applied it to the highly educated Wall Street bankers whose chicanery threw millions of their fellow citizens out of work during the Great Recession.[21]

In the spring of 2017, in the wake of Trump's election, I published a piece for *Harvard Magazine* suggesting that the instinct of many of my liberal friends to detest Trump voters was a big mistake, horrified as I was by Trump. While it might be comforting for us Clinton supporters to feel morally superior, it was important in a democracy to know why so many of our fellow Americans were so frustrated that they were willing to gamble on a candidate bent on blowing up the system.[22]

I found the thinking of political commentator Van Jones insightful. He said that the idea of "if you voted for a bigot, you are a bigot" is oversimplified. One Democratic pollster found that many working-class white voters were up for grabs. About 15 percent were reliably liberal, half were reliably conservative, and about 35 percent (twenty-three million voters) were moderate and persuadable.[23]

While racial preferences were not an overt issue in the 2016 campaign, they symbolized an approach that drove away persuadable white working-class voters. In her 2016 book *Strangers in Their Own Land*, sociologist Arlie Hochschild of UC Berkeley found that racial preferences remained unpopular with working-class white respondents, who saw them as a form of "cutting in line."[24] A 2017 *Atlantic* poll found that more than half (52 percent) of working-class white respondents (compared with 30 percent of college-educated white respondents) believed discrimination against white people had become as big a problem as discrimination against Black people and other minorities. In a society where African Americans continued to suffer racial discrimination in the criminal justice system, housing, employment, and even catching a taxicab, the only plausible reading of these results was that working-class white individuals equated affirmative action in education and employment with discrimination against them.[25]

Important research by a Duke political scientist found that Trump's rise was explained in part by an increase in "white identity politics," a phenomenon fostered by "threat to one's group." Part of the perceived threat was driven by demographic change, but surveys also found that three-quarters of white respondents said it was at least somewhat likely that "members of their racial group are denied jobs because employers are hiring minorities instead." More than three-quarters also said it was at least somewhat important "for members of their group to work together in order to change laws unfair to whites."[26] There was little doubt that issues of racial and class identity, fairly or unfairly, could move polls. Barack Obama said that when he told a press conference that white Cambridge, Massachusetts, police officer James Crowley "acted stupidly" in a dispute with Black Harvard professor Skip Gates, it caused "a huge drop in my support among white voters, bigger than would come from any single event during the eight years of my presidency."[27]

To my mind, Trump's election helped raise the stakes for avoiding policies that ignored working-class concerns and inadvertently caused feelings of white identity to spike. The exclusion of low-income and working-class students from selective campuses had long been a serious moral concern for me, but the 2016 election created a genuine crisis in American democracy. The failure to provide more avenues of success for lower-middle-income white citizens, combined with the embrace of explicit racial preferences by elites, epitomized an approach that helped create an opening for America's first presidential-level demagogue.[28] The advocacy for class- rather than race-based affirmative action wasn't an endorsement of Trump, but an attempt to shield against the rise of more politicians like him.

Discovering How Harvard Admissions Really Worked

At the outset of the Harvard litigation, the SFFA and Harvard lawyers met with federal district court judge Allison Burroughs to lay out a schedule and procedure. In the first phase, through the "discovery" process, Harvard would turn over reams of documentation and data about its admissions procedures and allow SFFA lawyers to depose various university officials about how the admissions process worked. In the next phase, Harvard's and SFFA's experts would each write two reports: an opening report and then a rebuttal report responding to the other side.

There were four expert witnesses in the case. SFFA's other expert was Peter Arcidiacono, a highly respected economist from Duke University. Harvard, the world's richest university, hired two very well-regarded experts: UC Berkeley economist David Card, who would later go on to win a Nobel Prize; and Ruth Simmons, the former president of Brown University and the first Black president of an Ivy League institution.

The first big question was to lift the mystery around what counted in admissions at Harvard. Colleges hide behind "holistic admissions," a complex evaluation method that takes into consideration numerous criteria carefully weighed by admissions officers. With Harvard's records, however, it was possible to derive the secret sauce and discover what really mattered in deciding who got in.

The results were eye-popping. If you wanted a fair system that measured "true merit" by taking into account the obstacles overcome, Carnevale's findings suggested that a significant emphasis on socioeconomic disadvantage would be necessary. The last thing you'd do is to give preference to advantaged students such as children of alumni, faculty, or wealthy donors. But Harvard's own documents and Arcidiacono's careful analysis of the data over several admissions cycles showed that Harvard's system was rigged for the wealthy in numerous ways.

One document Harvard was compelled to turn over in the legal discovery process was a May 2013 report of its Office of Institutional Research. Researchers examined the preferences in admissions provided to students in the classes of 2009–2016. Looking at data from 192,359 applicants, the Harvard researchers ran what's known as a "logistic regression" to detect the weight accorded to various preferences for students who were otherwise equally qualified (based on factors like the strength of their academic and extracurricular records). The larger the coefficient, the bigger the preference. A negative coefficient meant the students incurred a penalty. Harvard's data showed it gave the biggest preference for recruited athletes (6.33); large preferences for legacies (2.40), Black students (2.37), and Native American students (1.73); more modest preferences for Hispanic students (1.27) and low-income students (0.98); and actually penalized Asian American students (−0.37). The researchers concluded, "Compared to athletes and legacies, the size of the advantage for low income students is relatively small."

Peeking Behind the Admissions Curtain

Among students receiving the highest academic ratings (typically SATs of 680 or above on both the Math and Verbal sections), the Harvard researchers found that:

- Recruited athletes received a sixty-seven-percentage-point boost (83 percent chance of admission vs. 16 percent for nonathletes).
- Legacies received a forty-percentage-point boost (55 percent chance of admission vs. 15 percent for nonlegacies).
- Low-income students received a nine-percentage-point boost (24 percent chance of admission vs. 15 percent for non-low-income).[29]

In addition to Harvard's internal research, Arcidiacono conducted his own analysis, using a more recent set of data and employing additional factors in the admissions model. He reviewed data from 160,638 applicants in the admissions cycles for students scheduled to graduate four years later (the classes of 2014–2019). The data showed who was admitted and rejected. There was granular information not only about the race and socioeconomic status of applicants and their high school grades and standardized test scores, but also about their legacy status and family connections to faculty or staff. Moreover, Harvard had to produce detailed information about the quantitative ratings students were assigned that evaluated more subjective criteria, such as their athletic ability, their extracurricular activities, and a measure of their perceived "personal" strength as individuals (seeking to capture such qualities as integrity).

After examining admissions decisions for thousands of candidates with varying profiles, Arcidiacono estimated the extent of admission preferences employed by Harvard, with the largest numbers suggesting the largest boost. The preference is expressed as a "logit estimate," indicating the increased or decreased odds of admissions associated with various characteristics.[30] In rank order of importance, his results showed the relative weight of certain preferences in Harvard's admissions.

A Shockingly Biased System Stacked Toward Wealthy White Students

The results painted a devastating picture. The system systematically tended to favor wealthy and white students. Large preferences were provided to recruited athletes (7.859), including those playing boutique sports like fencing and squash, legacies (1.840), faculty children (1.704), and those who applied early in the admissions process (1.282). To produce racial diversity on campus, Harvard then had to compensate by also providing large racial preferences to Black (2.659) and Hispanic (1.419) students—boosts larger in magnitude than those provided to individuals who had overcome odds associated with economic disadvantage (1.083) or being first-generation college students (0.023). And Arcidiacono's analysis confirmed Harvard's internal study that Asian American students (−0.271) were penalized in admissions.

I found the results very depressing, not only because they showed how unfair the system was at a prominent elite college, but also because this was personal for me. I'd been raised in an exceedingly pro-Harvard family. When I was growing up, my father was pretty obsessed with the institution. A member of the class of 1952, Dad would tell me what it was like to share an undergraduate experience with fellow students who became luminaries, such as Vietnam War whistleblower Daniel Ellsberg and novelist John Updike. He talked a great deal about Harvard's ethos of public service and Dean Wilbur Bender's message to students that the privilege of a Harvard education incurred obligation.[31] When I was admitted to Harvard College in 1981, it was one of the rare times I saw my father cry. When high school classmates told me that Harvard was a school for rich kids, I took umbrage and said it was for smart kids.

My own undergraduate experience in the 1980s was very positive. During my first year, I met my wonderful wife, Rebecca, who lived upstairs in Weld Hall. I made some of the best friends of my life, some of whom I still meet annually for hiking adventures. A number of professors had helped shape my thinking and were instrumental in advancing my career. Three of my daughters also had positive experiences at Harvard graduate schools.

I had many reasons to be grateful to Harvard for what it had offered me and my family. And as a professional fighting for socioeconomic diversity, I had been initially impressed by the efforts of Bill Fitzsimmons and Larry Summers to lead a national conversation on improving access for disadvantaged students. But there was no mistaking what the data were showing in stark terms: Harvard was not a bastion of privilege because it picked the best candidates. It was a bastion of privilege because the deck was stacked.

The finding of anti-Asian bias was also deeply troubling. Although my expert reports would focus on Harvard's ability to achieve racial diversity without resorting to racial preferences, I was still disturbed that Harvard's internal analysis revealed that Asian students were being penalized.

Anti-Asian discrimination at Harvard received a lot of attention in the press, and I was distressed that some liberals, who would normally be attuned to anti-Asian bias, were quick to come up with excuses for Harvard in the name of defending affirmative action. But the evidence was damning. Asian applicants to Harvard on average had higher academic qualifications than white students. But in an apparent effort to cap Asian representation, Harvard frequently rated Asian applicants as less likely to have subjective attributes like "integrity, helpfulness, courage, kindness, fortitude, empathy, self-confidence, leadership ability, maturity, or grit."[32]

The district court judge in the case would later make a tortured effort to clear Harvard of the anti-Asian bias claim. But as *New Yorker* staff writer Jay Caspian Kang noted, the evidence of anti-Asian discrimination at Harvard was "frankly, overwhelming. Asian applicants to Harvard routinely scored significantly lower than students of other races on their 'personal scores,' a metric cobbled together from alumni interviews, essays and teacher recommendations."[33] There were only two possible explanations, both disturbing: Harvard was discriminating, or it believed Asian applicants, as a group, tended to lack qualities such as empathy and leadership ability.

Admissions counselors often advised Asian students applying to Harvard and other elite universities to downplay activities like playing the violin or piano, to avoid seeming too stereotypically Asian. One University of Pennsylvania professor observed, "Imagine if we learned that our Hispanic candidates were discouraged from seeming too Hispanic, or Black students from seeming too Black. That would trigger huge protests on our campuses, followed by heartfelt mea culpas from our admissions offices. But the fact that Asian American students hide aspects of themselves—to avoid appearing too Asian—barely registers on our outrage meters."[34]

The pattern of Asian admissions before and after the lawsuit was striking. Before the litigation was instigated in late 2014, Harvard's admitted class consistently ranged between 18 percent and 20 percent Asian American for the classes of 2009–2018. (The class of 2018 was admitted in the spring of 2014.)[35] After the lawsuit was filed and Harvard came under intense scrutiny for anti-Asian bias, Asian admissions steadily rose. By the class of 2027 (admitted in 2023), the Asian American population had risen to 30 percent.[36]

Much closer to the issue of my expert reports on whether Harvard could create racial diversity without employing racial preferences was an examination of the various boosts Harvard gave to mostly wealthy and white applicants. If Harvard eliminated those preferences and provided a meaningful advantage to economically disadvantaged students of all races, resulting in sufficient racial diversity, then Harvard could have a set of "workable" race-neutral alternatives. Therefore, much of the back-and-forth with Harvard's experts was about whether the school really needed to keep its preferences for legacies, donors, children of faculty, and students who applied early in the process.

Peeking Behind the Admissions Curtain

The first battle was over legacy preferences. It was public knowledge that Harvard had a long and shameful history of favoring the children of alumni. The practice began in the early twentieth century as a strategy for reducing the admissions of Jewish students, whose strong academic records were qualifying them in numbers that were unsettling to old-line Harvard Protestants. Because the legacy preference boosted the chances of those whose fathers had attended, new Jewish immigrants would be screened out.[37]

As I dug into the internal reports and depositions of Harvard officials, it became clear just how sordid the practice continued to be. Harvard claimed it provided a "slight tip" in admissions for legacies, which it sometimes referred to as a tiebreaker, but the school's internal research showed that legacy applicants received a forty-percentage-point boost, an edge much larger than that provided to disadvantaged students. If Harvard was engaging in "class-based affirmative action," it was much more pronounced for the affluent than for those who had surmounted life's hurdles. Overall, 34 percent of legacy applicants were admitted compared with 6 percent of nonlegacies. In total, 14 percent of the admitted classes of 2014–2019 were legacies.[38]

Despite positioning itself as a champion of diversity, Harvard's internal files showed that legacy preferences benefited white students at the expense of Asian American, Black, and Hispanic students. In the Harvard classes of 2014–2019, 70 percent of the admitted legacy students were white. Just 4 percent were Black, 6 percent Hispanic, and 11 percent Asian American, a much smaller share than in the general student population. Of all admitted white students, 20 percent were legacies, compared with 5 percent of Black admits. Arcidiacono's modeling suggested that eliminating legacy would have a positive influence on Black, Hispanic, and Asian representation, while white representation would decline.[39]

Legacies also diminished Harvard's socioeconomic diversity. While Harvard under Summers and Fitzsimmons had been emphasizing the importance of achieving socioeconomic diversity, its internal data showed that for the classes of 2009–2014, an astonishing 76 percent of legacies did not apply for *any* financial aid, meaning their families had no trouble paying Harvard's high sticker price. According to a *Harvard Crimson* survey of the class of 2019, 41 percent of legacies came from families making more than $500,000 a year, compared with 15 percent of students in the class overall.[40]

Having edited a book on legacy preferences, I was eager to see how Harvard justified them. In particular, I was curious to know what Harvard expert Ruth Simmons might say. I'd met Simmons years earlier when we served together on a panel on affirmative action at the New York Public Library, and I considered her a modern-day hero. She was an enormously impressive figure. Raised as the youngest of twelve children by sharecroppers in Jim Crow–era Texas, she grew up in a "rat-and-roach infested house." Yet she overcame poverty and discrimination to rise through sheer brilliance and determination, ultimately becoming the first Black president of an Ivy League institution.[41]

An expert is not required to address every issue or say things that go against their beliefs, so I thought Simmons might duck the legacy preferences issue, given how they tended to negatively affect Black, Hispanic, and economically disadvantaged applicants. (In the parallel litigation in the University of North Carolina, UNC's expert did not provide much of a defense of legacy preferences and acknowledged that the practice hurt students of color.)

But Simmons dove right in. In her expert report, she claimed that ending legacy preferences would entail "substantial costs" for Harvard, based on her "experience." She said that "paying attention to legacy status in admissions can play an important role in maintaining alumni allegiance and interest." Tellingly, Simmons cited not a single study or empirical analysis in her opening report. In her rebuttal report, she cited one study from Middlebury College and one from Marquette University but gave no evidence that Harvard had analyzed the relationship between legacy preferences and levels of alumni giving. She claimed that alumni preferences were necessary to enhance the "enthusiasm" of alumni networks. Moreover, she pointed out that if an institution wanted to rise in the *U.S. News & World Report*'s rankings, it needed high levels of alumni giving. But nowhere did she explain why it was necessary to bribe alumni with a preference for their children to generate such "enthusiasm." Nor did she explain why excellent institutions such as Caltech, UC Berkeley, Oxford, and Cambridge—all of which ranked among the ten best universities in the world—managed to survive without heaping preferences on the children of alumni.[42]

In fact, the empirical evidence mostly ran in the other direction. One analysis of the top one hundred universities in *U.S. News & World Report* found "no evidence that legacy preference policies themselves exert an influence on giving behavior." Another interesting study from researchers at Princeton and Stanford found that alumni increased their giving when their children were in high school, but then lowered or eliminated it entirely if the students were rejected. Alumni were outraged to be told that even with a preference, their children were not good enough. As universities became increasingly competitive, alumni children were being rejected at higher rates than in the past. Yet Harvard provided no evidence that it had researched the issue. In his testimony, for example, admissions dean Bill Fitzsimmons suggested that providing legacy preferences is "essential to Harvard's well-being" but could not point to any empirical evidence that legacy preferences had boosted alumni giving at Harvard. Notably, Harvard Faculty of Arts and Sciences dean Michael Smith testified that he did not think of legacy admissions as tied to alumni giving.[43]

Harvard's other argument in favor of legacy preferences was truly stunning. My jaw dropped while reading the deposition of Dean Rakesh Khurana, who tried to justify legacy preferences using the language of "diversity." He suggested it was important for Harvard to favor the children of alumni to bring together students who "have more experience with Harvard" with "others who are less familiar with Harvard." The ability of these different groups to "exchange perspectives, points of view," he claimed, would make "them more effective citizens and citizen leaders for society." I didn't know how quite to respond to this preposterous argument, so I went with understatement: "I am aware of no research to support this claim."[44]

Many universities used legacy preferences, but Harvard put the system on steroids. In his 2006 book *The Price of Admission*, reporter Daniel Golden documented that Harvard formalized a system for wealthy donors through the creation of the Committee on University Resources (COUR). He found that 336 children of COUR members have gone on to attend Harvard, "an astonishing enrollment rate of one child per major donor."[45]

The depositions and documents Harvard turned over during the lawsuit now provided additional insights. Harvard created a special "dean's interest list" each year that included applicants who were related to or of interest to big donors. These students constituted 9.5 percent of the admitted class. The admission rate was 42 percent for students on the dean's admissions list, compared with 6 percent for those not on it; 68 percent of these students were white, and just 3 percent were Black. If a white student had a 10 percent chance of admission on the merits, those odds shot up to 75 percent if they were on the dean's interest list.[46]

Internal emails and testimony showed how the system worked. In one email, with the subject line "My Hero," David Ellwood, dean of Harvard's Kennedy School, expressed appreciation to admissions dean Bill Fitzsimmons. "Once again you have done wonders. I am simply thrilled about the folks you were able to admit," Ellwood said. "[Redacted] and [redacted] are all big wins. [Redacted] has already committed to a building."[47]

In another email, a Harvard official noted that an applicant's family had donated $8.7 million in the past, but in recent years had given less. The email read, "[Redacted] was a devoted [redacted] Chair and generous donor. Going forward, I don't see a significant opportunity for further major gifts. [Redacted] had an art collection which conceivably could come our way."[48]

Peeking Behind the Admissions Curtain

Harvard went so far as to assign a rating system to quantify the size of donations associated with applicants. If the applicant had a relative with an art collection, their rating was 2. By contrast, an applicant whose family was likely to provide a larger "financial contribution" would receive a 1. Not surprisingly, the system tended to benefit white students. Fully 13 percent of admitted white students were on the dean's interest list, compared with 2 percent of admitted Black applicants.[49]

Although most donors seeking special treatment for their children to Harvard were alumni, not all were. In 1998, real estate developer Charles Kushner, a New York University graduate, pledged $2.5 million to Harvard just as his son Jared (the future son-in-law of Donald Trump) was applying. An official from Jared Kushner's high school said he was not in the toughest classes and his test scores were not up to par, but he was nevertheless admitted. The official said, "There were at the time other kids we thought should really get in on the merits, and they did not."[50]

Golden's book also documented Harvard's peculiar admissions process known as the "Z-list," which favored students who agreed to take a gap year between high school and college. As Golden explained, "If wealthy or well-connected applicants aren't admitted to Harvard in the standard fashion, they need not despair. . . . They may be placed on the 'Z-list'—a Harvard admissions office term for a little-known policy that compromises standards in the interest of alumni and donors, enabling their children to enter America's most famous university by a side door."[51]

Harvard internal admissions data—which I included in my expert report—provided additional details about who got in through the Z-list. In the classes of 2014–2019, Harvard admitted on average almost sixty students each year through this special process. While Harvard boasted of having a majority-minority student population overall, 70 percent of Z-list students were white, 14 percent were Asian, 4 percent were Hispanic, and just 2 percent were Black. About 60 percent were on the special dean's interest list and almost half were legacies. Just 1 percent were economically disadvantaged, and 2 percent were first-generation college students. A former Harvard admissions officer explained that the Z-list was not designed for students of modest means: "We had concerns of lower-income, under-resourced students not knowing what to do for a year, for a year off of traditional schooling." Academically, Z-list admits fell far below the typically admitted student.[52]

The discovery process revealed that Harvard also provided a substantial preference in admissions to the children of faculty and staff. According to Arcidiacono's analysis, the boost provided to this favored category of applicants was bigger than that provided to Hispanics, disadvantaged students, and first-generation students. The admission rate for faculty and staff children was 47 percent, compared with 7 percent for those not children of faculty and staff. Around 80 percent of the admitted students in this category were white or Asian, and just 1 percent were Black and 5 percent were Hispanic.[53]

In Ruth Simmons's expert report defending Harvard, she claimed that there were "strong reasons" to employ preferences for the children of faculty to retain talent, "based on my experience." She claimed that eliminating this special treatment for privileged applicants "would threaten to impose substantial costs in terms of faculty and staff morale." In Simmons's rebuttal report, she relayed her own experiences at Brown University, which underlined the seediness of the process: "During my time at Brown, I was involved in situations where I tried to recruit a new professor or faculty member to the school. Inevitably, if that individual had a child near college age, the individual would ask whether their child would be able to go to Brown. If we did not see a possibility of admitting their child based on a preview of their qualifications, the recruit often chose to go in a different direction."[54] She suggested that elite universities were helpless in fending off the process by which potential faculty recruits tried to leverage their status to extract admissions preferences for their kids—a process that hurt Black and Hispanic applicants, particularly at places like Harvard.

Peeking Behind the Admissions Curtain

Harvard also provided a large preference to recruited athletes, whose admission rate was an astonishing 86 percent, compared with 6 percent for nonathletes. Recruited athletes made up 10 percent of the admitted classes. While high-profile sports like football and basketball tend to be economically and racially diverse, Harvard also provided these preferences for students playing exclusive sports such as fencing, squash, and crew that are often the province of the wealthy. As a result, athletic preferences at Harvard disproportionately benefited wealthy and white students. About 69 percent of admitted athletes were white. In the six-year period for Harvard's classes of 2009–2014, 53 percent of varsity athletes were wealthy enough to not require any financial aid. According to a *Harvard Crimson* survey for the class of 2019, 25 percent of athletic recruits came from families making more than $500,000 a year, compared with 15 percent of the Harvard class overall.[55]

The cumulative effect of preferences for these four groups—recruited athletes, legacies, those on the dean's interest list, and children of faculty and staff (known in Harvard lingo as "ALDCs")—was a huge boon to white and wealthy students. Fully 43 percent of admitted white students were ALDCs, compared with less than 16 percent of admitted Black, Hispanic, and Asian American students. Harvard admitted more than one and a half times as many white ALDCs as Black students of any background.[56]

The ALDC preference was quite large. Without the preference they received, approximately three-quarters of white ALDC admits would not have been accepted. In a research paper, Arcidiacono and colleagues wrote, "We find that a white non-ALDC applicant with a 10% chance of admission would see a five-fold increase in admissions likelihood if they were a legacy; more than a seven-fold increase if they were on the dean's interest list; and that they would be admitted with near certainty if they were a recruited athlete."[57]

On top of ALDC preferences, the documents disclosed by Harvard revealed a fifth preference for the advantaged. Like many schools, Harvard provided a leg up to those who applied through the "early action" practice, which required applicants to apply to only one school, usually by November 1, rather than the regular admissions process, which allowed students to apply to multiple schools, usually by January 1. (Some colleges were even worse than Harvard and used an "early decision" policy, which required students to commit to attending the school if admitted, which low-income students hesitated to do because it prevented them from comparing financial aid packages.)

According to Arcidiacono's model, students applying early action to Harvard received a bigger boost in admissions compared to that given to first-generation college and disadvantaged students. On the national level, one study found that after controlling for a student's other characteristics, "early application is associated with a 20 to 30 percentage point increase in acceptance probability, about the same as 100 additional points on the SAT."[58]

Research has found that early admission programs, like Harvard's, typically have favored wealthier and better-informed students, who have the resources to submit their applications early. Students from private high schools are more than three times as likely to apply early as those from public schools. When Harvard terminated early admissions in 2006, university president Derek Bok explained, "We hope that doing away with early admission will improve the process and make it simpler and fairer. Early admission programs tend to advantage the advantaged. . . . Students from more sophisticated backgrounds and affluent high schools often apply early to increase their chances of admissions, while minority students and students from rural areas, other countries and high schools with fewer resources miss out." Similarly, Dean Fitzsimmons supported ending early admissions, noting, "An early admission program that is less accessible to students from modest economic backgrounds operates at cross-purposes with our goal of finding and admitting the most talented students from across the economic spectrum."[59]

Nevertheless, in 2011, Harvard reversed course and reinstated early admissions. The university did so because it was concerned about the decline in its yield rate (which represents the number of students who accept its offer of admission). The decline occurred among white and Hispanic students, while yield among African American students remained steady and increased for Asian students. Internal documents revealed that Harvard was occasionally losing to other colleges in the competition for students from schools that had historically sent a significant number of students to Harvard. One internal document noted, "At some of Harvard's most productive 'feeder' high schools ... up to 90 percent of students apply early somewhere. By not offering an admission option, therefore, Harvard has placed itself at odds with trends in the market."[60] Harvard did not explain why a college committed to finding talent from all walks of life had "feeder" schools at all, or why it was so important to recruit heavily from the likes of tony prep schools such as Andover, Exeter, and St. Paul's.

Yet Harvard's data showed that even without early admissions, it was beating out Yale, Stanford, and Princeton for two-thirds of the students who were accepted to one of those other universities. And its own internal data showed that after early action was reinstated, white students and legacy students were more likely to exploit the early admissions boost than Black, Hispanic, and first-generation college students.[61]

Several other selective colleges, including the University of Michigan and University of California schools, did not employ early admissions. Nevertheless, Ruth Simmons defended the practice, just as she did legacy preferences and preferences for the children of faculty, writing, "It is my opinion that eliminating early action would have substantial costs for a university like Harvard." She cited no evidence to support her claim.[62]

Racial Diversity and Economic Segregation

What was the result of this deeply unfair regime of preferences that tended to benefit white and wealthy students—and was then coupled with a system of racial preferences to compensate? The internal documents, along with some publicly available studies, showed a shocking lack of socioeconomic diversity.

For the classes of 2007 to 2016, the evidence revealed that Harvard had more legacy students (who received a forty-percentage-point boost in their chance of admissions) than it did first-generation college students. Although there were 382 times as many American adults aged twenty-five and older without a college degree (143 million) as adults in the world with a Harvard degree (375,000), the number of admitted students whose parents had attended Harvard exceeded the number of first-generation students in the undergraduate student body. Despite 68 percent of American adults aged twenty-five and older not having a four-year college degree, only 10 percent of Harvard students in the classes of 2007 to 2016 were first-generation college students on average. If African American students had been as underrepresented in Harvard's population as first-generation college students were, they would have constituted just 2.25 percent of the undergraduate student body.[63]

The income distribution of Harvard students was also heavily skewed toward the wealthy. In 2017, as I was preparing my expert reports, Harvard professor Raj Chetty and colleagues published a stunning study that examined a unique dataset of thirty million college students and financial data from the IRS (also discussed above, in Chapter 4). The researchers found that in the class of 2004, Harvard had *twenty-three times* as many high-income students as low-income students, with about as many drawn from the top 1 percent of the income distribution as the bottom 60 percent. Several years later, in the class of 2013, Harvard had more students who came from the most affluent 10 percent of the population than from the bottom 90 percent.[64]

Data discovered in the litigation process also revealed what I had long suspected: even the Black, Hispanic, and Native American students at Harvard tended to be pretty economically advantaged. At Harvard, 71.8 percent of underrepresented minority students hailed from the most advantaged one-fifth of the Black, Hispanic, and Native American populations nationally. And the white and Asian students were even more advantaged.[65]

This tilt toward advantaged minority students was by design. Arcidiacono's data revealed Harvard did *not* give disadvantaged Black students a double preference (separately for race and low socioeconomic background), but it *did* give a double preference to Black legacies. If a Black student had a 10 percent chance of admission, being a legacy would increase their chances to 30 percent, and being a double legacy (both parents being alumni) would raise it to 46 percent. But being socioeconomically disadvantaged made virtually no difference, as admissions rose just one percentage point, reaching a total of 11 percent.[66] This practice was a perfect illustration of what social critics call a "racial trickle-down approach," which told working-class Black people that they should be satisfied by the psychological boost that comes when more privileged Black people advance.[67]

How Well Would Race-Neutral Alternatives Work?

I was personally appalled by Harvard's system of admissions, stacked as it was toward the privileged, but the legal question was different. Harvard was under no obligation to create a fair admissions system. But it was required to use race as a "last resort."[68] As noted above, under the *Fisher I* decision, seven members of the Supreme Court had held that universities bear "the ultimate burden of demonstrating, before turning to racial classifications, that available workable race-neutral alternatives do not suffice."[69]

The Supreme Court was trying to strike a balance with this rule. On the one hand, it recognized that racial diversity was a valuable part of a campus experience, and universities were right to want to create racially integrated environments. On the other hand, the Court acknowledged that the use of race entailed costs, such as stigmatizing beneficiaries and creating racial hostility in a multiracial society. Therefore, if there were workable alternative ways to create racial diversity short of racial preferences, universities could not use race.

As I dug through the documents and depositions of Harvard officials, I wanted to know: What had they done to comply with the *Fisher I* command that they explore workable race-neutral alternatives? This requirement had been widely discussed in the academic community. Indeed, in a 2013 *Chronicle of Higher Education* article, Harvard professor Thomas Kane and Harvard Education School dean James Ryan noted that the *Fisher* decision meant that "to consider race in admissions . . . institutions must prove to courts that race-neutral alternatives—such as relying on socioeconomic status or where students live—will not work." They suggested that universities run simulations using past applicants to see if using factors like socioeconomic status might produce acceptable levels of racial diversity. However, they warned that if universities "fail to prepare convincing answers, they will lose" in the courts.[70] Harvard's internal documents revealed that Kane and Ryan sent a draft of the article to Dean Fitzsimmons for his input in advance of publication. Despite all this, Harvard witnesses testified that Harvard conducted no formal analysis of how race-neutral alternatives might work at the college or what would happen if the school transitioned to a race-blind system. Harvard's failure to investigate alternatives was particularly troubling, as it did not have to start from scratch. Over the years, universities in states where racial preferences had been banned had developed a clear menu of options to consider.[71]

In the litigation, Arcidiacono and I ran several simulations of race-blind admissions, as did Harvard's expert David Card. Both sides agreed that eliminating the use of race *without* adopting new, race-neutral strategies would result in a large decrease in racial diversity. Because race counted a lot in admissions, Card found that "the share of African-American students in the admitted class would drop from 14% to 6%. The fraction of Hispanic or Other students would fall from 14% to 9%."[72] To me, that would have been unacceptable.

Peeking Behind the Admissions Curtain

But the highly detailed data Harvard provided during the litigation allowed Arcidiacono and me to simulate what would happen if Harvard "turned off" the preference not only for race, but *also* for factors like legacy status, and boosted the preference for students who were socioeconomically disadvantaged. We ended up running seven simulations, and Harvard's expert David Card ran a number of simulations as well.

The most intriguing for me was Simulation D, later discussed by justices of the U.S. Supreme Court. Arcidiacono built off a model Card constructed about how Harvard's admissions system worked. The simulation was then altered to provide a preference for socioeconomically disadvantaged students that was about half the magnitude of Harvard's existing preference for athletes. It also "turned off" Harvard's preferences for race, legacy status, and faculty children.[73] (The model kept athletic preferences in place because I thought some might consider it unrealistic for universities to eliminate these preferences entirely, especially for sports that generate school spirit, such as football, basketball, and hockey.)[74]

In most respects, diversity improved under Simulation D. Socioeconomic representation increased, with the share Harvard labeled as socioeconomically "disadvantaged" (those from roughly the bottom two-thirds of the socioeconomic distribution) rising from 18 percent to 49 percent. The percentage of first-generation college students rose from 7 percent (120 students) to 24 percent (400 students). This would be a big step forward in an institution notoriously slanted toward the wealthy. Racial diversity also increased in most respects. Without legacy preferences, white shares declined from 40 percent to 33 percent, while Asian admissions increased from 24 percent to 31 percent. Black admissions declined from 14 percent to 10 percent, a point Harvard would emphasize. However, as discussed below, this potential decline was by no means inevitable if Harvard took additional steps. Meanwhile, Hispanic admissions increased from 14 percent to 19 percent, a significant development at an institution that received an F rating on Latino representation from the Education Trust.[75] The overall share of underrepresented minority students held steady at 28 percent.[76]

The incoming class in the simulation maintained an excellent level of academic quality. High school GPA was identical to the students in Harvard's admitted class, and SATs shifted only slightly, from the ninety-ninth percentile to the ninety-eighth. It was remarkable that the incoming class would have such stellar academic credentials even though many students admitted under the simulation have overcome significant socioeconomic obstacles.[77]

Addressing Harvard's Objections

Harvard set up a special committee on race-neutral alternatives, consisting of three senior Harvard officials—Faculty of Arts and Sciences Dean Michael D. Smith; Admissions Dean Bill Fitzsimmons; and Harvard College Dean Rakesh Khurana—to evaluate the simulations. They raised three central objections to the various simulations, including Simulation D.

First, while the Smith Committee did not object to the overall levels of racial diversity produced, it did raise the "diversity within diversity" argument advanced by the University of Texas at Austin, which suggested that race-neutral strategies did not admit enough privileged Black and Hispanic students. The fact that "many of the non-White students would come from modest socioeconomic circumstances," the committee claimed, could "undermin[e] rather than advanc[e] Harvard's diversity-related educational objectives."[78]

I thought this argument was absurd. Under the simulation, Black, Hispanic, and Native American students from the richest one-fifth of the population would still occupy 21 percent of the seats—roughly perfect representation.[79] The availability of space for more high-achieving Black and Hispanic working-class students, such as Edmund Kennedy,

Tony Jack, and Ana Barros, was a big step forward and not a cause for concern.

The Smith Committee's second objection was that race-neutral alternatives failed to maintain "the standards of excellence that Harvard seeks in its student body." If a socioeconomic preference had been too big, there could have been a legitimate concern about academic standards. But in this case, Harvard's objection was hard to take seriously. The committee complained that there would be a modest decline in the share of students who received an academic rating of 1 or 2 (a ten-percentage-point drop, from 76 percent to 66 percent). But I pointed out that we could achieve racial diversity even if we modified the model to admit all students with an academic 1 rating. While those receiving an academic 2 rating would decline some, these students were hardly must-have geniuses. As it was, Harvard rejected 80 percent of such students. And Harvard acknowledged that the socioeconomic obstacles faced by students should be considered in evaluating their academic credentials. For years, Ivy League colleges said that most students who applied could do well academically; it was absurd to now say there was no play in the joints. Overall, the simulation showed that students would have superb academic preparation despite many of them having overcome considerable hurdles.[80]

Third, the Smith Committee raised a concern that "Harvard could not significantly increase its financial aid budget without detracting from other commitments." I was frankly astonished that Harvard raised this issue. In depositions, Harvard officials had repeatedly said that the institution could handle the expenses related to providing financial aid for more economically disadvantaged students. David Card had concluded that the extra expenses in financial aid for one of our simulations would cost $62 million for a university with a financial aid budget of $171 million and a total endowment of $37 billion.[81] If this were the best Harvard could do in response, I felt confident we could win the argument in court.

The Deposition and Trial

Once the expert witness reports were completed, the next step was for me to be cross-examined by Harvard's lawyers in a deposition. Legal depositions are conducted in advance of trials to find out what witnesses are going to say about particular issues and to create a record that prevents them from easily retracting statements during the actual trial, in case of errors. I had prepared at length with SFFA attorneys Tom McCarthy and Patrick Strawbridge (a former Clarence Thomas clerk), but it was hard to know what the other side would ask. I had served as an expert witness twice before, discussing socioeconomic integration as an engine for promoting school achievement in cases involving Chicago and Little Rock public schools. But the Harvard litigation was a much bigger deal because we were creating a record for a potential U.S. Supreme Court case.

In May 2018, I went with McCarthy and Strawbridge to the fancy digs of Harvard's lawyers from the D.C. law firm WilmerHale. As we entered the offices, we walked past an enormous, ostentatious fountain, a signal meant to convey that the firm was so rich and powerful that it had money to burn. (Harvard and UNC would outspend SFFA by more than six to one.)[82] When we arrived at the conference room, two WilmerHale lawyers were present to grill me—Felicia Ellsworth and Seth Waxman. Ellsworth, an experienced litigator, had been editor in chief of the *University of Chicago Law Review* and a clerk to Chief Justice John Roberts. Waxman, who served as the solicitor general of the United States during Bill Clinton's second term, was, according to the firm's website, "universally considered to be among the country's premier Supreme Court and appellate advocates."[83]

Ellsworth asked almost all the questions, though Waxman was present throughout. Like some of my liberal friends, Ellsworth wanted to know more about my relationship with SFFA's Edward Blum. We also discussed some of the nice things I'd said about Bill Fitzsimmons's and Larry Summers's efforts to promote socioeconomic diversity, though she did not ask me to recount the nice things they had said about me.

Ellsworth tried to pin me down to say precisely what level of racial diversity was "sufficient" to make a race-neutral alternative viable. This was one of the tricky questions left open by the *Fisher I* decision. I suggested there were various guideposts in the *Grutter* case about Michigan's diversity levels, and said that Harvard's past levels of racial diversity were relevant. I also pointed to the Smith Committee's discussion of the issue. The committee had said that a 6 percent Black representation was unacceptably low but had voiced no complaints about a race-neutral strategy that produced a 10 percent representation. The deposition—which ran from about 9:00 a.m. to 5:30 p.m.—was exhausting and nerve-wracking. But after it was over, McCarthy and Strawbridge said they were pleased.

The case finally moved to trial in October 2018. When I arrived at the federal courthouse in Boston on October 22 to appear before Judge Allison Burroughs, the room was crowded with members of the national media, who were reporting daily on the trial. Journalists from the *New York Times*, *Politico*, Bloomberg, the *Boston Globe*, and NPR were all covering the proceedings.

Strawbridge conducted my direct testimony, in which he walked through my background, including my college thesis on Robert Kennedy, and we discussed the various simulations that Arcidiacono and I had conducted, which showed that Harvard could achieve racial diversity by employing socioeconomic preferences.[84]

At one juncture, Strawbridge asked me about Harvard's complaint that it might be too expensive to admit more highly talented economically disadvantaged students as a way of promoting both economic and racial diversity. I said it should not be a problem: "To begin with, Harvard University is literally the richest university in the entire country. Its $37 billion endowment is bigger than the gross domestic product of half the world's countries. They recently raised $9 billion in a campaign.

And in the *Chronicle of Higher Education*, someone said this was like beating the four-minute mile."

At this point Harvard's attorney, eminent trial lawyer Bill Lee, objected: "Your Honor, the *Chronicle of Higher Education*, the capital campaign, is neither in his report [n]or relevant to the issues here."

Judge Burroughs responded, "Let's just leave it at Harvard is rich."

The audience broke into laughter. And Lee conceded, "We'll stipulate."[85]

Then Strawbridge turned me over for cross-examination to Lee, who began by trying to make a big deal of the fact that I had known Edward Blum—"who is sitting right back here"—for fifteen years. He also tried to suggest that my opinion should be written off as predictable because I had been associated with research demonstrating the viability of class-based affirmative action for many years—as if consistency were somehow a bad thing.[86]

During my cross-examination, the big issue that Lee homed in on was that in Simulation D, Harvard's Black representation would drop from 14 percent to 10 percent. Lee said that "the racial group that bears the burden of race neutral alternatives is African American students." I understood this concern and, as outlined below, suggested how Harvard could address the issue. At the same time, this emphasis represented an important change in tactics on Harvard's part. The Smith Committee had raised no objections to the 10 percent Black representation level produced. Indeed, it said the simulations produced a "significant degree of diversity" and objected instead to an alleged lack of academic preparedness among the students. When asked specifically if he would reject a race-neutral alternative that produced a class in which 10 percent of students identified as African American, Dean Michael Smith testified, "We were not looking for any particular number."[87]

Another reason I was taken aback when Lee objected to the 10 percent Black representation level at trial was that for most of the affirmative action era, the Black share of students at Harvard was *lower* than 10 percent. Antidiscrimination laws, and then affirmative action, helped boost the Black population at Harvard from about 1 percent in the early 1960s to 7–8 percent in the 1970s and early 1980s. During this time, Harvard's affirmative action program was held up by the Supreme Court as a model for the country, and the university itself boasted that "diversity is the hallmark of a Harvard education." In more recent years, for example the class of 2016, Harvard's Black representation was 10 percent of admitted students.[88]

Harvard never explicitly said why 14 percent representation was so important, compared to 10 percent. But if 14 percent has some intuitive appeal, it may have been related to the fact that about 14 percent of the U.S. school-aged population was Black. If that were the thinking behind Harvard's benchmark, perhaps based on Ibram Kendi's theory (discussed in Chapter 9) that all racial disparities are the result of discrimination, then Harvard was wise to keep that rationale quiet. After all, Asian American students represented about 5 percent of the American school population, but 24 percent of the Harvard admitted class of 2019. A belief that fairness required proportionality would imply that Asian shares should be cut by almost 80 percent, even though Brookings researchers found that Asian American high school students on average spent twice as much time studying as white high school students, and four times as much as Black high school students. The proportionality assumption at elite colleges also hurt young women, who on average excelled in high school at higher levels than young men. To promote gender proportionality, Brown University, for example, admitted about 7 percent of male applicants, compared with just 4 percent of female applicants. At Wesleyan, a former admissions officer noted, a desire for gender balance meant that young women from disadvantaged backgrounds lost out to young men of privilege.[89]

Moreover, at trial, I took pains to emphasize that in the real world, Harvard could easily achieve more than 10 percent Black representation if it took a few additional steps that Arcidiacono and I could not include in Simulation D, mostly because Harvard did not turn over all the data we needed. These supplemental policy changes could make the admissions system fairer and boost Black representation. Most importantly, Harvard could give a preference to students from low-wealth families, which would help many Black applicants because the racial wealth gap in America is enormous.[90] Harvard could increase Black enrollment in the simulation by providing us with more detailed data on family income and whether students were raised in a single-parent household.[91] If Harvard did a better job of recruiting low-income students to apply and eliminated early admissions, it could increase Black admissions in a way not reflected in Simulation D.[92] Finally, Harvard could boost Black enrollment by increasing its dismal community college transfer rate. The Aspen Institute found that each year, thousands of high-achieving low- and moderate-income community college students fail to transfer to a four-year institution, even though they could succeed at "the most competitive schools." If Harvard admitted the same proportion of community college students as Amherst, it could have accepted three hundred students over six years. Harvard's actual number of community college transfers over that period? Two.[93]

In sum, there were several avenues open to Harvard to boost the share of Black students above 10 percent. Each would have required additional costs to Harvard's treasury, but the college had plenty of money to invest.

Looking back after the trial, I marveled at the system Harvard had created. I realized that the university had pulled off the same trick played by wealthy white suburbanites that my Harvard professor Robert Coles had described during the Boston desegregation busing crisis. During the 1970s, liberal white families in the suburbs had exempted themselves from school desegregation and, from their safe perch, had lectured working-class Irish residents in Boston about the need to be more open-minded. Decades later, Harvard was using the same arrangement. Legacy preferences shielded wealthy white applicants from having to sacrifice as part of Harvard's effort to allocate seats for Black and Hispanic students through racial preferences. And, like the Irish in Boston, Asian American kids, many of them from working-class backgrounds, such as those at Stuyvesant High School in New York City, were the ones asked to cede ground. The most nefarious thing about the whole arrangement was that liberal white legacy applicants could be admitted to Harvard and at the same time signal their virtue by lecturing less advantaged Asian applicants about the importance of not being so small-minded and intolerant.

The Varsity Blues Scandal

District courts can take a while to issue decisions—especially on highly contentious and high-profile issues like the Harvard lawsuit—and it would be almost a year before Judge Burroughs would render her judgment. In the meantime, during the spring of 2019, in the same courtroom where we had discussed Harvard's tawdry system of admissions, another scandal broke.

In March 2019, several wealthy individuals, including Hollywood celebrities Felicity Huffman and Lori Loughlin, were indicted by federal prosecutors in Boston for conspiring to illegally secure admissions for their children in elite colleges. The Varsity Blues scandal involved cheating on standardized tests and bribing athletic coaches to falsely recruit nonathletes as athletes.

William Rick Singer, the mastermind behind the scheme, told one donor there were three doors through which a student could enter an elite college: the "front door" of merit; the "back door" of donating to an institution; or the "side door," which Singer opened by bribing athletic coaches. Singer told his clients that the side door was comparatively less expensive than the back door. One FBI agent said that those indicted "had a role in fostering a culture of corruption and greed that created an uneven playing field for students trying to get into these schools the right way."[94]

The prosecutors drew a clear legal line between the back door and the side door. "We're not talking about donating a building so that a school is more likely to take your son or daughter," the U.S. attorney for the District of Massachusetts declared.[95] But to a lot of Americans, the moral distinction between bribing a coach and bribing an institution was a matter of degree rather than kind.

After all, by justifying legacy preferences as a fundraising tool, wasn't Harvard essentially suggesting that it was soliciting bribes? To build a system to elicit donations, Harvard couldn't just give every legacy candidate an equally sized preference. Otherwise, there would be no incentive for alumni to increase their giving. For the system to pay off, there had to be an extra boost for the children of alumni who made significant donations. As one admissions officer at an elite university told journalist Daniel Golden, there are two types of alumni: "trough drinkers" and "trough fillers." The cost of educating students at elite universities tended to exceed the amount of tuition charged, so even the full-pay students were being subsidized. In that sense, every graduate who does not donate is a trough drinker and not particularly valued. The official told Golden, "Just because you drank at a trough that others filled does not entitle your child to drink at the same trough." (Data from Raj Chetty would later confirm that at several elite colleges, legacies from the wealthiest families received a much bigger admissions boost than legacies as a whole.)[96]

The two sets of trials—those involving Varsity Blues, and the one involving Harvard—raised the question: Rather than drawing a distinction between those who got in through Harvard's back door and Rick Singer's side door, why not make all students go through the front door?[97]

The Judge's Disappointing Ruling

On September 30, 2019, Judge Allison Burroughs rendered her long-awaited decision in the Harvard case. She upheld what she called Harvard's "very fine admissions program," despite considerable evidence that it is anything but that. The court claimed that Harvard's system of admissions complied with existing Supreme Court precedent on the use of race. With respect to my piece of the case, she concluded that there were three reasons that "race-neutral alternatives" wouldn't work at Harvard.[98]

First, the court objected to my suggestion that Harvard boost diversity by getting rid of its substantial preferences that help wealthy white students, saying doing so would "come at considerable costs" to the university. Doing away with preferences for the children of alumni and other privileged groups, the court claimed, would damage Harvard's ability to "achieve desired benefits from relationships with its alumni and other individuals who have made significant contributions to Harvard." I was disappointed, given all the evidence we'd presented at trial about superb universities like Caltech, Oxford, and Cambridge that did not employ legacy preferences. Instead, the judge said it was too much to ask Harvard to end its shakedown of alumni.[99]

Second, the court suggested that admitting greater numbers of high-achieving disadvantaged students would "require Harvard to sacrifice the academic strength of its class." In particular, the court pointed to an estimated 53–71 point class-wide decline out of 2,400 possible SAT points. The judge ignored the fact that this was just a one-percentage-point change (from the ninety-ninth percentile to ninety-eighth) among an impressive group of students who had achieved very high scores, many in the face of considerable economic obstacles.[100]

Third, the court said that under a system of socioeconomic preferences, Harvard would be "less diverse than it is currently." But as I noted in my testimony, that was not true in most measures. The simulation showed that using economic affirmative action would maintain the overall share of underrepresented minorities (Black, Hispanic, and Native American), while tripling the share of first-generation college students. This would surely enhance classroom discussions at an institution like Harvard, where the rich outnumbered the poor by such a huge margin.[101]

The judge ended her decision by quoting moving remarks on the benefits of diversity made by Harvard's expert Ruth Simmons, who, as the judge observed, had a father who worked as a janitor and a mother who worked as a maid. If Harvard officials were truly dedicated to advancing people like the young Ruth Simmons, then naturally, I would have been cheering them on. But the reality was very different. By supporting Harvard's system of racial preferences, which in turn buttressed its system of legacy preferences and faculty child preferences, the judge was making it far *less* likely that the children of maids and janitors would ever have a chance to attend the prestigious university.[102]

My experience as an expert witness in the Harvard trial was unlike any other I had encountered. To move from academic observer to participant required an awkward alliance with conservatives with whom I disagreed on many issues, and it became even more uncomfortable after Donald Trump was elected president. At the same time, I felt that Trump's election made it even more important to root out a system that routinely favored wealthy students of all colors.

Having been an undergraduate and a law student at Harvard, I was shaken to learn the extent to which the system was stacked against Asian American applicants and working-class students of all races. The evidence showed that Harvard's use of racial preferences wasn't necessary. Rather, it was used to counteract a deeply unfair system that hurt Black and Hispanic students in the first place. For years, research involving a large group of selective universities showed that class-based affirmative action could work to create a fairer system that would produce ample racial and economic diversity while upholding rigorous academic standards. And now the granular evidence at Harvard showed it could work even at one of the most elite universities on the planet.

CHAPTER 8

Lifting the Admissions Veil at the "People's University" in North Carolina

EDWARD BLUM'S STUDENTS FOR FAIR ADMISSIONS ACTIVISM extended beyond Harvard, the nation's oldest private college, to a lawsuit challenging racial preferences at the University of North Carolina at Chapel Hill, the nation's oldest public college. I served in a similar capacity as expert witness. The UNC case drew less press attention than the case against Harvard, but it raised a number of distinct and interesting questions: Should one expect that UNC, as a public university, would be more open to working-class students than Harvard? As a state institution that, by law, admitted at least 82 percent of its students from North Carolina, would a Texas-style percentage plan work as a supplement to socioeconomic preferences in a way that it might not at Harvard? And would UNC take a more generous view of the academic abilities of working-class students than Harvard had? I became especially intrigued by that last question when I learned that UNC had hired as one of its experts Stanford professor Caroline Hoxby,

211

whose famous 2013 study found that there were tens of thousands of high-achieving low-income students who could flourish at selective colleges, but did not even apply.

Going into the UNC case, I had a positive view of Chapel Hill. I had spoken at UNC several times at conferences on inequality in education and been impressed by James Moeser, chancellor of UNC–Chapel Hill from 2000 to 2008, who had created the Carolina Covenant financial aid program for low-income students. I considered UNC to be a leader on equal opportunity and one of the good actors committed to doing the right thing.

What Counts in Getting into UNC?

As I dug through the files and wrote three reports in the case, the sheen quickly wore off. As in the Harvard case, the first step in figuring out whether race-neutral alternatives might work at UNC was to assess the relative weights provided to various preferences in the existing admissions process. Duke's Peter Arcidiacono reviewed 162,857 in-state and out-of-state applicants, primarily from the class of 2016 to the class of 2021 admissions cycles.[1]

The in-state and out-of-state systems were quite different, so Arcidiacono modeled each separately. The out-of-state admissions process was more competitive because UNC received more applications from out-of-state students than from in-state, and those students had to compete for just 18 percent of the school's seats. For the class of 2021, 14 percent of out-of-state students were admitted, compared to 46 percent of in-state students.[2]

In rank order of importance, Arcidiacono's results show the relative weight of various preferences in UNC's admissions for both sets of applicants. (He omitted recruited athletes, who constituted less than 2 percent of domestic admits and were essentially guaranteed admission, at a 97 percent rate.)[3] The preferences are expressed as logit estimates, which indicate the increased odds in admission associated with given traits. The big takeaway for in-state applicants was that race (being African American [4.687] or Hispanic [2.623]) counted a lot more than class (being first-generation college [1.251] or qualifying for an application fee waiver because of low-income status [0.205]). For in-state applicants, being a legacy (0.435) or an early applicant (0.355) had a relatively small impact.

For the much more competitive out-of-state applicant pool, the same basic pattern held, but with a twist. African Americans (7.090) and Hispanics (3.483) received larger preferences than first-generation applicants (2.428) or low-income students qualifying for fee waivers (0.165). However, unlike the in-state pool, large preferences were provided to out-of-state legacy applicants (5.637) and a moderate preference was given to early applicants (0.967).[4]

The "People's University" Stacks the Deck

As Arcidiacono and I delved into the admissions system at UNC, it became clear that UNC wasn't quite as bad as Harvard: there was no anti-Asian bias or Z-list for the wealthy. But a place that prided itself on being the "university of the people" followed Harvard's practices in most respects. It privileged the wealthy in several ways. Then, to create racial diversity, it sought to compensate by providing large preferences to economically advantaged students of color.[5]

For the highly competitive out-of-state student competition for seats, UNC provided a substantial boost to the children of alumni, more than twice as large as the preference for first-generation college students. A nonresident student with a 25 percent chance of admission would see their odds skyrocket to 97 percent if they were a legacy. Substantial numbers of out-of-state legacies were admitted. In the class of 2019, for example, the number of out-of-state legacy admits was comparable to the number of out-of-state Black and Latino admits.[6]

UNC provided substantial legacy preferences, even though it disproportionately benefited white students to the detriment of Asian

American, Black, and Hispanic students. Admitted out-of-state white students were more than four times as likely to be the children of alumni as admitted out-of-state Black, Hispanic, or Asian students.[7]

UNC did not put up much of a defense of legacy preferences. Unlike Harvard's expert Ruth Simmons, UNC's expert Bridget Terry Long, dean of Harvard's Education School, conceded that legacy preferences hurt the cause of diversity. And while Harvard insisted it needed legacy preferences for financial reasons, UNC provost Jim Dean appeared to discount that consideration: "There may be on the margin some sense about alumni giving to the university. But the effect is—is relatively small, so it's—I'm not sure how material it actually is."[8]

Like Harvard, UNC also had an early admissions program that increased the likelihood of admissions and tended to benefit advantaged students. According to Arcidiacono's model, for both in-state and out-of-state applicants, the preference for applying early was *larger* than that provided to low-income students (i.e., those receiving an application fee waiver). UNC stuck with the policy, even though the preference tended to benefit white students and hurt Black and Hispanic students. Economically advantaged students were also more likely to apply early than disadvantaged students.[9]

And, like Harvard, UNC also provided a preference to faculty children that was larger than the preference for students qualifying for application fee waivers—despite the fact that doing so undercut racial diversity. Some 82 percent of children of faculty applicants were white or Asian, and only 12 percent were Black or Hispanic.[10]

These preferences for the privileged helped explain why UNC ended up with a Harvard-like skew toward the wealthy in its student body. Despite UNC's claim to be the "university of the people," some people (those in the top income quintile) were sixteen times as likely to be found on campus as those who came from the bottom quintile. The median family income of a student from UNC–Chapel Hill was more than twice the median household income for North Carolina residents.[11]

First-generation college students were also grossly underrepresented at UNC. Stunningly, there were more legacy students at UNC than first-generation students, in a nation where there were *451 times* more American adults age twenty-five and older without a college degree compared to adults in the world who had graduated from UNC–Chapel Hill.[12]

As with Harvard's student body, the Black and Hispanic students at UNC were disproportionately well-off. The data showed they were more than twice as likely as the Black and Hispanic families statewide to come from socioeconomically advantaged families.[13]

Failing to Try Race-Neutral Strategies

As was true with Harvard, the legal issue in the UNC case was whether eliminating legacy and faculty child preferences and adopting socio-economic and geographic preferences might produce the educational benefits of racial and economic diversity without using racial prefer-ences. UNC had the legal duty to demonstrate that race-neutral strat-egies would not suffice, but, like Harvard, it did little to explore those options. In an agreement with the U.S. Department of Education's Office of Civil Rights, UNC committed to completing an analysis of race-neutral alternatives by September 30, 2013. In fact, a working group it created did not issue a report until 2016, about two and a half years late. Even then, the group applied the wrong legal standard. The *Fisher* case said race-neutral strategies had to work "about as well" as race to be viable, yet the working group said that any race-neutral strat-egy had to work *at least as well* as racial preferences to be considered via-ble. And the group only focused on high school grade percentage plans and did not even analyze the viability of a preference for socioeconomi-cally disadvantaged students.[14]

Given North Carolina's demographics, a socioeconomic preference looked to be a promising option. Although Black admitted students were pretty well-off compared to Black students throughout the state, they were still three times more likely to be economically disadvantaged than white students. And yet, Arcidiacono's analysis found that UNC relied far more heavily on racial preferences than economic preferences. For in-state applicants, being Black carried nearly *four times* the weight of being a first-generation college student and almost *twenty-three times* the weight of being eligible for an application fee waiver due to limited income. For out-of-state applicants, preferences for Black students were about three times the size of those for first-generation college students, and forty-three times the weight for students eligible for fee waivers.[15]

The evidence showed that UNC had another option available: admitting a top percentage of students from every high school in North Carolina. Whereas Harvard drew on a national pool of applicants, making a percentage plan more challenging (though not impossible), UNC had the ability to follow Texas, California, and Florida in implementing a plan devoted to geographic diversity, primarily with the 82 percent of in-state students.[16] Indeed, in the 2012 *Fisher* case, UNC filed an amicus brief noting that a class rank plan at UNC would actually *raise* the representation of underrepresented minority students (from 15 percent to 16 percent), though UNC claimed a modest decline in SAT scores (from the ninety-first to eighty-sixth percentile) would have a "devastating educational effect" and cause students to flock "to remedial courses."[17] When asked about that claim under oath, UNC's admissions dean testified, "I don't agree with that statement."[18] The claim about the importance of SAT scores was also at odds with UNC's own findings that high school grades were much more important to student success at UNC than SAT scores, and weighed more heavily in the admissions process as a result.[19]

One concept not mentioned in UNC's amicus brief was that SAT scores are an important factor in *U.S. News & World Report* rankings— a fact that UT Austin leadership highlighted in expressing a desire to curb Texas's Top 10 Percent plan.[20] It was hard to know how big a role that played in UNC's thinking. However, it was undeniable that UNC cited its *U.S. News* rankings on its website and, like other schools, cared about its position in the magazine's annual list.[21]

In any event, UNC seemed wedded to its existing system, which was dominated by a small number of feeder schools. Arcidiacono found that slightly more than half of in-state UNC admitted students came from just 8 percent of North Carolina high schools. And just 7 percent of North Carolina's private high schools accounted for nearly 60 percent of all admitted private high school students at UNC.[22]

In addition, UNC could have better promoted community college transfers as a way to increase racial and socioeconomic diversity. UNC operated a pilot program aimed at supporting transfers for highly qualified disadvantaged students, and pointed to the program's success, but the endeavor involved just ten of North Carolina's fifty-eight community colleges. Overall, community college transfers constituted just 5 percent of the incoming class at UNC, one-quarter of UC Berkeley's community college transfer representation.[23]

Overall, UNC did a poor job of encouraging applications from economically disadvantaged students, many of whom were underrepresented minorities. Arcidiacono found that first-generation students made up less than one-quarter of all in-state applicants, even though about three-quarters of North Carolina adults lacked a college degree.[24]

I was intrigued to see how UNC's expert, Caroline Hoxby, would reply to the concern that UNC could do a better job at recruiting high-achieving low-income students, given that she was perhaps the nation's best-known proponent of the idea that there was a large, untapped pool of talented, low-income students who were not applying to selective colleges. Hoxby's main response was that most high-ability, low-income students in North Carolina were white or Asian. But I pointed out that there was no legal prohibition to stop UNC from specifically targeting Black and Hispanic low-income high achievers from *applying*, and that this could be a rich source of diversity. Arcidiacono's data found that there were actually more high-achieving low-income Black and Hispanic students in North Carolina public schools who did not even apply to UNC than there were Black and Hispanic students admitted to UNC from *all* economic backgrounds.[25]

How Would a Percentage Plan or Economic Preferences Work at UNC?

As in the Harvard case, the rich data from UNC allowed Arcidiacono and me to simulate what would happen if UNC stopped using racial preferences and implemented alternatives. In Simulation 13, we provided a socioeconomic preference (equivalent in size to an out-of-state legacy preference) to students who came from disadvantaged families, neighborhoods, and schools. We also eliminated the unfair preferences based on factors like being a legacy or faculty child. The results showed that UNC would do about as well in terms of racial diversity and academic readiness, and better on socioeconomic diversity. Black shares went from 9.0 percent to 8.8 percent, and Hispanic shares from 5.0 percent to 5.3 percent. SAT scores went from about the ninety-first percentile to the ninetieth percentile. High school GPA held steady, going from 4.67 to 4.66. Socioeconomic diversity increased from 24.8 percent of admitted students coming from disadvantaged families to 34.3 percent.[26]

We also modeled a Texas-style percentage plan in Simulation 8. As in Texas, we allocated most of the seats for students who ranked at the top of their high school class and filled the others with high-performing applicants. To keep the UNC class size steady, students would have to be in the top 4.5 percent of their class. Both racial and socioeconomic diversity under the plan *increased*. The Black share increased from 9 percent to 10 percent, the Hispanic share held steady at 5 percent, and the share from socioeconomically disadvantaged families increased from 25 percent to 30 percent. Average SAT scores declined from 1311 to 1280 (about the ninetieth percentile to the eighty-eighth), and high school GPA dipped just a little (from 4.67 to 4.61).[27]

Addressing UNC's Objections

The results of the simulations were very positive, but UNC objected. In their rebuttal reports, UNC's experts Caroline Hoxby and Bridget Terry Long raised a couple of big complaints. First was the often-raised concern that socioeconomic preferences were not "efficient" in producing racial diversity. After all, if a school wanted to obtain a certain racial diversity level, the most direct way to do so was through the use of racial preferences. Long said that it was standard university practice to "admit the best-qualified candidates within each racial or ethnic group. . . . Without taking race into account explicitly, they would no longer be able to pick the best candidates within each race."[28]

But there were two problems with this line of thinking. First, the practice Long was advocating was akin to "race norming"—adjusting scores to take the top applicants within each racial group—which was a violation of federal civil rights law.[29] The courts have never been interested in promoting the most efficient means of achieving a given racial result. Quotas, which are the most direct means, are also illegal. Courts required universities to first try race-neutral alternatives because they recognized there are significant costs to using racial preferences, such as the imposition of stigma on recipients and increased racial antagonism in society. So, if a university could achieve the desirable goal of racial diversity without using race, that was the required option.[30]

The second troubling element to Hoxby and Long's contention that socioeconomic preferences were "inefficient" is that they accorded no independent value to socioeconomic diversity itself. Socioeconomic preferences were seen solely as "proxies" for race. Their only conceivable value was to indirectly promote racial diversity. Hoxby's framing of the issue was particularly stark. She described the admission of "a poor white student" to be "a false positive." Such an admission decision would be a mistake, she said, akin to a university seeking basketball players instead admitting a "tall person" who was "not a basketball player" and did not "actually contribute to the basketball team."[31] This view was at odds with UNC's stated belief that in evaluating the benefits of diversity, race should be "a single element" within a "larger definition of diversity" that was defined "broadly" to include "differences in social background [and] economic circumstances."[32]

Hoxby and Long also objected to the socioeconomic approach as impractical. In my reports, I emphasized the importance of considering family wealth in admissions. The simulations did not include wealth data because UNC did not provide them, but Hoxby and Long argued it was not pragmatic to consider wealth as a factor. Hoxby, for example, claimed that "accurate wealth data are not only *not* possessed by the university but would be extremely difficult if not impossible to obtain."[33]

I responded that UCLA Law School had for decades used wealth as a factor in admissions. Furthermore, I noted that the standard federal student aid form, known as the FAFSA, required students to provide extensive information about family wealth. UNC also required applicants to fill out an additional form created by the College Board that demanded even more information, including data on small businesses and primary residence home equity.[34] Some families might not complete these forms due to their high-wealth status, but that wasn't a flaw. After all, those applicants would not qualify for a socioeconomic preference anyway. Other than perhaps mortgage lenders, I noted, colleges had access to as much financial information on applicants as any major institution in American society.[35] The significant penalties for knowingly submitting false information discourage dishonesty.[36]

The Trial and Court Ruling

With the reports of the experts completed, in November 2020 we moved on to the trial, which was held before Judge Loretta Biggs in Winston-Salem, North Carolina. It was no fun, as noted in the prologue, being cross-examined by UNC's lawyer, the experienced former prosecutor Patrick Fitzgerald, or being questioned by an attorney from the Lawyers' Committee for Civil Rights. UNC criticized my simulations for being allegedly unrealistic because they assumed that the same types of students who applied in the past would apply in the future. I didn't think much of the complaint because simulations, by their nature, had to make assumptions, and we had also prepared a separate set of simulations where the applicant pool changed.[37]

Almost a year later, in October 2021, Judge Biggs ruled in favor of UNC. On the viability of race-neutral alternatives, I was disappointed that the court bought hook, line, and sinker the defense's complaint about methodology. The judge quoted uncritically Hoxby's claim that my simulations rested on "terribly unrealistic" assumptions, including the applicant pool remaining the same despite a new admissions system.[38] I was incredulous. It was impossible to know exactly how an applicant pool might change in response to a new set of admissions policies, which was why, in the Harvard case, both sides had used the existing applicant pool for their simulations.[39] If, as a matter of methodology, using the existing applicant pool was good enough for Harvard's expert David Card, who would go on to win the Nobel Prize in economics, it was good enough for me. My reading of the court's opinion in the UNC case was that the judge seemed intent on reaching a certain result and unwilling to let anything get in her way.

With Judge Biggs's ruling, SFFA had lost both cases at the district court level. SFFA also lost the Harvard case in the First Circuit Court of Appeals. The SFFA lawyers took the setbacks in the lower courts in stride, however, because changes were afoot where it mattered most: the Supreme Court of the United States. Donald Trump had appointed three new conservative justices—Neil Gorsuch to replace Antonin Scalia, Brett Kavanaugh to replace Anthony Kennedy, and Amy Coney Barrett to replace Ruth Bader Ginsburg.

Two of the four justices in the 4–3 majority in *Fisher II*, Kennedy and Ginsburg, were no longer on the Court. SFFA appealed the First Circuit decision to the Supreme Court and—rather than taking the UNC district court opinion to the Fourth Circuit—asked the Supreme Court to take the UNC case directly from the district court, a fairly unusual move. The question now was whether the U.S. Supreme Court would accept SFFA's appeals.

My involvement in the University of North Carolina litigation was eye-opening. Although UNC had a sparkling progressive reputation and had won national accolades for its financial aid program, it turned out to be virtually as elitist as Harvard in its admissions practices for the advantaged. The resulting student body composition was similarly skewed toward the wealthy. My simulations showed that UNC had two viable alternatives for producing a racially and economically diverse class while maintaining academic excellence: economic preferences for students of all races, and a percentage plan modeled after Texas's successful efforts. The evidence continued to build that there was a better path forward.

CHAPTER 9

Racism, Antiracism, and the Search for Sanity in the Age of Trump and Biden

DURING THE YEARS THE HARVARD AND UNC CASES WERE being litigated and moving forward to the Supreme Court, America was engaging in a fractious debate over race that undoubtedly would color the way the justices viewed the issue of racial preferences. The debates also demonstrated how much was at stake in the litigation. The use of racial preferences at Harvard and UNC was not just about college admissions; it raised a much bigger set of issues. In a multiracial democracy that has a terrible history of racial exclusion, did racial preference policies help heal wounds, open new ones, or do both things at once? Did racial preferences help to increase the salience of racial identity not only among beneficiaries, but also among white people? Was that a good thing or a bad thing for American democracy?

During the decade in which the SFFA cases were litigated, beginning in 2014, racial debates played out in four stages. First came a frightening rise in white nationalism, epitomized by the emergence of a Republican presidential nominee in 2016 who embraced racism more openly than any major candidate in decades. Second came a salutary racial justice movement, supported by communities of color and millions of white people, who were repulsed by a neo-Nazi rally in Charlottesville, Virginia, and a series of highly publicized police killings of unarmed Black people. Third came an overreach, especially among some highly educated white liberals, who began to see virtually every issue singularly through the lens of racial oppression and were willing to suspend long-standing norms around the importance of free speech, nondiscrimination, and the need for public order. Fourth came a course correction against some of the more extreme left-wing stances—such as "defund the police"—as large numbers of Americans of all races sought a middle ground.

The Rise of White Nationalism Under Donald Trump

The vicious cycle started on the far right. The growing demographic change in the country fed the disturbing idea in some quarters that white Christians constituted "real" Americans. These extremists suggested that something important was being lost as the racial, ethnic, and religious makeup of the citizenry diversified. They feared that Black, Brown, Asian, Jewish, and Muslim Americans were somehow "replacing"—rather than coming to live alongside—white Christians.

Astonishingly, these white nationalist views, long confined to the margins, were given voice in the presidential candidacy of Donald Trump. Trump had a long history of racism and fueled the racist idea that President Barack Obama, born in Hawaii, was not an American citizen.[1]

While border security and illegal immigration were legitimate issues to raise, in announcing his candidacy, Trump famously whipped up animosity against Mexican immigrants, whom he branded as criminals and "rapists." Trump then advocated a religious test for immigration and proposed "a total and complete shutdown of Muslims entering the United States." He also called for heavy surveillance of Muslim communities and their houses of worship, which the ACLU noted "would infringe upon American Muslims' First Amendment right to exercise their religion freely without fear or intimidation."[2]

During the 2016 presidential campaign, Trump also gained notoriety for his criticism of a federal judge presiding over a lawsuit against Trump University, specifically targeting the judge's ethnicity. He suggested an Indiana-born jurist of Mexican heritage, Gonzalo Curiel, was incapable of being neutral in the suit solely due to his ethnic origins. Republican Speaker of the House Paul Ryan said, "Claiming a person can't do their job because of their race is sort of like the textbook definition of a racist comment."[3]

After his election, Trump intensified his emphasis on racial exclusion. In August 2017, he said there were "very fine people" among those who marched in the Charlottesville neo-Nazi "Unite the Right" rally.[4] In January 2018, he said he wanted to limit immigration to America for people who lived in what he called "shithole" countries.[5]

During the years of the Trump presidency, many Americans were also horrified by a string of high-profile police killings of unarmed Black people, most notably Breonna Taylor in Louisville, Kentucky, in March 2020, and George Floyd in Minneapolis, Minnesota, in May 2020.

The Healthy Awakening of White People

In response, particularly to George Floyd's murder by a sadistic white officer, a multiracial coalition of tens of millions of Americans participated in Black Lives Matter demonstrations across the country. The protests were mostly peaceful, and many white Americans began, some for the first time in their lives, to acknowledge the corrosive effects of pervasive anti-Black racism in American history. People began to question why there were so many monuments to Confederate soldiers who betrayed the country in the name of defending a system of chattel slavery. Presidential candidate Joe Biden put Trump's comments about

Charlottesville at the center of his 2020 campaign to "heal the soul" of America.

As part of the healthy response to Trump's racially offensive comments, I saw in many people a new openness to some of the racial and economic justice work I had been participating in for many years, particularly around school integration. Since the publication of my 2001 book *All Together Now*, I'd been championing public school choice as a way to integrate schools by economic status and race. But in the pre-Trump era, the path had often been blocked on both the left and the right. The Bush administration favored the testing and accountability approach embodied by the No Child Left Behind Act, while Obama administration education secretary Arne Duncan argued that rather than tackling segregation, the focus should be on improving high-poverty schools by changing school governance rules (such as creating nonunion charter schools) and doubling down on Bush's testing and teacher accountability ideas. There were pros and cons to these policies, but I thought they ignored a fundamental finding in the social science research: that separate schools for rich and poor, as well as for Black and white, were almost never equal. For several years, I'd run up against a bipartisan consensus that school integration was simply too big of a political lift.

But in the run-up to Trump's presidency, the interest in racial and economic integration in schools began to increase. I found a strong ally in journalist Nikole Hannah-Jones. It was a little surprising for me to be rowing in the same direction as she was. I'd crossed swords with Hannah-Jones on affirmative action a few years earlier, when she had written an article that unfairly suggested my colleague Tony Carnevale and I were on opposite sides of the debate. (We responded forcefully.)[6] But Hannah-Jones recognized that school integration was one of the few measures that improved the life chances of low-income and Black and Hispanic students, and she had a talent for vividly illustrating her point with powerful stories of individual Black students who were harmed by segregation. In 2016, Hannah-Jones and I supported each other while serving on panels together at the SXSW EDU Conference in Austin and the Education Writers Association conference in Boston. Integration became more of a mainstream strategy, as exemplified by a 2016 article in *The Atlantic* observing that "school integration is being publicly debated in a way not seen in nearly 40 years."[7]

Trump's astonishing victory in 2016, which relied on a platform that demonized Mexican immigrants and Muslims, reminded policymakers and activists why school integration was so important. If more voters had come to know Mexican Americans and Muslim Americans as classmates and friends, it would have been much harder for a demagogue to run a cruel campaign against such groups.

The new openness to school integration was particularly evident in New York City. New York State schools were ranked the most segregated in America—worse than Alabama or Mississippi. And yet, for years, attempts by me and others to spark discussions about change fell flat. During the Trump era, however, student activists began pushing for reform, and in 2017, New York City mayor Bill de Blasio created a School Diversity Advisory Group to make recommendations for reducing school segregation in city schools. I was appointed to a five-member executive committee of the group, along with civil rights leaders Maya Wiley of the New School, Hazel Dukes of the NAACP, Jose Calderon of the Hispanic Federation, and researcher Amy Hsin. We assembled a larger group of about forty researchers, civil rights activists, and school officials to consider what could be done.[8]

The effort received a big boost when Mayor de Blasio appointed a new schools chancellor, Richard Carranza, the former superintendent in Houston, Texas, and a strong integrationist. In a 2018 interview with *The Atlantic*, Carranza committed to honoring the 1954 Supreme Court decision in *Brown v. Board of Education* outlawing segregation: "We've been admiring this issue for 64 years! Let's stop admiring and let's start acting."[9]

Our advisory group made a number of recommendations. We recognized that school integration wouldn't work everywhere in New

York, but that a subset of the city's community school districts—educating more than three hundred thousand students—had enough of an economic and racial mix to make integration work.[10] The mayor and chancellor agreed to implement almost all the recommendations. The effort received a fair amount of attention, and Carranza and I discussed the plan together on a panel at Harvard Law School. Soon after, the Los Angeles Unified School District asked me to be part of a similar effort to offer recommendations regarding school integration. Trump's openly hostile racial rhetoric had awakened liberals in some communities to the need to get their own houses in order.

The Unhealthy Rise of Race Essentialism and Illiberalism Among Left Elites

But among New York City's School Diversity Advisory Group—particularly the younger, academic members—there were also disturbing signs of overreach. Some wanted to abolish all gifted and talented programs, saying they were "tools of white supremacy." I argued that the group should be against segregation and for merit—which was the path I'd pushed a decade earlier in Chicago Public Schools, where I helped design a program under which Chicago's elite exam schools would consider in their admissions decisions not only exam scores and grades but also the socioeconomic challenges students had overcome. As Brookings researchers later found, this system produced far more racial diversity in its elite schools than most public school systems.[11] I had an ally in Hazel Dukes, who told me, "We can't be against merit."

But some members of the advisory group were adamant that we should eliminate the whole idea of selective schools. I objected that doing so could end up backfiring and driving middle-class families from New York City public schools, which would further concentrate poverty. We needed to strike a balance. Others responded that if privileged white families left the public schools, good riddance.

Racism, Antiracism, and the Search for Sanity

While leftists in the group spoke of a system that benefited white people, the truth in New York City was more complicated. At the most elite public school, Stuyvesant High School, Asian American students made up 75 percent of the student body, and 44 percent of students were from low-income families.[12] This was not a school for rich white students. However, some on the left viewed Asian Americans as "white adjacent," so they were part of the problem. I was deeply troubled in June 2018 when Carranza commented on the selective school admissions debate by saying, "I just don't buy into the narrative that any one ethnic group owns admission to these schools."[13] It was hard to interpret that comment as anything other than anti-Asian.

Similar overreach took place in other parts of the country. The KIPP charter school network abandoned its "Work Hard. Be Nice" slogan, allegedly a reflection of "white supremacy culture," even though polls found that 80 percent of parents, across racial lines, liked the idea of their kids working hard and being nice.[14] California Community Colleges adopted a policy that faculty should employ the principles of diversity, equity, inclusion, and accessibility, including the idea that "merit is embedded in the ideology of Whiteness and upholds race-based structural inequality."[15] In some circles, saying the best qualified person deserves the job became seen as a "microaggression."[16] In San Francisco, leftists on the school board said that student admissions to Lowell High School, which had long been based on merit, should instead be decided by lottery. The San Francisco school board made headlines when it proposed changing the name of a school honoring Abraham Lincoln. Despite being considered America's most heroic president, liberator of the enslaved, and preserver of the Union, school officials said that his mistreatment of Native Americans outweighed all those considerations.[17]

The San Francisco school board decision was widely ridiculed, but another reinterpretation of American history as fundamentally racist won surprisingly widespread accolades—including the coveted Pulitzer Prize. In 2019, the *New York Times* unveiled the 1619 Project, led by

Nikole Hannah-Jones. The project, which started as a series of magazine articles before being developed into a book, claimed that we should identify 1619, the year enslaved people came to America, as our true founding because racism was what defined America.[18]

To its credit, the 1619 Project included some research that was illuminating and helped broaden our understanding of the past, but there was also a great deal that was misleading. The endeavor was widely debunked by both mainstream historians and numerous critics for falsely claiming that the preservation of slavery was a primary motivation for declaring independence from England.[19] Many on the right called out the exaggerations, but so did liberal outlets such as the *Washington Post* and the *New York Times* itself.

While Hannah-Jones put slavery at the very center of the American story and said 1619 provided "the seed of so much of what has made us unique," critics noted that such thinking failed to capture what made America different. The *New York Times Book Review*'s analysis of the 1619 Project volume, by Adam Hochschild, acknowledged that the book could leave readers "with the impression that the heritage of slavery is uniquely American. It is not. . . . From ancient Egypt to czarist Russia, from sub-Saharan Africa to the Aztecs, forms of slavery have blighted nearly every continent."[20]

Critic Carlos Lozada noted in the *Washington Post* that part of the problem was that the 1619 Project was history with a clear political goal: cash reparations for Black people: "The *New York Times*'s 1619 Project is now enlisted in the service of a policy agenda and a political worldview." He quoted Hannah-Jones's concluding chapter: "It is one thing to say you do not support reparations because you did not know the history, that you did not understand how things done long ago helped create the conditions in which millions of Black Americans live today. But you now have reached the end of the book, and nationalized amnesia can no longer provide the excuse."[21]

The 1619 Project's call for reparations was part of a larger campaign that gained traction during this time period. A Duke professor called for $10.7 trillion in cash reparations to Black people whose ancestors were enslaved.[22] A California commission recommended compensating Black residents with up to $1.2 million each, which would result in a total cost to the state of more than $500 billion. A San Francisco commission recommended $5 million per Black resident at a cost of $100 billion to the city.[23]

On college campuses, the valid idea that race matters in American society was taken to an extreme, setting off a series of dominoes that undercut fundamental principles of liberal democracy. During the reign of Senator Joe McCarthy in the 1950s, higher education leaders proudly opposed the idea that faculty should take loyalty oaths as a condition of employment. But over time, colleges began routinely asking prospective candidates to take a twenty-first-century loyalty oath to diversity, equity, and inclusion (DEI). While the idea that professors should value diversity and inclusivity seems reasonable, in practice it too often became a political litmus test that forced would-be faculty members to endorse the idea that racial preferences were the only fair path forward for America. Those who didn't could face dire consequences.[24]

DEI programs sometimes embraced deeply troubling practices. At Penn State, one white faculty member in the English department alleged that DEI officials created a hostile work environment by requiring that faculty watch a video titled "White Teachers Are a Problem." In a preliminary ruling, a Black federal judge and Obama appointee named Wendy Beetlestone let the case proceed in part based on allegations that on several occasions, the plaintiff "was obligated to attend conferences or trainings that discussed racial issues in essentialist and deterministic terms—ascribing negative traits to white people or white teachers without exception and as flowing inevitably from their race."[25]

The hard left also began clamping down on free speech on campus, particularly when it came to issues of race and identity. In 2021, MIT disinvited a University of Chicago geophysicist from giving a lecture about climate science because he did not believe race should be a factor in college admissions—a position supported by 73 percent of Americans in one Pew survey. "In other words," wrote David Brooks, "the views of the large majority of Americans are not even utterable in certain academic parts of the progressive subculture."[26]

Students argued that certain views constituted a form of "violence," which made them feel "unsafe," and therefore justified shouting down speakers. When students tried to prevent people holding conservative views from speaking on campus, the subject matter was rarely labor policy, taxes, or the environment. Left-wing illiberalism was sparked by issues that touched on identity, such as race, gender, or sexual orientation. That was why the University of Virginia's school newspaper endorsed the cancellation of a speech by former vice president Mike Pence, who took conservative positions on gay rights. However, student groups did not target people like political activist Grover Norquist for his conservative position on taxes.[27]

Disturbingly, these anti–free speech attitudes were most prevalent among students at elite colleges, who would one day disproportionately make up America's leadership class. According to a survey of students by the Foundation for Individual Rights in Education, 72 percent of those at the top twenty colleges in the *U.S. News* rankings said shouting down speakers was sometimes justified. Half the students at these schools said it was sometimes justifiable to prevent peers from attending a campus presentation, and 30 percent said violence could be justified to block speech.[28]

I got a fleeting taste of college culture in November 2019 when I participated in a debate with Harvard Law professor Randall Kennedy about affirmative action.[29] Kennedy, whom I deeply respected for his nuanced and honest defense of racial preferences, arrived with me at Middlebury College to debate the pros and cons of race-based versus class-based affirmative action. Before the event started, the organizers said some people had been objecting to the forum, complaining the very idea of debating affirmative action was "offensive." Kennedy and I both shook our heads.

Racism, Antiracism, and the Search for Sanity

When Kennedy and I made our way to the forum, we were alarmed to see a phalanx of police officers ready to address any disruptions. Middlebury was taking precautions because a few years earlier, a mob had shouted down American Enterprise Institute's Charles Murray—author of the notorious *Bell Curve* book—with students chanting, "Racist, sexist, antigay: Charles Murray, go away!" The crowd then turned menacing. When Murray's interviewer, Allison Stanger, who is a Democrat and a Middlebury professor, sought to calm the crowd and model an exchange of ideas, she was physically attacked and ended up with whiplash and a concussion.[30]

To my great relief, and Kennedy's, there was no repeat of the protests during our debate. The agitators did not materialize, and we had productive back-and-forth in which we agreed on the end goal of racial and economic diversity, but respectfully disagreed on how to achieve it. When Kennedy and I had dinner with a small group of students, though, they explained that shouting down speakers wasn't the primary way to quash debate on campus. Social pressure was far more powerful. If someone raised a question about affirmative action either in a class discussion or in a more informal setting, we were told, the result was "social death." If you wanted to get a date on campus, staying quiet was the best course of action.

It was not just on college campuses, however, that the left felt emboldened on the issue of racial preferences. Particularly after the horrific murder of George Floyd, policymakers and nonprofits moved to embrace preferences more aggressively than they had in the past. In June 2020, California lawmakers passed legislation to place on the November 2020 ballot a proposition that would repeal the state's 1996 ban on racial preferences. In March 2021, the federal government created the Restaurant Revitalization Fund, which provided a limited number of post-COVID relief grants and prioritized those going to women and people of color. Asian businesses were favored over white ones, even though Asian Americans earn more than white Americans on average. In Minnesota and New York, state officials prioritized scarce COVID treatments for racial minorities, rather than, as one Brookings scholar noted, prioritizing the direct risk factors that are correlated with race such as socioeconomic status and obesity. In Congress, the lead Democrat on housing policy proposed a $25,000 down payment assistance program for first-generation homebuyers in 2021 that would exclude low-income white people. Chicago mayor Lori Lightfoot said she would only take questions from reporters of color. Evanston, Illinois, officials, meanwhile, reopened schools for in-person classes to students of color before doing so for white students.[31]

Progressive organizations began elevating identity to the point of determining "the order of who should be allowed to speak based on the perceived degree of marginalization."[32] My longtime friend Ruy Teixeira, a political analyst who emphasizes broad-based economic programs over a narrow identity-based politics, left the Center for American Progress, a prominent Washington, D.C., think tank. In explaining his departure, he said it was impossible to have conversations about how to bring together working-class white and Black voters. "People were leery of talking about the white working class, as if it was de facto racist," he told *Politico*. Younger staffers were particularly insistent on seeing everything through the lens of identity, while the more seasoned leaders, who should have known better, tolerated it, because there was nothing worse than feeling old and irrelevant. "It's just cloud cuckoo land. The fact that nobody is willing to call bullshit, it just freaks me out," Teixeira said.[33]

Unions, which normally prize economic solidarity across racial lines, got into the act as well. The U.S. Supreme Court years earlier had outlawed laying people off based on race. Failing to be hired because of racial criteria was one thing, but being fired based on skin color imposed a much bigger burden, the Court reasoned. Nevertheless, in 2022, the Minneapolis teachers' union pushed a contract that interjected race as a factor in decisions about teacher layoffs.[34] Teacher unions had moved dramatically left on racial preferences since the days of Albert Shanker.

Paradoxically, corporations had their own reasons to jump on board. Some corporate leaders, properly horrified by the murder of George

Floyd, surely acted on their good instincts. But just as universities used racial preferences to hide larger economic inequalities in their student body that would be expensive to address, so private firms had their own interests to pursue. The Starbucks coffee chain was emblematic. Officials announced their virtue on issues of race by saying they would tie executive compensation to meeting the goal of a "30% BIPOC workforce," even while fiercely resisting efforts of their employees—BIPOC or white—to unionize.[35]

More broadly, parts of the left began to champion policies that challenged law enforcement agencies as inherently discriminatory toward minorities. Slogans such as "abolish ICE" (the U.S. Immigration and Customs Enforcement) and "defund the police" became popular among leftists. Activists in Seattle, Washington, for example, unlawfully established a new, "police-free" neighborhood known as the Capitol Hill Autonomous Zone. One Black Lives Matter activist in Chicago argued that looting was a form of reparations. After a group of people pillaged stores in the Chicago Loop, Ariel Atkins said it was justifiable behavior. "I don't care if somebody decides to loot a Gucci or a Macy's or a Nike store because that makes sure that person eats," she said. "That makes sure that person has clothes. That is reparations."[36]

What was behind these policies that challenged meritocracy, reinterpreted America as fundamentally racist, rejected free speech, embraced racial preferences, and opposed institutions aimed at maintaining public order? Two bodies of academic work—critical race theory, embodied by thinkers like Derrick Bell; and antiracism, embodied by researchers like Ibram Kendi—had gained widespread acceptance among elites in progressive nonprofits, media outlets, and education establishments, as students of these theories now began to hold positions of power.

In contrast to the aspirational approach of Martin Luther King Jr. or Barack Obama, critical race theory (CRT) held a deeply pessimistic view of race in America. It said America was defined by racism, and always would be. Racism wasn't something that people struggled with and tried to overcome. It was endemic and permanent. Given that premise, many of the major advancements of the Enlightenment were suspect: the importance of debate through free speech; advancement based on merit rather than nepotism or other factors; the idea of a neutral rule of law that did not depend on the identity of the parties involved in a dispute; and the development of the scientific method, which sought to establish objective truth beyond subjective feelings. These values and norms, CRT suggested, should not be respected as white people used them to maintain their power. A leading CRT theorist, Richard Delgado, wrote that CRT "questions the very foundations of the liberal order, including equality theory, legal reasoning, Enlightenment rationalism, and neutral principles of constitutional law."[37]

Antiracism, meanwhile, posited that there could be no neutrality on race, or any aspiration of color blindness and nondiscrimination. A person was either racist or antiracist. A racist is defined as anyone who does not support racial preferences. Indeed, anyone who believes the government should treat everyone the same, regardless of race, was engaging in "colorblind racism."[38] Kendi argued that all racial disparities were the result of racial discrimination.[39] If Stuyvesant High School was 75 percent Asian and 58 percent of college students were female—as was true—something nefarious was afoot.[40] If discrimination were the explanation, then racial preferences would be the only appropriate response. Kendi argued that the "only remedy to past discrimination is present discrimination. The only remedy to present discrimination is future discrimination."[41] Kendi's approach went far beyond the already unpopular idea that racial preferences should provide a *temporary* remedy to past discrimination. Instead, he advocated a dystopian vision—perpetual rounds of back-and-forth discrimination—in which society treats people not as individuals, but as members of racial tribes, possibly for generations to come.[42]

Under the new theory, "white supremacy," a belief long associated with noxious groups like the KKK, was redefined more broadly. The *New York Times* reported that DEI trainings at elite private schools suggested that "characteristics of white supremacy" include "individualism, worship of the written word and objectivity."[43] For a time, even the venerable Smithsonian Institution posted a bizarre chart describing "objectivity," being on time, and appreciating the written word as particular aspects of "white culture."[44]

Sometimes the media would portray CRT and antiracism as a continuation of the civil rights movement—an uncontroversial effort to make Americans more fully recognize that the legacy of slavery and segregation persists. But that missed the truly radical nature of the movements. The long transition from Martin Luther King Jr. and Thurgood Marshall to Ibram Kendi and Richard Delgado was head-spinning. It began with the change from advocating "integration" (which emphasized commonality) to "diversity" (which emphasized difference). And it concluded by saying that racial preferences were not a temporary remedy for past discrimination and that color blindness would never be the end goal because racism was permanent.

The Eerie Parallels Between the Far Left and Far Right on Race

While coming from very different places, antiracist and CRT thinking on the far left had some strange and unsettling parallels with the white nationalism that Donald Trump had been elevating; "one is the yin to the other's yang," one social critic noted.[45] To begin with, it was not hard to imagine KKK members nodding their heads about leftist racial essentialism that posited there was something distinctively white about being on time. Racists had long thought that Black people were not cut out for rigorous programs like Advancement Placement (AP) classes, which emphasize developing a student's writing skills and might indeed be said to "worship the written word."

For this reason, some Black educators were deeply disturbed by antiracist trainings. A *New York Times* reporter who profiled the white antiracist theorist Robin DiAngelo, author of the bestselling *White*

Fragility, interviewed Deonca Renee, a Black educator working to expand access to AP classes in New York City to disadvantaged communities. Renee told the reporter, "The city has tens of millions invested in A.P. for All, so my team can give kids access to A.P. classes, and help them prepare for A.P. exams that will help them get college degrees, and we're all supposed to think that writing and data are white values?"[46] The disagreement between Renee and DiAngelo was not a one-off. Surveys found that white liberals had moved further to the left on issues of race than Black people.[47]

The hard left's theories about race paralleled Trump's in other ways as well. Race essentialists on the left and right agreed that by far the most important thing about individuals was not their common identity as Americans, but rather their race or ethnicity. Whereas schools used to emphasize what students of all backgrounds share in common as Americans, in liberal Montgomery County, Maryland, for example, policymakers proposed a new social studies curriculum that "strengthens students' sense of racial, ethnic and tribal identities."[48] If Trump believed that a Mexican American judge's heritage would inevitably bias his views, CRT agreed that race was an enormously powerful force in shaping a person's thinking, to the point where "rational neutrality" was just a cover for advancing white interests. The new overlap in thinking was astonishing. As one author noted, "Since the Enlightenment, liberals and progressives have insisted that there's a common humanity that goes beyond differences of tribes and clans." Universalism was "the very first principle that distinguishes left from right," but now some on the left had abandoned that core belief.[49]

There was also a strange overlap between the far left and far right on the issue of free speech. Advocates of CRT shared with Donald Trump a skepticism about the need for open dialogue. During the 2016 campaign, Trump promised to "open up" the nation's libel laws to make it easier for politicians to sue the press. He also revoked the press credentials of critical reporters from the *Washington Post* and *Politico*, which the *New York Times* noted was "an almost unheard-of practice for a modern presidential candidate."[50] For their own reasons, race essentialists on the left were equally skeptical of free speech. At William & Mary, students with Black Lives Matter blocked an ACLU official from speaking, chanting, "Your free speech hides beneath white sheets."[51] The idea wasn't, as Dr. King argued, that free speech and assembly could be used to highlight injustice and move the country's conscience to reform. Rather, free speech was a tool of white supremacy, and therefore it was perfectly justified to shout down speakers with dangerous ideas that made students feel unsafe.

There was also agreement around skepticism of school integration. The far right had never liked desegregation and fought it tooth and nail, often violently and with massive resistance. CRT founders, drawing on ideas of the Black Power movement, also rejected school integration.[52] They did not share King's belief that racial integration of schools and neighborhoods was necessary to dispel myths. In fact, Derrick Bell argued that integration subjected Black people to more intense discrimination by white people. School desegregation wasn't a means, as Thurgood Marshall argued, for people to come learn what they have in common. Instead, CRT preached that white people would never accept Black people.

Finally, there was overlap on the far left and the far right about the validity of merit. Trump, who placed family members in key positions in his administration and was skeptical of experts who were part of what he called the "deep state," was more impressed by power than merit. So too, as Bell had told me years earlier, CRT rejected the idea of merit as a "smokescreen." While Black political figures like Barack Obama had epitomized what was possible in a meritocracy, CRT dismissed the concept of merit as a clever ploy used by white people to maintain dominance.

To be sure, the overlap between far left and far right was not complete. The *motivation* of far-left activists to improve the lives of Black Americans who had suffered so much in the United States stood in sharp contrast to the motivation of far-right activists to maintain white power. But some underlying beliefs and conclusions about the essential nature of race and the discrediting of central advances of the Enlightenment coincided in disturbing ways.

Rediscovering a Middle Ground

During the presidencies of both Trump and Biden, as far-right and far-left extremists gained more attention, many average Americans pushed back against both sides. Most opposed right-wing racism. Just as it had been wrong to assume that after Barack Obama's election, America had entered a "postracial" era, it is wrong to say that the election of Trump signaled that America was shot through with racism. Polls showed that 94 percent of white Americans rejected white nationalist views.[53] As political analyst Ruy Teixeira noted in 2017, research showed that "the underlying trend toward racial liberalism continues."[54]

Most Americans also rejected left-wing thinking on race. In one poll, about five times as many white people said people were "too sensitive" in conversations about race than "not sensitive enough."[55] In another poll, 80 percent of Americans, including large proportions of communities of color, said that "political correctness is a problem in our country."[56]

Although Americans detested Trump's stoking of racial tensions and were horrified by cell phone videos of police officers committing heinous acts of violence against unarmed Black men, they also wanted to broaden the lens and recognize that economic inequality was taking a toll on working-class Americans, across racial lines.[57] Researchers noted a stunning decline in life expectancy among working-class white individuals, brought on by "deaths of despair"—opioid addiction, alcoholism, and suicide. While other groups held steady on life expectancy, white women without a high school diploma experienced a decrease of six years in life expectancy and white men lacking a high school diploma lost three years.[58]

Political strategists found that the most appealing messages across racial lines called out how wealthy interests used racial appeals to divide working-class people. The winning messages emphasized that "we need elected leaders who will reject the divide-and-conquer tactics of their opponents and put the interests of working people first, whether we're white, Black or Brown."[59]

Even in liberal bastions like San Francisco, average voters began to rebel against left-wing extremism. In a city where Joe Biden won 85 percent of the vote in 2020, just over a year later, 70 percent of voters, including large numbers of Asian Americans, supported an effort to recall the school board members who had vilified Abraham Lincoln and abolished merit-based admissions to Lowell High School.[60]

Likewise, while support for racial preferences had hardened among liberal white elites, rank-and-file California voters, including many Democrats, had a different view. The Democratic and business establishments in the state supported the restoration of racial preferences in the November 2020 referendum, outspending opponents nineteen to one. Despite voters supporting Joe Biden over Donald Trump by twenty-nine points, the effort to restore racial preferences was defeated by fourteen points. The margin of opposition to racial preferences was four points *larger* than it had been in 1996, when the state population was much whiter. Asian American opposition to racial preferences was eight percentage points higher than white opposition.[61]

Likewise, while commissions in California and San Francisco backed large cash reparations for Black residents, the idea did not have much appeal to most voters. In 2021, Pew found that 68 percent of Americans (including majorities of Hispanics and Asians) opposed reparations for the descendants of enslaved people. Savvy politicians, like Rep. James Clyburn (D-SC), focused instead on policies that provided repair by channeling federal aid to economically disadvantaged counties.[62]

Nationally, Americans continued to reject racial preferences, just as they had when I first wrote a book on affirmative action in 1996. Over the intervening quarter century, public opinion had shifted dramatically on a number of issues, perhaps the most prominent being same-sex marriage. At the same time, the demographics of the country changed substantially—from 72 percent to 59 percent non-Hispanic white. Yet throughout this period, public opposition to racial preferences at selective colleges had not budged. Polls taken in the mid-1990s showed that a majority of Americans held this view, and a *Washington Post* poll conducted in October 2022 similarly found that 63 percent of Americans opposed considering race in admissions.[63] These respondents were not coldhearted. The same *Washington Post* poll also found that 64 percent supported additional measures—such as providing a leg up to economically disadvantaged students—to increase racial diversity in colleges.[64]

During the presidencies of Donald Trump and Joe Biden, Americans navigated a turbulent period regarding matters of race. The rise of Trump and white nationalism and the police killing of unarmed Black people initially spawned a healthy reaction and awakening on the part of white people. In some elite circles, however, there was an overreaction that espoused a deeply pessimistic view on race. This development paradoxically elevated race in a manner that had unsettling parallels with right-wing views. During this period, many Americans refused to embrace either extreme and sought a middle ground that restored liberal democratic values. All these discussions raised a question: Could the U.S. Supreme Court put the country back on a healthier path, where individuals were treated not as members of racial groups, but as Americans?

CHAPTER 10

Students for
Fair Admissions in
the High Court

O N JANUARY 24, 2022, THE U.S. SUPREME COURT ANNOUNCED that it would hear the Harvard case and pull the UNC case directly from the district court, bypassing the usual step of going through the Fourth Circuit. It was an interesting move and may have been related to an important difference between the two cases. Harvard, as a private institution, was bound by a statute, the 1964 Civil Rights Act, whereas UNC, as a public institution, was bound by the U.S. Constitution. A Supreme Court ruling in the Harvard case could in theory be overturned by a congressional amendment to the Civil Rights Act. A ruling in the UNC case, by contrast, would require an unhappy Congress and a group of state legislatures to overturn the decision through a constitutional amendment, a much more arduous task than amending a law.

It was a momentous development. The Supreme Court heard fewer than 2 percent of the cases that were appealed to it, and the press immediately recognized the cases could yield blockbuster rulings.[1] Oral arguments were set for late October 2022.

Rebutting Misleading Amicus Briefs
from California and Michigan

Because the Supreme Court now had a 6–3 conservative majority, the higher education establishment was panicked that racial preferences would not survive. And the press, seeing the writing on the wall, became more interested in the question of what might replace racial preferences—and how well those alternatives would work.

The business and military establishment came out again for racial preferences. Sixty major corporations, including Apple, Google, and Starbucks, and thirty-five retired generals filed amicus briefs supporting Harvard's use of racial preferences.[2]

Predictably, elite higher education trotted out its old arguments that alternatives to racial preferences couldn't preserve racial diversity. The University of Michigan and University of California systems claimed in amicus briefs that after racial preferences were banned in their states, they tried economic preferences, percentage plans, and boosts to financial aid, but nothing worked.[3]

Less predictable was that leading news organizations, whose reporters are trained to be skeptical, would accept at face value the universities' claims that the only way to achieve racial diversity was through racial preferences—the path that just happened to be cheapest for them. In August 2022, the *New York Times* ran a major article claiming that despite the investment of "hundreds of millions of dollars," race-neutral strategies to produce racial diversity "have fallen abysmally short."[4] The story was enormously misleading. It was true that universities facing bans on racial preferences often saw *short-term* drops in racial diversity. But once universities implemented race-neutral strategies, they typically were able to restore diversity to robust levels.

Students for Fair Admissions in the High Court

In response to questions from other reporters, who took their cue from the *Times*, I pointed out numerous holes in the amicus briefs filed by lawyers for the California and Michigan university systems. To begin with, while the attorneys' amicus briefs were pleading failure, the college admissions offices had been telling a different story. In 2021, UCLA said it admitted the highest proportion of underrepresented minority students "in over 30 years." UCLA's Hispanic population had long exceeded its representation before the ban on racial preferences. And while UCLA's Black first-year enrollment dropped from 264 in 1995 to 144 in 1998, it had rebounded to more than 250 by 2014. Black representation continued to improve over time. Without employing racial preferences, UCLA achieved a 6 percent Black student representation in 2019, in a state with a high school population that was about 5 percent Black. UCLA's Black share subsequently climbed to 7 percent in 2022, and the university "ended up more racially diverse than it had been when affirmative action was allowed." Nor could the ban on racial preferences be said to have benefited white students. UCLA in 2022 had just a 25 percent white population. Asian students outnumbered white students at UCLA, in a state where there were more than twice as many white students as Asian students in the public schools.[5]

UC Berkeley, likewise, reported in 2020 that it had "the most ethnically diverse freshman admitted class in more than 30 years." The one-percentage-point gap between Berkeley's share of Black students (4 percent) and the statewide 5 percent Black high school population was much smaller than UNC's gap. At Chapel Hill, the use of racial preferences resulted in an 8 percent Black population in a state that is 22 percent Black. And UC Berkeley's white freshman population was just 31 percent in the fall of 2022, compared to 52 percent for Asian Americans.[6]

At the graduate level, UC Davis Medical School—the subject of the original *Bakke* lawsuit—also showed that race-neutral alternatives could be viable. Davis created a race-neutral "adversity scale" that considered a variety of socioeconomic factors and was lauded as a model at the national level. Although the school was highly selective—accepting just 2 percent of applicants—84 percent came from disadvantaged backgrounds, 42 percent were first-generation college graduates, and the entering class was 14 percent Black and 30 percent Hispanic, both of which exceeded the national average for medical schools.[7]

Finally, while the University of Michigan lawyers were complaining about the ban on racial preferences in Michigan's amicus brief, the admissions office said its 2021 incoming class was "among the university's most racially and ethnically diverse classes, with 37% of first-year students identifying as persons of color." And the data in the amicus brief itself found that while Black representation had declined, the overall underrepresented minority population had increased from 12.9 percent (before the ban on racial preferences) to 13.5 percent in 2021. Meanwhile, at the University of Michigan Law School, the class starting in the fall of 2022 had "a record-setting 42 percent people of color." Black students constituted 10.4 percent of the entering class and Hispanic students 11.3 percent—shares that were both *higher* than when racial preferences were employed.[8]

When delving deeper, the stories from California and Michigan proved to be even more encouraging than at first glance. To begin with, their racial diversity numbers were a floor, not a ceiling, because the schools could have done more to boost diversity if they had chosen to do so. Unlike state universities in Texas and Florida, Michigan had no percentage plan to admit top high school students. Unlike Texas A&M or the University of Georgia, Michigan hadn't eliminated legacy preferences. Michigan also provided substantial "merit" aid to wealthy students, thereby diverting funds from need-based aid. As a result, Michigan had only about half as many students eligible for federal Pell Grants as UT Austin. Indeed, Raj Chetty's data found students at Michigan came from families with the *highest* median income of its twenty-seven peer institutions, with a ratio of eighteen wealthy students to every poor student.[9]

Although UC Berkeley and UCLA did a better job than Michigan in pursuing race-neutral strategies, they could have done even more. Most notably, they employed family income and education—but not wealth—as a measure of socioeconomic disadvantage. Since wealth, in addition to income, would more effectively capture economic and racial disadvantage, these institutions could have achieved even greater racial diversity.[10]

Additionally, while critics correctly observed that Berkeley and Michigan had a reduced number of Black students utilizing race-neutral methods compared to before the ban on racial preferences was implemented, the comparison was unjust. For one thing, in Berkeley's case, the Black population in California declined over time (from 7.7 percent in 1980 to 5.5 percent in 2018). Moreover, in 2010, the U.S. Department of Education changed its methodology for categorizing students by race and ethnicity, requiring colleges to report separately students who belonged to two or more racial groups. That had important implications for tracking racial numbers over time. A *Chronicle of Higher Education* article noted that "a drop in the number of black students reported at a university from 2009 to 2010 doesn't *necessarily* mean that there were actually fewer black students." In fact, when the new "mark one or more" races methodology was proposed, civil rights groups raised concerns that it artificially decreased Black and Hispanic representation in government statistics.[11]

Consider the case of the University of Virginia, which was not subject to a voter-imposed ban on racial preferences, and continued to use race as a factor in admissions. In 2008, before students could use the multirace category, UVA enrolled 1,199 African American students. After the change in categories was implemented in 2012, the number of African Americans dropped dramatically by 21.1 percent to 946. However, with the inclusion of the 206 students who identified as African American and another ethnicity in the 2012 data (resulting in a total of 1,152 African American students under the old methodology), the decrease was 3.9 percent. In other words, about 80 percent of the apparent decline in Black enrollment at UVA was due to reporting changes.[12]

In addition, as noted above, it was important to remember that selective universities in states where racial preferences were barred had been fighting for talented underrepresented minority students with one hand tied behind their backs. UC Berkeley, for example, couldn't use racial preferences, but most of its twelve peer institutions could. Given the tilted playing field, it was remarkable that Michigan, Berkeley, and UCLA had achieved as much racial diversity as they did.

Finally, in telling the full story about diversity at universities employing race-neutral strategies, it was crucial to recognize that socioeconomic diversity typically increased at selective colleges employing race-neutral strategies—a point the press often neglected. At the UC schools, the impact of the ban on racial preferences was noticeable, as both UCLA and UC Berkeley abandoned legacy preferences and increased the admissions advantage given to economically disadvantaged students from all ethnic backgrounds. Under this admissions system, UC Berkeley and UCLA consistently had the highest percentage of students receiving federal Pell Grants among the top twenty-five *U.S. News* universities—double the level of many other such institutions.[13]

I spent much of the summer and fall of 2022 talking with reporters and refuting the misinformation that higher education elites were spewing about how they couldn't create diversity in new ways. To me, the most telling line in the UC amicus brief was the assertion that the 1996 ban on race had forced them over the decades to spend "over a half-billion dollars" on race-neutral strategies such as outreach programs.[14] That, I argued, was the biggest reason the higher education establishment was fighting so hard to preserve racial preferences.

Supreme Court Oral Arguments

On October 31, the date of the Supreme Court's oral arguments, I woke up early, eager to finally glean some hints of what the justices thought of the cases that I and others had been working on for almost eight years. As I entered the Supreme Court's august chambers, I felt the competing pulls of my strange involvement in the case. I shyly nodded to friends I saw there from the civil rights community, such as former NAACP Legal Defense and Education Fund attorney Anurima Bhargava and David Hinojosa of the Lawyers' Committee for Civil Rights, as well as Harvard's admissions dean Bill Fitzsimmons. At the same time, I sat in the audience with critics of racial preferences—Edward Blum, Peter Arcidiacono, UCLA Law professor Richard Sander, and former *New York Times* Supreme Court reporter Stuart Taylor Jr.

As the justices filed in, there were familiar faces I'd seen in earlier Supreme Court oral arguments—Thomas, Sotomayor, Alito, Roberts, and Kagan. And there were the new faces—Gorsuch, Kavanaugh, Barrett, and the newest of all, Biden appointee Ketanji Brown Jackson, whom I'd found enormously impressive in her confirmation hearings.

As I settled in for what would be a five-hour oral argument in the Harvard and UNC cases, I wondered, Would this finally be the time when opponents of racial preferences on the Court held firm, or would a Powell, O'Connor, or Kennedy emerge among the conservatives, deferring to elite institutions? What would the justices say about the race-neutral alternatives that Arcidiacono and I developed? Some liberal friends of mine had warned that if conservatives struck down racial preferences, they would go after class-based affirmative action next. Would the justices delve at all into that next-generation issue?

On the first big question—whether a conservative would blink—it quickly became clear that the right-leaning justices were unsympathetic to Harvard and UNC. Justices Thomas and Alito appeared highly critical of racial preferences, as expected. Chief Justice Roberts had famously sided with liberals on occasion, as demonstrated by his refusal to overturn *Roe v. Wade* and his support for the Affordable Care Act. But it became evident that Roberts had little sympathy for the liberal position on racial preferences. As noted in the introduction, probably the most widely cited exchange came when Seth Waxman, representing Harvard, explained that just as being a good oboe player can help a student get in, so can their race. The press ate up the Chief Justice's tart response: "We did not fight a Civil War about oboe players. We did fight a Civil War to eliminate racial discrimination."[15]

The three new conservative justices who had been appointed to the Court after the 2016 *Fisher II* decision did not have much of a public record on racial preferences. But before long, Justices Barrett and Kavanaugh were hammering UNC and Harvard lawyers on the question of when racial preferences should end. Meanwhile, Justice Gorsuch did not seem willing to take Harvard's word that it was doing all it could to achieve racial diversity without racial preferences. He noted that Harvard provided preferences that seemed to work against diversity—a leg up in admissions for "legacies," students on "the squash team," and the offspring of those who might donate to a "museum." For emphasis, he added, "I'm not making it up. It's in the record."[16]

Most of the conservatives seemed to want to stake out the middle ground occupied by the American public, acknowledging the importance and validity of diversity while rejecting racial preferences as the sole means of achieving it. UNC's lawyer, Ryan Park, inadvertently highlighted this third way when he mentioned my testimony. Park noted that even as I testified in favor of race-neutral strategies, I also championed the importance of racial diversity. Park noted that "SFFA's own expert . . . conceded and agreed enthusiastically" that diversity "leads to a deeper and richer learning environment."[17]

Several of the justices focused on Simulation D, which Arcidiacono and I prepared in the Harvard case. Sotomayor was skeptical. She skipped over the fact that Hispanic, Asian, and low-income student admissions increased, and white representation declined under the model, and instead focused on the change in Black shares from 14 percent to 10 percent. SFFA's lawyer, Cameron Norris, was ready, and on three separate occasions noted that I had testified that the lack of access to wealth data from Harvard meant the simulation underestimated the potential for race-neutral strategies to boost Black enrollment.[18]

The liberal justices raised another complaint about Simulation D. Justice Sotomayor pointed out that Simulation D "reduces SAT score averages." Norris responded that the average SAT would move from the ninety-ninth to the ninety-eighth percentile, which would still be superb: "That's not sacrificing academic excellence. That's moving Harvard from Harvard to Dartmouth. Dartmouth is still a great school."[19]

In a moment of levity that also underlined the clubby nature of the justices—all of whom attended elite schools—Kagan quipped about Norris's reference to Dartmouth, "There are those who love it."[20] There was laughter in the courtroom in response to Kagan's reference to a Supreme Court argument made by Daniel Webster in the 1819 case of *Dartmouth v. Woodward*. In a story well-known to Dartmouth alumni, when the state of New Hampshire sought to force Dartmouth to become public, Webster, a Dartmouth graduate, referred to it as "a small college, and yet there are those who love it."[21]

I was pleased that while President Biden's solicitor general, Elizabeth B. Prelogar, frequently criticized race-neutral strategies, she recognized an important truth. "There are nine states," she noted, "that have barred the use of race in college admissions, and many of the universities and colleges in those states have been able still to achieve enrollment of diverse student bodies." She continued, "I think that it's incumbent on every college and university around the nation to study from and learn from those examples."[22]

Among the justices, there appeared to be so much opposition to racial preferences that some members of the Court started exploring the next generation of challenges to race-neutral alternatives in a future case. If programs like class-based affirmative action aimed to produce racial diversity, was that illegal? SFFA attorney Patrick Strawbridge's answer was reassuring. While SFFA would likely oppose "a pure proxy for race" such as a preference for the descendants of slaves, other programs—such as socioeconomic or geographic preferences—would be legal because there would be a "race-neutral justification" for adopting those plans. Strawbridge declared, "If the only reason to do it [adopt a race-neutral strategy] is through the narrow lens of race and there is no other race-neutral justification . . . that's the only scenario where it would create problems."[23] The key was that new plans would need to have an independent rationale. In the case of socioeconomic preferences, for example, a university could appropriately say that it desired economic diversity both for its own sake and as a means to promote racial diversity, because it enriched classroom discussions and students who overcame socioeconomic obstacles were likely to show more promise than their academic records might indicate.

The liberal justices struggled against the onslaught from conservatives. Justice Jackson, for example, kept emphasizing that race was just one of "forty factors" at the University of North Carolina, when evidence from the trial showed that race was by far the biggest preference in admissions—almost four times the size of preferences given to in-state, first-generation college students, for example.[24] And the liberal justices never resolved a central contradiction: even as they said race was a minor factor in admissions, they simultaneously claimed that eliminating racial preferences would have disastrous results on racial diversity levels.

The evening of the oral arguments, Students for Fair Admissions sponsored a dinner at Morton's restaurant on Connecticut Avenue in Washington, D.C. I congratulated Strawbridge on his oral argument in the UNC case and thanked him for making clear that SFFA would not contest valid race-neutral alternatives. And I thanked attorney Cameron Norris for mentioning that the Black shares at Harvard would have been higher if the simulations could use wealth data. The group felt good about how the argument went, though the celebratory mood was tinged by a deep sadness as one of the architects of the litigation, Will Consovoy, was gravely ill with brain cancer. (He would die a few months later at the age of forty-eight.)[25]

Students for Fair Admissions in the High Court

Although people routinely claimed that Edward Blum was just using Asian Americans in the Harvard case to advance the interests of white Americans, many Asian American activists at the dinner expressed enormous gratitude to SFFA lawyers for championing their cause.[26] (Nationally, 63 percent of Asian Americans opposed racial preferences.)[27] At one point, an Indian American gentleman came up to one SFFA attorney and thanked him profusely. "You are our Gandhi," he said. If the praise seemed a bit over the top, it certainly rebutted the fashionable argument in elite circles that SFFA's position in favor of color blindness was just a covert plot to advance white supremacy.

Rising Hopes for Working-Class Students of All Races

During the months-long wait for the Supreme Court's ruling, some groups supportive of racial preferences were pragmatic enough to show a new openness to class-based affirmative action. I was invited to speak at meetings with the Russell Sage Foundation and the Education Department's Office for Civil Rights, and at seminars sponsored by George Washington University, the Aspen Institute, and, in a delicious irony, even Harvard. I also met with admissions officials at Georgetown and Johns Hopkins University who wanted to create a plan B.

During this period, I also wrote an article with the civil rights lawyer John Brittain on ten ways to pursue diversity without racial preferences. And I coauthored another article with Melvin Oliver, former president of Pitzer College, and Peter Dreier of Occidental College about using wealth in admissions instead of race. I tried to reach conservative readers with an article in *National Affairs*, and liberal readers with an article in *Dissent*.[28]

The biggest signal that my ideas were finally being taken seriously came in late March 2023, when the *New York Times* ran a front-page story about my work as a "liberal maverick" fighting for affirmative action based on class rather than race. The tagline read, "For decades, Richard Kahlenberg has pushed for a class-conscious approach to college admissions. He may finally get his wish, but it comes at a personal cost."[29]

I'd spent a lot of time over the previous couple of months with the *Times* reporter Anemona Hartocollis, who I thought did a good job of explaining the paradox: that I was the son of a liberal minister, motivated by the idealism of Robert Kennedy and Martin Luther King Jr., who found himself in the uncomfortable position of working with conservatives like Edward Blum to advance the cause of cross-racial, class-based politics and public policy. I had lost friends along the way, the article explained.

Being the subject of a page 1 profile is a heady experience, but it also could be cringe-inducing. When Hartocollis asked about whether I had received a legacy preference myself, instead of just answering yes, I gave a convoluted and embarrassing response, which she decided to quote in full: "This will sound incredibly insecure or something, but I was gratified that I got into Yale and Princeton, because it made me feel like, OK, it wasn't just legacy, hopefully."

But overall, the article did a nice job of explaining how my views, which were once received respectfully by many liberals, had now become anathema among elites as "universities and politicians and activists have hardened their positions on affirmative action." Times had changed. Back in the day, there had been nothing "maverick" about a liberal supporting affirmative action based on class. For Kennedy, King, Bayard Rustin, Lyndon B. Johnson, and William O. Douglas, the position I advocated was simply that taken by many mainstream liberals. In more recent years, Bill Clinton and Barack Obama had tested the waters around the issue before pulling back. Now advocating class-based affirmative action made me liberalism's maverick, and to some, a "lino, a liberal in name only."[30] I received some hateful emails, including one from a person who accused me of being a "racist Jew." In just two words, the reader had managed to be doubly wrong and expose himself as an anti-Semite to boot.

Students for Fair Admissions in the High Court

On the whole, the reaction was quite positive, and I was touched by several emails from people identifying themselves as coming from working-class backgrounds. A few said they were moved to tears by seeing someone fighting for working people of all races. Also interesting was the response of many rank-and-file *New York Times* readers. A week later, Hartocollis posted an audio version of the article, and in the introduction, she said that she was surprised by the reaction in the comment section and via email. "A lot of people are really intrigued by what he is proposing and a lot of people really support it, and I wasn't particularly expecting that," she said.[31]

As the Supreme Court's decision approached, the pending ruling was front of mind for students across the country, including those in a class I was teaching at the George Washington University's Trachtenberg School of Public Policy on "Civil Rights and Economic Inequality." In the course, we discussed the pros and cons of affirmative action based on race and class. Virtually all the students favored race-based affirmative action, but one came up to me after class to relay a long conversation she had with a good friend of hers, a Black PhD student at Johns Hopkins University named Benvindo "Tye" Chicha. The student told me Chicha felt deeply isolated on campus because affirmative action had not addressed important issues of economic disadvantage. I was curious to learn more, so in late May 2023, Chicha and I had lunch, and he agreed to share his story with me.[32]

Chicha told me he was thrilled when he was awarded a special fellowship in February 2022, designed to support outstanding students from historically Black colleges and universities and minority-serving institutions who wished to pursue PhDs in the sciences at Johns Hopkins University. A graduate of Bowie State University in Maryland, Chicha had always excelled academically and was fascinated by science. Studying cell, molecular, and developmental biology and biophysics at one of the world's most renowned universities was a wonderful opportunity. The scholarship was made possible by a $150 million gift from Bloomberg Philanthropies to address the underrepresentation of minority scholars in science, technology, engineering, and math.

The road to Johns Hopkins had not been easy for Chicha, one of three children of a highly determined mother employed as a social worker and community outreach activist. Though Chicha had some contact with his father, an immigrant from the African nation of Cabo Verde, he was primarily raised by his mother. She valued education, he said. However, after giving birth to her three children between the ages of nineteen and twenty-three, she had to set aside her own education to support her family, and as a result, she was unable to earn a bachelor's degree.

Chicha grew up mostly in three working-class Massachusetts communities: Lowell, Brockton, and Fall River. The family made just enough to stay off public assistance but moved a great deal, sometimes every six months. At various points during Chicha's young life, when money became especially tight, the family had to move in with friends or relatives. "We always had a roof over our heads," he said, "but sometimes it was someone else's roof."

He recalled that living in other people's homes could be uncomfortable at times. On one such occasion, when his family had no other place to live, Chicha and his little brother stayed in their aunt's basement. Chicha joined the track-and-field team during high school so that he could spend as little time at home as possible. Working as a store cashier and cart collector allowed him to save up a few thousand dollars. He liked to carefully count the large stack of cash, because it was the first time in his life he had extra money. It was fun to imagine what he could do with it. For example, he thought about how much pizza he could now afford to buy. He didn't actually use much of the cash. He recalled being "paranoid about spending money because you're worried about the next time you'll need it." But he ultimately decided to use the funds to help his family rent a place of their own.

At one point, the family moved to Easton, a town that was more affluent and heavily white than others in which Chicha had resided.

Chicha faced unique challenges as one of only three Black students in his middle school. He sensed that some white students weren't thrilled that he was excelling academically, and he was picked on and needed to stand up for himself. In one altercation, Chicha got into a fistfight and was unfairly expelled as the aggressor and severely punished.

He attended Brockton High School, where he kept his head down, worked hard, and managed to graduate in the top 4 percent of his class. He impressed his teachers and got a big break in his senior year when two of his physics teachers recommended him for an internship at the Dana-Farber Cancer Institute after graduation. There, Chicha participated in a project doing brain-mapping for safe tumor removal using functional magnetic resonance imaging. "This was *Star Wars* stuff," he recalled, and the experience inspired him to study science further.

Chicha was accepted to Northeastern University in Boston, but the scholarship they offered was limited and would have required him to take out more than $100,000 in student loans. Meanwhile, Chicha was recruited to run track at Bowie State University, a historically Black institution in Prince George's County, Maryland, outside Washington, D.C. Although initially recruited as an athlete, he was offered a full scholarship based on his academic record and subsequently admitted to the honors program.

Given his financial situation, Chicha said he had no real choice but to go to Bowie State. Chicha had never heard of Bowie State and wasn't thrilled to go because the institution, he said, does not have a great reputation and is underresourced. "Bowie is no one's first choice," he lamented. "I hated that I had to go there" purely for financial reasons, he said, "but at the end of the day, the experience is what you make of it."

While Chicha never grew to like Bowie State all that much, he did have some excellent professors who he believes could have taught at more prestigious universities, but were personally committed to helping underserved students. He majored in bioinformatics, a specialty that uses computers to analyze and interpret biological data. He once again excelled academically.

Class Matters

In the fall of 2022, after Chicha had graduated from college, he began his program at Johns Hopkins with nineteen other PhD scholars from minority-serving institutions. He said that he was struck by the affluence of his fellow students, no matter their race. At Hopkins, a world-famous university, "no one had ever heard of Bowie," even though the two institutions were only about thirty miles apart.

On the one hand, Chicha reveled in the wealth of resources and opportunities at Johns Hopkins—the chance to learn from leading scholars through a program with free tuition, health care, and a $40,000 stipend. The Bloomberg-funded Vivien Thomas Scholars Initiative was named after a leading Black researcher who overcame odds in the Jim Crow South to teach pioneering medical techniques to surgeons and scientists at Johns Hopkins. But while Chicha said he was grateful for the special opportunity, he also could feel out of place.

He told me that within his cohort of twenty Black and Hispanic scholars who were part of the Thomas Scholars program at Hopkins, he didn't believe anyone he met shared his economic background. One of the Thomas Scholars, for example, had enough money to purchase a house. In Chicha's experience, having $2,000 or $3,000 was "a lot of money," so the wealth of his fellow Hopkins students seemed unimaginable. Some other Thomas Scholars had parents who were doctors or had PhDs. "They live in a different world," he said. Chicha said he was surrounded by "people who look like me," but their economic station was radically different. "It feels kind of lonely," he said.

The differences sometimes surfaced when he talked to fellow minority students about the challenges he faced growing up. He noticed the reactions were so different from those he received when he recounted the same stories among friends back home. There, stories of struggle were common, and people reacted with a sense of recognition. But at Hopkins, when he talked about the time when he had nowhere to stay and had to move in with his aunt, people would reply, "That's so sad." They reacted with "sympathy more than empathy," he

258

said, showing a sense of pity rather than understanding. He wanted to respond, "That's just life."

On one level, Chicha said he wanted to celebrate the Black wealth he found on campus. America needed more wealthy Black families, and Chicha wouldn't mind becoming wealthy himself one day. And to be sure, he said, the white and Asian students at Hopkins who were not in the Thomas program could be even wealthier. But even among the Thomas Scholars, the experience was "socially isolating." The difference between them and him, he said, is that "if I mess up, I don't know what I'd fall back on."

After speaking with Chicha, I thought more about the decision the Supreme Court would soon be rendering. The simulations in the Harvard case showed that under race-based affirmative action, just 28 percent of the underrepresented minority students came from the bottom *four-fifths* of the socioeconomic distribution of Black and Hispanic students nationally—much less Chicha's truly working-class background. On the other hand, if Harvard adopted the class-based approach, students like Chicha would be much more likely to be part of a cohort of Black students who were socioeconomically diverse—and the same would be true for the white, Asian, and Hispanic students. It was exciting to think about.

The Supreme Court Ruling

In June 2023, while at my mother's summer house in Chautauqua Institution in Upstate New York, I received news of the Supreme Court's decision in the Harvard and UNC cases. CNN had me on standby for reaction, giving me only a few minutes to race through the decision. But from a quick skim, it was clear that racial preferences were coming to an end. By a 6–2 vote in the Harvard case and a 6–3 vote in the UNC case, a convincing majority of justices had declared that elite colleges had violated the Civil Rights Act of 1964 and the Equal Protection Clause of the Fourteenth Amendment. In the words of Chief Justice John Roberts, "Eliminating racial discrimination means eliminating all of it."[33]

Part of me couldn't believe it. I thought, based on the oral arguments, that racial preferences were ending, but stranger things had happened in the past. Some had speculated that two of the Court's conservative justices—Kavanaugh and Barrett—might play the roles Lewis Powell, Sandra Day O'Connor, and Anthony Kennedy had in earlier decisions and surprise observers by supporting Harvard and UNC. Some noted that Kavanaugh had made it a point over the years to hire Black law clerks in substantial numbers, while others noted that Barrett had adopted children who were Black and might be sympathetic to preserving racial preferences. And yet these two justices joined the full opinion without reservation.

I was elated. For universities that cared about racial diversity (virtually all of them), this would mean new types of programs that recognize economic disadvantage. In the thirty years I'd been researching and writing about affirmative action, there had been several moments when I thought the country might shift from racial preferences back to King and Douglas's racially inclusive approach for the disadvantaged students of all races: in 1995, when Clinton floated the idea of shifting to class; in 2003, when it looked like O'Connor might provide the fifth vote to force change in the *Grutter* case; in 2004, when Larry Summers and Tony Marx seemed to be ushering in a new focus on socioeconomic diversity in higher education; in 2008, when Barack Obama said his own daughters didn't deserve a preference, but working-class students did; and in 2016, when it looked like Justice Kennedy would force universities to use alternatives before resorting to race in the *Fisher II* case. On these five separate occasions over three decades, I'd had my hopes raised, only to see them dashed. And now, change was finally coming.

When asked for my reaction on CNN, I said the decision spelled the end of racial preferences, but not the end to all forms of affirmative action. Instead, it would usher in something better—a fairer form of affirmative action that looked at economic disadvantages. In that sense, the decision was a big win for working-class students, I argued. Harvard and UNC had been pushing racial justice on the cheap by recruiting wealthy and upper-middle-class students of all races. Now, to achieve racial diversity, they would have to do the hard work of giving a break to economically disadvantaged students of all races. While my fellow liberals were decrying the decision, I believed the conservative U.S. Supreme Court decisions striking down the use of race in admissions would yield a progressive public policy outcome. At long last, universities would have to face up to long-entrenched issues of class inequality that they had managed to ignore.

After an initial foray of interviews on television, radio, and with print outlets, I had a chance to sit down and read the decision and truly grasp the enormity of its critique of racial preferences. This was a judicial earthquake. While the Supreme Court in the past had been highly deferential to elite institutions—colleges and universities that most of the justices had themselves attended—the ruling saw through the charade the higher education establishment had engaged in for the past four decades.[34] In critiquing Harvard and UNC's rationale for using race as a factor in student admissions, the six-member majority opinion, authored by Chief Justice Roberts, cited four fundamental flaws.

First, the universities' justifications for using race—such as "training future leaders," "better educating its students through diversity," and promoting "cross racial understanding"—while "commendable," were not "sufficiently measurable" to allow courts to scrutinize them in a way that could justify treating students differently based on race. (In the Harvard case, for example, the institution was unable to explain why it was necessary to break the general rule that people shouldn't be treated differently based on race to boost Black enrollment above the 10 percent mark.) Because the interests advanced were "inescapably imponderable," courts could not validate them under the "strict scrutiny standard," which requires a powerful justification anytime the government wants to treat people differently based on their racial identity.

Moving forward, while a college could theoretically come up with a more measurable standard that was better than those Harvard and UNC posited, this was highly unlikely. The dissenting opinion, written by Justice Sotomayor, recognized that the majority's requirement of more measurable standards would be fatal to racial affirmative action programs in practice. The majority had set a trap, the dissent said, "designed to ensure all race-conscious plans fail." If a university failed to explain why it needed more than a 10 percent Black representation to achieve "cross racial understanding," for example, its goal was "imponderable." But if it tried to make the case that it needed 14 percent Black representation to achieve its goals, it would be accused of creating a racial quota, which the Supreme Court has long found to be unconstitutional.[35]

Second, the justices in the majority said that in the selective college admissions context, the positive use of race for some students necessarily meant a "negative" use of race for others (nonbeneficiaries). While a racial preference policy might be aimed at helping Black and Hispanic students, that inevitably meant it was hurting white and Asian students. "College admissions are zero-sum," the majority opinion observed. "A benefit provided to some applicants but not others necessarily advantages the former group at the expense of the latter."[36] The old standard under *Grutter* had been that white and Asian students could be made to bear some burden, but not an "undue burden." In the context of employment, an undue burden would include firings based on race. Now, it appeared that the new standard said that white and Asian students could not be forced to bear any burden whatsoever.[37] Once again, this objection seemed almost impossible for a university to overcome.

Third, the majority suggested, there was no "logical end point" to Harvard and UNC's use of race in admissions, in violation of the Equal Protection Clause and Title VI of the Civil Rights Act. The Supreme Court has always required that racial preferences be temporary in nature, as they violate the general rule that institutions cannot discriminate based on race. The majority rejected the dissent's contention that racial preferences should remain until racial equality has been achieved in the larger society. Complete equality of racial group results in different fields of endeavor is a condition few societies in human history had ever achieved, so such a requirement would likely mean racial preferences would be perpetuated far into the future.[38]

Fourth, the majority said Harvard and UNC's programs engaged in impermissible stereotyping about the meaning of a student's race. The Court said that "Harvard's admissions process rests on the pernicious stereotype that 'a black student can usually bring something that a white student cannot offer.'" UNC, the Court said, improperly "argues that race itself 'says [something] about who you are.'"[39]

By leveling these four objections, the Court gutted the *Grutter* ruling, which had held that the educational benefits of diversity provided a compelling rationale for using race. Although *Grutter* was not expressly overruled, Justice Thomas acknowledged that "*Grutter* is, for all intents and purposes, overruled."[40] The dissenting justices agreed, writing, "Overruling decades of precedent," the *Students for Fair Admissions* decision "strikes at the heart of *Bakke*, *Grutter*, and *Fisher* by holding that racial diversity is an 'inescapably imponderable' objective" and "overrides its longstanding holding that diversity in higher education is a compelling value."[41] The fact that Harvard's diversity program, which was lauded by Justice Lewis Powell in the 1978 *Bakke* decision as a national model, was struck down in the 2023 *Students for Fair Admissions* case underlined the dramatic change in the law.[42]

At the end of the opinion, the Supreme Court said that while it had struck down the use of racial preferences, universities could still consider a student essay that discussed how race shaped an applicant's life. The majority opinion provided that "nothing in this opinion should be construed as prohibiting universities from considering an applicant's discussion of how race affected his or her life, be it through discrimination, inspiration, or otherwise."[43] The Court then provided two examples: a university might provide "a benefit to a student who overcame racial discrimination," showing "courage or determination"; or "a benefit to a student whose heritage or culture motivated him to assume a leadership role or attain a particular goal," showing a "unique ability to contribute to the university."[44] Because a student of any race could conceivably make these arguments, this consideration could be considered "race-neutral."[45] However, as discussed in Chapter 11, the Supreme Court quickly put sharp parameters around the essay loophole, and both the majority and the dissent warned universities not to make too much of this provision.

There was one other big issue I was watching out for in the Court's decision. There had always been a small chance that the *Students for Fair Admissions* opinion would go too far, raising questions about the legality of the race-neutral alternatives I'd been fighting for. Some on the extreme right argued that the Court should flip from considering diversity as a "compelling" interest to regarding it as an impermissible goal. If that were true, then race-neutral alternatives like socioeconomic preferences could themselves be struck down as "proxy discrimination," given that part of their purpose was to enhance racial diversity.[46]

I was relieved that the Court in *Students for Fair Admissions* did nothing of the kind. While it invalidated racial preferences as a *means*, it did nothing to negate the *goal* of racial diversity. As discussed further in Chapter 11, six of the justices—including some of the most conservative—explicitly called out ways universities might consider socioeconomic disadvantage and other race-neutral strategies to produce racial diversity. In a concurring opinion, Justice Gorsuch, for example, noted my expert testimony that "Harvard could nearly replicate the current racial composition of its student body without resorting to race-based practices if it: (1) provided socioeconomically disadvantaged applicants just half of the tip it gives recruited athletes; and (2) eliminated tips for the children of donors, alumni and faculty."[47] Simply put, while racial preferences were struck down by the Court, race-neutral alternatives were given a green light.

Stepping back, I thought about why, after so many years of narrowly supporting racial preferences, the Supreme Court in 2023 reversed course. The most obvious answer was that the current justices were more conservative than their predecessors; this was a Court that had overturned *Roe v. Wade*, after all. But I think there were two additional factors. First, Supreme Court justices, as human beings, are inevitably influenced not only by the facts of a case and their judicial philosophy, but also by the cultural developments in the country at large. And it was certainly possible that some conservative justices wanted to stop what they saw as perhaps well-intentioned but deeply misguided trends around race: the decision of unions to use race in layoff decisions; the practice of teaching young children that being on time was a manifestation of white supremacy; and government programs that allocated COVID relief funds by race. In short, the justices may have been pushing back out of a fear that wacky academic ideas—like Ibram Kendi's belief that "the only remedy to past discrimination is present discrimination"—were seeping into the American mainstream.

Second, I think the Supreme Court was emboldened by the egregious facts in the litigation before them, particularly in the Harvard case. While Harvard argued that it could only achieve racial diversity through significant racial preferences, its history of providing big preferences to mostly wealthy, white students through the Z-list, legacy preferences, faculty preferences, and a special dean's interest list—coupled with the relatively small boosts provided to economically disadvantaged students—contradicted Harvard's claims. Moreover, the evidence that Harvard's use of a personal rating that routinely denigrated Asian Americans suggested the model that Justice Lewis Powell had held up in the *Bakke* case—"the Harvard Plan"—was in fact deeply corrupt.

Class Matters

The Supreme Court ruling in *Students for Fair Admissions* was deeply gratifying for me. Despite the misinformation from the higher education establishment's amicus briefs, the evidence was overwhelming that race-neutral alternatives could work if universities were willing to invest in them. After decades of the establishment winning—defeating efforts to move toward class-based affirmative action in *Bakke*, *Grutter*, and *Fisher II*—the Supreme Court had at long last struck down racial preferences that tended to benefit upper-middle-class students of color and supported a larger infrastructure of preferences that helped wealthy white students. The path was now cleared for universities to welcome more people like Tye Chicha, enormously talented working-class students who had mostly been shut out of elite higher education.

CHAPTER 11

What Next?

From Diversity to Adversity

THE REACTIONS TO THE SUPREME COURT DECISION WERE FAS-
cinating to watch and fell into three buckets. I was sad to see the
far left call for outright defiance of the court, or for sneaking racial
preferences back into admissions through the personal essay loophole,
despite the Court's stern warning not to do so. I was even more disturbed that some on the far right urged the Supreme Court to go much
further than it had in the *Students for Fair Admissions* decision. They
claimed that class-based affirmative action was just as bad as racial preferences because it was a form of proxy discrimination. However, I was
pleased to note that most observers—from President Biden to prominent university leaders—backed a third path: reinventing admissions
around overcoming adversity. The U.S. Supreme Court's decision in
Students for Fair Admissions had created a crisis—and, in the words of
National Association for College Admissions Counseling CEO Angel
Perez, higher education shouldn't "let a crisis go to waste." Colorado
College president Song Richardson argued, "Affirmative action made

us complacent. Now that tool is gone, and I'm optimistic that all of us can work together to fix our broken system." Most signs pointed to a revival of the King, Kennedy, and Douglas path of focusing on supporting the economically disadvantaged of all races.[1]

The Far-Left Reaction: Defy the Supreme Court or Cheat Through the Personal Essay Loophole

One of the most troubling reactions came from my friend Richard Rothstein, author of a well-regarded book on housing segregation called *The Color of Law*. Rothstein and I had known each other since the late 1990s, when I edited a volume on educational inequality to which he contributed. I was astonished when Rothstein, writing in *The Atlantic*, flatly declared that in the face of a negative ruling, universities "should continue to implement race-specific affirmative action, in defiance of the Supreme Court."[2]

It was possible that some rogue university administrators, in a fit of self-righteousness, would take up Rothstein's call for lawlessness. It would not be the first time. In 2023, for example, an investigation at the University of Washington showed that the psychology department had defied a state ban on using race by hiring a Black professor, who was ranked third, over a white professor who was ranked first. The administrators then sought to cover their tracks. One email read, "I advise deleting the statement below as it shows that URM [underrepresented minority] applicants were singled out and evaluated differently than non-URM applications (which is not allowed . . .)."[3]

Although university leaders have not publicly said they will simply break the law, some admissions officers may, in their good-faith enthusiasm for sustaining racial diversity, be tempted to stretch the *Students for Fair Admissions* ruling's personal essay loophole in a way that the Court has forbidden. One Cornell Law professor raised a concern that universities such as Harvard would take the essay loophole and "drive an affirmative action truck right through it."[4]

What Next?

Many selective institutions, including Harvard, the University of Maryland, Princeton, Northwestern, and Rice, began requiring that applicants answer new essay questions that seemed designed to elicit stories about race. Harvard, for example, began requiring that all applicants answer the following prompt: "Harvard has long recognized the importance of enrolling a diverse student body. How will the life experiences that shape who you are today enable you to contribute to Harvard?"[5]

But going forward, universities need to be careful in how they use the essay—as all nine justices warned in the *Students for Fair Admissions* decision. The Supreme Court had little choice but to allow students to discuss their race in essays and to allow admissions officers to read them. As one critic noted, it would have been untenable to require that an essay detailing how a student had overcome racial discrimination be "heavily redacted because the college must censor all references to an applicant's race." Even SFFA did not call for this type of censorship in its arguments before the Court.[6] At the same time, all the justices clearly cautioned that universities should not make too much of the essay loophole.

In the Supreme Court oral argument in the UNC case, Chief Justice Roberts had raised a concern about colleges abusing the use of student essays to reengineer racial preferences. He asked what "if all of a sudden the number of essays that talk about the experience of being an African American in society rises dramatically . . . ?" In the majority opinion, the justices raised an important caution sign for colleges. Immediately after noting the ability to consider essays, the majority said, "Universities may not simply establish through application essays or other means the regime we hold unlawful today. . . . What cannot be done directly cannot be done indirectly." The majority opinion made clear that educational institutions should focus on "challenges bested, skills built, or lessons learned" by students, not "the color of their skin."[7]

The dissent, likewise, minimized the importance of universities considering a student's discussion of race in their essay. The three dissenting justices said that the Court's decision "rolls back decades of precedent and momentous progress," arguing that the student essay provision in the decision was "an attempt to put lipstick on a pig." The dissenters further suggested that the essay exception was "a false promise" used by the majority to "save face and appear attuned to reality. No one is fooled." The dissent concluded—the Court's essay "loophole" notwithstanding—that "the devastating impact of this decision cannot be overstated." Justice Jackson charged the majority with employing "let-them-eat-cake obliviousness," saying that the decision's use of the Equal Protection Clause to "obstruct our collective progress . . . is truly a tragedy for all of us."[8] These are not the words of justices who think that universities can easily exploit the use of essays to accomplish significant levels of racial diversity.

If universities are allowed to consider student essays about race, but can't push it too far, where is the line dividing permissible and impermissible uses of the essay? The key principle is that universities should consider a characteristic they value in essays—such as grit—equally across racial lines. If they admire students who have overcome racial discrimination because it shows resilience, they should also admire students of all races who surmount economic hurdles, given evidence that socioeconomic disadvantages present academic obstacles that are seven times greater than racial ones in today's world.[9] If universities are attracted to a Black or Hispanic student who writes an essay about how they came to appreciate their heritage by learning cooking from their grandmother, they should admire that same quality in a Greek or Korean student. If, on the other hand, universities selectively apply their consideration of qualities found in personal essays to applicants from an underrepresented racial group, they are applying covert racial preferences.[10]

The Far-Right Reaction: Strike Down Class-Based Affirmative Action as Proxy Discrimination

If the far left has been thinking of ways to defy the Supreme Court's ruling or exploit the essay loophole to the point of cheating, the far right has also been pushing the envelope in the opposite direction. Whereas those on the right had long said they preferred economic preferences over racial ones, now some have begun attacking socioeconomic affirmative action and percentage plans as a form of "proxy" discrimination.[11] Under this extreme theory, if a university were to eliminate legacy preferences with even the partial intention of boosting racial diversity, the racial motive would render the move illegal.[12] I was struck that the right was making the same mistake Justice Ginsburg had made in her *Fisher I* dissent back in 2013, when she suggested there was no real difference between the Texas Top 10 Percent plan and the use of racial preferences, as both aimed to enhance racial diversity. Both Ginsburg then and the right wing now missed enormous distinctions: that percentage plans for students with the best grades in a high school impose no stigma; that percentage plans fostered exciting cross-racial political alliances, not hostility; and that they tended to help the most disadvantaged students who had overcome odds.[13]

I thought that the right-wing attack was far-fetched. In general, the courts treat policies that classify people by race and those that classify them by economic status very differently. They have long held that distinctions based on income are broadly permissible. For example, the progressive income tax, which imposes a higher marginal tax rate on the wealthy, presents no constitutional problem, while a tax system that imposed a higher marginal rate on white people than Black people would likely be struck down. Whereas the use of race by the government is subject to "strict scrutiny," requiring the government to have a "compelling" justification and use means that are "narrowly tailored" to reach the goals, the government's use of economic status need meet only the more relaxed "rational basis" test, which requires that policymakers have a "legitimate" interest and employ means that have a rational connection to the goals.[14]

But some smart people I respect a great deal, like Harvard Law School's Randall Kennedy, warned that the Supreme Court might go after class-based affirmative action. A few weeks before the Court decision, he wrote a *New York Times* op-ed warning against those who "declare confidently that race-neutral strategies for facilitating racial diversity will be in the clear. They insist that wealth-based, or income-based, or ZIP-code-based affirmative action will be immune to judicial attack because such markers are not expressly racial, though if tweaked carefully they can dependably yield substantial numbers of Black beneficiaries. That view is naïve."[15]

But when the *Students for Fair Admissions* decision was handed down, there was nothing in the opinion to hint that the Court was considering outlawing race-neutral strategies. To the contrary, the Supreme Court appeared to leave the door open to universities employing a variety of "race-neutral" alternatives to promote the goal of racial diversity in admissions. While the Supreme Court appeared to reject the idea that diversity provides a *compelling* justification for using race in admissions, it said nothing to suggest that pursuing the educational benefit of racial diversity through race-neutral means was an *impermissible* goal. To the contrary, the majority opinion called the larger goals Harvard and UNC sought to achieve, such as promoting cross-racial understanding, "commendable" and "worthy."[16]

Moreover, the majority opinion, the dissents, and various concurring opinions all gave a thumbs-up to race-neutral alternatives like the use of socioeconomic status and geography. The majority opinion, for example, noted that considering geography is perfectly legal. Chief Justice Roberts wrote, "The entire point of the Equal Protection Clause is that treating someone differently because of their skin color is *not* like treating them differently because they are from a city or from a suburb."[17] In addition, six members of the court—Justices Thomas, Gorsuch, and Kavanaugh in concurring opinions, and Justices Sotomayor, Kagan, and Jackson in the dissent—discussed and endorsed other race-neutral admissions policies.[18]

It was not long before the Supreme Court had a chance to weigh in on the arguments about "proxy" discrimination. In *Coalition for TJ*

What Next?

v. Fairfax County School Board (2023), the Pacific Legal Foundation, a conservative group, challenged the use of geographic and socioeconomic considerations (but not race) in admissions to Thomas Jefferson High School (TJ), a highly selective magnet school located in northern Virginia. TJ drew primarily from Fairfax County, whose public schools were 37 percent white, 27 percent Hispanic, 20 percent Asian, 10 percent Black, and 30 percent low-income. But for years the proportion of Black, Hispanic, and low-income students remained tiny.[19]

In response, TJ adopted a race-neutral diversity plan. Students in the top 1.5 percent by grade point average in each middle school gained admission; for the remaining seats, the plan provided a boost for talented, economically disadvantaged students. Diversity increased, as hoped, compared to the prior system that relied solely on traditional criteria such as grades and test scores. The proportion of Black students accepted under the new plan rose from 1 percent to 7 percent, Hispanic students increased from 3 percent to 11 percent, and disadvantaged students increased from 1 percent to 25 percent. White students saw a modest increase from 18 percent to 22 percent, and Asian representation declined from 73 percent to 54 percent.[20]

A conservative federal district court judge in Virginia struck down the plan as discriminatory, citing the decline in Asian American student representation, which struck me as bizarre, as if any deviation from a quota of 73 percent were somehow problematic. Fortunately, the Fourth Circuit reversed, noting that conservative justices have been advocating that educational institutions employ *precisely* the type of race-neutral factors Thomas Jefferson High School did, instead of relying on race.[21]

I did not think the Court would have the appetite to take the case, but people whom I respect disagreed. For example, the *New York Times* Supreme Court reporter Adam Liptak wrote, "It is a decent bet that the Supreme Court will agree to hear an appeal."[22] I was delighted in February 2024 when the Court announced it would let stand the Fourth

Circuit decision in support of race-neutral alternatives. Given all the past statements from even the most conservative justices, I hoped for a unanimous decision not to hear the case. But Justice Alito wrote a fiery dissent, joined by Justice Thomas. To my mind, it represented a clear reversal of their past endorsements of the Texas Top 10 Percent plan and socioeconomic preferences.

But my frustration was outweighed by the more important point that seven justices—including Roberts, Gorsuch, Kavanaugh, and Barrett—had declined to join Alito's dissent. Although the Court had not ruled on the merits, Alito's vigorous dissent suggested the decision to bypass the case was significant. The ruling in *Students for Fair Admissions*, coupled with its decision not to hear the Thomas Jefferson case, appeared to align the Court precisely with the American public's position: in opposition to racial preferences, but supportive of using race-neutral means to produce racial diversity.[23]

The use of race-neutral alternatives not only appears to provide a legally viable path, but could also provide an affirmative shield for universities in fending off litigation. If a university were to achieve racial diversity *without* adopting race-neutral strategies, it might be suspected of cheating and using the personal essay loophole in ways not intended by the Supreme Court. By announcing the adoption of alternatives and demonstrating a rise in socioeconomic diversity, a university could provide evidence that its racial diversity was achieved legitimately. A university with good racial diversity numbers without any new race-neutral programs, by contrast, could be placing a litigation target on its back.

Announcing new, race-neutral alternative programs could also signal to underrepresented minority students that the university is serious about diversity and willing to pay for it. This inclusive message to students could result in increased applications from talented socioeconomically disadvantaged students, including underrepresented minorities.

What Next?

The Mainstream Reaction: Begin Rewarding Students Overcoming Adversity

While the far left was calling for defiance of the Supreme Court and the far right was seeking to challenge authentic race-neutral strategies, many university leaders, as well as the president of the United States, took a better approach. In the immediate aftermath of the Supreme Court's *Students for Fair Admissions* decision, President Joe Biden said he disagreed with the ruling, but he didn't spend much time denouncing it. Unlike the Supreme Court's unpopular decision in *Dobbs v. Jackson Women's Health Organization* overturning *Roe v. Wade* a year earlier, Gallup found that a whopping 68 percent of Americans *supported* the Supreme Court's ruling in *Students for Fair Admissions*. About 52 percent of Black Americans also supported the decision, including 62 percent of young Black people (between the ages of eighteen and thirty-nine). In another poll, 58 percent of Democrats supported the Supreme Court striking down racial preferences.[24]

In response to the decision, Biden advocated what he called "a new standard where colleges take into account the adversity a student has overcome," whether the student is from Appalachia or Atlanta.[25] He held a summit of college leaders and issued a sixty-six-page report outlining this idea.[26] Biden was the first Democratic president in decades to have the political freedom to advance an adversity approach. Bill Clinton and Barack Obama had made noises about shifting the basis of affirmative action from race to class, but they were unable to achieve this due to interest group politics. Now, because the courts had forced the issue, Biden was able to revive the long-buried adversity approach outlined by William O. Douglas in the courts and broadly embraced by Robert Kennedy and Martin Luther King Jr. in politics.

Transitioning from race to class preferences—from an emphasis on diversity to overcoming adversity—was a natural for Biden. When he became president, Biden had placed small statues of King and RFK in the Oval Office. Early in his career, he had fully recognized that racial preferences could be highly divisive. However, as the Democratic Party leadership shifted on that issue, he had gone along.[27] The Court decision ushering in the post-racial-preference era had given Biden a unique chance to move to more favorable political terrain. For the previous half century, Democrats had been on the defensive about racial preferences. They believed they had to support a deeply unpopular policy because Black leaders (though not necessarily Black rank-and-file voters) passionately supported the policy.[28]

As the argument shifted to whether universities should embrace class-based affirmative action or do nothing, it would be Republicans who were on the defensive. A GOP that gleefully exploited the unpopularity of racial preferences for its own political gain would now be torn between the far right, which wanted to challenge class-based preferences, and the general public, which had long favored economic affirmative action. Democrats had been handed an opportunity to create something better—an affirmative action policy that reminded working people of what they have in common, not what divides them.[29]

Would universities actually adopt these programs? Some were strongly urging them to. In the aftermath of the decision, David Brooks of the *New York Times* applauded the effort "to devise a system where a kid growing up in West Virginia or a poor area of New Orleans has the ability to compete with a kid who grew up in Beverly Hills or Santa Monica or Manhattan. And so [Richard Kahlenberg has] built models of how to do this. These are models that schools like Harvard or the University of North Carolina can use." Brooks noted, "He's found that if you take into account things like 'What neighborhood did you grow up in?' 'How much family wealth do you have?' you get a class with the same level or even more racial diversity by using the Kahlenberg system than under the current system. But you also get many, many, many more first-generation students whose parents didn't go to college at all."[30]

Others were not so sure that it would happen. In September 2023, a *Politico* reporter wrote, "Perhaps the day is coming when Rick Kahlenberg's dream comes true, where colleges get rid of legacies and dean's lists for rich donor parents and instead give a large admission bump to kids from poor families. But it's not coming any time soon."[31] I was struck by the reporter's certitude.

I always thought, based on the experience of states like California, Texas, and Florida, that universities would not simply give up on racial diversity and would instead adopt new programs. But I couldn't be sure, so I was elated when, soon after the *Students for Fair Admissions* decision, colleges began announcing a host of new strategies that grew into a steady stream.

To begin with, many colleges declared that they were doing away with practices that tended to benefit white and wealthy students at the expense of low-income and minority students. Numerous schools announced they were ending legacy preferences, including Wesleyan, Occidental, Carleton, the University of Minnesota, and Virginia Tech.[32] (The president of Wesleyan called the practice "obscene.")[33] An analysis by one think tank found that in the months following the oral arguments in *Students for Fair Admissions*, several other prominent institutions abandoned legacy preferences, including American University, Boston University, Carnegie Mellon, Davidson, Kenyon, New York University, University of Maryland, and University of Michigan.[34]

Although some Ivy League institutions were staying quiet about whether they would eliminate legacy preferences, pressure was mounting. Former Harvard president Larry Summers jettisoned his prior support for legacy preferences and said they should now be eliminated, along with preferences for aristocratic sports.[35] Former Harvard president Derek Bok went further and called for eliminating legacy preferences, faculty child preferences, donor preferences, and athletic preferences. Bok had done nothing to eliminate these policies during his more than twenty years as Harvard's president. What had changed? He was candid: universities could no longer get away with it. The efforts to employ preferences for wealthy applicants "in hopes these practices will not be noticed have not succeeded. The admissions policies of leading universities have been clearly exposed to public view through lawsuits over racial preferences." The jig was up, he noted, and continuing to employ these preferences would only invite government action (an issue discussed further below).[36]

Early admissions policies also came under attack. After the Supreme Court decision, Virginia Tech ended its early decision program.[37] And in what was called an "elegant" twist, Wake Forest decided to allow only first-generation college students to apply early action.[38]

And, in timing that seemed connected to the Court's then-pending ruling in *Students for Fair Admissions*, a number of elite graduate programs ended their cooperation with the *U.S. News & World Report* ranking system. The arguments cited for ceasing to participate with *U.S. News*—including the complaint that the rankings penalize institutions that admit low-income students—had been true for decades, but never previously prompted action.[39] The announcements preceding the *Students for Fair Admissions* decision suggested that some universities may have been planning to admit more working-class students as a race-neutral alternative to racial affirmative action, but did not want to lose their competitive edge if other institutions did not follow suit.

Other university practices that tended to favor wealthy white students were eliminated. For example, Lafayette College announced that it would reduce the number of extracurricular activities admissions counselors would consider. College president Nicole Hurd said that amassing a long list was particularly burdensome for low-income students who may need to care for family members or work multiple jobs.[40]

In addition to eliminating detrimental practices, a number of universities adopted new race-neutral strategies. About a week after the Court's ruling, UNC announced that it would increase its financial aid budget substantially, providing free tuition to every North Carolina undergraduate coming from families making less than $80,000 a year (in a state where the median household income is roughly $61,000).[41] This was a remarkable development. In the trial, a UNC official had testified that "the university faces really serious financial challenges and those financial challenges make it hard for us to expand financial aid at will."[42] Once racial preferences were declared illegal, however, resources became available. Around the time of the Supreme Court's decision, Duke University also announced that incoming students from North and South Carolina (two states with large Black populations) would be offered free tuition, provided their families made less than $150,000 a year.[43] Stanford, UVA, Dartmouth, Princeton, and Vanderbilt also all significantly expanded financial aid, leading one reporter to ask, "Is financial aid the new affirmative action?"[44] The improved financial aid policies appeared to result in a rise in the number of applicants.[45]

Others announced efforts to boost diversity in new ways. For instance, the University of Virginia unveiled a new plan to enhance recruitment at forty high schools that had historically sent few applicants.[46]

Dartmouth reinstated its requirement that students submit their SAT scores to better identify strivers who had overcome odds. While some refer to the SAT as a "wealth test," meaning it really just measures how rich students' families are, researchers have found that all the other criteria (such as essays, recommendations, and extracurricular activities) are probably "even more" related to privilege. Because grades are inflated, admissions officers may be unwilling to take a risk on low-income students without knowing their SAT scores.[47] Dartmouth researchers found that test-optional programs had backfired. There were "hundreds of less-advantaged applicants with scores in the 1400 range who should be submitting scores to identify themselves to Admissions, but do not under test-optional policies." These students would have "twice the probability of admissions of more advantaged students," because Dartmouth was assessing SAT scores in the context of obstacles overcome. The researchers found that "students with standardized test scores at or above the 75th percentile of test-takers from their respective high schools are well prepared to succeed" at Dartmouth. Yale, Harvard, and Caltech soon reinstated SAT scores, citing the same reasoning.[48]

Percentage plan approaches, modeled after Texas's Top 10 Percent plan, also became more popular, including in deeply conservative red states where supporters of racial preferences had feared universities would give up on racial diversity. About a month after the Supreme Court ruling, the University of South Carolina announced a plan to admit the top 10 percent of students with the best grades from every high school throughout the state.[49] A month later, the University of Tennessee adopted a top 10 percent plan for its flagship Knoxville campus.[50] In New York, Governor Kathy Hochul also proposed a top 10 percent plan for the State University of New York and City University of New York systems, and the Wisconsin legislature passed a top 5 percent plan for the University of Wisconsin at Madison.[51] To complete the ideological span, the chair of the Congressional Progressive Caucus, Rep. Pramila Jayapal (D-WA), also endorsed the percentage plan approach.[52]

In response to the Supreme Court's decision, some four-year institutions adopted a new program known as "direct admissions." In 2023, seventy schools in twenty-eight states agreed to participate in a program sponsored by the Common Application for high-achieving, first-generation college, and low-income students. Students above a certain academic threshold who are socioeconomically disadvantaged and fill out basic information on the Common App are automatically admitted, without applying, to such institutions as the New School in New York City and George Mason in northern Virginia.[53]

Meanwhile, in September 2023, Yale University, in settling a lawsuit with Students for Fair Admissions, agreed not only that it would curtail its use of race in admissions in several ways but also announced that it was launching a number of new race-neutral strategies. Yale said it would begin using data from the Opportunity Atlas, which provides a measure of economic mobility in every census tract in America, as part of its admissions process. Yale also hired two new admissions officers to work with college-access organizations to increase recruitment of disadvantaged students. Yale's dean of undergraduate admissions and financial aid said some of the new initiatives had been under consideration for years, but "now we are extremely motivated."[54] Harvard's dean of admissions and financial aid William Fitzsimmons announced that in light of the Supreme Court decision, "we are expanding our use of tools that help readers [of applications] identify financial and educational challenges some applicants face" and "expanding our recruitment efforts"— two steps SFFA and I had urged Harvard to take.[55]

Princeton University announced that "in the changed legal environment, the University's greatest opportunity to attract diverse talent pertains to socioeconomic diversity." It committed to increasing the proportion of students receiving financial aid to at least 70 percent, increasing its Pell percentage to at least 22 percent, and boosting the number of students transferring from community colleges.[56]

Others doubled down on the community college approach. Occidental College, for example, announced it would "deepen its relationships with community colleges to attract more transfer students."[57] And in the fall of 2023, following the *Students for Fair Admissions* decision, the National Student Clearinghouse found that "highly selective institutions" increased their enrollment of community college transfer students by 13.3 percent from low-income neighborhoods and 20.4 percent from middle-income neighborhoods.[58]

I also noticed a substantial change in tone from higher education about the viability of race-neutral strategies to produce diversity. Right before the decision, I appeared at the Aspen Institute with an official from the University of Michigan who said race-neutral efforts had been a disaster. But the evening of the Supreme Court decision, I was on *PBS NewsHour* with University of Michigan president Santa Ono, whose stance was very different. He said that while the university had suffered losses in racial diversity because of the ban on racial preferences, "we're really making significant progress now" and have "started to increase Black and Latino and Native American enrollment recently."[59] Likewise, prior to the Court's decision the Biden administration and institutions like the University of California argued in amicus briefs that race-neutral alternatives could not work. However, by September 2023, the chancellor of UCLA conceded that the university had more racial diversity after the ban on racial preferences took effect, and U.S. education secretary Miguel Cardona pointed to UCLA as evidence that "colleges can achieve diversity without affirmative action."[60]

Preliminary Admissions Results After the Supreme Court's Ruling

In the fall of 2024, the results of the first admitted classes of selective colleges were announced. During the litigation, some were predicting disaster if racial preferences were outlawed. Yale Law's Justin Driver, writing in the *New York Times*, said that "a decision banning affirmative action would be catastrophic for the presence of marginalized racial groups on the nation's leading campuses."[61] David Card predicted Black shares at Harvard would drop from 14 percent to 6 percent.[62] Likewise, a brief filed by about thirty liberal arts colleges cited research predicting that without racial preferences, Black student admissions would drop to 2.1 percent at selective colleges, a return to "early 1960s levels."[63] The Supreme Court dissenters had similarly claimed the *Students for Fair Admissions* decision would have a "devastating impact."[64]

I was skeptical of these dire predictions because universities had a massive financial incentive to exaggerate the effect of a racial preference ban in an attempt to persuade the justices to maintain the status quo. And, sure enough, when the results were released, I was very pleased that most (though not all) selective colleges had in fact found new ways to create racial diversity.

At Harvard, the share of Black students did not decline to 6 percent or 2 percent. Instead, the figure reported was 14 percent, a modest decrease from the previous year.[65] Hispanic representation actually grew from 14 percent to 16 percent, and Asian representation held steady at 37 percent.[66]

At UNC, the modeling suggested that if the college ended racial preferences without adding a socioeconomic boost, Black shares in the admitted class of 2019 would fall from 9 percent to 5 percent and Hispanic representation from 7 percent to 4 percent.[67] In fact, when the results were released, UNC showed 8 percent Black enrollment (down from 10.5 percent the previous year), and Hispanic enrollment held fairly steady at 10 percent (down slightly from 11 percent the previous year).[68]

Harvard and UNC appeared to do better on racial diversity than supporters of racial preferences predicted in some measure because both institutions adopted at least parts of the playbook on race-neutral alternatives that I advocated during the litigation. Around the time Students for Fair Admission filed the suit against Harvard, only 7 percent of Harvard's class was made up of first-generation college students; by 2024, that share had essentially tripled to 21 percent.[69] Likewise, UNC's newfound ability after the Supreme Court ruling to greatly expand financial aid may have had a positive impact on the college's ability to forestall large drops in racial diversity.

Having said that, Harvard and UNC could have done even better promoting racial diversity if they had enacted the full menu of options that I laid out in my expert reports. Whereas a number of top colleges jettisoned legacy preferences in the wake of the Supreme Court's affirmative action decision, for example, Harvard stubbornly clung to them. And, unlike flagship colleges in California, Florida, Texas, South Carolina, Tennessee, and Wisconsin, UNC refused to adopt a high school percentage plan. That may help explain why UNC's first-generation college shares have not budged since the litigation.[70]

How did other selective colleges do? As the numbers began to roll out, it became clear that many of them had maintained high levels of racial diversity despite the Supreme Court's ban on racial preferences. Princeton, Dartmouth, the University of Pennsylvania, the University of Virginia, and Emory all announced they had succeeded in keeping racial diversity at roughly the *same level* as they had achieved in the past employing racial preferences. At Yale, Black and Hispanic representation stayed even at 14 percent and 19 percent respectively.[71] Duke actually saw an *increase* in Black enrollment from 12 percent to 13 percent and in Hispanic enrollment from 13 percent to 14 percent.[72] Williams, Bowdoin, Bates, and Caltech all increased Black enrollment as well.[73]

To be sure, some selective institutions saw significant drops in Black enrollment—a development that tended to garner much more public attention than those institutions that held steady because change constitutes "news" while continuity generally does not. MIT, Johns Hopkins, Brown, Columbia, and Amherst all saw significant declines.[74] While MIT tried to put the blame on the Supreme Court, the list of institutions that were much more successful in sustaining diversity despite the Court's ruling suggested colleges that fell short were not without blame. MIT's president Sally Kornbluth acknowledged, "We need to seek out new approaches."[75]

The million-dollar question became: Why did so many universities succeed in maintaining racial diversity where some others failed? Given the disparities in how different universities fared, some conservatives immediately jumped to the conclusion that the highly successful colleges must have cheated and employed covert racial preferences.

It is difficult to know for sure what went on behind closed doors because admissions processes remain notoriously opaque. And it is quite possible that some colleges have been exploiting the personal essay loophole to consider race in a way not intended by the Supreme Court. Litigation will likely expose any cheating.[76] But early evidence emerged, as I'd fervently hoped, that many institutions were adopting authentic race-neutral strategies.

At the University of Virginia, for example, new financial aid programs and partnerships with high schools appeared to pay off. UVA increased its share of Pell Grant eligible students from 14 percent five years earlier to 24 percent.[77] At Duke, the share of Pell students doubled in just two years, from 11 percent to 22 percent. Enhancing economic diversity, Duke's admissions dean said, "was clearly helpful to us in terms of racial diversity in enrollment." He said, "I think there will be considerable interest this coming year from colleges in thinking about what was successful and how to recreate that."[78]

At Yale, the admissions dean announced that "the class of 2028 includes the greatest representation of first-generation and low-income students on record."[79] Dartmouth also said it increased its share of first-generation college students to a "record-setting level," and its share of Pell Grant recipients increased five percentage points in a single year to an "all time high."[80]

Over time, it seems likely that socioeconomic and racial diversity could continue to rise. To begin with, some universities, such as UNC, said their racial and socioeconomic results might have been temporarily depressed because the U.S. Department of Education faced major delays in processing FAFSA financial aid awards in the 2023–2024 cycle, which could have discouraged racial minorities from applying.[81] In addition, as a reporter for the *Chronicle of Higher Education* noted, it will take time for admissions officers to modify their approaches after employing racial preferences for several decades; "their adjustments have just begun."[82]

Moving forward, there is an additional reason for universities to adopt legal, race-neutral strategies to achieve diversity: political necessity. Higher education, particularly elite higher education, is in political trouble. In the past few decades, the erosion of support among Republicans has been particularly dramatic. Between 2015 and 2023, the proportion of Republicans who said they had a "great deal" or "quite a lot" of confidence in higher education declined from 56 percent to less than one in five.[83] The top reason Republicans cited for losing their faith was that colleges had become "too liberal/political."[84] (At top liberal arts colleges, one study found Democrats outnumbered Republicans by forty-eight to one among English department faculty members, and seventeen to one among philosophy, history, and psychology professors.)[85] Democrats have remained more supportive of higher education, but that sympathetic attitude could erode if universities don't take steps to ensure they remain racially inclusive. As Anthony Carnevale notes, affirmative action provided "a shield" for elite higher education against populist attacks from the left. But after the Supreme Court decision, "their shield is down."[86] If elite higher education does not retain the support of progressive Democrats, their armament against Republican attacks will disappear.

While some universities had stubbornly held on to legacy preferences, shortfalls on racial diversity will likely put additional pressure on them to reform.[87] At the end of the day, there is a clear blueprint for universities to create diversity in a new, sustainable form that is both legally and politically sound. In fact, new studies emerged from Brookings and Stanford in the wake of the Supreme Court decision showing that racial diversity could be achieved in new ways.[88] It is up to universities to choose whether to make diversity a priority.

Paying for Class-Based Affirmative Action

Some questioned how colleges would be able to pay for class-based affirmative action. Sure, Harvard could afford it, but what about all the colleges that didn't have Harvard's wealth? The evidence suggests there are several avenues available. Colleges can cut administrative bloat, which has reached extraordinary levels.[89] They can redirect financial aid dollars away from non-need "merit" aid toward those who actually need it.[90] University leaders, who have long regarded themselves as champions of racial justice, can make clear that opposing these changes will be seen as insensitive to the needs of Black and Hispanic students.[91] Universities can also make new fundraising appeals that emphasize the need for donations to stave off the resegregation of higher education—a tactic that was highly successful after UCLA initially saw a steep decline in Black representation after the use of race was barred in California's public universities.[92] "It's a great campaign," says Anthony Carnevale. "You go to your alumni and you say, 'We want diversity, and we want kids from every kind of family in America.' That will sell."[93]

What Next?

In cases where universities cannot secure the funds needed to preserve racial diversity, federal and state sources will need to step into the breach. The good news is that in the past, when states banned racial preferences, legislators typically found resources to increase financial aid because class-based affirmative action is more popular than racial preferences.[94] A 2012 analysis found that in eight of nine states where racial preferences were banned (often by voter referendum), financial aid programs were beefed up to preserve diversity.[95] The funding increases occurred not only in blue states, but also in red states such as Texas, Florida, Nebraska, and Arizona. This happened because legislators across the board had a strong desire to open opportunities for disadvantaged students of all races and also to avoid significant drops in racial representation.[96]

Public Policies to Encourage the Transition to Class-Based Affirmative Action

If universities are slow in making the transition to new paths to diversity, federal and state actors can step in. The federal government can increase the endowment tax at colleges that are failing to serve the public interest in promoting racial and economic diversity.[97] There may well be bipartisan support for this move, as conservatives desire to tame elite higher education institutions, which they see as centers of radicalism, and liberals want to pressure institutions to preserve diversity based on race in new ways.[98]

Legacy preferences have also come under increasing fire since the Supreme Court's decision in *Students for Fair Admissions* from civil rights groups, which had previously condoned the practice.[99] Proposals to end legacy preferences or penalize institutions using them have been introduced in Massachusetts and New York.[100] In Virginia, a proposal to ban legacy preferences at public universities—including UVA and William & Mary—was unanimously passed in both the Senate and the

House and signed into law by a Republican governor.[101] In Maryland, few politicians were willing to defend legacy preferences either. The House of Delegates voted to ban the practice by a vote of 133–4, and the measure was subsequently signed into law.[102] California and Illinois also passed legislation banning legacy preferences.[103] In the U.S. Senate, Indiana Republican Todd Young teamed up with Virginia Democrat Tim Kaine to introduce the MERIT Act, which would amend the Higher Education Act to prohibit preferences for legacies and children of donors.[104]

———

The post-racial-preference environment in higher education has mostly shaped up as I anticipated. The far left was still trying to cling to covert racial preferences by exploiting the student essay loophole beyond what the Supreme Court intended, while the far right was overreaching and seeking to outlaw class-based affirmative action as "proxy discrimination." But both extremes appeared unlikely to prevail in the long term. The reaction from Joe Biden and many leading college presidents was heartening. They said it was time to begin retiring long-standing practices that unfairly benefited wealthy white students, especially legacy preferences. And they supported a boost in social mobility programs for low-income and working-class students of all races. It looked at long last like a better affirmative action was beginning to emerge.

EPILOGUE

Opening the Doors
a Third Time

LOOKING FORWARD, I AM EXCITED ABOUT THE FUTURE OF affirmative action as it shifts to an economic grounding. I remain inspired by the examples set sixty years ago by Robert Kennedy, Martin Luther King Jr., and Bayard Rustin, who charted a path toward a "solidarity liberalism" where working-class white, Black, Hispanic, and Asian voters could come together to harness large majorities of the American public for social change.[1] We've been on a long detour since then. In a fateful turn that has had catastrophic consequences for the country, Democrats pivoted away from solidarity toward "charity" liberalism. This approach has attracted upper-middle-class white liberals and people of color, but has not built a durable majority in a country where swing voters tend to be socially moderate and economically liberal.[2]

Over the years, various issues drove white working-class voters away from the Democratic Party, including immigration, national security, patriotism, and crime. But politics often boils down to whether voters think a political party has their best interests at heart. The use of class-blind racial preferences in college admissions, employment, and government contracting sent the worst possible message. If you were white or Asian, whether rich or poor, you were privileged; if you were Black or Hispanic, you were disadvantaged, even if your father was the president of the United States.

Most Americans never supported this class-blind policy. While Americans don't like to talk about economic class, they understand it in their bones. They know that America has become, in the words of Matthew Desmond, "one of the most unequal societies in the history of the world." Our concentrations of wealth and poverty are unrivaled among the thirty-eight most developed countries.[3] Only 36 percent of Americans still believe the American dream is possible.[4] Telling working-class white and Asian voters that race was the only thing that mattered made no sense to them. They knew that even in America— especially in America—class matters.[5]

Over the past several decades, some liberals recognized this, and I was eager and excited to work for a time with officials in the Clinton and Obama administrations, and then with college presidents like Larry Summers and Anthony Marx, to create a system of affirmative action based on economic need. But when those efforts failed, foiled by interest group politics within the Democratic Party and elite universities, I felt I had no choice but to forge an unlikely alliance with conservatives to challenge racial preferences in cases that went all the way to the U.S. Supreme Court.

The Court's 6–3 decision to end America's fifty-five-year experiment with racial preferences in college admissions was widely popular with the American public and has emboldened conservatives to challenge racial preferences in employment and government contracting as well.[6] In March 2024, a federal court struck down one race-based program providing preferences to minority-owned firms, noting that under the law, "Oprah Winfrey is presumptively disadvantaged," while white firms, even if disadvantaged, "are not."[7] It is now possible to imagine a better future for affirmative action, where the demise of racial preferences opens the door to a more robust and racially inclusive set of economic affirmative action policies in several spheres of American life.

Opening the Doors a Third Time

In the coming years, the new effort to create class-based affirmative action has the chance to scramble traditional political alliances in a way that would please Kennedy and King, who were determined to overcome divide-and-conquer racial politics. For decades, preferences have divided working-class Americans of different races into separate groups of the favored and disfavored, which sowed resentment. However, in the coming years, debates over class-based affirmative action could promote the opposite political dynamic. The exciting coalition of legislators representing working-class white and working-class Black and Hispanic districts that came together in Texas to support the Top 10 Percent plan could be replicated again and again across the country.[8]

We know that in other policy domains, cross-racial working-class alliances have emerged when shared interests are highlighted. In California, Oregon, Massachusetts, and Texas, for example, working-class voters and their representatives have coalesced across racial lines to end snob zoning in wealthy residential areas. It turns out that working-class white voters, just like working-class Black and Hispanic voters, don't like exclusionary zoning laws that tell teachers, firefighters, lawn care workers, and childcare providers that they are welcome to work, but not to live, in exclusive communities.[9] The same coalitions could develop around efforts to combat legacy preferences and support affirmative action for working-class people.

The shift in the coming debates will have broader implications for social cohesion in America as well. One of the terrible, unintended consequences of racial preferences is that economically struggling groups in America have become more and more divided, adversarial, and alienated. When policies divide people by race, it leads to the hardening of social divides and an escalation of political polarization. Upending those animosities won't be easy, but we have enough examples of success that it is possible to imagine a different path forward.

Finally, it's thrilling to think of a future in which a greater number of talented working-class students—including those who are Black and Hispanic—have a chance to attend elite colleges. Evidence suggests that graduating from these institutions can transform their lives and diversify America's leadership class.[10] Imagine if, in the next generation, working-class students like those whose stories are shared in this book—Tye Chicha at Hopkins, Edmund Kennedy and Tony Jack at Amherst, Heather Berg at the University of Virginia, and the young Anthony Carnevale at Colby and Michael Dannenberg at Boston University—weren't isolated exceptions, but a common sight across all college campuses.

Some say selective colleges have always been bastions of wealth and will never change. But elite colleges can and have changed for the better. In the early 1960s, it was hard to believe that Harvard would one day have a majority-minority population and elite, all-male colleges would begin admitting women. But both of those things happened. In a changed legal environment, universities will be under tremendous pressure to usher in a new era for selective higher education in which the final barrier—class disadvantage—begins to fall. And just as the addition of women and people of color in an earlier era enhanced higher education, so will opening the door a third time to include a new multiracial cohort of low-income and working-class students.[11]

It won't happen right away. There will be bumps along the road. But a decade from now, I think the Supreme Court decision will be viewed with less doom and gloom than it is by elite liberals today. When I think back on the 2016 gathering I attended at Harvard, which brought together 350 first-generation students from a variety of selective colleges, I am filled with hope. I think of Ana Barros, the daughter of a janitor, and how she felt so out of place at a setting like Harvard. I consider how future students like her might feel less isolated. The audience that day included kids of every imaginable race, and yet they were all pulling in the same direction, calling for selective colleges to remove the barriers that kept their numbers so abysmally low. This highly talented group of students, who persevered to overcome obstacles, represents the future of affirmative action.

Class Matters

Reader's Guide to Answering Ten Common Concerns

B ECAUSE THIS BOOK IS PRESENTED AS A NARRATIVE JOURNEY rather than as a thematic argument, this section raises ten common concerns I've heard over the years about my support for affirmative action based on economic need rather than race. I then point readers to book sections that discuss those issues in greater detail.

1. Why not add class-based affirmative action on top of race-based affirmative action? Why does it have to be either/or?

This is by far the most common question I get, especially from my liberal friends. I believe that class and race both shape opportunity in America in distinct ways, and I also believe it is important that universities maintain diversity in both aspects. So why not simply layer class preferences on top of race preferences?

At one point, I did work with colleges to supplement racial preferences with class preferences (see pages 106–114). But the effort failed (115–122). Elite universities say they care about both racial and economic diversity, but they typically focus almost exclusively on race and give short shrift to economic diversity because of financial considerations and the greater emphasis placed on race by university stakeholders (23, 87–88, 110–111, 122–126, 201).

Research finds that selective universities give much bigger preferences based on race than class (91–92, 107–111, 182–184, 212–213, 252). As a result, they end up racially diverse but economically segregated (89–90, 195–196, 214–215). And even the underrepresented minority students tend to be fairly advantaged socioeconomically (89–90, 143, 196–197, 215, 255, 258–259). The only time universities provide economic preferences is when they can't use race and therefore turn to class preferences as a plan B to indirectly produce racial diversity (126–127).

The other big reason for not simply adding racial preferences on top of class preferences is that economic preferences can produce the benefits of racial preferences without the costs. Well-conceived economic preferences, if shaped properly, can recognize history and produce racial diversity. (See the discussion under Question 3 below.)

And racial preferences entail a number of costs. They fracture the progressive political coalition of working people (32–45, 131, 156, 157, 180–181, 289–290). They can impose stigma on beneficiaries (131, 136, 155). They can increase racial resentment and social strife (155–156, 180–181). And they help provide cover for an unfair system of preferences for legacies, children of faculty, and donors (102, 141–142, 168–169, 182–195, 207–208, 212–215).

Having said that, I do support taking race and class into consideration in a few particular instances. As the Supreme Court recognized, it is entirely appropriate for a university to consider the fact that a Black or Hispanic student faced and overcame racial discrimination, because doing so shows drive and character (263–264, 270). Moreover, in extremely rare instances, when class preferences might not produce sufficient racial diversity—say, because the college is located in a predominantly white rural area and struggles to achieve racial diversity—I favor an institution first considering economic disadvantage and then using race, only as a very last resort (175–176). (This is not something the Supreme Court allows.)

2. Racial oppression is America's original sin, not class inequality. Isn't class-based affirmative action just dancing around the real issue?

Race matters a great deal in American society, and dismantling racial discrimination remains an important challenge. That is why we need strong antidiscrimination laws that combat both intentional discrimination and unjustified policies that disproportionately hurt vulnerable racial groups (56). I also hope universities will provide an admissions boost to talented Black and Hispanic students who outline in their personal essays how they have faced—and overcome—discrimination in their lives (270).

Racial oppression also leaves an enormous economic legacy today. It is no accident that Black people continue to have huge inequalities by wealth and neighborhood, and I support efforts to uplift those who are low wealth and live in high-poverty neighborhoods, which will disproportionately benefit the victims of past and present discrimination (66, 93–95, 160, 253).

But class disadvantage also has a tremendous impact on a student's life chances. A Black student who grows up hungry in a tough neighborhood faces vastly different odds than a Black child who is raised by a wealthy lawyer and attends a tony private school. And it is important to acknowledge the extensive evidence finding that the impact of race and class has shifted over time. Whereas race once played the predominant role, today it is class. Residential segregation by race is declining, while class segregation is rising. Additionally, the academic achievement gap by income is now twice as large as the academic achievement gap by race—the reverse of fifty years ago (9–10, 70–71, 143–145, 157–158). Careful research finds that when looking at predicted SAT scores, socioeconomic obstacles are seven times more significant than those based purely on race (143–144, 270).

The public understands these dynamics, which is why large majorities oppose racial preferences in public opinion polls and voter referenda, while also supporting class-based affirmative action for the economically disadvantaged of all races (22, 29, 74, 101, 130, 175, 232, 241, 275).

3. Won't class-based affirmative action end up helping mostly poor white and Asian students?

Not if structured fairly. It is true that America has many poor white and Asian students who would benefit from class-based affirmative action, as they should. But there are two big reasons that class-based affirmative action can also produce robust levels of racial diversity.

First, universities can avoid a zero-sum game where poor white and Asian students squeeze out poor Black and Hispanic students by making room for both. By eliminating preferences for legacies, faculty children, and students who play boutique sports, a university can free up seats. This can be done without hurting academic standards (see Question 4). Second, universities should look at socioeconomic obstacles that go beyond family income. On average, Black and Hispanic students are more likely than white students of the same income bracket to have low levels of wealth and to live in neighborhoods and attend schools with high poverty levels. Counting these extra disadvantages is not only fair, but will also increase the "racial dividend" of class-based affirmative action (92–95, 160–161).

The results in states that banned affirmative action suggest that class-based and geographic-based alternatives can produce high levels of racial diversity (97, 140, 147–148, 244–248, 251, 282). So does the evidence from national simulations (85, 92–95, 160, 286). And so does the evidence from the Harvard (197–200, 204–206) and UNC cases (218).

4. What's wrong with merit-based admissions? Why have affirmative action of any kind? Shouldn't we just fix K–12 education instead? And won't students admitted through a class preference flunk out?

It would be better if we achieved genuine equal opportunity at the K–12 level, and I've spent a lot of my career thinking about ways to do that (137–138, 226–228). But I'm not holding my breath for it to happen anytime soon. So, in the meantime, it is important for colleges to consider the strength of an applicant in light of obstacles overcome.

I'm a big believer in merit, and for me, "true merit" requires looking at the context in which a student achieved their record. That means looking at not only the distance traveled, but also where a student ends up (75, 84, 182).

There are limits to this approach. It does no one any good if students are in over their heads. However, there are tens of thousands of high-achieving low-income students who could be attending selective colleges but currently do not (108, 150–151, 168). Indeed, the proportion coming from the bottom socioeconomic half could almost quadruple, and selective institutions would maintain high graduation rates (92–93). In state flagships where more low-income students were admitted, they did well academically (168). National simulations showed the same result (18, 108). And additional simulations found that it was possible to maintain high academic standards at both Harvard (200–201, 251) and UNC (218) while increasing socioeconomic diversity and sustaining racial diversity.

5. What makes you think that without the ability to use race, universities will shift to class preferences, rather than just settling for less racial diversity?

Thirty years ago, it was an open question whether universities would shift to class-based affirmative action or just give up (77). But over the years, in the nine states where racial preferences were eliminated (usually by voter initiative), virtually all of them came up with alternative programs to sustain diversity (78–80, 146–147). Moreover, the early signs suggest that in the aftermath of the U.S. Supreme Court decision striking down racial preferences, universities have been devising a variety of race-neutral strategies to boost diversity (275–281).

There are two reasons to be optimistic that universities won't just retreat from their commitment to diversity. First, most selective colleges now have a fundamental commitment to the idea that diversity is part of an excellent education (122, 205). Moreover, as a practical matter, elite higher education is in political trouble, especially with conservatives, and so has a powerful interest in not losing liberal support. If universities allow for a steep decline in racial diversity, they risk losing their only ideological allies (285–286).

6. Conservatives have supported class-based affirmative action only as a political talking point to attack racial preferences. Now that they've won in the Supreme Court, they will go after class-based affirmative action as "proxy discrimination" in the courts.

It is true that some on the extreme right are already bringing proxy discrimination cases (270–271). But this effort will almost surely lose in the courts (251–252, 264–265, 271–274). Politically, while conservatives have historically shown modest concerns about working-class people, they now have a reason to support class-based affirmative action (which is far more popular than racial affirmative action) due to the Republican base's shift to working-class white voters who for the first time can benefit from economic preference programs (287).

7. Although Students for Fair Admissions raised the issue of anti-Asian bias at Harvard, the organization was just using Asian Americans to advance the interests of white people.

I found the argument that Asians were being "used" by white people in the affirmative action litigation against Harvard to be both inaccurate and condescending to Asian Americans. Powerful evidence was presented at trial that Harvard, in its efforts to engineer a particular racial balance in the student body, discriminated against Asian students, who were overrepresented among top applicants (182–186, 206–207). I don't think Asian families were "duped" by white leaders on this question; many Asian Americans have been strongly opposed to efforts that devalue merit (241, 253). They recognized the logic that if all racial disparities were the result of discrimination, as some on the left were arguing, then Asian overrepresentation at elite universities would be seen as deeply suspect (12–13, 146, 205, 236).

The idea that ending racial preferences was designed to benefit white people more than Asian Americans was also undermined by the data. In California, where race was banned in admissions, Asian students outnumbered white students at both Berkeley and UCLA, even though white residents outnumber Asian ones in the state by more than two to one (245). And the simulations in the Harvard case showed that moving from race- to class-based affirmative action would increase Asian representation and decrease white representation (199).

8. How can universities afford your program of eliminating legacy preferences and providing a meaningful boost to socioeconomically disadvantaged students?

Class-based affirmative action will indeed cost more than racial preferences (286). But because most colleges are not selective and don't use affirmative action, the new costs in financial aid will be manageable in the larger scheme of things (10). The wealthiest colleges will be able to afford it on their own, and others can reduce administrative bloat and shift funds from non-need merit aid to students who genuinely require it (286). Moreover, in the past, any drop in minority admissions has set off alarm bells that have launched successful private fundraising efforts to restore diversity (286). And in both red and blue states, legislatures have stepped up to increase financial aid after racial preferences were ended. The reason for this happening was that if racial preferences were politically unpopular, so too was the idea of resegregating higher education (287). Democrats traditionally have been supportive of financial aid increases, and Republicans will be hesitant to oppose funding for class-based affirmative action, as they have recently gained support from their base of working-class white voters. As for ending legacy preferences, numerous superb institutions, including MIT, Johns Hopkins, Amherst, UC Berkeley, Oxford, and Cambridge, have done so, and their reputations for excellence have not diminished (189).

9. Why are you obsessed with who gets into a small number of universities? Shouldn't we be more concerned about making sure that places like community colleges, which educate most working-class students, provide an excellent education?

I both agree and disagree with this point. I have spent a great deal of professional time working on efforts to improve community colleges precisely because that is where the greatest numbers of poor and working-class students and students of color are educated (174). But it also matters who attends elite colleges, in part because, rightly or wrongly, these institutions provide about half the nation's government and industry leaders (10–11).

10. How could a good liberal like you, who has worked with civil rights leaders on K–12 school integration, housing desegregation, and labor rights, get mixed up with conservatives like Edward Blum?

Actually, class-based affirmative action has a strong liberal pedigree. The broader themes were advanced by Robert F. Kennedy (32–40) and Martin Luther King Jr. (40–43) in the 1960s, Justice William O. Douglas in the 1970s (45–48), and Bayard Rustin in the 1980s (43–44, 47, 49, 53–54).

I tried working with the Democratic administrations of Bill Clinton in the 1990s (59–66) and Barack Obama in the 2000s (130–136) when they discussed shifting to class-based affirmative action. But I was told that Democratic interest groups play such a powerful role in party politics that the courts would have to compel Democrats to adopt a different model (134). That's why I teamed up with Blum in the 2010s (173–176). I was pleased when Joe Biden, forced by the courts, announced he was coming out against legacy preferences and expressed his support for rewarding students who overcame adversity (275–276).

Reader's Guide

The fact that class-based affirmative action has also received support from conservatives over the years, such as Bob Dole (72), Jack Kemp (72), George W. Bush (95–98), Antonin Scalia (53), and Neil Gorsuch (264), is a good thing. When a pantheon of leading liberals like Kennedy, King, and Douglas can find common grounds with leading conservatives like Scalia, Bush, and Gorsuch, that's something to celebrate.

Acknowledgments

Writing is solitary, but producing a book is very much of a community effort. I'm deeply grateful to a number of people.

First, I'd like to thank those individuals who generously shared their personal stories with me for this book: Heather Berg, John Brittain, Anthony Carnevale, Benvindo "Tye" Chicha, Michael Dannenberg, and Chase Sackett.

I'd also like to thank my new colleagues at the Progressive Policy Institute (PPI), especially Will Marshall and Lindsay Lewis, who provide a wonderfully hospitable home for left-of-center thinkers who sometimes take unorthodox views. PPI prizes vigorous debate and intellectual curiosity at a level unusual for Washington, D.C., think tanks.

Thanks, too, to my students at the George Washington University Trachtenberg School of Public Policy and Public Administration, where I teach a class on "Civil Rights and Economic Inequality." Affirmative action is one of the topics we address in the seminar each year, and my students always offer fresh and innovative insights on the issue.

Warm appreciation to my agent, Lisa Adams of the Garamond Agency, who provided smart advice and keen thinking about how to shape an appealing book proposal. John Mahaney, my editor for the second consecutive book, provided enormously valuable edits for which I am terribly grateful. Thanks as well to Nicholas Taylor, who provided superb copy edits.

Most of all, I want to thank my (growing!) family. My mother, Jeannette Kahlenberg, taught me to write and so much more. My sisters, Trudi and Joy, and their husbands, Joe and Bob, provided loving

Acknowledgments

support for this book, even when they may have disagreed with some of my public policy conclusions. My fabulous daughters, Cindy, Jessica, Caroline, and Amanda, and my sons-in-law, Matt and Jason, bring me great joy and have given me encouragement on this topic during difficult times. My grandchildren, Adam, Hailey, David—and the latest, Bennett—are delights. And my wife, Rebecca, is a wondrously kind and generous soul, who knows all the ideas in this book without reading it, because (God help her) she has lived with them since we began dating as freshmen in college. She lives the best values found in this book.

Notes

PROLOGUE

1. Portions of the prologue draw on Richard D. Kahlenberg, "The Affirmative Action That Colleges Really Need," *The Atlantic*, October 26, 2022, www.theatlantic.com/ideas/archive/2022/10/supreme-court-harvard-affirmative-action-legacy-admissions-equity/671869.
2. Jack Newfield, *Robert Kennedy: A Memoir* (New York: Bantam Books, 1969), 287.
3. Richard D. Kahlenberg, *The Remedy: Class, Race, and Affirmative Action* (New York: Basic Books, 1996), ix.

INTRODUCTION

1. Evan Mandery, *Poison Ivy: How Elite Colleges Divide Us* (New York: The New Press, 2022), 227–229.
2. John R. Logan and Brian Stults, "The Persistence of Segregation in the Metropolis: New Findings from the 2020 Census," Diversity and Disparities Project, Brown University, August 12, 2021, 2, https://s4.ad.brown.edu/Projects/Diversity/Data/Report/report08122021.pdf (finding the Black–white dissimilarity index, in which 100 is apartheid and 0 is perfect integration, declined from 79 in 1970 to 55 in 2020); Sean F. Reardon and Kendra Bischoff, "The Continuing Increase in Income Segregation, 2007–2012," Stanford Center for Educational Policy Analysis, 2016, https://cepa.stanford.edu/content/continuing-increase-income-segregation-2007-2012.
3. Sean Reardon, "The Widening Academic Achievement Gap Between Rich and Poor: New Evidence and Possible Explanations," in *Whither Opportunity? Rising Inequality, Schools, and Children's Life Chances*, ed. Greg J. Duncan and Richard J. Murnane (New York: Russell Sage Foundation and the Spencer Foundation, 2011), 93, 98.
4. Robert D. Putnam, *Our Kids: The American Dream in Crisis* (New York: Simon and Schuster, 2015), 18.
5. Sarah Reber, Gabriela Goodman, and Rina Nagashima, "Admissions at Most Colleges Will Be Unaffected by Supreme Court Ruling on Affirmative Action," Brookings Institution, November 7, 2023, www.brookings.edu/articles/admissions-at-most-colleges-will-be-unaffected-by-supreme-court-ruling-on-affirmative-action.
6. Peggy Noonan, "Biden Can't Resist the 'River of Power,'" *Wall Street Journal*, September 14, 2023, www.wsj.com/articles/biden-cant-resist-the-river-of-power-politics-election-voters-2024-president-nominee-5ee64e04 (citing Richard Ben Cramer's *What It Takes: The Way to the White House* [New York: Vintage, 1993]).
7. Kevin Carey, "Can College Diversity Survive the End of Affirmative Action?," *Vox*, June 29, 2023, www.vox.com/scotus/2023/6/29/23767756/affirmative-action-college-admissions-race-sffa-ruling.
8. Derek Bok, *Attacking the Elites: What Critics Get Wrong—and Right—About America's Leading Universities* (New Haven, CT: Yale University Press, 2024), 22.
9. Daniel Lippman, "Biden Stocks His White House with Ivy Leaguers," *Politico*, May 2, 2021, www.politico.com/news/2021/05/02/biden-white-house-ivy-league-479298.

Notes to Introduction

10. Thomas R. Dye, *Who's Running America? The Obama Reign* (Boulder, CO: Paradigm, 2014), 180 (Table 8.2). The twelve institutions are Harvard, Yale, Princeton, Columbia, University of Pennsylvania, Stanford, University of Chicago, University of California at Berkeley, Johns Hopkins, MIT, Cornell, and Northwestern. See also Richard D. Kahlenberg, "Achieving Better Diversity: Reforming Affirmative Action in Higher Education," Century Foundation, December 3, 2015, Figure 1, https://tcf.org/content/report/achieving-better-diversity.

11. Anthony P. Carnevale and Jeff Strohl, "How Increasing College Access Is Increasing Inequality, and What to Do About It," in *Rewarding Strivers: Helping Low-Income Students Succeed in College*, ed. Richard D. Kahlenberg (New York: Century Foundation Press, 2010), 112 (the most selective institutions spent $92,000 per student, compared with $12,000 at nonselective colleges).

12. Mandery, *Poison Ivy*, xiv.

13. Raj Chetty, John N. Friedman, Emmanuel Saez, Nicholas Turner, and Danny Yagan, "Mobility Report Cards: The Role of Colleges in Intergenerational Mobility," July 2017, https://web.archive.org/web/20240527070720/www.equality-of-opportunity.org/papers/coll_mrc_paper.pdf ("Rates of upper-tail [bottom quintile to top 1%] mobility are highest at elite colleges, such as Ivy League universities"); Richard D. Kahlenberg, "Who Benefits Most from Attending Top Colleges?," *Chronicle of Higher Education*, March 10, 2011, www.chronicle.com/blogs/innovations/who-benefits-most-from-attending-top-colleges (citing research by Princeton's Alan Krueger and Stacey Dale of Mathematica Policy Research).

14. Daniel DeVise and Lexi Lonas, "Are Legacy Admissions on the Way Out?," *The Hill*, September 4, 2023, https://thehill.com/homenews/education/4183749-are-legacy-admissions-on-the-way-out.

15. Heather McGhee, *The Sum of Us: What Racism Costs Everyone and How We Can Prosper Together* (New York: One World, 2021), 288.

16. Ibram X. Kendi, "'When I See Racial Disparities, I See Racism': Discussing Race, Gender and Mobility," *New York Times*, March 27, 2018, www.nytimes.com/interactive/2018/03/27/upshot/reader-questions-about-race-gender-and-mobility.html ("A racist policy yields racial disparities. An anti-racist policy reduces or eliminates racial disparities. . . . As an anti-racist, when I see racial disparities, I see racism").

17. Arlie Russell Hochschild, *Strangers in Their Own Land: Anger and Mourning on the American Right* (New York: The New Press, 2016), 137–139.

18. Richard D. Kahlenberg, "How to Fix College Admissions Now: Focus on Class, Not Race," *New York Times*, July 5, 2023, www.nytimes.com/interactive/2023/07/05/opinion/affirmative-action-college-admissions.html.

19. *Regents of the University of California v. Bakke*, 438 U.S. 265, 316 (1978).

20. Kahlenberg, "Affirmative Action That Colleges Really Need."

21. "Economic Diversity and Student Outcomes at Amherst College," *New York Times*, January 18, 2017, www.nytimes.com/interactive/projects/college-mobility/amherst-college.

22. Vianney Gomez, "As Courts Weigh Affirmative Action, Grades and Test Scores Seen as Top Factors in College Admissions," Pew Research Center, April 26, 2022, www.pewresearch.org/fact-tank/2022/04/26/u-s-public-continues-to-view-grades-test-scores-as-top-factors-in-college-admissions.

23. "Brief of Oklahoma and Thirteen States as Amici Curiae in Support of Petitioner, *Students for Fair Admissions v. Harvard*," U.S. Supreme Court, March 31, 2021, iv, www.supremecourt.gov/DocketPDF/20/20-1199/173604/20210331161510903_2021.03.31%20Amicus%20of%20OK%20et%20al..pdf (noting that nine states eliminated racial preferences).

24. Halley Potter, "Transitioning to Race-Neutral Admissions: An Overview of Experiences in States Where Affirmative Action Has Been Banned," in *The Future of Affirmative Action: New Paths to Higher Education Diversity After Fisher v. Texas*, ed. Richard D. Kahlenberg (New York: Century Foundation; Indianapolis: Lumina Foundation, 2014), 75–90.

25. "Brief of Harvard University, Brown University, the University of Chicago, Dartmouth College, Duke University, the University of Pennsylvania, Princeton University, and Yale University as

Notes to Introduction

Amici Curiae Supporting Respondents, *Grutter v. Bollinger and Gratz v. Bollinger*," U.S. Supreme Court, February 18, 2003, 23, https://ogc.brown.edu/sites/default/files/2003-2-18%20Grutter%20v.%20Bollinger%20-%20Amicus%20Brief.pdf.

26. *Grutter v. Bollinger*, 539 U.S. 306 (2003).

27. William G. Bowen, Martin A. Kurzweil, and Eugene M. Tobin, *Equity and Excellence in American Higher Education* (Charlottesville: University of Virginia Press, 2005), 105 (Table 5.1), 289 (Appendix Table 5.1).

28. See discussion in Chapter 4.

29. Mandery, *Poison Ivy*, xvi.

30. Chetty et al., "Mobility Report Cards."

31. Richard D. Kahlenberg and Halley Potter, "A Better Affirmative Action: State Universities That Created Alternatives to Racial Preferences," Century Foundation, 2012, 26–61, https://tcf.org/content/report/a-better-affirmative-action.

32. Anthony Carnevale, Stephen Rose, and Jeff Strohl, "Achieving Racial and Economic Diversity with Race-Blind Admissions Policy," in Kahlenberg, *Future of Affirmative Action*, 192 (Table 15.1); Sigal Alon, *Race, Class, and Affirmative Action* (New York: Russell Sage Foundation, 2015), 254–256 (Figure 11), 268–269 (Table A8.2).

33. Oral argument transcript, *Fisher v. University of Texas*, U.S. Supreme Court, December 9, 2015, 41, 84, www.supremecourt.gov/oral_arguments/argument_transcripts/2015/14-981_onjq.pdf.

34. *Fisher v. University of Texas*, 579 U.S. 365, 385 (2016).

35. See Chapter 7; and "Economic Diversity and Student Outcomes at Harvard University," *New York Times*, January 18, 2017, www.nytimes.com/interactive/projects/college-mobility/harvard-university (for students who were born in 1991, mostly the class of 2013).

36. See Chapter 8; and "Economic Diversity and Student Outcomes at the University of North Carolina, Chapel Hill," *New York Times*, January 18, 2017, www.nytimes.com/interactive/projects/college-mobility/university-of-north-carolina-chapel-hill.

37. Ibram X. Kendi, *How to Be an Anti-Racist* (New York: One World, 2019), 19.

38. Gomez, "As Courts Weigh Affirmative Action."

39. Stephanie Saul, "Affirmative Action Was Banned at Two Top Universities. They Say They Need It," *New York Times*, August 26, 2022, www.nytimes.com/2022/08/26/us/affirmative-action-admissions-supreme-court.html.

40. Janet Gilmore, "UC Berkeley's Push for More Diversity Shows in Its Newly Admitted Class," *Berkeley News*, July 16, 2020, https://news.berkeley.edu/2020/07/16/uc-berkeleys-push-for-more-diversity-shows-in-its-newly-admitted-class.

41. "UCLA 2021 Freshman Class Is Most Diverse, Academically Accomplished in History, School Says," *ABC Eyewitness News*, July 19, 2021, https://abc7.com/ucla-admission-freshman-class-2021-admissions/10897823. See also Teresa Watanabe, "UC Admits Largest, Most Diverse Class Ever, but It Was Harder to Get Accepted," *Los Angeles Times*, July 20, 2021, www.latimes.com/california/story/2021-07-19/uc-admissions-new-diversity-record-but-harder-to-get-in.

42. Richard D. Kahlenberg, "A Middle Ground on Race and College," *National Affairs*, no. 59 (Spring 2023), https://nationalaffairs.com/publications/detail/a-middle-ground-on-race-and-college.

43. *Students for Fair Admissions v. Harvard*, 600 U.S. 181, 206 (2023).

44. Michael Lind, "Charity vs. Solidarity: Exploring Two Philosophies of Liberalism. The Debate over Affirmative Action Reveals a Split Among Liberals That Goes Back a Century," *Salon*, June 25, 2013, www.salon.com/2013/06/25/liberalisms_mortal_danger.

45. Bayard Rustin, "The King to Come," *New Republic*, March 9, 1987, https://newrepublic.com/article/72534/king-come.

46. Caroline Hoxby and Christopher Avery, "The Missing 'One-Offs': The Hidden Supply of High-Achieving, Low Income Students," Brookings Papers on Economic Activity, Spring 2013, www.brookings.edu/articles/the-missing-one-offs-the-hidden-supply-of-high-achieving-low-income-students.

Notes to Introduction

47. Kahlenberg, "How to Fix College Admissions Now."

CHAPTER 1

1. Emily Bazelon, "Why Is Affirmative Action in Peril? One Man's Decision," *New York Times Magazine*, February 15, 2023, www.nytimes.com/2023/02/15/magazine/affirmative-action-supreme-court.html.

2. William Bowen and Derek Bok would later document that in the entering class of 1989, 89 percent of Black students at twenty-eight elite colleges were middle or upper class, and that the white students were even wealthier, with 98 percent coming from the middle or upper class. See Bowen and Bok, *The Shape of the River* (Princeton, NJ: Princeton University Press, 1998), 341 (Table B.2), xxviii–xxix (listing the twenty-eight institutions). See also Anthony Carnevale, Peter Schmidt, and Jeff Strohl, *The Merit Myth: How Our Colleges Favor the Rich and Divide America* (New York: The New Press, 2020), 155.

3. Stanley B. Greenberg, *Middle Class Dreams: The Politics and Power of the New American Majority* (New York: Times Books, 1995), 25, 40.

4. Jack Newfield, *Robert Kennedy: A Memoir* (New York: Bantam, 1969).

5. John DiIulio Jr., email message to author, December 5, 2023; John J. DiIulio Jr., "The Case for a Second New Deal," *Claremont Review of Books*, Winter 2023/24, https://claremontreviewofbooks .com/the-case-for-a-second-new-deal; University of Pennsylvania, "John DiIulio," accessed July 5, 2024, https://live-sas-www-polisci.pantheon.sas.upenn.edu/people/standing-faculty/john-diiulio.

6. Richard D. Kahlenberg, "Harvard's Class Gap," *Harvard Magazine*, May/June 2017, www .harvardmagazine.com/2017/04/harvards-class-gap.

7. Kahlenberg.

8. Kahlenberg.

9. Kahlenberg.

10. William Vanden Heuvel and Milton Gwirtzman, *On His Own: RFK, 1964–1968* (Garden City, NY: Doubleday, 1970), 348–349. In later years, their critique was picked up by Ronald Steel and Gary Wills.

11. Richard D. Kahlenberg, "The Inclusive Populism of Robert Kennedy," Century Foundation, March 16, 2018, https://tcf.org/content/report/inclusive-populism-robert-f-kennedy.

12. David Halberstam, *The Unfinished Odyssey of Robert Kennedy* (New York: Random House, 1968), 41.

13. Newfield, *Robert Kennedy*, 287–288.

14. Kahlenberg, "Inclusive Populism of Robert Kennedy."

15. Kahlenberg.

16. Halberstam, *Unfinished Odyssey*, 128–129.

17. Editorial, "Soak the Rich," *Wall Street Journal*, May 21, 1968.

18. Robert Kennedy, "A Program for a Sound Economy," May 12, 1968, in Douglas Ross, *Robert Kennedy: Apostle for Change* (New York: Trident Press, 1968), 547–548.

19. Jeff Greenfield, interview with author, January 30, 1985.

20. Kahlenberg, "Inclusive Populism of Robert F. Kennedy."

21. David Paul Kuhn, *The Hardhat Riot: Nixon, New York City, and the Dawn of the White Working-Class Revolution* (New York: Oxford University Press, 2020), 26–27.

22. Kahlenberg, "Inclusive Populism of Robert F. Kennedy."

23. Kahlenberg.

24. Michael Lind, *The Next American Nation: The New Nationalism and the Fourth American Revolution* (New York: The Free Press, 1995), 109.

25. Peter Brown, *Minority Party: Why Democrats Face Defeat in 1992 and Beyond* (Washington, D.C.: Regnery Gateway, 1991), 25; Hugh Davis Graham, *The Civil Rights Era: Origins and Development of National Policy, 1960–1972* (Oxford: Oxford University Press, 1990), 106–107.

Notes to Chapter 1

26. Chris Matthews, *Bobby Kennedy: A Raging Spirit* (New York: Simon and Schuster, 2017), 215 (citing John Seigenthaler, John F. Kennedy Presidential Library, Oral History Collection).

27. Kahlenberg, "Inclusive Populism of Robert F. Kennedy" (citing Leo Casey).

28. Richard D. Kahlenberg, *Excluded: How Snob Zoning, NIMBYism, and Class Bias Build the Walls We Don't See* (New York: PublicAffairs, 2023).

29. Arthur Schlesinger Jr., interview with author, January 31, 1985.

30. Paul Cowan, "Wallace in Yankee Land," *Village Voice*, July 18, 1968.

31. Halberstam, *Unfinished Odyssey*, 173–174, 195.

32. Martin Luther King Jr., *Why We Can't Wait* (New York: New American Library, 1964), 134. See also Richard D. Kahlenberg, "A Path Forward on Reparations?," *Democracy Journal*, September 16, 2020, https://democracyjournal.org/magazine/a-path-forward-on-reparations.

33. King, *Why We Can't Wait*, 137.

34. King, 138.

35. Richard D. Kahlenberg and Moshe Marvit, *Why Labor Organizing Should Be a Civil Right* (New York: Century Foundation Press, 2012), 96.

36. McGhee, *Sum of Us*, 108–109.

37. McGhee, 10.

38. Ta-Nehisi Coates, "The Case for Reparations," *The Atlantic*, June 2014, www.theatlantic.com/magazine/archive/2014/06/the-case-for-reparations/361631.

39. Jamelle Bouie, "The Irony in the 'Rich Men North of Richmond,'" *New York Times*, August 19, 2023, www.nytimes.com/2023/08/19/opinion/rich-men-north-of-richmond-history.html. See also McGhee, *Sum of Us*, 170.

40. McGhee, 121 (citing W. E. B. Du Bois, *Black Reconstruction in America: 1860–1880* [New York: Harcourt Brace, 1935]).

41. Stephen B. Oates, *Let the Trumpet Sound: The Life of Martin Luther King, Jr.* (New York: New American Library, 1982), 434.

42. David Garrow, *Bearing the Cross: Martin Luther King, Jr., and the Southern Christian Leadership Conference* (New York: Morrow, 1986), 312.

43. King, *Why We Can't Wait*, 142.

44. Richard D. Kahlenberg, "He Had a Dream Too: When Civil Rights Leader Bayard Rustin Dared to Question Affirmative Action, the Black Establishment Erased Him from History," *Washington Monthly*, April 1997, 50.

45. John David Skrentny, *The Ironies of Affirmative Action: Politics, Culture, and Justice in America* (Chicago: University of Chicago Press, 1996).

46. Matthew Yglesias, "Martin Luther King, Jr.'s Plan for Class Struggle," *Slow Boring*, January 17, 2022, www.slowboring.com/p/martin-luther-king-jrs-plan-for-class.

47. Dwight Garner, "The Content of His Character," review of *King: A Life*, by Jonathan Eig, *New York Times Book Review*, May 8, 2023, www.nytimes.com/2023/05/08/books/the-new-definitive-biography-of-martin-luther-king-jr.html.

48. Richard D. Kahlenberg, "Bayard Rustin at 100," *Chronicle of Higher Education*, March 16, 2012, www.chronicle.com/blogs/innovations/bayard-rustin-at-100 (citing *I Must Resist: Bayard Rustin's Life in Letters*, ed. Michael G. Long [San Francisco: City Lights Books, 2012]).

49. Kahlenberg, "He Had a Dream Too," 50 (citing Garrow, *Bearing the Cross*).

50. Bayard Rustin, "From Protest to Politics: The Future of the Civil Rights Movement," *Commentary*, February 1965, www.commentary.org/articles/bayard-rustin-2/from-protest-to-politics-the-future-of-the-civil-rights-movement.

51. Terry Gross, "Martin Luther King's Last Campaign for Equality," *Fresh Air*, April 4, 2008, www.npr.org/2008/04/04/89372561/martin-luther-kings-last-campaign-for-equality.

52. Kahlenberg, "Bayard Rustin at 100" (citing Rustin, "From Protest to Politics," *Commentary*, February 1965).

53. Jervis Anderson, *Bayard Rustin: Troubles I've Seen* (New York: HarperCollins, 1997), 284.

Notes to Chapter 1

54. Lyndon B. Johnson, "Commencement Address at Howard University: 'To Fulfill These Rights,'" *American Presidency Project*, June 4, 1965, www.presidency.ucsb.edu/documents /commencement-address-howard-university-fulfill-these-rights.

55. Lee Rainwater and William L. Yancy, eds., *The Moynihan Report and the Politics of Controversy* (Cambridge, MA: MIT Press, 1967), 278.

56. Margaret Weir, *Politics and Jobs: The Boundaries of Employment Policy in the United States* (Princeton, NJ: Princeton University Press, 1992), 108; Graham, *Civil Rights Era*, 278.

57. Exec. Order No. 11246, 3 C.F.R. 339 (1964–65), www.dol.gov/agencies/ofccp/executive -order-11246/as-amended.

58. *DeFunis v. Odegaard*, 416 U.S. 312, 324 (1974); James Fishkin, *Justice, Equal Opportunity, and the Family* (New Haven, CT: Yale University Press, 1983), 90.

59. Jacob S. Hacker and Paul Pierson, "The Wisconsin Union Fight Isn't About Benefits, It's About Labor's Influence," *Washington Post*, March 6, 2011, www.washingtonpost.com/wp-dyn /content/article/2011/03/04/AR2011030402416.html.

60. Richard D. Kahlenberg, *Tough Liberal: Albert Shanker and the Battles over Schools, Unions, Race, and Democracy* (New York: Columbia University Press, 2007), 116–117, 194–195.

61. Kahlenberg, 196 (citing Bayard Rustin, "Where We Stand," advertisement in the *New York Times*, August 25, 1974).

62. Long, *I Must Resist*, 394–396 (citing Rustin's March 25, 1974, letter to the editor of the *Wall Street Journal*). See also Bayard Rustin, "The Blacks and the Unions," *Harper's*, May 1971, 81.

63. Adam Cohen, *Supreme Inequality: The Supreme Court's Fifty-Year Battle for a More Just America* (New York: Penguin, 2020), 13; *Edwards v. California*, 314 U.S. 160, 176 (1941); *Gideon v. Wainwright*, 372 U.S. 335 (1963); *Harper v. Virginia State Board of Elections*, 383 U.S. 663 (1966).

64. *DeFunis v. Odegaard*, 416 U.S. at 331 (Douglas, dissenting).

65. Kahlenberg, *Tough Liberal*, 217.

66. Kahlenberg, 217–218.

67. Kahlenberg, 217–218.

68. *Regents of University of California v. Bakke*, 438 U.S. at 395.

69. Bazelon, "Why Is Affirmative Action in Peril?"

70. *Regents of University of California v. Bakke*, 438 U.S. at 415 (Stevens, concurring in part and dissenting in part).

71. *Regents of University of California v. Bakke*, 438 U.S. at 407 (Blackmun, concurring in part and dissenting in part).

72. McGeorge Bundy, "The Issue Before the Court: Who Gets Ahead in America," *The Atlantic*, November 1977, www.theatlantic.com/past/docs/politics/race/bundy.htm.

73. Cohen, *Supreme Inequality*, 101–102.

74. *Regents of University of California v. Bakke*, 438 U.S. at 316.

75. Michael Sandel, *Liberalism and the Limits of Justice* (New York: Cambridge University Press, 1982), 141.

76. The *Washington Post* adopted this slogan in 2017 during Donald Trump's presidency. Paul Farhi, "The *Washington Post*'s New Slogan Turns Out to Be an Old Saying," *Washington Post*, February 24, 2017, www.washingtonpost.com/lifestyle/style/the-washington-posts-new-slogan-turns -out-to-be-an-old-saying/2017/02/23/cb199cda-fa02-11e6-be05-1a3817ac21a5_story.html.

77. *Students for Fair Admissions v. Harvard*, 600 U.S. at 222 (showing little variation year to year between the class of 2009 and the class of 2018).

78. Lind, *Next American Nation*, 109.

79. Antonin Scalia, "Commentary: The Disease as Cure: 'In Order to Get Beyond Racism, We Must First Take Race into Account,'" *Washington University Law Quarterly* 147 (1979): 153–154.

80. *City of Richmond v. Croson*, 488 U.S. 469 (1989).

81. *City of Richmond v. Croson*, 488 U.S. at 526, 509–510.

Notes to Chapter 2

82. Edward Koch, "Equal Opportunity—Without Minority Set Asides," *New York Times*, February 20, 1989, www.nytimes.com/1989/02/20/opinion/equal-opportunity-without-minority-set -asides.html.

83. Rustin, "King to Come."

84. Kendi, *How to Be an Anti-Racist*, 79.

85. Eric Pace, "Bayard Rustin Is Dead at 75; Pacifist and a Rights Activist," *New York Times*, August 25, 1987, www.nytimes.com/1987/08/25/obituaries/bayard-rustin-is-dead-at-75-pacifist -and-a-rights-activist.html.

86. Alan Dershowitz and Laura Hanft, "Affirmative Action and the Harvard College Diversity-Discretion Model: Paradigm or Pretext?," *Cardozo Law Review* 1 (1979): 416n114.

87. Richard D. Kahlenberg, "President Clinton's Race Initiative: Promise and Disappointment," in *One America? Political Leadership, National Identity and the Dilemmas of Diversity*, ed. Stanley A. Renshon (Washington, D.C.: Georgetown University Press, 2001), 93 (citing Brown, *Minority Party*, 146–147).

88. "Nomination of Judge Clarence Thomas to Be Associate Justice of the Supreme Court of the United States," Hearings Before the Committee on the Judiciary, United States Senate, September 10, 11, 12, 13, 16, 1991, 358–360, www.govinfo.gov/content/pkg/GPO-CHRG-THOMAS/pdf /GPO-CHRG-THOMAS-1.pdf.

CHAPTER 2

1. Brown, *Minority Party*, 145–146.

2. Thomas Edsall, "Clinton Admits '60s Marijuana Use," *Washington Post*, March 30, 1992; Thomas Edsall, "The Special Interest Gambit," *Washington Post*, January 3, 1993.

3. George Stephanopoulos, *All Too Human: A Political Education* (New York: Little, Brown, 1999), 38–39.

4. Editorial, "Bill Clinton in Black and White," *New York Times*, March 11, 1992, www.nytimes .com/1992/03/11/opinion/bill-clinton-in-black-and-white.html.

5. William Julius Wilson, "The Right Message," *New York Times*, March 17, 1992, www.nytimes .com/1992/03/17/opinion/the-right-message.html.

6. Bill Clinton and Al Gore, *Putting People First: How We Can All Change America* (New York: Times Books, 1992), 64.

7. David Broder, "Diversity Was Paramount in Building the Cabinet," *Washington Post*, December 25, 1992, www.washingtonpost.com/archive/politics/1992/12/25/diversity-was-para mount-in-building-the-cabinet/871a2574-af6b-498e-beb5-7bb9274caf69.

8. Leon Wieseltier, "Covenant and Burling," *New Republic*, February 1, 1993, 77–80.

9. Iver Peterson, "Justice Dept. Switches Sides in Racial Case: Backs Board on Layoff of New Jersey Teacher," *New York Times*, August 14, 1994, www.nytimes.com/1994/08/14/nyregion /justice-dept-switches-sides-in-racial-case.html.

10. Linda Greenhouse, "Settlement Ends High Court Case on Preferences: Tactical Retreat," *New York Times*, November 22, 1997, www.nytimes.com/1997/11/22/nyregion/affirmative-action -settlement-overview-settlement-ends-high-court-case.html.

11. Kahlenberg, "President Clinton's Race Initiative," 95 (citing pollster Geoffrey Garin).

12. R. Jeffrey Smith, "GOP Senators Begin Studying Repeal of Affirmative Action," *Washington Post*, February 6, 1995.

13. *Adarand v. Peña*, 515 U.S. 200, 227 (1995).

14. Mickey Kaus, "Class Is In: Class-Based Affirmative Action," *New Republic*, March 27, 1995 (noting that Clinton was facing "the prospect of a voter revolt in California" over affirmative action); Nicholas Lemann, *The Big Test: The Secret History of the American Meritocracy* (New York: Farrar, Straus and Giroux, 1999), 293, 296.

Notes to Chapter 2

15. Lemann, 296–297.

16. Ann DeVroy, "In Shift, President Supports Affirmative Action Based on Needs," *Washington Post*, March 4, 1995, www.washingtonpost.com/archive/politics/1995/03/04/clinton-cites -gop-hostility/04af0609-4bd2-4c4d-8092-0bc31738fb3b.

17. Charles Murray and Richard J. Herrnstein, "Race, Genes and I.Q.—an Apologia: The Case for Conservative Multiculturalism," *New Republic*, October 31, 1994, https://newrepublic.com /article/120887/race-genes-and-iq-new-republics-bell-curve-excerpt.

18. Martin Peretz, *The Controversialist: Arguments with Everyone: Left, Right, and Center* (New York: Wicked Son, 2023), 304–305.

19. Richard D. Kahlenberg, "Class, Not Race: A Liberal Case for Junking Old-Style Affirmative Action in Favor of Something That Works," *New Republic*, April 3, 1995.

20. Michael Kinsley, "Class, Not Race: It's a Poor Basis for Affirmative Action," *Washington Post*, August 1, 1991.

21. Kahlenberg, "Class, Not Race."

22. Nathan Glazer, "Race, Not Class," *Wall Street Journal*, April 5, 1995.

23. Abigail Thernstrom, "A Class-Backwards Idea: Why Affirmative Action for the Needy Won't Work," *Washington Post*, June 11, 1995, www.washingtonpost.com/archive/opinions/1995 /06/11/a-class-backwards-idea/94a7254a-43b5-4083-b1b7-2a1db1818bfc.

24. Stephanopoulos, *All Too Human*, 362.

25. Kevin Merida, "Worry, Frustration Build for Many in Black Middle Class," *Washington Post*, October 9, 1995.

26. Stephanopoulos, *All Too Human*, 365, 364, 370.

27. Stephanopoulos, 370.

28. Kahlenberg, "President Clinton's Race Initiative," 103.

29. Stephanopoulos, *All Too Human*, 370.

30. William Julius Wilson, *The Truly Disadvantaged: The Inner City, the Underclass, and Public Policy* (Chicago: University of Chicago Press, 1987), 110–111.

31. Kahlenberg, *Tough Liberal*, 347.

32. Kahlenberg, 347; Albert Shanker, interview with author, September 20, 1995.

33. Kahlenberg, *Tough Liberal*, 63–64, 100–103. See also Richard D. Kahlenberg, "A School Strike That Never Quite Ended," *New York Times*, November 17, 2018, www.nytimes.com/2018/11 /17/opinion/teachers-strike-liberals-ocean-hill-brownsville.html (on the close relationship between Shanker and Rustin in the 1968 Ocean Hill–Brownsville teachers strike).

34. Lemann, *Big Test*, 299.

35. Kahlenberg, "President Clinton's Race Initiative," 96.

36. Richard D. Kahlenberg, "Class-Based Affirmative Action," *California Law Review* 84 (July 1996): 1048–1056.

37. Kahlenberg, "President Clinton's Race Initiative," 97.

38. William Julius Wilson, *The Declining Significance of Race: Blacks and Changing American Institutions* (Chicago: University of Chicago Press, 1978); Justin McCarthy, "U.S. Approval of Interracial Marriage at New High of 94%," Gallup, September 10, 2021, https://news.gallup.com /poll/354638/approval-interracial-marriage-new-high.aspx; Putnam, *Our Kids*, 34–44.

39. See Robert Putnam and Shaylin Romney Garrett, *The Upswing: How America Came Together a Century Ago and How We Can Do It Again* (New York: Simon and Schuster, 2020), 211, 68 (Figure 2.19) (showing rise and decline of economic equality), and 212 (Figure 6.4) (showing leveling off of Black gains in income relative to whites around the time economic inequality begins to rise).

40. Lind, *Next American Nation*, 177–178.

41. Kahlenberg, "President Clinton's Race Initiative," 107.

42. Richard D. Kahlenberg, "Goal Line," *New Republic*, October 7, 1996, 27.

Notes to Chapter 2

43. Richard Bernstein, "Racial Discrimination and Righting Past Wrongs?," *New York Times*, July 13, 1994, www.nytimes.com/1994/07/13/us/racial-discrimination-or-righting-past-wrongs.html.

44. *Hopwood v. Texas*, 78 F.3d 932 (5th Cir. 1996).

45. *Hopwood v. Texas*, 78 F.3d at 932.

46. Doug Lederman, "Colleges Forced to Consider Ending Use of Race in Admissions," *Chronicle of Higher Education*, July 19, 1996, www.chronicle.com/article/colleges-forced-to-consider-ending-use-of-race-in-admissions.

47. "California Proposition 209," Digital History, 1996, www.digitalhistory.uh.edu/disp_textbook.cfm?smtID=3&psid=4099.

48. Ward Connerly, *Creating Equal: My Fight Against Race Preferences* (San Francisco: Encounter Books, 2000); Richard D. Kahlenberg, "Class Action: The Good and the Bad Alternatives to Affirmative Action," *Washington Monthly*, July/August 2000, 39–43.

49. Amy Wallace, "He's Either Mr. Right or Mr. Wrong: What Drives Ward Connerly in His Crusade to End Affirmative Action?," *Los Angeles Times*, March 31, 1996, www.latimes.com/archives/la-xpm-1996-03-31-tm-53137-story.html.

50. William J. Clinton, "Remarks in Oakland, California," American Presidency Project, October 31, 1996, www.presidency.ucsb.edu/documents/remarks-oakland-california.

51. Ballotpedia, "California Prop. 209: Affirmative Action Initiative (1996)."

52. Kahlenberg, "President Clinton's Race Initiative," 100; "1996," American Presidency Project, accessed June 26, 2024, www.presidency.ucsb.edu/statistics/elections/1996.

53. "Bush Steals Connerly's Wind," *Tampa Bay Times*, November 16, 1999, www.tampabay.com/archive/1999/11/16/bush-steals-connerly-s-wind.

54. Center for Educational Outreach and Innovation and Columbia Law School, "Reinventing Merit: The Future of Affirmative Action on Campus," Teachers College, Columbia University, New York, April 25, 1997.

55. Richard D. Kahlenberg, "Standardized Tests Are Weakening Our Democracy: In Tyranny of the Meritocracy, Lani Guinier Argues That the SATs Have Become 'Accurate Reflectors of Wealth and Little Else,'" *The Nation*, January 6, 2015, www.thenation.com/article/archive/standardized-tests-are-weakening-our-democracy.

56. Kahlenberg; Lani Guinier, *The Tyranny of Meritocracy: Democratizing Higher Education in America* (Boston: Beacon Press, 2015), xi, xiii.

57. Guinier, 23, 33, 39–41; Kahlenberg, "Standardized Tests Are Weakening Our Democracy."

58. Derrick Bell, "The Racism Is Permanent Thesis: Courageous Revelation or Unconscious Denial of Racial Genocide," in *The Derrick Bell Reader*, ed. Richard Delgado and Jean Stefancic (New York: New York University Press, 2005), 309–313.

59. Yascha Mounk, *The Identity Trap: A Story of Ideas and Power in Our Time* (New York: Penguin, 2023), 57.

60. Derrick Bell, *Race, Racism, and American Law*, 3rd ed. (Boston: Little, Brown, 1992), 640–641.

61. My experience was typical. See Jelani Cobb, "The Man Behind Critical Race Theory," *New Yorker*, September 13, 2021, www.newyorker.com/magazine/2021/09/20/the-man-behind-critical-race-theory (noting that even conservative white men got along with Bell at New York University Law School because of his respect for different views).

62. Kahlenberg, "Achieving Better Diversity." See also Matthew Watkins and Neena Satija, "The Price of Admission: How an Attempt to Boost Diversity at Texas Colleges Could Kill Affirmative Action," Part 1, *Texas Tribune*, March 29, 2016, https://apps.texastribune.org/price-of-admission.

63. Kahlenberg and Potter, "Better Affirmative Action," 35. Unlike the Texas plan, the California percentage plan guarantees admission to the UC system, but not to any particular campus.

64. Richard Sander and Stuart Taylor Jr., *Mismatch: How Affirmative Action Hurts Students It's Intended to Help, and Why Universities Won't Admit It* (New York: Basic Books, 2012), xii–xiii.

Notes to Chapter 2

65. Richard D. Kahlenberg, "In Search of Fairness: UCLA Shows That Class-Based Affirmative Action Won't Lead to a 'Whiteout,'" *Washington Monthly*, June 1998, 27.

66. Richard D. Kahlenberg, introduction to Kahlenberg, *Future of Affirmative Action*, 13.

67. Potter, "Transitioning to Race-Neutral Admissions," 78 (Table 6); Richard D. Kahlenberg, "Expert Report, *Students for Fair Admissions v. University of North Carolina*," January 12, 2018, 57, https://affirmativeactiondebate.files.wordpress.com/2021/06/kahlenberg-report-jan-2018.pdf.

CHAPTER 3

1. Anthony Carnevale, interview with author, January 15, 2023. See also Peter Schmidt, "ETS Accused of Squelching New Approach on Racial Bias: Plan Was an Alternative to Using Race in Admissions; Testing Service Denies the Charge," *Chronicle of Higher Education*, November 10, 2006, www.chronicle.com/article/ets-accused-of-squelching-new-approach-on-racial-bias; and Peter Schmidt, *Color and Money: How Rich White Kids Are Winning the War over College Affirmative Action* (New York: Palgrave Macmillan, 2007), 156.

2. Amy Dockser Marcus, "New Weights Can Alter SAT Scores: Family Is Factor in Determining Who's a 'Striver,'" *Wall Street Journal*, August 31, 1999, www.wsj.com/articles/SB9360 61265207782969.

3. Carnevale, interview with author. See also Schmidt, *Color and Money*, 152 (working-class parents).

4. Carnevale, interview with author.

5. "Anthony P. Carnevale," Georgetown University Center on Education and the Workforce, accessed June 26, 2024, https://web.archive.org/web/20240325164940/https://cew.georgetown.edu/about-us/staff/anthony-p-carnevale.

6. Marcus, "New Weights Can Alter SAT Scores."

7. Carnevale, interview with author.

8. Linda F. Wightman, "The Threat to Diversity in Legal Education: An Empirical Analysis of the Consequences of Abandoning Race as a Factor in Law School Admission Decisions," *New York University Law Review* 72, no. 1 (April 1997): 41–42.

9. Richard D. Kahlenberg, "The Colleges, the Poor, and the SATs," *Washington Post*, September 21, 1999.

10. Schmidt, "ETS Accused of Squelching New Approach"; Schmidt, *Color and Money*, 156. As discussed below, Carnevale's subsequent research would confirm the critical importance of employing wealth as a factor in admissions. See Carnevale and Strohl, "How Increasing College Access Is Increasing Inequality," 165.

11. Schmidt, "ETS Accused of Squelching New Approach"; Schmidt, *Color and Money*, 157.

12. Carnevale, interview with author.

13. David J. Hoff, "Former DuPont Executive New Head of ETS," *Education Week*, July 12, 2000, www.edweek.org/teaching-learning/former-dupont-executive-new-head-of-ets/2000/07; Carnevale, interview with author.

14. Harvard Journal on Legislation Symposium, "Affirmative Action in Higher Education," Harvard Law School, Cambridge, MA, March 12, 2002. For background on Carl Cohen, see "Obituary—Carl Cohen," University of Michigan Record, September 15, 2023, https://record.umich.edu/articles/obituary-carl-cohen.

15. *Gratz v. Bollinger*, 539 U.S. at 270.

16. *Grutter v. Bollinger*, 539 U.S. at 308.

17. Richard D. Kahlenberg, introduction to *America's Untapped Resource: Low-Income Students in Higher Education*, ed. Richard D. Kahlenberg (New York: Century Foundation Press, 2004), 14 (citing 2003 polls from the *Los Angeles Times*, *Newsweek*, and Epic/MRA).

18. Charles Lane, "U-Michigan Gets Broad Support on Using Race," *Washington Post*, February 11, 2003, www.washingtonpost.com/archive/politics/2003/02/11/u-michigan-gets-broad-support-on-using-race/1436edd4-8a61-4d79-bc0c-4066aa64243e.

Notes to Chapter 3

19. Kahlenberg, *Excluded*, 98–99.

20. "Brief of Harvard University, Brown University, the University of Chicago, Dartmouth College, Duke University, the University of Pennsylvania, Princeton University, and Yale University as Amici Curiae Supporting Respondents," 22n13.

21. Richard D. Kahlenberg, "Style, Not Substance: Affirmative Action Is Not as Liberal as You Think," *Washington Monthly*, November 2008, 45–48 (reviewing *The Shape of the River*).

22. Bowen and Bok, *Shape of the River*, 50.

23. Bowen and Bok, 341 (Table B.2). See also Kahlenberg, "Style, Not Substance."

24. Susanto Basu and David Barkan, "A View from the Top: An Interview with Derek Bok," *Harvard Political Review*, Spring 1985, 9.

25. Richard D. Kahlenberg, "The Conservative Victory in *Grutter* and *Gratz*," *Jurist*, September 5, 2003, https://web.archive.org/web/20111107134130/http://jurist.law.pitt.edu/forum/symposium-aa/kahlenberg-printer.php.

26. Sander and Taylor, *Mismatch*, 249 (Figure 16.1).

27. Bowen and Bok, *Shape of the River*, 47. See also Peter Passell, "Surprises for Everyone in a New Analysis of Affirmative Action," *New York Times*, February 27, 1997, www.nytimes.com/1997/02/27/business/surprises-for-everyone-in-a-new-analysis-of-affirmative-action.html (citing research by Thomas Kane).

28. Anthony Carnevale and Stephen Rose, "Socioeconomic Status, Race/Ethnicity, and Selective College Admissions," in Kahlenberg, *America's Untapped Resource*, 135. The document was originally published in March 2003; see https://files.eric.ed.gov/fulltext/ED482419.pdf.

29. Carnevale and Rose, 142; Kahlenberg, introduction to Kahlenberg, *America's Untapped Resource*, 9 (under a system of grades and test scores, the share of students from the lower socioeconomic half of the national distribution would rise to 11 percent, compared with 10 percent under the status quo).

30. Carnevale and Rose, "Socioeconomic Status, Race/Ethnicity, and Selective College Admissions," 108 (Table 3.1).

31. David Leonhardt, "Top Colleges, Largely for the Elite," *New York Times*, May 25, 2011, www.nytimes.com/2011/05/25/business/economy/25leonhardt.html.

32. Kahlenberg, introduction to Kahlenberg, *America's Untapped Resource*, 10. For subsequent research, see Hoxby and Avery, "Missing 'One-Offs.'"

33. Carnevale and Rose, "Socioeconomic Status, Race/Ethnicity, and Selective College Admissions," 150–151.

34. Thomas J. Kane, "Racial and Ethnic Preferences in College Admissions," in *The Black–White Test Score Gap*, ed. Christopher Jencks and Meredith Phillips (Washington, D.C.: Brookings Institution Press, 1998), 448–450.

35. Richard D. Kahlenberg, *All Together Now: Creating Middle-Class Schools Through Public School Choice* (Washington, D.C.: Brookings Institution Press, 2001); Raj Chetty and Nathaniel Hendren, "The Impacts of Neighborhoods on Intergenerational Mobility: Childhood Exposure Effects and County-Level Estimates," National Bureau of Economic Research, May 2015, https://scholar.harvard.edu/files/hendren/files/nbhds_paper.pdf.

36. John R. Logan, Brian D. Stults, and Rachel McKane, "Less Separate, No Less Equal," Brown University, September 27, 2022, https://s4.ad.brown.edu/Projects/Diversity/data/report/report0727.pdf.

37. Kahlenberg, introduction to Kahlenberg, *America's Untapped Resource*, 14.

38. Kahlenberg, 10 (Carnevale and Rose included in the disadvantaged pool students who came from the bottom 40 percent by family socioeconomic status—income, education, and occupation—or attended a high-poverty high school).

39. Carnevale and Rose, "Socioeconomic Status, Race/Ethnicity and Selective College Admissions," 150–151. See also Peter Schmidt, "Report Urges Colleges to Adopt Income-Based Affirmative-Action Policies," *Chronicle of Higher Education*, March 31, 2003, www.chronicle.com/article/report-urges-colleges-to-adopt-income-based-affirmative-action-policies; Daniel Golden, "Could

There Be Diversity If Affirmative Action Ends? Admissions Preferences Based on Economics, Not Race, Could Also Help Achieve Diversity," *Wall Street Journal*, March 31, 2003, www.wsj.com /articles/SB104906938428478400.

40. Richard D. Kahlenberg, "Affirmative Action: There's a Third Way," *Washington Post*, March 31, 2003, www.washingtonpost.com/archive/opinions/2003/03/31/affirmative-action-theres-a-third -way/207b21a9-0a64-4a8a-ab36-c3a578733249/.

41. Kahlenberg.

42. Kahlenberg, introduction to Kahlenberg, *America's Untapped Resource*, 14 (citing 2002 data). These disparities continue to this day. See Emily Moss, Kriston McIntosh, Wendy Edelberg, and Kristen Broady, "The Black–White Wealth Gap Left Black Households More Vulnerable," Brookings Institution, December 8, 2020, www.brookings.edu/articles/the-black -white-wealth-gap-left-black-households-more-vulnerable.

43. Schmidt, *Color and Money*, 158.

44. Schmidt, "ETS Accused of Squelching New Approach."

45. Richard D. Kahlenberg, ed., *Public School Choice vs. Private School Vouchers* (New York: Century Foundation Press, 2003); Richard D. Kahlenberg, ed., *Improving on No Child Left Behind* (New York: Century Foundation Press, 2008).

46. U.S. Department of Education Office for Civil Rights (OCR), "Race-Neutral Alternatives in Postsecondary Education: Innovative Approaches to Diversity," March 2003, 35, 38; Richard D. Kahlenberg, "Expert Report, *Students for Fair Admissions v. University of North Carolina*," January 12, 2018, 57, https://affirmativeactiondebate.org/wp-content/uploads/2021/06/kahlenberg -report-jan-2018.pdf.

47. OCR, "Race-Neutral Alternatives in Postsecondary Education," 39.

48. Kahlenberg, "In Search of Fairness," 27; Kahlenberg, introduction to Kahlenberg, *America's Untapped Resource*, 15.

49. OCR, "Race-Neutral Alternatives in Postsecondary Education," 29, 33–34; Sander and Taylor, *Mismatch*, 255.

50. Lind, *Next American Nation*, 109.

51. "Transcript of Argument in *Grutter v. Bollinger*," *New York Times*, April 1, 2003, www .nytimes.com/2003/04/01/politics/transcript-of-arguments-in-grutter-v-bollinger.html.

52. Linda Greenhouse, "On Affirmative Action, High Court Seeks Nuance," *New York Times*, April 1, 2003, www.nytimes.com/2003/04/01/politics/on-affirmative-action-high-court-seeks-nu ance.html.

53. Kahlenberg, "Conservative Victory in *Grutter* and *Gratz*."

54. Sander and Taylor, *Mismatch*, 208.

55. Schmidt, *Color and Money*, 178.

56. Kahlenberg, "Conservative Victory in *Grutter* and *Gratz*."

57. *Grutter v. Bollinger*, 539 U.S. at 297 (Souter, dissenting).

58. *Grutter v. Bollinger*, 539 U.S. at 343.

59. Kahlenberg, "Conservative Victory in *Grutter* and *Gratz*."

60. Stephen L. Carter, "Affirmative Distraction," *New York Times*, July 6, 2008, www.nytimes .com/2008/07/06/opinion/06carter.html.

61. Lane, "U-Michigan Gets Broad Support on Using Race."

62. Kahlenberg, "Conservative Victory in *Grutter* and *Gratz*" (citing three polls from January and February 2003: a *Los Angeles Times* survey found that 56 percent of Americans opposed racial preferences, but 59 percent supported preferences for economically disadvantaged students; a *Newsweek* survey found that 68 percent of Americans opposed preferences for Black people in admissions, but 65 percent favored socioeconomic preferences; and an Epic/MRA poll found 63 percent opposition to Michigan's race preferences, but 57 percent support for low-income preferences).

63. Nat Hentoff, "Sandra Day O'Connor's Elitist Decision," *Village Voice*, July 29, 2003, www .villagevoice.com/sandra-day-oconnors-elitist-decision.

Notes to Chapter 4

64. *Grutter v. Bollinger*, 539 U.S. at 368 (Thomas, dissenting).

65. Lani Guinier, "Saving Affirmative Action," *Village Voice*, July 1, 2003, www.villagevoice.com /saving-affirmative-action.

66. Jedediah Britton-Purdy, "Tocqueville's Uneasy Vision of American Democracy: American Government Succeeded, Tocqueville Thought, Because It Didn't Empower the People Too Much," *New Republic*, April 22, 2022, https://newrepublic.com/article/165923/olivier-zunz-tocqueville -book-review-uneasy-vision-american-democracy.

67. Carnevale, interview with author. See also Schmidt, *Color and Money*, 211.

68. Ronald Roach, "Class-Based Affirmative Action," *Diverse Issues in Higher Education*, June 19, 2003, www.diverseeducation.com/home/article/15079324/class-based-affirmative-action.

CHAPTER 4

1. Kahlenberg, "In Search of Fairness," 28.

2. "President Lawrence H. Summers' Remarks at ACE: 'Higher Education and the American Dream,'" Harvard University, February 29, 2004, www.harvard.edu/president/news-speeches -summers/2004/president-lawrence-h-summers-remarks-at-ace-higher-education-and-the -american-dream. See also Richard D. Kahlenberg, "Toward Affirmative Action for Economic Diversity," *Chronicle of Higher Education*, March 19, 2024, www.chronicle.com/article /toward-affirmative-action-for-economic-diversity.

3. "President Lawrence H. Summers' Remarks at ACE."

4. Kahlenberg, "Toward Affirmative Action for Economic Diversity."

5. The April 2004 lectures were the basis for a 2005 book. See William G. Bowen, Martin A. Kurzweil, and Eugene M. Tobin, *Equity and Excellence in American Higher Education* (Charlottesville: University of Virginia Press, 2005), 9 (referencing April 2004 lectures).

6. Schmidt, *Color and Money*, 212.

7. Bowen, Kurzweil, and Tobin, *Equity and Excellence*, 105 (Table 5.1), 289 (Appendix Table 5.1).

8. Richard D. Kahlenberg, "Class Action: Why Education Needs Quotas for Poor Kids," *Washington Monthly*, May 2005, 53–54.

9. Bowen, Kurzweil, and Tobin, *Equity and Excellence*, 115; Bowen and Bok, *Shape of the River*, 77.

10. Bowen, Kurzweil, and Tobin, *Equity and Excellence*, 115.

11. Anthony Marx, email message to author, August 1, 2003.

12. Anthony W. Marx, "Venture Capitalists of the Mind," May 23, 2004, www.amherst.edu /news/magazine/issue-archive/2004_summer/venture.

13. Sara Rimer, "Elite Colleges Open New Door to Low-Income Youths," *New York Times*, May 27, 2007, www.nytimes.com/2007/05/27/education/27grad.html. See also Richard D. Kahlenberg, "Anthony Marx's Legacy at Amherst," *Chronicle of Higher Education*, October 14, 2010, www .chronicle.com/blogs/innovations/anthony-marx's-legacy-at-amherst.

14. Bowen relayed this anecdote (without naming Summers) in Bowen, Kurzweil, and Tobin, *Equity and Excellence*, 176.

15. Lani Guinier, "The Real Bias in Higher Education," *New York Times*, June 24, 1997, www .nytimes.com/1997/06/24/opinion/the-real-bias-in-higher-education.html; Ethan Bronner, "Dividing Lines: Colleges Look for Answers to Racial Gap in Testing," *New York Times*, November 8, 1997, www.nytimes.com/1997/11/08/us/dividing-lines-special-report-colleges-look-for-answers-ra cial-gaps-testing.html (citing unpublished dissertation from the Harvard Graduate School of Education).

16. See the Consortium on Financing Higher Education website at https://web.mit.edu/cofhe /index.html.

17. Clayton Spencer, Tony Carnevale, and Tony Broh, in conversation with author, June 23, 2004.

Notes to Chapter 4

18. Richard D. Kahlenberg, "National Imperative for Educating Low-Income Students," College Board Forum, Chicago, November 1, 2004.

19. Richard D. Kahlenberg, introduction to Kahlenberg, *Rewarding Strivers*, 3.

20. Alexandra A. Chaidez, Molly C. McCafferty, and Aidan F. Ryan, "'This Is Not Who I Am': For Harvard Admissions Dean, the Trial Is Personal," *Harvard Crimson*, October 22, 2018, www.thecrimson.com/article/2018/10/22/fitzsimmons-faces-personal-reckoning; Alan Finder and Karen Arensen, "Harvard Ends Early Admission," *New York Times*, September 12, 2006, www.nytimes.com/2006/09/12/education/12harvard.html; "Harvard to Eliminate Early Admission," *Harvard Gazette*, September 12, 2006, https://news.harvard.edu/gazette/story/2006/09/harvard-to-eliminate-early-admission; Alan Finder, "Princeton Stops Its Early Admissions, Joining Movement to Make Process Fairer," *New York Times*, September 19, 2006, www.nytimes.com/2006/09/19/education/19admit.html; Susan Kinzi, "U-Va. Ends Early Decision Admissions," *Washington Post*, September 26, 2006, www.washingtonpost.com/archive/local/2006/09/26/u-va-ends-early-decision-admissions/a5ced4fe-a037-4a87-92db-10fbb58c19fe.

21. William G. Bowen and Michael McPherson, *Lesson Plan: An Agenda for Change in American Higher Education* (Princeton, NJ: Princeton University Press, 2016), 35.

22. James Fallows, "The Early-Decision Racket," *The Atlantic*, September 2001, www.theatlantic.com/magazine/archive/2001/09/the-early-decision-racket/302280 (citing research by Christopher Avery, Andrew Fairbanks, and Richard Zeckhauser, *The Early Admissions Game* [Cambridge, MA: Harvard University Press, 2003]).

23. For example, Harvard did so in 2011. See Richard D. Kahlenberg, "The Restoration of Early Admissions," *Chronicle of Higher Education*, February 25, 2011, www.chronicle.com/blogs/innovations/the-restoration-of-early-admissions.

24. Richard D. Kahlenberg, introduction to *Affirmative Action for the Rich: Legacy Preferences in College Admissions*, ed. Richard D. Kahlenberg (New York: Century Foundation Press, 2010), 8, 2; Richard D. Kahlenberg, "Elite Colleges, or Colleges for the Elite?," *New York Times*, September 29, 2010, www.nytimes.com/2010/09/30/opinion/30kahlenberg.html; Frederick M. Hess and Richard D. Kahlenberg, "Why It's Time for Legacy College Admissions to Go," *Time*, May 8, 2023, https://time.com/6276372/legacy-college-admissions-democrat-republican.

25. Daniel Golden, *The Price of Admission: How America's Ruling Class Buys Its Way into Elite Colleges—and Who Gets Left Outside the Gates* (New York: Crown, 2006), 232.

26. Michael Dannenberg, interview with author (interview notes confirmed in email to author, March 11, 2024).

27. Michael Dannenberg, "New Paths to Racial and Economic Diversity on Campus," National Association for College Admission Counseling, Baltimore, September 21, 2023; Michael Dannenberg, email message to author, January 26, 2024.

28. Michael Dannenberg, "Affirmative Action for the Rich? Legacy Preferences in College Admissions," National Press Club, Washington, D.C., September 22, 2010.

29. Richard D. Kahlenberg, introduction to Kahlenberg, *Affirmative Action for the Rich*, 10.

30. John Brittain, interview with author, February 1, 2024; "S.C. Dobbs, 81, Dies: Coca-Cola Ex-Head," *New York Times*, November 2, 1950, www.nytimes.com/1950/11/02/archives/sc-dobbs-81-dies-cocacola-exhead-former-president-of-company-had.html.

31. Richard D. Kahlenberg, "A Civil Rights Hero Is Honored," Century Foundation, April 1, 2022, https://tcf.org/content/commentary/a-civil-rights-is-honored; James Traub, "Can Separate Be Equal?," *Harper's Magazine*, June 1994, 40.

32. Kahlenberg, "Civil Rights Hero Is Honored." The meetings were held in Washington, D.C., on February 26 and May 27, 2010.

33. Dannenberg, interview with author; *Students for Fair Admissions v. Harvard*, 600 U.S. at 386 (Jackson, dissenting) (citing a white student who would be "the seventh generation to graduate from UNC" and arguing that a Black student should similarly have his race considered).

Notes to Chapter 4

34. Anemona Hartocollis and Amy Harmon, "Affirmative Action Ruling Shakes Universities over More Than Race," *New York Times*, July 26, 2023, www.nytimes.com/2023/07/26/us/affirmative-action-college-admissions-harvard.html.

35. *Grutter v. Bollinger*, 539 U.S. at 368 (Thomas, dissenting).

36. Thomas J. Espenshade and Alexandria Walton Radford, *No Longer Separate, Not Yet Equal* (Princeton, NJ: Princeton University Press, 2009), 92 (Table 3.5), 411–412 (at highly selective private institutions, the boost provided to African American applicants is worth 310 SAT points on a 1600 scale, compared with 130 points for poor students and 70 points for working-class applicants relative to middle-class pupils, according to 1997 data); Sean F. Reardon, Rachel Baker, Matt Kasman, Daniel Klasik, and Joseph B. Townsend, "Can Socioeconomic Status Substitute for Race in Affirmative Action College Admissions Policies? Evidence from a Simulation Model," Educational Testing Service, 2015, 6, www.ets.org/Media/Research/pdf/reardon_white_paper.pdf (study of forty selective colleges using 2004 data, which concludes that "racial affirmative action plays (or played, in 2004) some role in admissions to highly selective colleges but SES-based affirmative action did not"); Kahlenberg, "Expert Report, *Students for Fair Admissions v. University of North Carolina*"; Richard D. Kahlenberg, "Expert Report, *Students for Fair Admissions v. Harvard*," October 16, 2017, 26–27, https://studentsforfairadmissions.org/wp-content/uploads/2018/06/Doc-416-1-Kahlenberg-Expert-Report.pdf (race counted much more than economic status in admissions for the class of 2019, which was admitted in 2015).

37. Espenshade and Radford, *No Longer Separate, Not Yet Equal*, 98 (Figure 3).

38. Richard D. Kahlenberg, "The Dismal Pell Numbers at Wealthy Colleges," *Chronicle of Higher Education*, April 1, 2011, www.chronicle.com/blogs/innovations/the-dismal-pell-numbers-at-wealthy-colleges; Leonhardt, "Top Colleges, Largely for the Elite"; Jennifer Giancola and Richard D. Kahlenberg, "True Merit: Ensuring Our Brightest Students Have Access to Our Best Colleges and Universities," Jack Kent Cooke Foundation, January 11, 2016, www.jkcf.org/research/true-merit-ensuring-our-brightest-students-have-access-to-our-best-colleges-and-universities.

39. Beckie Supiano and Andrea Fuller, "Elite Colleges Fail to Gain More Students on Pell Grants," *Chronicle of Higher Education*, March 27, 2011, www.chronicle.com/article/elite-colleges-fail-to-gain-more-students-on-pell-grants.

40. Giancola and Kahlenberg, "True Merit," 5 (Table 1), 6 (Figure 2), 40. See also Michael Bastedo, "Enrollment Management and the Low-Income Student," American Enterprise Institute, August 4, 2015, 1, www.aei.org/research-products/report/enrollment-management-low-income-student; Paul Fain, "Finding the Right Match," *Inside Higher Ed*, August 4, 2015, www.insidehighered.com/news/2015/08/05/conference-and-new-research-takes-broader-look-college-match-challenge.

41. Melissa Korn, "Many Colleges Fail in Push to Boost Enrollment of Lower-Income Students," *Wall Street Journal*, September 14, 2022, www.wsj.com/articles/many-colleges-fail-in-push-to-boost-enrollment-of-lower-income-students-11663164001.

42. Richard D. Kahlenberg, "How Much Do You Pay for College?," *Chronicle of Higher Education*, February 11, 2013, www.chronicle.com/article/how-much-do-you-pay-for-college.

43. David Deming, "The Single Biggest Fix to Inequality at Elite Colleges," *The Atlantic*, December 5, 2023, www.theatlantic.com/ideas/archive/2023/12/legacy-admissions-inequality-elite-colleges/676233 (noting that a few elite schools such as Princeton and Yale increased the proportion of Pell students by more than 60 percent between 2011 and 2021, but also that focusing on Pell eligibility is much less illuminating than showing income quintiles).

44. Jason Delisle, "The Pell Grant Proxy: A Ubiquitous but Flawed Measure of Low-Income Student Enrollment," Brookings Institution, October 12, 2017, www.brookings.edu/articles/the-pell-grant-proxy-a-ubiquitous-but-flawed-measure-of-low-income-student-enrollment. See also Paul Tough, *The Years That Matter Most: How College Makes or Breaks Us* (New York: Houghton Mifflin Harcourt, 2019), 119; Deming, "Single Biggest Fix" (bottom half of the income distribution).

Notes to Chapter 4

45. Tough, *Years That Matter Most*, 119–121; Caroline Hoxby and Sarah Turner, "Measuring Opportunity in U.S. Higher Education" (NBER Working Paper Series 25479, National Bureau of Economic Research, Cambridge, MA, 2019), www.doi.org/10.3386/w25479.

46. Richard D. Kahlenberg, "Reflections on Richard Sander's *Class in American Legal Education*," *Denver University Law Review* 88 (September 2011): 719.

47. Richard H. Sander, "Class in American Legal Education," *Denver Law Review* 88 (September 2011): 649.

48. Chetty et al., "Mobility Report Cards"; "Some Colleges Have More Students from the Top 1 Percent Than the Bottom 60. Find Yours," *New York Times*, January 18, 2017, www.nytimes.com /interactive/2017/01/18/upshot/some-colleges-have-more-students-from-the-top-1-percent-than -the-bottom-60.html.

49. Mandery, *Poison Ivy*, 25.

50. "Economic Diversity and Student Outcomes at Harvard University," *New York Times*, January 18, 2017, www.nytimes.com/interactive/projects/college-mobility/harvard-university; "Economic Diversity and Student Outcomes at Princeton University," *New York Times*, January 18, 2017, www.nytimes.com/interactive/projects/college-mobility/princeton-university; "Economic Diversity and Student Outcomes at Amherst College," *New York Times*, January 18, 2017, www.nytimes .com/interactive/projects/college-mobility/amherst-college.

51. David Brooks, "What If We're the Bad Guys Here?," *New York Times*, August 2, 2023, www .nytimes.com/2023/08/02/opinion/trump-meritocracy-educated.html.

52. Rob Henderson, "'Luxury Beliefs' That Only the Privileged Can Afford," *Wall Street Journal*, February 9, 2024, www.wsj.com/us-news/education/luxury-beliefs-that-only-the-privileged -can-afford-7f6b8a16.

53. Sara Goldrick-Rab, "Promoting Economic Diversity for College Affordability," in Kahlenberg, *Future of Affirmative Action*, 35–36 (noting that while it is true that elite higher education is the domain of the wealthy because it is so expensive, the reverse is also true: that catering to the demands of wealthy students further drives up the cost of college).

54. John Rosenberg, "Aiming for Excellence," *Harvard Magazine*, July/August 2022, www .harvardmagazine.com/2022/06/montage-aiming-for-excellence (citing Colin Diver).

55. Alan Blinder, "Why Colleges Can't Quit the U.S. News Rankings," *New York Times*, September 16, 2023, www.nytimes.com/2023/09/16/us/us-news-rankings-medical-schools-colleges.html.

56. Emily Bazelon, "Selective Colleges Are Shockingly Bad at Recruiting Poor Kids of All Races," *Slate*, June 25, 2013, https://slate.com/news-and-politics/2013/06/supreme-court-affirma tive-action-case-colleges-are-shockingly-bad-at-recruiting-poor-kids.html. After the U.S. Supreme Court decision striking down racial preferences, elite colleges that were planning to switch to class had an incentive to push *U.S. News* to give more value to socioeconomic diversity in the rankings, which the magazine did. See discussion below in Chapter 11.

57. Carnevale, interview with author.

58. Walter Benn Michaels and Adolph Reed, *No Politics but Class Politics* (London: ERIS Press, 2023), 198.

59. Lilah Burke, "Faculty More Likely to Have Wealthier, Highly Educated Parents," *Inside Higher Ed*, March 28, 2021, www.insidehighered.com/quicktakes/2021/03/29/faculty-more-likely -have-wealthier-highly-educated-parents.

60. Michael J. Sandel, *The Tyranny of Merit: What's Become of the Common Good?* (New York: Farrar, Straus and Giroux, 2020), 95–96 (citing Toon Kuppens, Russell Spears, Antony S. R. Manstead, Bram Spruyt, and Matthew J. Easterbrook, "Educationalism and the Irony of Meritocracy: Negative Attitudes of Higher Educated People Towards the Less Educated," *Journal of Experimental Social Psychology* 76 [May 2018]: 441–442).

61. Bowen, Kurzweil, and Tobin, *Equity and Excellence*, 105 (Table 5.1), 289 (Appendix Table 5.1).

62. Walter Benn Michaels, *The Trouble with Diversity: How We Learned to Love Identity and Ignore Inequality* (New York: Metropolitan Books, 2006), 81.

Notes to Chapter 5

63. Michaels and Reed, *No Politics but Class Politics*, 298.

64. Libby Sander, "Students Try to Break Taboo Around Social Class on Campus," *Chronicle of Higher Education*, May 17, 2013, www.chronicle.com/article/students-try-to-break-taboo-around -social-class-on-campus; Heather Berg, interview with author, March 14, 2024.

65. Berg, interview with author.

66. Justin Pope, "Affirmative Action Sparks Debate over Race v. Class," *Diverse Issues in Higher Education*, June 17, 2013, www.diverseeducation.com/home/article/15093287/affirmative-action -case-sparks-debate-over-race-vs-class.

67. Chase Sackett, interview with author, February 22, 2024.

68. Chase Sackett and Grant Damon, eds., "Class/Action: A Report on Socioeconomic Class as Experienced by Students at Yale Law School," March 2013, 8, https://law.yale.edu/sites/default /files/area/department/studentaffairs/2013class_action_report.pdf; Camille L. Ryan and Kurt Bauman, "Educational Attainment in the United States: 2015," U.S. Census Bureau, March 2016, Table 1, www.census.gov/content/dam/Census/library/publications/2016/demo/p20-578.pdf.

69. Richard Sander, "The Use of Socioeconomic Affirmative Action at the University of California," in Kahlenberg, *Future of Affirmative Action*, 99.

70. Kate Antonovics and Ben Backes, "The Effect of Banning Affirmative Action on College Admissions Policies and Student Quality," *Journal of Human Resources* 49, no. 2 (Spring 2014): 306.

71. Sander, "Use of Socioeconomic Affirmative Action," 105.

72. David Leonhardt, "California's Upward-Mobility Machine," *New York Times*, September 16, 2015, www.nytimes.com/2015/09/17/upshot/californias-university-system-an-upward-mobil ity-machine.html; Kahlenberg and Potter, "Better Affirmative Action."

73. Supiano and Fuller, "Elite Colleges Fail to Gain More Students on Pell Grants."

74. Carnevale and Strohl, "How Increasing College Access Is Increasing Inequality," 170 (Table 3.7) (finding that class barriers are seven times as powerful as race barriers in predicting SAT scores).

CHAPTER 5

1. Richard D. Kahlenberg, "Time for a New Strategy," *Inside Higher Ed*, November 10, 2006.

2. "Brief of Oklahoma and Thirteen States as Amici Curiae in Support of Petitioner, *Students for Fair Admissions v. Harvard*."

3. Barack Obama, "Keynote Address at the 2004 Democratic National Convention," July 27, 2004, www.presidency.ucsb.edu/documents/keynote-address-the-2004-democratic-national-con vention.

4. John B. Judis and Ruy Teixeira, *Where Have All the Democrats Gone? The Soul of the Party in the Age of Extremes* (New York: Henry Holt, 2023), 89.

5. Timothy Shenk, "A Lost Manuscript Shows the Fire Barack Obama Couldn't Reveal on the Campaign Trail," *New York Times*, October 7, 2022, www.nytimes.com/2022/10/07/opinion /obama-lost-book-manuscript.html.

6. Nicholas Lemann, "Can Affirmative Action Survive?," *New Yorker*, July 26, 2021, www .newyorker.com/magazine/2021/08/02/can-affirmative-action-survive.

7. Richard D. Kahlenberg, "Obama's RFK Moment," *Slate*, February 4, 2008, www.slate.com /articles/news_and_politics/politics/2008/02/obamas_rfk_moment.html. For Obama's support as a legislator, see Richard D. Kahlenberg, "A Touch of Class," *The Guardian*, May 23, 2008 (noting that Obama campaigned against the Michigan affirmative action ban in 2006).

8. "Transcript: Barack Obama's Speech on Race," National Public Radio, March 18, 2008, www .npr.org/templates/story/story.php?storyId=88478467; Richard D. Kahlenberg, "Barack Obama and Affirmative Action," *Inside Higher Ed*, May 12, 2008.

9. Kahlenberg, "Barack Obama and Affirmative Action"; Richard D. Kahlenberg, "What's Next for Affirmative Action?," *The Atlantic*, November 2008, www.theatlantic.com/magazine/archive /2008/11/what-s-next-for-affirmative-action/307122; Kahlenberg, "Obama's RFK Moment."

Notes to Chapter 5

10. Rachel Swarns, "For Obama, a Delicate Path on Race and Class," *New York Times*, August 3, 2008, www.nytimes.com/2008/08/03/world/americas/03iht-obama.1.14965389.html.

11. Swarns.

12. Kahlenberg, "What's Next for Affirmative Action?"

13. Kahlenberg, "Touch of Class."

14. Marian Wright Edelman, "Voting," *Politico*, November 4, 2008, https://web.archive .org/web/20120105215443/http://www.politico.com/arena/perm/Marian_Wright_Edelman _3D2A213C-D36A-4D72-8E71-CA8956B95358.html.

15. Matt Schudel, "Cassandra Q. Butts, Obama Law School Classmate and Adviser, Dies at 50," *Washington Post*, May 28, 2016, www.washingtonpost.com/politics/cassandra-q-butts-obama-law -school-classmate-and-adviser-dies-at-50/2016/05/28/20950d2c-24e1-11e6-9e7f-57890b612299 _story.html.

16. Jess Bravin, "Government Court Brief Backs Race-Based Admissions," *Wall Street Journal*, March 31, 2010, www.wsj.com/articles/SB10001424052702303601504575153502859094306.

17. Richard D. Kahlenberg and John C. Brittain, "10 Ways Colleges Can Diversify After Affirmative Action," *Chronicle of Higher Education*, November 9, 2022, www.chronicle.com /article/10-ways-colleges-can-diversify-after-affirmative-action?.

18. Steve Benen, "Limbaugh, Health Care, and 'Reparations,'" *Washington Monthly*, February 23, 2010, https://washingtonmonthly.com/2010/02/23/limbaugh-health-care-and-reparations.

19. Jesse C. Baumgartner, Sara R. Collins, David C. Radley, and Susan L. Hayes, "How the Affordable Care Act Has Narrowed Racial and Ethnic Disparities in Access to Health Care," Commonwealth Fund, January 16, 2020, www.commonwealthfund.org/publications/2020/jan/how -ACA-narrowed-racial-ethnic-disparities-access.

20. "Obama on Racism: He's Been Mistaken for a Valet, Waiter," *Chicago Sun-Times*, December 17, 2014, https://chicago.suntimes.com/politics/2014/12/17/18614554/obama-on-racism-he -s-been-mistaken-for-a-valet-waiter.

21. Phil McCombs, "The Civil Struggles of Linda Chavez," *Washington Post*, January 30, 1984, www.washingtonpost.com/archive/lifestyle/1984/01/30/the-civil-struggles-of-linda-chavez /4a69466c-0c73-4db0-b4b4-1f643a95c5f1.

22. *Parents Involved in Community Schools v. Seattle*, 551 U.S. 701, 748 (2007).

23. Jeffery Toobin, *The Nine: Inside the Secret World of the Supreme Court* (New York: Doubleday, 2007), 336 (citing Breyer).

24. Kennedy invalidated the Seattle and Louisville programs because "the schools could have achieved their stated ends through different means." *Parents Involved in Community Schools v. Seattle*, 127 S. Ct. 2738, 2793 (2007). Kennedy also joined the Court's plurality opinion, which found that in Seattle, several race-neutral alternatives had been rejected "with little or no consideration" and that Jefferson County (Louisville) "failed to present any evidence that it considered alternatives." 127 S. Ct. at 2760.

25. Kahlenberg, *All Together Now*. See also Century Foundation Task Force on the Common School, *Divided We Fail: Coming Together Through Public School Choice* (New York: Century Foundation Press, 2002).

26. Halley Potter and Michelle Burris, "Here Is What School Integration in America Looks Like Today," Century Foundation, December 2, 2020, https://tcf.org/content/report/school -integration-america-looks-like-today.

27. "Education, Industry Leaders See Legal Threats to Diversity in Higher Ed S&T Programs," *AAAS News*, February 2008.

28. "Expanding Inclusion in Higher Education," Ford Foundation, New York, April 11, 2008.

29. Kahlenberg, "What's Next for Affirmative Action?"

30. "College for All Texans: Automatic Admissions—Top 10% Rule," Texas Higher Education Coordinating Board, accessed June 28, 2024, www.collegeforalltexans.com/index.cfm?objectid =24937C2A-D8B0-34EB-1FC5AF875A28C616; Richard D. Kahlenberg, "Will the Supreme Court

Notes to Chapter 5

Kill Diversity?," *Chronicle of Higher Education*, February 22, 2012, www.chronicle.com/blogs/innova
tions/will-the-supreme-court-kill-diversity (on socioeconomic factors employed).

31. Richard D. Kahlenberg, "Diversity or Discretion?," *Inside Higher Ed*, October 22, 2012,
www.insidehighered.com/views/2012/10/22/essay-questions-motives-u-texas-affirmative-action
-case. UT Austin began the system of capping the percentage plan at 75 percent of seats in 2009.

32. Kahlenberg, "Will the Supreme Court Kill Diversity?"

33. *Fisher v. University of Texas*, 133 S. Ct. 2411, 2416 (2013); Kahlenberg and Potter, "Better Affirmative Action," 26–30; Bridget Terry Long, "Expert Report, *Students for Fair Admissions v.
University of North Carolina*," January 12, 2018, 20, https://admissionslawsuit.unc.edu/wp-content
/uploads/sites/841/2019/01/Exhibit-030.pdf.

34. Kahlenberg, "Diversity or Discretion?"

35. James C. McKinley Jr., "Texas Vote Curbs a College Admission Guarantee Meant to Bol-
ster Diversity," *New York Times*, May 30, 2009, www.nytimes.com/2009/05/31/education/31texas
.html?.

36. Kahlenberg, "Diversity or Discretion?"

37. David G. Savage, "Supreme Court to Revisit Affirmative Action in Texas Case," *Los Angeles
Times*, September 27, 2012, www.latimes.com/world/la-xpm-2012-sep-27-la-na-court-affirmative
-20120928-story.html.

38. Kahlenberg, "Diversity or Discretion?"

39. Richard D. Kahlenberg, "The University of Texas's Weak Affirmative-Action Defense,"
Chronicle of Higher Education, August 8, 2012, www.chronicle.com/blogs/innovations/the-uni
versity-of-texass-weak-affirmative-action-defense.

40. Sander, "Class in American Legal Education."

41. Carnevale and Rose, "Socioeconomic Status, Race/Ethnicity, and Selective College Admissions," 142; Carnevale, Rose, and Strohl, "Achieving Racial and Economic Diversity with Race-Blind
Admissions Policy," 194–195.

42. Richard D. Kahlenberg, "The Achilles Heel of Affirmative Action," *Chronicle of Higher
Education*, October 11, 2012, www.chronicle.com/blogs/conversation/the-achilles-heel-of-affir
mative-action.

43. Carnevale and Strohl, "How Increasing College Access Is Increasing Inequality," 170 (Table
3.7).

44. Carnevale and Strohl, 165, 170 (noting that the wealth measure was restricted to savings of
between $0 and $40,000, yielding a penalty of forty-one points, and that "if a wealthy family saves
$175,000 for college, the gap between rich and poor would increase to −175 points").

45. Kahlenberg, introduction to Kahlenberg, *Rewarding Strivers*, 14.

46. Sean Reardon, "The Widening Academic Achievement Gap," Center for Education
Policy Analysis, 93, 98, https://cepa.stanford.edu/content/widening-academic-achievement-gap
-between-rich-and-poor-new-evidence-and-possible.

47. Putnam, *Our Kids*, 125–126.

48. Eric Levitz, "How Anti-Racist Is Anti-Racism?," *New York*, July 23, 2021, https://nymag
.com/intelligencer/2021/07/how-anti-racist-is-ibram-x-kendis-anti-racism.html.

49. Kahlenberg, *Excluded*, 98–99.

50. See discussion below in Chapter 10 of Black representation at the University of North
Carolina.

51. *Regents of University of California v. Bakke*, 438 U.S. at 407 (Blackmun, concurring).

52. Kahlenberg and Potter, "Better Affirmative Action," 4; Richard D. Kahlenberg, "A New Kind
of Affirmative Action to Ensure Diversity," *Chronicle of Higher Education*, October 3, 2012, www
.chronicle.com/article/a-new-kind-of-affirmative-action-can-ensure-diversity.

53. Kahlenberg and Potter, "Better Affirmative Action," 11, 76.

54. Kahlenberg and Potter, 12, 26–61; Ray Rodrigues and Samuel J. Abrams, "The Florida Way:
Diversity Without Affirmative Action," *RealClearEducation*, August 7, 2023, www.realclearedu

Notes to Chapter 5

cation.com/articles/2023/08/07/the_florida_way_diversity_without_affirmative_action_9709
83.html.

55. Richard L. McCormick, "Converging Perils to College Access for Racial Minorities: Examples of Responses That Work from Washington State and New Jersey," in Kahlenberg, *Future of Affirmative Action*, 118.

56. *Johnson v. Board of Regents*, 106 F. Supp. 2d 1362 (S.D. Ga. 2000).

57. Nancy G. McDuff and Halley Potter, "Ensuring Diversity Under Race-Neutral Admissions at the University of Georgia," in Kahlenberg, *Future of Affirmative Action*, 126.

58. McDuff and Potter, 123; Kahlenberg and Potter, "Better Affirmative Action," 48–51.

59. Kahlenberg and Potter, 15.

60. See discussion below in Chapter 10.

61. Richard D. Kahlenberg, "A Liberal Critique of Racial Preferences," *Wall Street Journal*, October 10, 2012, www.wsj.com/articles/SB10000872396390444897304578046531385328710.

62. "Supreme Court Hears Affirmative Action Challenges by Public College Applicants," *PBS NewsHour*, October 10, 2012, www.pbs.org/newshour/show/supreme-court-hears-affirma tive-action-challenges#transcript.

63. Oral argument transcript, *Fisher v. University of Texas*, U.S. Supreme Court, October 10, 2012, 43, www.supremecourt.gov/oral_arguments/argument_transcripts/2012/11-345.pdf.

64. Kahlenberg, "Achilles Heel of Affirmative Action."

65. Richard D. Kahlenberg, "Why Socioeconomic Diversity?," Money at Midd Conference, Middlebury College, Middlebury, VT, November 28, 2012.

66. Kahlenberg, "How Much Do You Pay for College?"

67. Kahlenberg.

68. David Leonhardt, "Better Colleges Failing to Lure Talented Poor," *New York Times*, March 16, 2013, www.nytimes.com/2013/03/17/education/scholarly-poor-often-overlook-better-colleges.html?; Hoxby and Avery, "Missing 'One-Offs.'"

69. Leonhardt, "Better Colleges Failing to Lure Talented Poor"; Richard D. Kahlenberg, "The Untapped Pool of Low-Income Strivers," *Chronicle of Higher Education*, March 19, 2013, www.chronicle.com/blogs/conversation/the-untapped-pool-of-low-income-strivers.

70. Richard D. Kahlenberg, "Expert Rebuttal Report, *Students for Fair Admissions v. University of North Carolina*," April 6, 2018, 34, Appendix E, https://affirmativeactiondebate.files.wordpress.com/2021/06/2018.04.06-rebuttal-report-of-richard-kahlenberg.pdf (citing Caroline Hoxby, email message to Michael Petrilli, May 31, 2013). See also Carnevale, Schmidt, and Strohl, *Merit Myth*, 182 (noting that only 19 percent of high-scoring Black and Latino students go to selective colleges, compared with 31 percent of high-scoring white students).

71. David Leonhardt, "The Leading Liberal Against Affirmative Action," *New York Times*, March 9, 2013, https://archive.nytimes.com/economix.blogs.nytimes.com/2013/03/09/the-leading-liberal-against-affirmative-action.

72. "Looking Back, Moving Forward: A Conference on Race, Class, Opportunity, and School Boundaries in the Richmond Region," University of Richmond, Richmond, VA, March 14, 2013.

73. Gary Orfield, *Must We Bus? Segregated Schools and National Policy* (Washington, D.C.: Brookings Institution Press, 1978), 69. See also Gary Orfield and Chungmei Lee, *Why Segregation Matters: Poverty and Educational Inequality* (Cambridge, MA: Civil Rights Project at Harvard University, 2005), 8–9.

74. *Fisher v. University of Texas*, 570 U.S. 297, 312 (2013).

75. Mark Walsh, "Supreme Court's College Race Ruling Continues to Spur Debate," *Education Week*, July 19, 2013 (quoting my argument that the ruling was "a victory for racial diversity and a defeat for racial preferences").

76. *Fisher v. University of Texas*, 570 U.S. at 312.

77. Thomas Kane and James Ryan, "Why 'Fisher' Means More Work for Colleges," *Chronicle of Higher Education*, July 29, 2013, www.chronicle.com/article/why-fisher-means-more-work-for-colleges.

Notes to Chapter 6

78. *Fisher v. University of Texas*, 570 U.S. at 335 (Ginsburg, dissenting).

79. Kahlenberg, "Middle Ground on Race and College."

80. Glenn Loury, "Affirmative Distraction: Racial Preferences Won't Solve Racial Inequality," *City Journal*, Autumn 2022, www.city-journal.org/article/affirmative-distraction.

81. Anna Holmes, "Variety Show," *New York Times Magazine*, November 1, 2015, www.nytimes .com/2015/11/01/magazine/has-diversity-lost-its-meaning.html.

82. Loury, "Affirmative Distraction."

83. Paul M. Sniderman and Edward G. Carmines, *Reaching Beyond Race* (Cambridge, MA: Harvard University Press, 1997). See also Paul M. Sniderman and Thomas Leonard Piazza, *The Scar of Race* (Cambridge, MA: Harvard University Press, 1993), 102–104; and Robert P. Jones, Daniel Cox, Betsy Cooper, and Rachel Lienesch, "Anxiety, Nostalgia, and Mistrust: Findings from the 2015 American Values Survey," Public Religion Research Institute, November 17, 2015, 5, www.prri.org /research/survey-anxiety-nostalgia-and-mistrust-findings-from-the-2015-american-values-survey (finding resentment associated with racial preferences).

84. Kahlenberg, "Middle Ground on Race and College."

85. Long, "Expert Report, *Students for Fair Admissions v. University of North Carolina*," 4, 15–16.

86. John Judis, "Action Affirmed: A Heartwarming Tale of a Washington Policy Quixote," *New Republic*, July 15, 2013, https://newrepublic.com/article/113669/richard-kahlenberg-class -based-affirmative-action-prophet.

87. "New Paths to Higher Education Diversity After *Fisher v. University of Texas*," Lumina Foundation, Indianapolis, August 6–7, 2013.

88. Sheryll Cashin, *Place, Not Race: A New Vision of Opportunity in America* (Boston: Beacon Press, 2014), ix, xvi.

89. Richard D. Kahlenberg, "Affirmative Action Fail: The Achievement Gap by Income Is Twice the Gap by Race," *New Republic*, April 27, 2014, https://newrepublic.com/article/117529 /affirmative-action-fail-achievement-gap-income-twice-gap-r; Cashin, *Place, Not Race*, 78.

90. Kahlenberg, *Future of Affirmative Action*; Lumina Ideas Summit, "New Pathways to Higher Education Diversity," Washington, D.C., June 17, 2014; "New Paths to Higher Education Diversity," University of Michigan, Ann Arbor, August 13–14, 2014.

CHAPTER 6

1. Richard D. Kahlenberg, "Affirmative-Action Ruling Could Be Pyrrhic Victory for UT-Austin," *Chronicle of Higher Education*, July 17, 2014, www.chronicle.com/blogs/conversation /affirmative-action-ruling-could-be-pyrrhic-victory-for-ut-austin; *Fisher v. University of Texas*, 758 F.3d. 633 (5th Cir. 2014).

2. "Brief of Richard D. Kahlenberg as *Amicus Curiae* in Support of Neither Party, *Fisher v. University of Texas*," September 10, 2015, https://tarlton.law.utexas.edu/ld.php?content_id=19667238.

3. *Fisher v. University of Texas*, 758 F.3d at 656 (citing Bowen and Bok, *Shape of the River*, 51, referencing the work of Thomas Kane).

4. "Brief of Richard D. Kahlenberg," 29–31. See also Richard Sander and Aaron Danielson, "Thinking Hard About 'Race-Neutral' Admissions," *University of Michigan Journal of Law Reform* 47 (2014): 990–991 (finding that richer measures of socioeconomic status significantly increased the correlation between race and socioeconomic status and the racial dividend of class-based affirmative action).

5. Carnevale, Rose, and Strohl, "Achieving Racial and Economic Diversity with Race-Blind Admissions Policy"; David Leonhardt, "If Affirmative Action Is Doomed, What's Next?," *New York Times*, June 17, 2014, www.nytimes.com/2014/06/17/upshot/if-affirmative-action-is-doomed -whats-next.html.

6. Richard D. Kahlenberg, "What Sotomayor Gets Wrong About Affirmative Action," *Chronicle of Higher Education*, June 17, 2014, www.chronicle.com/article/what-sotomayor-gets -wrong-about-affirmative-action.

Notes to Chapter 6

7. Carnevale, Rose, and Strohl, "Achieving Racial and Economic Diversity with Race-Blind Admissions Policy," 192, Tables 15.1–15.2. Under the status quo, the mean SAT at these selective universities was 1230; under socioeconomic affirmative action, it would be 1322; and if one admitted the top 10 percent of test takers from every high school, the SAT mean would be 1254.

8. *Fisher v. University of Texas*, 758 F.3d at 657.

9. *Grutter v. Bollinger*, 539 U.S. at 324. See also *Regents of University of California v. Bakke*, 438 U.S. at 316.

10. *Grutter v. Bollinger*, 539 U.S. at 324, 330.

11. Steven A. Holmes, "Mulling the Idea of Affirmative Action for Poor Whites," *New York Times*, August 18, 1991, www.nytimes.com/1991/08/18/weekinreview/the-nation-mulling-the-idea -of-affirmative-action-for-poor-whites.html (citing Clyde Summers).

12. *Grutter v. Bollinger*, 539 U.S. at 332.

13. Kahlenberg, "Harvard's Class Gap."

14. Sandel, *Tyranny of Merit*, 95–96. See also Kahlenberg, "Harvard's Class Gap."

15. Dan Roberts, "Justice Scalia: Minority Students May Be Better Off Going to 'Lesser Schools,'" *The Guardian*, December 9, 2015, www.theguardian.com/law/2015/dec/09/supreme -court-affirmative-action-fisher-v-university-of-texas.

16. Richard D. Kahlenberg, "Right-Wing Judge for Working-Class Kids: In Praise of Samuel Alito's Stand on Affirmative Action in Higher Education," *New York Daily News*, December 11, 2015, www .nydailynews.com/2015/12/11/right-wing-judge-for-working-class-kids-in-praise-of-samuel -alitos-stand-on-affirmative-action-in-higher-education (citing Alito); Richard D. Kahlenberg, "Scalia's Rant and Alito's Reasoning: What Will Influence Anthony Kennedy and Determine the Fate of Affirmative Action in *Fisher*?," *Slate*, December 14, 2015, https://slate.com/news-and-politics/2015 /12/scalias-rant-and-alitos-reasoning-in-the-fisher-supreme-court-oral-arguments.html; oral argument transcript, *Fisher v. University of Texas*, U.S. Supreme Court, December 9, 2015, 41, 84.

17. Kahlenberg, "Scalia's Rant and Alito's Reasoning."

18. "Inter–Ivy League First Generation College Students Conference," Harvard University, Cambridge, MA, February 19–21, 2016; Richard D. Kahlenberg, "How Low-Income Students Are Fitting In at Elite Colleges," *The Atlantic*, February 24, 2016, www.theatlantic.com/education /archive/2016/02/the-rise-of-first-generation-college-students/470664.

19. bell hooks, "Confronting Class in the Classroom," in *The Critical Pedagogy Reader*, 4th ed., ed. Antonia Darder, Kortney Hernandez, Kevin D. Lam, and Marta Baltodano (New York: Routledge, 2023), http://doi.org/10.4324/9781003286080-13.

20. Kahlenberg, "How Low-Income Students Are Fitting In"; Laura Pappano, "First Gens United," *New York Times*, April 12, 2015, www.nytimes.com/2015/04/12/education/edlife/first -generation-students-unite.html.

21. Kahlenberg, "How Low-Income Students Are Fitting In."

22. Kahlenberg, "Harvard's Class Gap."

23. Kahlenberg, "How Low-Income Students Are Fitting In."

24. *Fisher v. University of Texas*, 579 U.S. at 365.

25. Emma Brown and Danielle Douglas-Gabriel, "Affirmative Action Advocates Shocked— and Thrilled—by Supreme Court's Ruling in University of Texas Case," *Washington Post*, June 23, 2016, www.washingtonpost.com/news/grade-point/wp/2016/06/23/affirmative-action-advocates -shocked-and-thrilled-by-supreme-courts-ruling-in-university-of-texas-case.

26. *Fisher v. University of Texas*, 579 U.S. at 389 (Alito, dissenting).

27. Kahlenberg, "Achieving Better Diversity" (citing Joan Biskupic).

28. Richard D. Kahlenberg, "Symposium: A Win for Wealthy Students," *SCOTUSblog*, June 23, 2016, www.scotusblog.com/2016/06/symposium-a-win-for-wealthy-students.

29. *Fisher v. University of Texas*, 579 U.S. at 381–382.

30. *Fisher v. University of Texas*, 579 U.S. at 385.

31. Sunny X. Niu and Marta Tienda, "Minority Student Academic Performance Under the Uniform Admission Law: Evidence from the University of Texas at Austin," *Educational Evaluation*

Notes to Chapter 7

and Policy Analysis 32, no. 44 (2010): abstract; Kalena E. Cortes, "Do Bans on Affirmative Action Hurt Minority Students? Evidence from the Texas Top 10% Plan," *Economics of Education Review* 29 (2010): 1110–1124.

32. "Brief of Richard D. Kahlenberg," 32 (citing Larry Faulkner, "The 'Top Ten Percent Law' Is Working for Texas," October 19, 2000).

33. "Four-Year Graduation Rate Rises from 51 to 66 Percent in Five Years," *UT News*, September 20, 2017, https://news.utexas.edu/2017/09/20/four-year-graduation-rate-rises-from-51-to-66 -percent (noting that four-year graduation rates had risen fifteen percentage points in the previous five years and set "a university record"; the six-year graduation rate was 82.9 percent).

34. Sander, "Use of Socioeconomic Affirmative Action at the University of California," 107.

35. Carnevale and Rose, "Socioeconomic Status, Race/Ethnicity, and Selective College Admissions," 148–149.

36. Alexandria Radford and Jessica Howell, "Addressing Undermatch: Creating Opportunity and Social Mobility," in Kahlenberg, *Future of Affirmative Action*, 134; Sander and Taylor, *Mismatch*, 254 (Figure 16.3).

37. *Fisher v. University of Texas*, 579 U.S. at 392 (Alito, dissenting).

38. *Fisher v. University of Texas*, 579 U.S. at 432–433 (Alito, dissenting).

39. Jack Stripling, "Admissions Report Chips at Austin Chief's Uncompromising Reputation," *Chronicle of Higher Education*, February 13, 2015, www.chronicle.com/article/admissions -report-chips-at-austin-chiefs-uncompromising-reputation; Richard D. Kahlenberg, "Affirmative Action for the Advantaged at UT-Austin," *Chronicle of Higher Education*, February 13, 2015, www .chronicle.com/blogs/conversation/affirmative-action-for-the-advantaged-at-ut-austin.

40. Sandel, *Tyranny of Merit*, 27.

CHAPTER 7

1. "Our Team," Consovoy McCarthy PLLC, accessed June 29, 2024, https://consovoy mccarthy.com/team/#open-overlay. In 2001, when Consovoy and McCarthy graduated from law school, George Mason Law ranked fortieth in the *U.S. News & World Report* poll. In 2024, it had risen to twenty-eight, an all-time high. See "Scholarship Fund Established in Memory of William S. Consovoy, '01," George Mason University Antonin Scalia School of Law, accessed June 29, 2024, www.law.gmu.edu/news/2023/will_consovoy_remembered_as_brilliant_jurist_dedicated _teacher; "Top 2000–2008 Law School Rankings," Prelaw Handbook, accessed June 29, 2024, www.prelawhandbook.com/law_school_rankings__2000_present; and Sarah Holland, "Mason Has 14 Graduate Programs in the Top 50 *U.S. News* Rankings," George Mason University, April 10, 2024, www.gmu.edu/news/2024-04/mason-has-14-graduate-programs-top-50-us-news-rank ings.

2. Century Foundation Task Force on Preventing Community Colleges from Becoming Separate and Unequal, *Bridging the Higher Education Divide: Strengthening Community Colleges and Restoring the American Dream* (New York: Century Foundation Press, 2013); Ned Resnikoff, "Keith Ellison Wants to Make Union Organizing a Civil Right," MSNBC, July 19, 2014, www.msnbc.com /msnbc/keith-ellison-union-organizing-civil-right-msna372951; Richard D. Kahlenberg, "Another Reason to Love John Lewis—His Stance on Labor," Century Foundation, August 3, 2020, https: //tcf.org/content/commentary/yet-another-reason-love-john-lewis-stance-labor.

3. Soledad O'Brien, in conversation with author, October 19, 2023.

4. Lulu Garcia-Navarro, "He Worked for Years to Overturn Affirmative Action and Finally Won. He's Not Done," *New York Times*, July 8, 2023, www.nytimes.com/2023/07/08/us/ed ward-blum-affirmative-action-race.html.

5. Peter Applebome, "Rights Movement in Struggle for an Image as Well as a Bill," *New York Times*, April 3, 1991, www.nytimes.com/1991/04/03/us/rights-movement-in-struggle-for-an-image -as-well-as-a-bill.html (citing Cornel West: "The power of the civil rights movement under Martin Luther King was its universalism").

Notes to Chapter 7

6. Nikki Graf, "Most Americans Say Colleges Should Not Consider Race or Ethnicity in Admissions," Pew Research Center, February 25, 2019, www.pewresearch.org/short-reads/2019/02/25/most-americans-say-colleges-should-not-consider-race-or-ethnicity-in-admissions.

7. See Chapter 10, below.

8. Theodore Roosevelt, "The Man in the Arena," Theodore Roosevelt Center, April 23, 1910, www.theodorerooseveltcenter.org/Learn-About-TR/TR-Encyclopedia/Culture-and-Society/Man-in-the-Arena.aspx.

9. Richard D. Kahlenberg and Clifford Janey, "Is Trump's Victory the Jump-Start Civics Education Needed?," *The Atlantic*, November 10, 2016, www.theatlantic.com/education/archive/2016/11/is-trumps-victory-the-jump-start-civics-education-needed/507293.

10. Charlie Savage, "Justice Dept. to Take on Affirmative Action in College Admissions," *New York Times*, August 1, 2017, www.nytimes.com/2017/08/01/us/politics/trump-affirmative-action-universities.html.

11. Richard D. Kahlenberg, "The Right Fix to Affirmative Action," *New York Daily News*, August 3, 2017.

12. Emma Brown and Sarah Larimer, "Trump Administration Reopens Volatile Debate over Race and College Admissions," *Washington Post*, August 2, 2017, www.washingtonpost.com/news/grade-point/wp/2017/08/02/trump-administration-reopens-volatile-debate-over-race-and-college-admissions.

13. Barton Swaim, "Politics: Timothy Shenk's 'Realigners,'" *Wall Street Journal*, October 7, 2022, www.wsj.com/articles/politics-book-review-timothy-shenks-realigners-11665153466 (citing Timothy Shenk, *Realigners: Partisan Hacks, Political Visionaries, and the Struggle to Rule American Democracy* [New York: Farrar, Straus and Giroux, 2022]). See also Jason Willick, "How the Degree Diploma Came to Dominate American Politics," *Washington Post*, October 1, 2023, www.washingtonpost.com/opinions/2023/10/01/understanding-electorate-diploma-divide (in 2020, Trump won 65 percent of working-class white votes, twenty points higher than George H. W. Bush's share in 1992).

14. Mark Lilla, "The End of Identity Liberalism," *New York Times*, November 18, 2016, www.nytimes.com/2016/11/20/opinion/sunday/the-end-of-identity-liberalism.html.

15. Ruy Teixeira, "An Insurance Policy for Democrats," *Liberal Patriot*, August 17, 2023, www.liberalpatriot.com/p/an-insurance-policy-for-democrats.

16. Sheri Berman, "How Identity Politics Aids the Right and Divides the Left," *Liberal Patriot*, April 19, 2023, www.liberalpatriot.com/p/how-identity-politics-ate-the-left.

17. McCarthy, "U.S. Approval of Interracial Marriage at New High of 94%"; Putnam and Garrett, *The Upswing*, 234 (Figure 6.9).

18. Thomas Edsall, "The Unsettling Truth About Trump's First Great Victory," *New York Times*, March 22, 2023, www.nytimes.com/2023/03/22/opinion/trump-racial-resentment-2016-2020.html.

19. Gideon Resnick, "Hillary Clinton on Election Night," *Daily Beast*, April 20, 2018, www.thedailybeast.com/hillary-clinton-they-were-never-going-to-let-me-be-president? (citing Amy Chozick, *Chasing Hillary: Ten Years, Two Presidential Campaigns, and One Intact Glass Ceiling* [New York: Harper, 2018]). In all, Trump won sixty-one million votes in 2016. See "2016 Presidential Election Results," *Politico*, December 13, 2016, www.politico.com/2016-election/results/map/president.

20. Aaron Blake, "Hillary Clinton Takes Her 'Deplorables' Argument for Another Spin," *Washington Post*, March 13, 2018, www.washingtonpost.com/news/the-fix/wp/2018/03/12/hillary-clinton-takes-her-deplorables-argument-for-another-spin.

21. Harold Meyerson, "The Democrats in Opposition," *American Prospect*, January 18, 2017, https://prospect.org/civil-rights/democrats-opposition.

22. Kahlenberg, "Harvard's Class Gap."

23. Guy Molyneux, "Mapping White Working-Class Voters," *American Prospect*, December 20, 2016, http://prospect.org/article/mapping-white-working-class.

Notes to Chapter 7

24. Hochschild, *Strangers in Their Own Land*, 137–139.

25. Daniel Cox, Rachel Lienesch, and Robert Jones, "Beyond Economics: Fears of Cultural Displacement Pushed the White Working Class to Trump," Public Religion Research Institute / *The Atlantic*, May 9, 2017, www.prri.org/research/white-working-class-attitudes-economy-trade-immigration-election-donald-trump.

26. Ashley Jardina, *White Identity Politics* (Cambridge: Cambridge University Press, 2019), 7, 11, 19, 66–67. See also Richard D. Kahlenberg, "The Rise of White Identity Politics," *Washington Monthly*, July 12, 2019, https://washingtonmonthly.com/2019/07/12/the-rise-of-white-identity-politics.

27. Barack Obama, *A Promised Land* (New York: Crown, 2020), 397.

28. Kahlenberg, "Harvard's Class Gap."

29. Kahlenberg, "Expert Report, *Students for Fair Admissions v. Harvard*," 26–27.

30. The increased odds are expressed in terms of the probability of being admitted divided by the probability of not being admitted.

31. Richard D. Kahlenberg, *Broken Contract: A Memoir of Harvard Law School* (New York: Hill and Wang, 1992), 117.

32. Kahlenberg, "Middle Ground on Race and College."

33. Jay Caspian Kang, "It's Time for an Honest Conversation About Affirmative Action," *New York Times*, January 27, 2022, www.nytimes.com/2022/01/27/opinion/affirmative-action-harvard.html.

34. Jonathan Zimmerman, "Affirmative Action and Anti–Asian American Bias," *Inside Higher Ed*, December 12, 2022, www.insidehighered.com/views/2022/12/12/addressing-alleged-anti-asian-biases-admissions-opinion.

35. *Students for Fair Admissions v. Harvard*, 601 U.S. 181, 222 (2023).

36. "Harvard Further Expands Financial Aid to Ease Access," *Harvard Gazette*, March 30, 2023, https://news.harvard.edu/gazette/story/2023/03/college-makes-regular-admission-offers-to-1220.

37. Peter Schmidt, "A History of Legacy Preferences and Privileges," in Kahlenberg, *Affirmative Action for the Rich*, 42.

38. Michelle Amponsah and Emma Haidar, "Could Losing Legacy Admissions Sustain Racial Diversity?," *Harvard Crimson*, September 22, 2023, www.thecrimson.com/article/2023/9/22/harvard-without-legacy (citing Harvard's admissions dean); Kahlenberg, "Expert Report, *Students for Fair Admissions v. Harvard*," 26–27; Peter Arcidiacono, Josh Kinsler, and Tyler Ransom, "Legacy and Athlete Preferences at Harvard" (NBER Working Paper 26316, National Bureau of Economic Research, Cambridge, MA, 2019), 40 (Table 1), 14, www.nber.org/system/files/working_papers/w26316/w26316.pdf.

39. David Card, "Racial Composition of Admitted ALDC Students in Each Class and Across Classes," Joint Appendix, *Students for Fair Admissions v. Harvard*, May 2, 2022, JA 1776, www.supremecourt.gov/DocketPDF/20/20-1199/222327/20220502145901917_20-1199%20Volume%20IV.pdf; Arcidiacono, Kinsler, and Ransom, "Legacy and Athlete Preferences at Harvard," 42 (Table 3), 49 (Table 11).

40. Kahlenberg, "Expert Report, *Students for Fair Admissions v. Harvard*," 32; Arcidiacono, Kinsler, and Ransom, "Legacy and Athlete Preferences at Harvard," 23 (citing *Harvard Crimson*).

41. Stacia L. Brown, "The Inspiring Story of the First Black Ivy League President," *Washington Post*, August 29, 2023, www.washingtonpost.com/books/2023/08/29/ruth-simmons-brown-memoir-review (reviewing Ruth Simmons, *Up Home: One Girl's Journey* [New York: Random House, 2023]).

42. Ruth Simmons, "Expert Report, *Students for Fair Admissions v. Harvard*," December 1, 2017, 20–22; Ruth Simmons, "Expert Rebuttal Report, *Students for Fair Admissions v. Harvard*," March 15, 2018, 7, 4; Kahlenberg, introduction to Kahlenberg, *Affirmative Action for the Rich*, 8.

43. Chad Coffman, Tara O'Neil, and Brian Starr, "An Empirical Analysis of Legacy Preferences on Alumni Giving at Top Universities," in Kahlenberg, *Affirmative Action for the Rich*, 113; Kahlenberg, introduction to Kahlenberg, *Affirmative Action for the Rich*, 8 (citing Jonathan Meer and Harvey S. Rosen, "Altruism and the Child-Cycle of Alumni Donations" [CEPS Working Paper 150,

Notes to Chapter 7

Princeton University, 2007], 48 [Figure 1], www.princeton.edu/~ceps/workingpapers/150rosen
.pdf); Kahlenberg, "Expert Report, *Students for Fair Admissions v. Harvard*," 33.

44. Kahlenberg, 33.

45. Golden, *Price of Admission*, 26.

46. Delano R. Franklin and Samuel W. Zwickel, "In Admissions, Harvard Favors Those Who
Fund It, Internal Emails Show," *Harvard Crimson*, October 18, 2018, www.thecrimson.com
/article/2018/10/18/day-three-harvard-admissions-trial; Arcidiacono, Kinsler, and Ransom, "Legacy and Athlete Preferences at Harvard," 14, 40 (Table 1), 48 (Table 9); Card, "Racial Composition
of Admitted ALDC Students," JA 1776.

47. Franklin and Zwickel, "In Admissions."

48. Franklin and Zwickel.

49. Franklin and Zwickel; Arcidiacono, Kinsler, and Ransom, "Legacy and Athlete Preferences
at Harvard," 42 (Table 3).

50. Golden, *Price of Admission*, 35.

51. Golden, 26, 37.

52. Kahlenberg, "Expert Report, *Students for Fair Admissions v. Harvard*," 35–36.

53. Arcidiacono, Kinsler, and Ransom, "Legacy and Athlete Preferences at Harvard," 40 (Table
1); Card, "Racial Composition of Admitted ALDC Students," JA 1776.

54. Simmons, "Expert Report, *Students for Fair Admissions v. Harvard*," 21; Simmons, "Expert
Rebuttal Report, *Students for Fair Admissions v. Harvard*," 9.

55. Arcidiacono, Kinsler, and Ransom, "Legacy and Athlete Preferences at Harvard," 40 (Table
1), 14, 5n8, 49 (Table 11) (finding that eliminating athletic preferences would result in fewer white
students, more Hispanic and Asian students, and roughly the same number of Black students), 23
(citing *Harvard Crimson*); Card, "Racial Composition of Admitted ALDC Students," JA 1776;
Kahlenberg, "Expert Report, *Students for Fair Admissions v. Harvard*," 47n162.

56. Arcidiacono, Kinsler, and Ransom, "Legacy and Athlete Preferences at Harvard," 16;
"Brief for Legal Scholars Defending Race-Conscious Admissions as Amicus Curiae, *Students for
Fair Admissions v. Harvard*," U.S. Supreme Court, August 1, 2022, 19, www.supremecourt.gov
/DocketPDF/20/20-1199/232386/20220801142646237_220703a%20Amicus%20Brief
%20for%20efiling.pdf.

57. Arcidiacono, Kinsler, and Ransom, "Legacy and Athlete Preferences at Harvard," 5.

58. Christopher Avery and Jonathan D. Levin, "Early Admissions at Selective Colleges" (NBER
Working Paper Series 14844, National Bureau of Economic Research, Cambridge, MA, 2009), 2,
www.nber.org/system/files/working_papers/w14844/w14844.pdf.

59. Alan Finder and Karen W. Arenson, "Harvard Ends Early Admission," *New York Times*, September 12, 2006, www.nytimes.com/2006/09/12/education/12harvard.html; Julie J. Park and M.
Kevin Eagan, "Who Goes Early? A Multi-Level Analysis of Enrolling via Early Action and Early
Decision Admissions," *Teachers College Record* 113, no. 11 (2011): 2345–2373; Michael Dannen-
berg, "Getting Rid of Legacy Preferences in College Admissions Would Be Satisfying: It's Not Nearly
Enough," *Slate*, April 14, 2023, https://slate.com/human-interest/2023/04/affirmative-action
-college-admissions-legacy-preference-abolition.html; Kahlenberg, "Expert Report, *Students for Fair
Admissions v. Harvard*," 43.

60. Kahlenberg, 43–44.

61. Kahlenberg, 44.

62. Christopher Avery and Jonathan Levin, "Early Admission at Selective Colleges" (SIEPR
Discussion Working Paper 08-31, Stanford Institute for Economic Policy Research, Stanford,
CA, 2009), 4n4, https://siepr.stanford.edu/publications/working-paper/early-admission-selective
-colleges; Simmons, "Expert Report, *Students for Fair Admissions v. Harvard*," 22.

63. Kahlenberg, 22. Of undergraduates, 56 percent did not have a parent with a bachelor's degree
or higher in 2015–2016. "First-Generation College Students," Center for First-Generation Student
Success, accessed July 2, 2024, https://firstgen.naspa.org/files/dmfile/FactSheet-01.pdf.

Notes to Chapter 7

64. Chetty et al., "Mobility Report Cards"; "Economic Diversity and Student Outcomes at Harvard University."

65. Kahlenberg, "Expert Report, *Students for Fair Admissions v. Harvard*," Appendix, Simulation 4; Richard D. Kahlenberg, "Supplemental Expert Report Regarding the Final Report of the Committee to Study Race-Neutral Alternatives, *Students for Fair Admissions v. Harvard*," April 26, 2018, 4–5, https://studentsfor.wpenginepowered.com/wp-content/uploads/2018/06/Doc-416-3-Kahlenberg-Errata.pdf; Andrew Howard Nichols and J. Oliver Schak, "Degree Attainment for Black Adults: National and State Trends," Education Trust, 2017, https://edtrust.org/wp-content/uploads/2014/09/Black-Degree-Attainment_FINAL.pdf.

66. Arcidiacono, Kinsler, and Ransom, "Legacy and Athlete Preferences at Harvard," 48 (Table 9).

67. Michaels and Reed, *No Politics but Class Politics*, 330, 343.

68. *City of Richmond v. Croson*, 488 U.S. at 519 (Kennedy, concurring in part and concurring in the judgment).

69. *Fisher v. University of Texas*, 133 S. Ct. at 2420.

70. Kane and Ryan, "Why 'Fisher' Means More Work for Colleges."

71. Kahlenberg, "Expert Report, *Students for Fair Admissions v. Harvard*," 16, 17–20, 23–36.

72. David Card, "Expert Report, *Students for Fair Admissions v. Harvard*," December 15, 2017, 103, https://affirmativeactiondebate.org/wp-content/uploads/2021/06/card-principal-report-redacted.pdf.

73. Kahlenberg, "Expert Rebuttal Report, *Students for Fair Admissions v. Harvard*," January 29, 2018, 22n85, 29–32, https://studentsforfairadmissions.org/wp-content/uploads/2018/06/Doc-416-2-Kahlenberg-Rebuttal-Report.pdf.

74. Kahlenberg, 32.

75. "'Segregation Forever?': The Continued Underrepresentation of Latino Undergraduates at the Nation's 122 Most Selective Private Colleges and Universities," Education Trust, February 28, 2024, 26 (Table 2), https://edtrust.org/resource/segregation-forever-the-continued-underrepresentation-of-black-undergraduates-at-the-nations-122-most-selective-private-colleges-and-universities.

76. Kahlenberg, "Expert Rebuttal Report, *Students for Fair Admissions v. Harvard*," Appendix (results from Simulation 7); Kahlenberg, "Expert Report, *Students for Fair Admissions v. Harvard*," 49, 22n75 (that "disadvantaged" covers more than two-thirds of American households).

77. Kahlenberg, "Expert Rebuttal Report, *Students for Fair Admissions v. Harvard*," Appendix (Simulation 7).

78. Richard D. Kahlenberg, "Expert Supplemental Report, *Students for Fair Admissions v. Harvard*," April 26, 2018, 4, https://studentsforfairadmissions.org/wp-content/uploads/2018/06/Doc-416-3-Kahlenberg-Errata.pdf.

79. Kahlenberg, 4–5.

80. Richard D. Kahlenberg, trial testimony transcript, *Students for Fair Admissions v. Harvard*, October 22, 2023, 52–53; Kahlenberg, "Expert Supplemental Report, *Students for Fair Admissions v. Harvard*," 2–3; Jessica Grose, "Why Those Super Low College Admissions Rates Can Be Misleading," *New York Times*, April 22, 2023, www.nytimes.com/2023/04/22/opinion/college-admissions.html? (citing a former Brown admissions officer estimating that between 60 percent and 85 percent of applicants were qualified).

81. Kahlenberg, "Expert Supplemental Report, *Students for Fair Admissions v. Harvard*," 5; Card, "Expert Report, *Students for Fair Admissions v. Harvard*," 153n220.

82. Adam Liptak, "Blunder in Affirmative Action Case May Cost Harvard $15 Million," *New York Times*, October 23, 2022, www.nytimes.com/2022/10/23/us/harvard-affirmative-action-litigation-cost.html (noting Harvard spent more than $27 million and UNC more than $24 million, while SFFA spent less than $8 million on the two cases combined).

83. "Felicia H. Ellsworth," WilmerHale, accessed July 2, 2024, www.wilmerhale.com/en/people

Notes to Chapter 7

/felicia-ellsworth; "Seth P. Waxman," WilmerHale, accessed July 2, 2024, www.wilmerhale.com/en /people/seth-waxman.

84. "Testimony of Richard D. Kahlenberg, *Students for Fair Admissions v. Harvard*," U.S. District Court, Boston, October 22, 2018, 8, 29–30.

85. "Kahlenberg Testimony, *Students for Fair Admissions v. Harvard*," JA 780–781, www .supremecourt.gov/DocketPDF/20/20-1199/222327/20220502145710361_20-1199 %20Volume%20II.pdf. This portion of the trial testimony was included in the Joint Appendix, but most of the trial testimony was not.

86. "Kahlenberg Testimony, *Students for Fair Admissions v. Harvard*," 60, 64.

87. "Kahlenberg Testimony, *Students for Fair Admissions v. Harvard*," 128, 51–52; Kahlenberg, "Supplemental Expert Report, *Students for Fair Admissions v. Harvard*," 2.

88. "Since 1980 Black Enrollments Have Increased at All but a Few of the Nation's Highest-Ranked Colleges and Universities," *Journal of Blacks in Higher Education*, 2006, www.jbhe.com/news _views/50_blackenrollments.html; Keith Butler, "Harvard's Black Admissions," *Harvard Crimson*, September 1, 1974, www.thecrimson.com/article/1974/9/1/harvards-black-admissions-pbibn-1968 -just; Dershowitz and Hanft, "Affirmative Action and the Harvard College Diversity-Discretion Model"; Jerome Karabel, *The Chosen: The Hidden History of Admission and Exclusion at Harvard, Yale, and Princeton* (Boston: Houghton Mifflin, 2005), 404; Elizabeth Bangs, "Harvard Adds Another 'Hallmark': 'Distinction and Diversity' Now Central to Your College Experience," *Harvard Crimson*, September 16, 1994, www.thecrimson.com/article/1994/9/16/harvard-adds -another-hallmark-pyou-may (noting Harvard's touting diversity "for years"); *Students for Fair Admissions v. Harvard*, 600 U.S. at 222 (class of 2016).

89. Kendi, "When I See Racial Disparities, I See Racism"; Kahlenberg, "Expert Report, *Students for Fair Admissions v. Harvard*," Appendix, Simulation 1, Status Quo; Maya Riser-Kositsky, "Education Statistics: Facts About American Schools," *Education Week*, January 9, 2024, www.edweek .org/leadership/education-statistics-facts-about-american-schools/2019/01 (Asian numbers); Michael Hansen and Diana Quintero, "Analyzing 'the Homework Gap' Among High School Students," Brookings Institution, August 10, 2017, www.brookings.edu/articles/analyzing-the -homework-gap-among-high-school-students; Susan Dominus, "Gone Guys: With Women Making Up a Majority of American Undergraduates, Some Colleges Are Going to Great Lengths to Enroll More Men," *New York Times Magazine*, September 10, 2023, www.nytimes.com/2023/09/08/maga zine/men-college-enrollment.html.

90. Phillip Levine and Dubravka Ritter, "The Racial Wealth Gap, Financial Aid, and College Access," Brookings Institution, September 27, 2022, Figure 1, www.brookings.edu/articles/the -racial-wealth-gap-financial-aid-and-college-access; William Darity Jr., "A New Agenda for Eliminating Racial Inequality in the United States: The Research We Need," William T. Grant Foundation, January 2019, 1, https://wtgrantfoundation.org/wp-content/uploads/2019/01/A-New-Agenda-for -Eliminating-Racial-Inequality-in-the-United-States_WTG-Digest-2018.pdf (noting that Black households headed by an individual with a bachelor's degree have just two-thirds of the wealth, on average, of white households headed by an individual who lacks a high school degree).

91. Harvard did not give us its information about the precise family income of financial aid applicants. Instead, we were given rough proxies that did not distinguish between members of the bottom half of the income distribution. This limitation was important because we could not give a bigger boost to impressive students from the bottom of the income distribution—students who were much more likely to be Black than white in America. See Kahlenberg, "Expert Report, *Students for Fair Admissions v. Harvard*," 52. Harvard also did not provide data on whether students were raised in a single-parent household. Students who grow up in homes with just one parent face extra obstacles, according to a broad body of research, and about two-thirds of Black children, compared with 25 percent of white children, were raised by a single parent in 2015. See Melissa S. Kearney, *The Two-Parent Privilege: How Americans Stopped Getting Married and Started Falling Behind* (Chicago: University of Chicago Press, 2023); and Annie E. Casey Foundation, "Children in

Notes to Chapter 7

Single-Parent Families by Race," Kids Count Data Center, 2018, http://datacenter.kidscount.org /data/tables/107-children-in-single-parent-families-by#detailed/1/any/false/573,869,36,868,867 /10,11,9,12,1,185,13/432,431.

92. Simulation D understated the possible racial dividend Harvard could achieve because it was limited to the existing pool of applicants—even though evidence suggested that Harvard did a poor job of recruiting disadvantaged students to apply. Harvard relied heavily on a relatively small number of "feeder" schools to fill a significant part of its class. For the classes of 2007–2016, 20.3 percent of matriculates and 12.9 percent of applicants came from schools that represented just 0.6 percent of American high schools. For the class of 2019, Harvard received applications from only 7,561 of the nation's 41,368 high schools. In other words, 82 percent of American high schools produced not a single applicant to Harvard, one of the world's best-known colleges. Harvard did a particularly poor job of recruiting first-generation college students, a disproportionate share of whom are Black. Although 68 percent of adults in the United States between the ages of forty-five and fifty-four lack a college degree, only 12.5 percent of Harvard applicants for the classes of 2007–2011 had parents without a college degree. For the class of 2009, nearly half of high-achieving, high-income students applied to Harvard, compared with less than a quarter of high-achieving low-income students. See Kahlenberg, "Expert Report, *Students for Fair Admissions v. Harvard,*" 39–40; and Card, "Expert Report, *Students for Fair Admissions v. Harvard,*" 130, Exhibit 48. In addition, in Simulation D, the preferences for early admissions were left in place. Another similar simulation that removed the early admissions preference saw a somewhat higher level of diversity. See Kahlenberg, "Expert Rebuttal Report, *Students for Fair Admissions v. Harvard,*" 32n124, Appendix (showing that Simulation D [aka Simulation 7] used the early admission preference, while Simulation 6, which turned it off, produced somewhat higher levels of diversity).

93. Tania LaViolet, Benjamin Fresquez, McKenzie Maxson, and Josh Wyner, "The Talent Blind Spot," Aspen Institute, June 27, 2018, www.aspeninstitute.org/publications/the-talent-blind-spot; Kahlenberg, "Expert Report, *Students for Fair Admissions v. Harvard,*" 41–42.

94. Richard D. Kahlenberg, "College Admissions Scandal Implicating Felicity Huffman and Lori Loughlin Reveals Elite Culture of Corruption," *NBC Think*, March 13, 2019, www.nbcnews .com/think/opinion/college-admissions-scandal-implicating-felicity-huffman-lori-loughlin -reveals-elite-ncna982961; Terry Nguyen, "College Officials Were Charged in the Admissions-Bribery Scheme: Now Their Campuses Are Cutting Ties," *Chronicle of Higher Education*, March 12, 2019, www.chronicle.com/article/college-officials-were-charged-in-the-admissions-bribery-scheme -now-their-campuses-are-cutting-ties.

95. Lauren Camera, "50 Charged in Largest College Admissions Scam Ever," *U.S. News & World Report*, March 12, 2019, www.usnews.com/news/education-news/articles/2019-03-12/50 -charged-in-largest-college-admissions-scam-ever.

96. Richard D. Kahlenberg, "Legacy Admissions Are Legalized Bribery," *New York Daily News*, March 12, 2019, www.nydailynews.com/2019/03/12/legacy-admissions-are-legalized-bribery; Claire Cain Miller and Aatish Bhatia, "How Big Is the Legacy Boost at Elite Colleges?," *New York Times*, July 27, 2023, www.nytimes.com/2023/07/27/upshot/ivy-league-legacy-admissions.html.

97. Kahlenberg, "College Admissions Scandal Implicating Felicity Huffman and Lori Loughlin."

98. Richard D. Kahlenberg, "There's a Better Way to Diversify Harvard," *Boston Globe*, October 3, 2019, www.bostonglobe.com/opinion/2019/10/04/there-better-way-diversify-harvard/zU8 GinH9WRhOEjTu7hrflK/story.html?; *Students for Fair Admissions v. Harvard*, 397 F. Supp. 3d 126, 177–183 (rejecting race-neutral alternatives) and 204 (a "very fine" admissions system) (D. Mass. 2019).

99. Kahlenberg, "There's a Better Way to Diversify Harvard."

100. Kahlenberg.

101. Kahlenberg.

102. *Students for Fair Admissions v. Harvard*, 397 F. Supp. 3d at 205; Kahlenberg, "There's a Better Way to Diversify Harvard."

Notes to Chapter 8

CHAPTER 8

1. Kahlenberg, "Expert Report, *Students for Fair Admissions v. University of North Carolina*," 32.

2. Kahlenberg, 32, 65.

3. Kahlenberg, 32n115.

4. Kahlenberg, 33–34.

5. "Brief by University Respondents in the Supreme Court of the United States, *Students for Fair Admissions v. University of North Carolina*," July 25, 2022, 1, www.supremecourt.gov /DocketPDF/21/21-707/230779/20220725144111091_21-707_Response%20brief.pdf.

6. Kahlenberg, "Expert Report, *Students for Fair Admissions v. University of North Carolina*," 55; Richard D. Kahlenberg, "Expert Reply Report, *Students for Fair Admissions v. University of North Carolina*," June 8, 2018, 38, https://affirmativeactiondebate.files.wordpress.com/2021/06 /final-kahlenberg-unc-reply-report-june-8-2018.pdf.

7. Kahlenberg, "Expert Report, *Students for Fair Admissions v. University of North Carolina*," 56 (showing 18 percent of out-of-state admitted white students were children of alumni, compared with 4 percent of Hispanic students, 4 percent of Black students, and 3 percent of Asian students).

8. Long, "Expert Report, *Students for Fair Admissions v. University of North Carolina*," 45; Kahlenberg, "Expert Report, *Students for Fair Admissions v. University of North Carolina*," 57n219.

9. Kahlenberg, "Expert Report, *Students for Fair Admissions v. University of North Carolina*," 62–63 (showing that for the admissions cycles for the classes of 2016–2021, 76 percent of white in-state applicants applied early, compared with 55 percent of Black applicants; among out-of-state students, 54 percent of white UNC applicants applied early, compared with 32 percent of Black applicants).

10. Kahlenberg, "Expert Rebuttal Report, *Students for Fair Admissions v. University of North Carolina*," 53–54.

11. "Economic Diversity and Student Outcomes at the University of North Carolina, Chapel Hill" (showing that for the class of 2013, 60 percent of UNC–Chapel Hill students came from the top 20 percent of the income distribution, compared with 3.8 percent from the bottom 20 percent of the income distribution; more students at UNC came from the top 5 percent than the bottom 60 percent by income); "Median Household Income by State," U.S. Census Bureau, Table H-8, last modified September 12, 2023, www.census.gov/data/tables/time-series/demo/income-poverty /historical-income-households.html. While family income can sometimes be higher than house-hold income, that methodological difference would not account for the more than two-to-one ratio found at UNC.

12. Kahlenberg, "Expert Report, *Students for Fair Admissions v. University of North Carolina*," 28–29 (showing that the proportion of students who were first-generation college students was just 17 percent among the first-year students admitted for the fall of 2017 despite the fact that statewide, 72 percent of adults lacked a four-year degree; there were 143 million Americans without a college degree, and 317,000 UNC–Chapel Hill alumni in the world).

13. Kahlenberg, 33–34.

14. Kahlenberg, 17–20.

15. Kahlenberg, 24, 33–34.

16. Potter, "Transitioning to Race-Neutral Admissions," 82–83 (referencing details about the Texas Top 10 Percent plan, the California top 9 percent plan, and the Florida top 20 percent plan; only the Texas plan guaranteed admission to the flagship institution).

17. "Brief of Amicus Curiae the University of North Carolina at Chapel Hill Supporting Respondents," *Fisher v. University of Texas*, August 9, 2012, 33–35, www.scotusblog.com/wp -content/uploads/2016/08/11-345-respondent-amicus-UNCCH.pdf.

18. Kahlenberg, "Expert Report, *Students for Fair Admissions v. University of North Carolina*," 40–41.

19. Kahlenberg, "Expert Report, *Students for Fair Admissions v. University of North Carolina*," 46–48.

Notes to Chapter 8

20. Robert Morse and Eric Brooks, "Best Colleges Ranking Criteria and Weights," *U.S. News & World Report*, September 11, 2017, www.usnews.com/education/best-colleges/articles/ranking-criteria-and-weights; Amy Scott, "'Top 10%' Rule for College Admissions Faces a New Challenge," *Marketplace*, National Public Radio, May 23, 2016, www.marketplace.org/2016/05/18/wealth-poverty/top-10-rule-faces-new-challenge-texas. See also "University of Texas Chancellor Opposes Top 10 Percent Admission Rule," Public University Honors, January 25, 2016, http://publicuniversityhonors.com/2016/01/25/university-of-texas-chancellor-opposes-top-10-percent-admission-rule.

21. Kahlenberg, "Expert Report, *Students for Fair Admissions v. University of North Carolina*," 51–52.

22. Kahlenberg, 38–39.

23. Kahlenberg, 61–62.

24. Kahlenberg, 58 (showing that first-generation students constituted 22 percent of all in-state applicants and 12 percent of out-of-state applicants, even though 73 percent of North Carolina adults and 68 percent of American adults lacked a college degree).

25. Kahlenberg, "Expert Rebuttal Report, *Students for Fair Admissions v. University of North Carolina*," 33–34; Caroline Hoxby, "Expert Rebuttal Report, *Students for Fair Admissions v. University of North Carolina*," April 6, 2018, 54, Exhibit 6, https://affirmativeactiondebate.files.wordpress.com/2021/06/2018.04.06-rebuttal-report-of-caroline-hoxby.pdf.

26. Joint Appendix, *Students for Fair Admission v. University of North Carolina*, May 2, 2022, JA 1148–1149, www.supremecourt.gov/DocketPDF/20/20-1199/222330/20220502151757578_21-707%20JA%20Vol%203.pdf. Even more racial diversity resulted when nonapplicants were included. See Joint Appendix, *Students for Fair Admissions v. University of North Carolina*, JA 1151 (showing Simulation 11).

27. Joint Appendix, *Students for Fair Admissions v. University of North Carolina*, JA 1152–1153; Kahlenberg, "Expert Reply Report, *Students for Fair Admissions v. University of North Carolina*," 57–61.

28. Long, "Expert Report, *Students for Fair Admissions v. University of North Carolina*," 12, 41, 42–43; Caroline Hoxby, "Expert Report, *Students for Fair Admissions v. University of North Carolina*," January 12, 2018, 56, https://affirmativeactiondebate.org/wp-content/uploads/2021/06/hoxby-expert-report-jan-2018.pdf.

29. Steven A. Holmes, "State Job Agencies May Not Give Edge to Minority Testees," *New York Times*, December 14, 1991, www.nytimes.com/1991/12/14/us/state-job-agencies-may-not-give-edge-to-minority-testees.html (noting that the 1991 Civil Rights Act made race norming illegal).

30. Kahlenberg, "Expert Report, *Students for Fair Admissions v. University of North Carolina*," 25.

31. Hoxby, "Expert Report," 38–39, 48, 51; Long, "Expert Report, *Students for Fair Admissions v. University of North Carolina*," 4, 30, 41.

32. Kahlenberg, "Expert Report, *Students for Fair Admissions v. University of North Carolina*," 44.

33. Hoxby, "Expert Rebuttal Report, *Students for Fair Admissions v. University of North Carolina*," 71.

34. Kahlenberg, "Expert Reply Report, *Students for Fair Admissions v. University of North Carolina*," 13–15 (noting that under the FAFSA, universities had extensive information about family wealth, including information about "brokerage accounts, CDs, stocks, bonds, mutual funds, money market accounts, college savings plans, trust funds, real estate, and other investments"). The FAFSA was subsequently revised to include the value of small businesses. See Danielle Douglas-Gabriel, "The New FAFSA Form for College Aid Is Out: Five Things to Know," *Washington Post*, December 31, 2023, www.washingtonpost.com/education/2023/fafsa-2024-25-application-release-details. While it was true, as Hoxby noted, that the FAFSA did not ask families for information about certain wealth factors, such as home equity and the value of small businesses, I noted that UNC was among almost four hundred colleges that also required parents seeking aid to fill out the College Board's

CSS Profile as a supplement to the FAFSA. The CSS, which was used by colleges to award institutional aid, generally required more information than the FAFSA.

35. Kahlenberg, "Expert Reply Report, *Students for Fair Admissions v. University of North Carolina*," 14–15. Those families who did not apply for financial aid at UNC (where the annual cost of attendance was $25,876 per student for North Carolina residents and $53,100 for out-of-state students in the 2017–2018 academic year) could safely be assumed to be among the wealthiest Americans in the nation.

36. "Federal Student Aid: The Importance of Submitting Accurate Information," U.S. Department of Education, accessed July 2, 2024, https://studentaid.gov/help/submitting-accurate-info (noting that families who knowingly submit false information on the FAFSA can be punished with a $20,000 fine and time in prison).

37. In the Harvard case, both Arcidiacono and Harvard's expert David Card used applicants from previous classes to simulate the effects of different policies. For UNC, however, Hoxby used a large database of North Carolina public high school students that might apply to UNC under the new admissions system. The advantage of Hoxby's approach was that it captured the benefits of UNC doing a better job of outreach to get more students to apply. Though we had test scores and grades for these students, the downside was that they had not actually applied to UNC. So, we did not have the rich set of ratings that UNC employed that go beyond grades and test scores to consider the rigor of classes taken, the strength of extracurricular activities, essay quality, and their personal qualities such as curiosity and integrity. Arcidiacono and I decided to try modeling both scenarios—existing applicants and all potential applicants—in considering how a socioeconomic preference and a North Carolina percentage plan would work. Simulations with actual applicants and their holistic ratings provided conservative estimates. Including nonapplicants, as Hoxby suggested, made it easier to achieve racial diversity while maintaining rigorous academic standards due to more highly qualified, socioeconomically disadvantaged students in the pool. Kahlenberg, "Expert Rebuttal Report, *Students for Fair Admissions v. University of North Carolina*," 37–38. When UNC objected to both approaches at trial, I responded that this was the way simulations were conducted. One had to make some sort of assumptions, and both sides in the Harvard case had used the current applicant pool as the basis for simulations, without any dissent. If simulations on both ends of that spectrum worked, then that should satisfy the range of possibilities. Moreover, I noted, it was Hoxby, not Arcidiacono and me, who had introduced the idea of using nonapplicants from the North Carolina public school database.

38. *Students for Fair Admissions v. University of North Carolina*, 567 F. Supp. 3d 580, 644–645 (M.D. N.C. 2021), https://casetext.com/case/students-for-fair-admissions-inc-v-university-of-north-carolina.

39. For a more complete discussion, see note 37 above.

CHAPTER 9

1. David Leonhardt and Ian Prasad Philbrick, "Donald Trump's Racism: The Definitive List, Updated," *New York Times*, January 15, 2018, www.nytimes.com/interactive/2018/01/15/opinion/leonhardt-trump-racist.html.

2. Leonhardt and Philbrick; Anthony D. Romero, "We Will Defend the Constitution Against a President Trump," *Washington Post*, July 13, 2016, www.washingtonpost.com/opinions/a-president-trump-would-threaten-our-constitutional-freedoms/2016/07/13/42b41048-4876-11e6-bdb9-701687974517_story.html.

3. Deirdre Walsh and Manu Raju, "Paul Ryan Rips Donald Trump Remarks as 'Textbook Definition of a Racist Comment,'" CNN, June 7, 2016, www.cnn.com/2016/06/07/politics/paul-ryan-donald-trump-racist-comment/index.html.

4. Leonhardt and Philbrick, "Donald Trump's Racism."

5. Eli Watkins and Abby Phillip, "Trump Decries Immigrants from 'Shithole Countries'

Notes to Chapter 9

Coming to US," CNN, January 12, 2018, www.cnn.com/2018/01/11/politics/immigrants-shithole
-countries-trump/index.html.

6. Nikole Hannah-Jones, "Class Action: A Challenge to the Idea That Income Can Integrate America's Campuses," *Pro Publica*, June 24, 2013, www.propublica.org/article/class-action-a
-challenge-to-the-idea-that-income-can-integrate-americas-cam; Anthony Carnevale and Richard D.
Kahlenberg, "Close Allies, Not Rivals, on Affirmative Action," Century Foundation, June 27, 2013,
https://tcf.org/content/commentary/close-allies-not-rivals-on-affirmative-action.

7. Matthew Delmont, "The Lasting Legacy of the Boston Busing Crisis," *The Atlantic*,
March 29, 2016, www.theatlantic.com/politics/archive/2016/03/the-boston-busing-crisis-was-ne
ver-intended-to-work/474264.

8. Valerie Strauss, "New York City Should Set Ambitious Diversity Goals for Public Schools:
New Report by Panel Commissioned by Mayor," *Washington Post*, February 12, 2019, www
.washingtonpost.com/education/2019/02/12/new-york-city-should-set-ambitious-diversity-goals
-public-schools-new-report-by-panel-commissioned-by-mayor.

9. Adam Harris, "Can Richard Carranza Integrate the Most Segregated System in the Country?," *The Atlantic*, July 23, 2018, www.theatlantic.com/education/archive/2018/07/richard-car
ranza-segregation-new-york-city-schools/564299.

10. Maya Wiley and Richard D. Kahlenberg, "The Integration Imperative: New York City's Public Schools Must Mix Student Populations Far More Effectively," *New York Daily News*, February 19,
2019, www.nydailynews.com/opinion/ny-oped-the-integration-imperative-20190218-story.html.

11. Richard V. Reeves and Ashley Schobert, "Elite or Elitist? Lessons for Colleges from
Selective High Schools," Brookings Institution, July 31, 2019, www.brookings.edu/articles/elite
-or-elitist-lessons-for-colleges-from-selective-high-schools.

12. Boaz Weinstein, "No Ethnic Group Owns Stuyvesant. All New Yorkers Do," *New York
Times*, June 13, 2018, www.nytimes.com/2018/06/13/opinion/de-blasio-stuyvesant-school.html.

13. Weinstein.

14. Frederick M. Hess and Michael Q. McShane, *Getting Education Right* (New York: Teachers
College Press, 2024), 82.

15. "'Antiracists' vs. Academic Freedom," *Wall Street Journal*, July 22, 2023, www.wsj.com
/articles/daymon-johnson-lawsuit-california-community-colleges-bakersfield-deia-faculty
-education-7fc2763e.

16. Judis and Teixeira, *Where Have All the Democrats Gone?*, 126.

17. Stella Chan and Amanda Jackson, "San Francisco School Board Votes to Rename 44 Schools,
Including Abraham Lincoln and George Washington High Schools," CNN, January 27, 2021, www
.cnn.com/2021/01/27/us/san-francisco-school-name-changes-trnd/index.html.

18. Nikole Hannah-Jones, "Our Democracy's Founding Ideals Were False When They Were
Written: Black Americans Have Fought to Make Them True," *New York Times Magazine*, August 14,
2019, www.nytimes.com/interactive/2019/08/14/magazine/black-history-american-democracy.html
("Anti-black racism runs in the very DNA of this country").

19. Leslie M. Harris, "I Helped Fact-Check the 1619 Project: The *Times* Ignored Me," *Politico*, March 6, 2020, www.politico.com/news/magazine/2020/03/06/1619-project-new-york-times
-mistake-122248; Len Gutkin, "Reviewing the '1619 Project' Four Years On," *Chronicle of Higher
Education*, January 30, 2023, www.chronicle.com/newsletter/the-review/2023-01-30 (discussing
the work of historians Daryl Michael Scott and Sandra E. Greene).

20. Nikole Hannah-Jones, preface to *The 1619 Project*, ed. Nikole Hannah-Jones, Caitlin Roper,
Ilena Silverman, and Jake Silverman (New York: One World, 2021), xxii; Adam Hochschild, "A
Landmark Reckoning with America's Racial Past and Present," *New York Times*, November 15, 2021,
www.nytimes.com/2021/11/15/books/review/the-1619-project-nikole-hannah-jones-caitlin
-roper-ilena-silverman-jake-silverstein.html.

21. Carlos Lozada, "The 1619 Project Started as History: Now It's Also a Political Program,"
Washington Post, November 19, 2021, www.washingtonpost.com/outlook/2021/11/19/1619-proj
ect-book-history; Nikole Hannah-Jones, "Justice," in Hannah-Jones et al., *1619 Project*, 475.

Notes to Chapter 9

22. William Darity Jr. and A. Kirsten Mullen, *From Here to Equality: Reparations for Black Americans in the Twenty-First Century* (Chapel Hill: University of North Carolina Press, 2020); Kahlenberg, "Path Forward on Reparations?"

23. Kurtis Lee, "California Panel Calls for Billions in Reparations to Black Residents," *New York Times*, May 6, 2023, www.nytimes.com/2023/05/06/business/economy/california-reparations.html; Emmanuel Felton, "Black San Francisco Residents Could Get $5 Million Each in Reparations," *Washington Post*, February 27, 2023, www.washingtonpost.com/nation/2023/02/27/san-francisco-reparations-black-5-million; Trip Gabriel, Maya King, Kurtis Lee, and Shawn Hubler, "Democrats Are in a Bind over Reparations Call," *New York Times*, May 27, 2023, www.nytimes.com/2023/05/27/us/politics/reparations-democrats-black-americans.html.

24. Komi Frey, "We Know Diversity Statements Are Political Litmus Tests: It's Time to End This Discriminatory Practice," *Chronicle of Higher Education*, January 4, 2024, www.chronicle.com/article/we-know-diversity-statements-are-political-litmus-tests; Richard D. Kahlenberg, "What Liberals Can Do to Root Out Illiberalism in Higher Education," *Liberal Patriot*, February 19, 2024, www.liberalpatriot.com/p/what-liberals-can-do-to-root-out.

25. Conor Friedersdorf, "'A Constant Drumbeat' of Racial Essentialism," *The Atlantic*, January 29, 2024, www.theatlantic.com/ideas/archive/2024/01/dei-lawsuit-penn-state/677268.

26. David Brooks, "The Self-Isolation of the American Left," *New York Times*, October 28, 2021, www.nytimes.com/2021/10/28/opinion/school-culture-wars.html.

27. Susan Svrluga, "Mike Pence Event Reignites a Debate over Free Speech at University of Virginia," *Washington Post*, April 11, 2022, www.washingtonpost.com/education/2022/04/11/uva-pence-free-speech.

28. Samuel J. Abrams, "Cancel Culture Is Real in Higher Education: But Its Degree Does Vary Significantly," *AEIdeas*, April 21, 2022, www.aei.org/politics-and-public-opinion/cancel-culture-is-real-in-higher-education-but-its-degree-does-vary-significantly.

29. "Race or Class? An Affirmative Action Debate Featuring Richard Kahlenberg and Randall Kennedy," Middlebury College, Middlebury, VT, November 22, 2019, https://vimeo.com/374968959.

30. Allison Stanger, "Understanding the Angry Mob at Middlebury That Gave Me a Concussion," *New York Times*, March 13, 2017, www.nytimes.com/2017/03/13/opinion/understanding-the-angry-mob-that-gave-me-a-concussion.html.

31. "California Proposition 16, Repeal Proposition 209 Affirmative Action Amendment (2020)," Ballotpedia, accessed July 3, 2024, https://ballotpedia.org/California_Proposition_16,_Repeal_Proposition_209_Affirmative_Action_Amendment_(2020); Stacy Cowley, "Judges Halt Race and Gender Priority for Restaurant Relief Grants," *New York Times*, June 14, 2021, www.nytimes.com/2021/06/14/business/restaurant-relief-fund-covid-sba.html; Yascha Mounk, *The Great Experiment: Why Diverse Democracies Fall Apart and How They Can Endure* (New York: Penguin, 2022), 264–265; Shadi Hamid, "Race-Based Rationing Is Real—and Dangerous," *The Atlantic*, January 30, 2022, www.theatlantic.com/ideas/archive/2022/01/race-based-covid-rationing-ideology/621405; Anne Kim, "The Wrong Way to Build Black Wealth," *Washington Monthly*, June 8, 2021, https://washingtonmonthly.com/2021/06/08/the-wrong-way-to-build-black-wealth; Craig Wall, "Mayor Lightfoot Only Granting Interviews to Reporters of Color Ahead of 2nd Anniversary," *ABC Eyewitness News*, May 19, 2021, https://abc7chicago.com/chicago-mayor-lori-lightfoot-black-reporters-brown/10663890; Douglas Belkin and Lee Hawkins, "Can School Be 'Antiracist'? A New Superintendent in Evanston Ill., Has a Plan," *Wall Street Journal*, October 6, 2020, www.wsj.com/articles/can-school-be-antiracist-a-new-superintendent-in-evanston-ill-has-a-plan-11601982001.

32. Joshua Green, "How Social Justice Activists Lost the Plot," *Washington Monthly*, September/October 2023, https://washingtonmonthly.com/2023/08/27/how-social-justice-activists-lost-the-plot (reviewing Fredrik deBoer, *How Elites Ate the Social Justice Movement* [New York: Simon and Schuster, 2023]).

33. Michael Shaffer, "'A Real Chilling Effect': A Lefty Scholar Is Dumping CAP—for AEI," *Politico*, July 15, 2022, www.politico.com/news/magazine/2022/07/15/capital-city-ruy-teixeira

-american-enterprise-institute-00045819; George Packer, *Last Best Hope: America in Crisis and Renewal* (New York: Farrar, Straus and Giroux, 2021), 137.

34. *Wygant v. Jackson Board of Education*, 476 U.S. 267 (1986); Amanda Su and Deena Zaru, "Minneapolis Public Schools Defends Policy to Prioritize Retaining Educators of Color When Determining Layoffs," *ABC News*, August 19, 2022, https://abcnews.go.com/US/minneapolis -public-schools-defends-policy-prioritize-retaining-educators/story?id=88491641.

35. Joanna Fantozzi, "Starbucks Links Executive Compensation to Company Diversity Goals, Commits to a Corporate Workforce of at Least 30% BIPOC by 2025," *Nation's Restaurant News*, October 14, 2020, www.nrn.com/quick-service/starbucks-links-executive-compensation -company-diversity-goals-commits-corporate; Steven Greenhouse, "How Corporations Crush New Unions," *New Republic*, December 18, 2023, https://newrepublic.com/article/177557/trader-joes -union-busting-bargaining-table-first-contract.

36. Katelyn Burns, "Seattle's Newly Police-Free Neighborhood, Explained," *Vox*, June 16, 2020, www.vox.com/identities/2020/6/16/21292723/chaz-seattle-police-free-neighborhood; Dahleen Glanton, "Reparations Are About Economic Stability, Not a Looted Pair of $120 Nikes," *Chicago Tribune*, August 17, 2020, www.chicagotribune.com/2020/08/17/column-reparations-are-about-eco nomic-stability-not-a-looted-pair-of-120-nikes.

37. Mounk, *Identity Trap*, 56; Francis Fukuyama, "The Long Arc of Historical Progress," *Wall Street Journal*, April 29, 2022, www.wsj.com/articles/the-long-arc-of-historical-progress -11651244262; William A. Galston, "How Adherents See 'Critical Race Theory,'" *Wall Street Journal*, July 13, 2021, www.wsj.com/articles/how-adherents-see-critical-race-theory-11626199490; William A. Galston, "A Deeper Look at Critical Race Theory," *Wall Street Journal*, July 20, 2021, www .wsj.com/articles/kimberle-crenshaw-critical-race-theory-woke-marxism-education-11626793272; David Brooks, "Universities Are Failing at Inclusion," *New York Times*, November 16, 2023, www .nytimes.com/2023/11/16/opinion/college-university-antisemitism-crt.html.

38. Meghan Burke, *Colorblind Racism* (New York: John Wiley and Sons, 2018).

39. Kendi, "When I See Racial Disparities, I See Racism."

40. Weinstein, "No Ethnic Group Owns Stuyvesant" (75 percent Asian); "Fast Facts: Enroll ment," National Center for Education Statistics, accessed July 3, 2024, https://nces.ed.gov/fastfacts /display.asp?id=98 (58 percent female).

41. Kendi, *How to Be an Anti-Racist*, 19.

42. Kahlenberg, "Middle Ground on Race and College."

43. Michael Powell, "New York's Private Schools Tackle White Privilege: It Has Not Been Easy," *New York Times*, August 27, 2021, www.nytimes.com/2021/08/27/us/new-york-private-schools -racism.html.

44. Marina Watts, "In Smithsonian Race Guidelines, Rational Thinking and Hard Work Are White Values," *Newsweek*, May 25, 2021, www.newsweek.com/smithsonian-race-guidelines -rational-thinking-hard-work-are-white-values-1518333.

45. Yascha Mounk, "The Insidious Lie That We Can't Understand Each Other," *Liberal Patriot*, October 4, 2023, www.liberalpatriot.com/p/the-insidious-lie-that-we-cant-understand.

46. Daniel Bergner, "Whiteness Lessons," *New York Times Magazine*, July 19, 2020, www .nytimes.com/2020/07/15/magazine/white-fragility-robin-diangelo.html.

47. Matthew Yglesias, "The Great Awokening," *Vox*, April 1, 2019, www.vox.com/2019/3 /22/18259865/great-awokening-white-liberals-race-polling-trump-2020; Nate Hochman, "The Doctrine of the Irreligious Right," *New York Times*, June 5, 2022, www.nytimes.com/2022/06/01 /opinion/republicans-religion-conservatism.html.

48. David Bernstein, "Teach '1619' and '1776' U.S. History: The Answer to Ideological Edu cation Isn't to Ban the Ideology but to Make Room for Alternative Views," *Wall Street Journal*, April 10, 2022, www.wsj.com/articles/1619-project-1776-history-america-crt-critical-race-theory -racism-woke-progressive-education-schools-virginia-youngkin-tennessee-11649595715.

49. Robert Kuttner, "A Conversation with Susan Neiman About Left and Woke," *American Prospect*, May 2, 2023, https://prospect.org/videos/05-02-2023-susan-neiman-left-woke.

50. Michael M. Grynbaum, "*Washington Post* Is Latest News Outlet Barred by Trump," *New York Times*, June 13, 2016, www.nytimes.com/2016/06/14/business/media/trump-kicks-phony-and -dishonest-washington-post-off-his-campaign.html.

51. Jeremy Bauer-Wolf, "Free Speech Advocate Silenced," *Inside Higher Ed*, October 5, 2017, www.insidehighered.com/news/2017/10/06/william-mary-students-who-shut-down-aclu-event -broke-conduct-code.

52. Galston, "How Adherents See 'Critical Race Theory'"; Galston, "Deeper Look at Critical Race Theory."

53. George Hawley, "Demography of the Alt-Right," Institute for Family Studies, August 9, 2018, https://ifstudies.org/blog/the-demography-of-the-alt-right.

54. Ruy Teixeira, "Things Look Bleak for Liberals Now: But They'll Beat Trump in the End," *Washington Post*, March 3, 2017, www.washingtonpost.com/posteverything/wp/2017/03/03/op timistic-leftist/?.

55. Ian Haney Lopez, *Merge: Fusing Race and Class, Winning Elections, and Saving America* (New York: The New Press, 2019), 30.

56. Yascha Mounk, "Americans Strongly Dislike PC Culture," *The Atlantic*, October 10, 2018, www.theatlantic.com/ideas/archive/2018/10/large-majorities-dislike-political-correctness/572581.

57. Scott Clement and David Nakamura, "Poll Shows Clear Disapproval of How Trump Responded to Charlottesville Violence," *Washington Post*, August 21, 2017, www.washingtonpost .com/politics/poll-shows-strong-disapproval-of-how-trump-responded-to-charlottesville-violence /2017/08/21/4e5c585c-868b-11e7-a94f-3139abce39f5_story.html.

58. Simon Greer and Richard D. Kahlenberg, "How Progressives Can Recapture Seven Deeply Held American Values," Century Foundation, February 26, 2020, https://tcf.org/content/report /progressives-can-recapture-seven-deeply-held-american-values.

59. Lopez, *Merge*, 45–53, 190.

60. Thomas Fuller, "'You Have to Give Us Respect': How Asian Americans Fueled the San Fran- cisco Recall," *New York Times*, February 17, 2022, www.nytimes.com/2022/02/17/us/san-francisco -school-board-parents.html; Peggy Noonan, "San Francisco Schools the Left," *Wall Street Journal*, February 19, 2022, www.wsj.com/articles/san-francisco-school-board-teachers-elections-recall-vote -racist-woke-closures-remote-learning-crt-11645130926 (Biden's 85 percent vote).

61. Michael Powell and Ilana Marcus, "California Vote Exposed a Divide amid Democrats," *New York Times*, June 11, 2023, www.nytimes.com/2023/06/11/us/supreme-court-affirmative -action.html; "California Proposition 16" (fourteen-point margin); "California Presidential Elec- tion Results 2020," *NBC News*, November 3, 2020, www.nbcnews.com/politics/2020-elections /california-president-results (twenty-nine point margin); John Ellis, "A More Diverse America Turns Against Racial Preferences," *Wall Street Journal*, October 15, 2022, www.wsj.com/articles/a-more -diverse-america-turns-against-racial-preferences-supreme-court-academia-college-admissions -students-polls-11665775782.

62. Carrie Blazina and Kiana Cox, "Black and White Americans Are Far Apart in Their Views of Reparations for Slavery," Pew Research Center, November 28, 2022, www.pewresearch.org /short-reads/2022/11/28/black-and-white-americans-are-far-apart-in-their-views-of-reparations -for-slavery; Tracy Jan, "Reparations, Rebranded," *Washington Post*, February 24, 2020, www .washingtonpost.com/business/2020/02/24/reparations-south-carolina-clyburn.

63. Kahlenberg, "Middle Ground on Race and College."

64. Kahlenberg.

CHAPTER 10

1. See United States Courts, "Supreme Court Procedures," accessed July 3, 2024, www.uscourts .gov/about-federal-courts/educational-resources/about-educational-outreach/activity-resources /supreme-1.

Notes to Chapter 10

2. Shira Scheindlin, "If the Supreme Court Abolishes Affirmative Action, Here's What Women Need to Do," *New York Times*, June 11, 2023, www.nytimes.com/2023/06/11/opinion/affirmative -action-supreme-court.html.

3. "Brief for the President and Chancellors of the University of California as Amici Curiae Supporting Respondents, *Students for Fair Admissions v. Harvard*," U.S. Supreme Court, August 1, 2022, www.supremecourt.gov/DocketPDF/20/20-1199/232355/20220801134931730_20-1199 %20bsac%20University%20of%20California.pdf; "Brief for the University of Michigan as Amicus Curiae in Support of Respondents, *Students for Fair Admissions v. Harvard*," U.S. Supreme Court, August 2022, https://record.umich.edu/wp content/uploads/2022/08/220804_AmicusBrief.pdf.

4. Stephanie Saul, "Affirmative Action Was Banned at Two Top Universities: They Say They Need It," *New York Times*, August 26, 2022, www.nytimes.com/2022/08/26/us/affirmative-action -admissions-supreme-court.html.

5. "UCLA 2021 Freshman Class Is Most Diverse, Academically Accomplished in History, School Says"; Watanabe, "UC Admits Largest, Most Diverse Class Ever"; Kahlenberg, "Expert Rebuttal Report, *Students for Fair Admissions v. University of North Carolina*," 8; Nick Anderson, "UC-Berkeley Can't Use Race in Admissions: Is It a Model for the Country?," *Washington Post*, November 27, 2022, www.washingtonpost.com/education/2022/11/27/uc-berkeley-admissions -race-diversity (5 percent Black High school population); "Undergraduate Admissions Summary," University of California, March 6, 2023, www.universityofcalifornia.edu/about-us/information -center/admissions-residency-and-ethnicity; Liam Knox, "A Political Standoff over Affirma- tive Action," *Inside Higher Ed*, September 29, 2023, www.insidehighered.com/news/admissions /traditional-age/2023/09/29/legislators-and-regulators-duel-affirmative-actions-wake (citing UCLA chancellor Gene Block); "Fingertip Facts on Education in California," California Department of Education, last modified May 16, 2024, www.cde.ca.gov/ds/ad/ceffingertipfacts.asp.

6. Gilmore, "UC Berkeley's Push for More Diversity Shows in Its Newly Admitted Class"; Scott Jaschik, "Affirmative Action Fight Shifts to UNC," *Inside Higher Ed*, January 21, 2019, www.insidehighered.com/admissions/article/2019/01/22/legal-fight-over-affirmative-action -shifts-unc-chapel-hill; "UC Berkeley Fall Enrollment Data for New Undergraduates," UC Berke- ley, last modified September 26, 2023, https://opa.berkeley.edu/uc-berkeley-fall-enrollment -data-new-undergraduates.

7. Stefanie Saul, "With End of Affirmative Action, a Push for a New Tool: Adversity Scores," *New York Times*, July 2, 2023, www.nytimes.com/2023/07/02/us/affirmative-action-university -of-california-davis.html.

8. Samuel Dodge, "Largest Ever Student Body at University of Michigan This Fall, Offi- cials Say," *MLive.com*, October 22, 2021, www.mlive.com/news/ann-arbor/2021/10/largest-ever -student-body-at-university-of-michigan-this-fall-officials-say.html; "Brief for the University of Michigan," 21–22; Sharon Morioka, "Meet Michigan Law's Class of 2025," University of Michi- gan Law School, September 7, 2022, https://michigan.law.umich.edu/news/meet-michigan-laws -class-2025; Linda Greenhouse, "Court to Revisit Colleges' Efforts to Gain Diversity," *New York Times*, December 3, 2002, www.nytimes.com/2002/12/03/us/court-to-revisit-colleges-efforts-to -gain-diversity.html (noting that Michigan Law, using racial preferences, had a student body that was 6.7 percent Black and 4.4 percent Hispanic). See also "Brief of Amici Curiae Oklahoma and 18 Other States in Support of Petitioner, *Students for Fair Admissions v. Harvard*," U.S. Supreme Court, May 9, 2022, 15, www.supremecourt.gov/DocketPDF/20/20-1199/222849/20220509155246082 _OkSFA%20Merits%20Amicus%20MAIN%20May%209%202022%20E%20File.pdf (noting that the total underrepresented student population increased from 14.5 percent of the entering class of 2000 to 2 percent in the law school's class of 2024).

9. Richard D. Kahlenberg, "A Fresh Chance to Rein in Racial Preferences," *Wall Street Journal*, October 13, 2013, www.wsj.com/articles/SB10001424052702304520704579125003614256882; "Economic Diversity and Student Outcomes at the University of Michigan, Ann Arbor," *New York Times*, January 18, 2017, www.nytimes.com/interactive/projects/college-mobility/university

343

-of-michigan-ann-arbor. Michigan did not end legacy preferences until after December 2022. See James Murphy, "The Future of Fair Admissions Issue Brief 4: Legacy Admissions Update," *Ed Reform Now*, December 2023, 10 (Table 2), "Prominent Colleges and Universities That Ended Legacy Admissions Since December 2022," https://edreformnow.org/wp-content/uploads/2023/12/The-Future-of-Fair-Admissions-Brief-4-FINAL-1.pdf.

10. Sander, "Use of Socioeconomic Affirmative Action at the University of California," 101 (noting that UC campuses look at parental education and income).

11. Lauren Hepler, "The Hidden Toll of California's Black Exodus," *CalMatters*, July 15, 2020, https://calmatters.org/projects/california-black-population-exodus; Jonah Newman, "What Does the Education Dept. Know About Race?," *Chronicle of Higher Education*, April 28, 2014, www.chronicle.com/blogs/data/what-does-the-education-dept-know-about-race; Kim M. Williams, *Mark One or More: Civil Rights in Multicultural America* (Ann Arbor: University of Michigan Press, 2008).

12. McGregor McCance, "Analysis of U.Va.'s Incoming Class Shows Consistent Quality with Dynamic Change," *UVA Today*, May 16, 2013.

13. Antonovics and Backes, "Effect of Banning Affirmative Action," 306 (on the increased weight accorded to socioeconomic disadvantage after California banned racial preferences); "Economic Diversity Among the Top 25 National Universities," *U.S. News & World Report*, accessed July 3, 2024, www.usnews.com/best-colleges/rankings/national-universities/economic-diversity-among-top-ranked-schools (showing that using fall of 2022 data, UCLA was first, with 28 percent Pell, and UC Berkeley second with 27 percent Pell; at the other extreme among the top 25, Georgetown had 11 percent Pell and Duke 12 percent).

14. "Brief for the President and Chancellors of the University of California as Amici Curiae Supporting Respondents, *Students for Fair Admissions v. Harvard*," 15.

15. Oral argument transcript, *Students for Fair Admissions v. Harvard*, U.S. Supreme Court, October 31, 2022, 67–68, www.supremecourt.gov/oral_arguments/argument_transcripts/2022/20-1199_bi7a.pdf.

16. Oral argument transcript, *Students for Fair Admissions v. University of North Carolina*, 80 (Barrett), 85 (Kavanaugh), www.supremecourt.gov/oral_arguments/argument_transcripts/2022/21-707_bb7j.pdf; oral argument transcript, *Students for Fair Admissions v. Harvard*, 23 (Gorsuch).

17. Oral argument transcript, *Students for Fair Admissions v. University of North Carolina*, 73.

18. Oral argument transcript, *Students for Fair Admissions v. Harvard*, 23, 35–36, 118.

19. Oral argument transcript, 38.

20. Oral argument transcript, 39.

21. John Hurd, "Did Wester Really Say It?," *Dartmouth Alumni Magazine*, January 1966, https://archive.dartmouthalumnimagazine.com/article/1966/1/1/did-webster-really-say-it.

22. Oral argument transcript, 102. See also oral argument transcript, *Students for Fair Admissions v. University of North Carolina*, 158.

23. Oral argument transcript, *Students for Fair Admissions v. University of North Carolina*, 15–16.

24. Oral argument transcript, 30 (forty factors); Kahlenberg, "Expert Report, *Students for Fair Admissions v. University of North Carolina*," 33.

25. Clay Risen, "William Consovoy Dies at 48; Took Conservative Cases to Supreme Court," *New York Times*, January 12, 2023, www.nytimes.com/2023/01/12/us/william-consovoy-dead.html.

26. Paul Butler, "This Right Court Will Doom Affirmative Action," *Washington Post*, January 27, 2022, www.washingtonpost.com/opinions/2022/01/27/i-once-told-supreme-court-justice-that-affirmative-action-got-me-into-harvard-yale-today-they-wouldnt-listen (that the goal was "to take this country back to the time where straight White men ruled everything"); Benjamin Chang, "Stop Using Asian Americans to Attack Other People of Color," *Washington Post*, February 4, 2022, www

Notes to Chapter 10

.washingtonpost.com/opinions/2022/02/04/harvard-asian-american-student-believes-in
-affirmative-action.

27. Gomez, "As Courts Weigh Affirmative Action."

28. Kahlenberg and Brittain, "10 Ways Colleges Can Diversify"; Peter Dreier, Richard D. Kahlenberg, and Melvin V. Oliver, "The Path to Diversity at College Now That the Supreme Court Has Struck Down Affirmative Action," *Slate*, February 8, 2023, https://slate.com/news-and -politics/2023/02/supreme-court-affirmative-action-wealth-admissions-factor.html; Kahlenberg, "Middle Ground on Race and College"; Richard D. Kahlenberg, "A New Path to Diversity," *Dissent*, March 23, 2023, www.dissentmagazine.org/online_articles/a-new-path-to-diversity.

29. Anemona Hartocollis, "The Liberal Maverick Fighting Race-Based Affirmative Action," *New York Times*, March 29, 2023, www.nytimes.com/2023/03/29/us/richard-kahlenberg-affirmative -action.html.

30. Paige Sutherland and Meghna Chakrabarti, "Can Focusing on Class Instead of Race Solve Our Country's Equity Issues?," *On Point*, WBUR, August 3, 2023, www.wbur.org/onpoint/2023/08/03 /can-class-based-preferences-over-race-solve-our-countrys-equity-issues.

31. "An Opposing View of Affirmative Action and More: The Week in Reporter Reads," *New York Times*, April 7, 2023, www.nytimes.com/2023/04/07/podcasts/affirmative-action-daft-punk -alaska.html.

32. Benvindo Chicha, interview with author, May 26, 2023.

33. *Students for Fair Admissions v. Harvard*, 600 U.S. at 206. The votes were 6–3 in the UNC case and 6–2 in the Harvard case because Justice Ketanji Brown Jackson participated in the UNC case but was recused in the Harvard case.

34. This section draws from Richard D. Kahlenberg, "New Avenues for Diversity After *Students for Fair Admissions*," *Journal of College and University Law* 48, no. 2 (2023): 283–324.

35. *Students for Fair Admissions v. Harvard*, 600 U.S. at 213–15; *Students for Fair Admissions v. Harvard* 600 U.S. at 366–367 (Sotomayor, dissenting).

36. *Students for Fair Admissions v. Harvard*, 600 U.S. at 218–219.

37. Vinay Harpalani, "Secret Admissions," *Journal of College and University Law* 48, no. 2 (2023): 327.

38. *Students for Fair Admissions v. Harvard*, 600 U.S. at 221–225, 227–228 (rejecting the idea that racial preferences should remain "indefinitely, until 'racial inequality will end'"); Thomas Sowell, "Race, Culture, and Equality," accessed July 4, 2024, www.tsowell.com/spracecu.html.

39. *Students for Fair Admissions v. Harvard*, 600 U.S. at 220.

40. *Students for Fair Admissions v. Harvard*, 600 U.S. at 287 (Thomas, concurring). See also *Students for Fair Admissions v. Harvard*, 600 U.S. at 307 (Gorsuch, concurring) ("If the Court's post-*Bakke* higher-education precedents ever made sense, they are now incoherent. Recognizing as much, the Court today cuts through the kudzu. It ends university exceptionalism").

41. *Students for Fair Admissions v. Harvard*, 600 U.S. at 357 (Sotomayor, dissenting).

42. *Students for Fair Admissions v. Harvard*, 600 U.S. at 210 (noting that Justice Powell pointed to Harvard as an "illuminating example" of how diversity policies should operate).

43. *Students for Fair Admissions v. Harvard*, 600 U.S. at 230.

44. *Students for Fair Admissions v. Harvard*, 600 U.S. at 231.

45. "Preliminary Guidance Regarding the U.S. Supreme Court's Decision in *Students for Fair Admissions v. Harvard* and *Students for Fair Admissions v. University of North Carolina*," Education Counsel, July 6, 2023, 3n4, https://educationcounsel.com/storage/seLGkbGgqeKNZ56fYV H9l4AT5U0cw88M2YwTomUc.pdf.

46. Brian Fitzpatrick, "Racial Preferences Won't Go Easily," *Wall Street Journal*, May 31, 2023, www.wsj.com/articles/racial-preferences-wont-go-easily-thomas-jefferson-harvard-unc-court -bfa302b3.

47. *Students for Fair Admissions v. Harvard*, 600 U.S. at 300 (Gorsuch, concurring).

CHAPTER 11

1. Liam Knox, "A National Summit on a Higher Education 'Low Point,'" *Inside Higher Ed*, July 27, 2023, www.insidehighered.com/news/admissions/traditional-age/2023/07/27/frustration -and-uncertainty-affirmative-action-summit. Portions of this chapter are drawn from Kahlenberg, "New Avenues for Diversity After *Students for Fair Admissions*."

2. Richard Rothstein, "Equalizing Educational Resources on Behalf of Disadvantaged Children," in *A Notion at Risk: Preserving Public Education as an Engine for Social Mobility*, ed. Richard D. Kahlenberg (New York: Century Foundation Press, 1998), 31–92; Richard Rothstein, "The Problem with Wealth-Based Affirmative Action," *The Atlantic*, June 1, 2023, www.theatlantic.com /ideas/archive/2023/06/affirmative-action-race-socioeconomic-supreme-court/674251.

3. Ryan Quinn, "U of Washington Faculty Search Weighed Race Inappropriately," *Inside Higher Ed*, November 3, 2023, www.insidehighered.com/news/faculty-issues/diversity-equity/2023 /11/03/u-washington-faculty-search-weighed-race.

4. William A. Jacobson, "SCOTUS 'Gave Universities a Narrow Opening, and Harvard Just Announced It's Going to Drive an Affirmative Action Truck Right Through It,'" *Legal Insurrection*, June 29, 2023, https://legalinsurrection.com/2023/06/scotus-gave-universities-a-narrow-opening -and-harvard-just-announced-its-going-to-drive-an-affirmative-action-truck-right-through-it.

5. Scott White, "College Diversity Actions After Supreme Court," *Forbes*, November 12, 2023, www.forbes.com/sites/scottwhite/2023/11/12/how-colleges-are-maintaining-diversity-after -supreme-court-decision; Steven McGuire, "Can Harvard Use Application Essays to Discriminate by Race?," *Wall Street Journal*, August 11, 2023, www.wsj.com/articles/can-harvard-use -application-essays-to-discriminate-by-race-unc-fair-admission-5638086f.

6. Elise C. Boddie, "A Damaging Bid to Censor Applications at Harvard," *New York Times*, October 10, 2018, www.nytimes.com/2018/10/10/opinion/harvard-affirmative-action-lawsuit.html; *Students for Fair Admissions v. Harvard*, 600 U.S. at 230 (noting that "all parties agree" that universities should not be barred from considering discussions of race in an essay).

7. Oral argument transcript, *Students for Fair Admissions v. University of North Carolina*, 42; *Students for Fair Admissions v. Harvard*, 600 U.S. at 231.

8. *Students for Fair Admissions v. Harvard*, 600 U.S. at 318, 363, 383 (Sotomayor, dissenting); *Students for Fair Admissions v. Harvard*, 600 U.S. at 407, 411 (Jackson, dissenting).

9. Carnevale and Strohl, "How Increasing College Access Is Increasing Inequality," 170 (Table 3.7).

10. For further discussion of the personal essay, see Kahlenberg, "New Avenues for Diversity After *Students for Fair Admissions*."

11. Fitzpatrick, "Racial Preferences Won't Go Easily."

12. Jonathan Feingold, Remarks, "What's Next? Diversity in Education After *Students for Fair Admissions v. Harvard/UNC*?," Journal of College and University Law Seminar, Rutgers University Law School and National Association of College and University Lawyers, online, September 29, 2023.

13. See discussion above in Chapter 5.

14. *Gratz v. Bollinger*, 539 U.S. at 270 (all racial classifications subject to strict scrutiny); *James v. Valtierra*, 402 U.S. 137, 141 (1971) (wealth classifications not subject to strict scrutiny).

15. Randall Kennedy, "The Truth Is, Many Americans Just Don't Want Black People to Get Ahead," *New York Times*, June 7, 2023, www.nytimes.com/2023/06/07/opinion/resistance-black -advancement-affirmative-action.html.

16. *Students for Fair Admissions v. Harvard*, 600 U.S. at 214–215.

17. *Students for Fair Admissions v. Harvard*, 600 U.S. at 220.

18. *Students for Fair Admissions v. Harvard*, 600 U.S. at 280–282, 284 (Thomas, concurring); at 300, 299 (Gorsuch, concurring); at 317 (Kavanaugh, concurring); at 365 (Sotomayor, dissenting). See also *Fisher v. University of Texas*, 579 U.S. at 426–427 (Alito, dissenting).

19. Richard D. Kahlenberg, "Alito's Furious Dissent in a New Admissions Case Is a Good Sign

for Student Body Diversity," *Slate*, February 22, 2024, https://slate.com/news-and-politics/2024/02/alito-thomas-jefferson-dissent-admissions-scotus.html.

20. Fairfax County Public Schools, "TJHSST Offers Admission to 550 Students," June 23, 2021, www.fcps.edu/news/tjhsst-offers-admission-550-students-broadens-access-students-who-have-aptitude-stem.

21. *Coalition for TJ v. Fairfax County School Board*, 68 F.4th 864 (4th Cir. 2023), www.justice.gov/d9/case-documents/attachments/2023/05/23/coalition_for_tj_v._fairfax_county_sch._bd._no._22-1280_4th_cir._05.23.23.pdf. For further background about the Thomas Jefferson case, see Kahlenberg, "Middle Ground on Race and College."

22. Adam Liptak, "Elite High School's Admissions Plan May Face Supreme Court Test," *New York Times*, May 29, 2023, www.nytimes.com/2023/05/29/us/politics/supreme-court-high-school-admissions.html.

23. Kahlenberg, "Alito's Furious Dissent."

24. Justin McCarthy, "Age Plays Key Role in Black Views of Affirmative Action Case," Gallup, January 16, 2024, https://news.gallup.com/poll/578645/age-plays-key-role-black-views-affirmative-action-case.aspx; Thomas Edsall, "The Liberal Agenda of the 1960s Has Reached a Fork in the Road," *New York Times*, November 15, 2023, www.nytimes.com/2023/11/15/opinion/abortion-dobbs-affirmation-action.html; Adam Liptak and Eli Murray, "The Major Supreme Court Decisions in 2023," *New York Times*, June 29, 2023, www.nytimes.com/interactive/2023/06/07/us/major-supreme-court-cases-2023.html.

25. "Remarks by President Biden on the Supreme Court's Decision on Affirmative Action," White House, June 29, 2023, www.whitehouse.gov/briefing-room/speeches-remarks/2023/06/29/remarks-by-president-biden-on-the-supreme-courts-decision-on-affirmative-action.

26. "Strategies for Increasing Diversity and Opportunity in Higher Education," U.S. Department of Education, September 2023, https://sites.ed.gov/ous/files/2023/09/Diversity-and-Opportunity-in-Higher-Education.pdf.

27. Richard D. Kahlenberg, "What Biden Should Do About Affirmative Action," *Liberal Patriot*, June 6, 2023, www.liberalpatriot.com/p/what-biden-should-do-about-affirmative; Matt Viser, "Biden's Tough Talk on 1970s School Desegregation Plan Could Get New Scrutiny in Today's Democratic Party," *Washington Post*, March 7, 2019, www.washingtonpost.com/politics/bidens-tough-talk-on-1970s-school-desegregation-plan-could-get-new-scrutiny-in-todays-democratic-party/2019/03/07/9115583e-3eb2-11e9-a0d3-1210e58a94cf_story.html (quoting a 1975 comment from Biden: "I don't feel responsible for the sins of my father and grandfather. I feel responsible for what the situation is today, for the sins of my own generation. And I'll be damned if I feel responsible to pay for what happened 300 years ago").

28. Gomez, "As Courts Weigh Affirmative Action."

29. Kahlenberg, "What Biden Should Do About Affirmative Action."

30. David Brooks, "Affirmative Action Is Dead: Campus Diversity Doesn't Have to Be," *New York Times*, June 29, 2023, www.nytimes.com/2023/06/29/opinion/affirmative-action-campus-diversity.html.

31. Marc Novicoff, "Why Won't Elite Colleges Deploy the One Race-Neutral Way to Achieve Diversity?," *Politico*, September 15, 2023, www.politico.com/news/magazine/2023/09/15/supreme-court-admissions-elite-schools-00116087.

32. Kahlenberg, "New Avenues for Diversity After *Students for Fair Admissions*," 320.

33. "Wesleyan University President on Legacy Admissions and Educational Opportunity," *Washington Post*, September 5, 2023, www.washingtonpost.com/washington-post-live/2023/09/05/wesleyan-university-president-legacy-admissions-educational-opportunity.

34. Murphy, "Future of Fair Admissions Issue Brief 4," 10 (Table 2).

35. Lawrence H. Summers, "The Affirmative Action Ruling Is Big: Now Elite Colleges Need to Think Bigger," *Washington Post*, July 1, 2023, www.washingtonpost.com/opinions/2023/07/01/lawrence-summers-affirmative-action-elite-colleges/; Richard D. Kahlenberg, "Larry Summers's

Notes to Chapter 11

Unsatisfying Proposal," *Chronicle of Higher Education*, July 16, 2012; Bari Weiss, "Rethinking Higher Ed with Harvard's Former President," *Free Press*, July 22, 2023, www.thefp.com/p/harvard -president-larry-summers-bari-weiss.

36. Bok, *Attacking the Elites*, 30–37; Richard D. Kahlenberg, "A Harvard Champion of Affirmative Action Accepts Reality," *Washington Monthly*, March 5, 2024, https://washingtonmonthly .com/2024/03/05/a-harvard-champion-of-affirmative-action-accepts-reality.

37. Liam Knox, "The Common App Enters an Uncommon Era," *Inside Higher Ed*, August 2, 2023, www.insidehighered.com/news/admissions/traditional-age/2023/08/02/colleges-change-essay -prompts-after-affirmative-action.

38. White, "College Diversity Actions After Supreme Court."

39. Dean Gerken, "Why Yale Law School Is Leaving the *U.S. News & World Report* Rankings," Yale Law School, November 16, 2022, https://law.yale.edu/yls-today/news/dean-gerken-why-yale -law-school-leaving-us-news-world-report-rankings (citing, among other things, that "the *U.S. News* rankings are profoundly flawed—they disincentivize programs that support public interest careers, champion need-based aid, and welcome working-class students into the profession").

40. Knox, "Common App Enters an Uncommon Era."

41. Korie Dean, "UNC to Offer Free Tuition to NC Students After Supreme Court Ruling," *Raleigh News and Observer*, July 7, 2023, www.newsobserver.com/news/local/education /article277105993.html.

42. Trial transcript, *Students for Fair Admissions v. University of North Carolina*, November 12, 2020, available in U.S. Supreme Court, Joint Appendix, *Students for Fair Admissions v. University of North Carolina*, JA 662, www.supremecourt.gov/DocketPDF/20/20-1199/222330/2022 0502150338804_21-707%20JA%20Vol%202.pdf.

43. Dean, "UNC to Offer Free Tuition" (noting Duke's program).

44. Liam Knox, "Is Financial Aid the New Affirmative Action?," *Inside Higher Ed*, April 22, 2024, www.insidehighered.com/news/admissions/traditional-age/2024/04/22/wealthy-colleges-boost -financial-aid-post-affirmative.

45. Liam Knox, "Colleges Begin to Welcome the Class of 2028," *Inside Higher Ed*, April 3, 2024, www.insidehighered.com/news/admissions/traditional-age/2024/04/03/colleges-release-some -acceptance-rates-and-application (noting, "At some colleges, applications appeared to rise in direct response to affordability initiatives," citing Duke and the University of Minnesota).

46. Jeffrey Selingo, "How Elite Colleges Will Work Around the Supreme Court Ruling," *Wall Street Journal*, July 8, 2023, www.wsj.com/articles/how-elite-colleges-will-still-seek-diversity -despite-the-supreme-courts-rejection-of-affirmative-action-a2c7f340.

47. Liz Mineo, "New Study Finds Wide Gap in SAT/ACT Scores Between Wealthy, Lower-Income Kids," *Harvard Gazette*, November 22, 2023, https://news.harvard.edu/gazette/story /2023/11/new-study-finds-wide-gap-in-sat-act-test-scores-between-wealthy-lower-income-kids (citing David Deming). See also David Leonhardt, "The Misleading SAT Debate," *New York Times*, January 8, 2024, www.nytimes.com/2024/01/08/briefing/sats-standardized-tests-college -admission.html.

48. "Update on Dartmouth's Standardized Testing Policy," Dartmouth College, February 5, 2024, https://admissions.dartmouth.edu/apply/update-testing-policy; "Report from Working Group on the Role of Standardized Test Scores in Undergraduate Admissions," Dartmouth College, January 30, 2024, https://home.dartmouth.edu/sites/home/files/2024-02/sat-undergrad-admissions .pdf; David Leonhardt, "A Top College Reinstates the SAT," *New York Times*, February 5, 2024, www.nytimes.com/2024/02/05/briefing/dartmouth-sat.html; Stephanie Saul, "Yale to Require Standardized Test Scores for Admissions," *New York Times*, February 22, 2024, www.nytimes.com /2024/02/22/us/yale-standardized-testing-sat-act.html; Anemona Hartocollis and Stephanie Saul, "Harvard and Caltech Will Require Test Scores for Admission," *New York Times*, April 11, 2024, www.nytimes.com/2024/04/11/us/harvard-test-scores-admissions.html.

49. Doug Lederman, "Admitting the Top 10%, for Geographic Diversity," *Inside Higher*

Notes to Chapter 11

Ed, August 2, 2023, www.insidehighered.com/news/admissions/traditional-age/2023/08/02/university-south-carolina-admit-top-10-state-residents.

50. Susan H. Greenberg, "University of Tennessee Guarantees Admission to Eligible Students," *Inside Higher Ed*, September 11, 2023, www.insidehighered.com/news/quick-takes/2023/09/11/eligible-students-guaranteed-admission-univ-tennessee.

51. "Governor Hochul Announces Initiatives to Increase Access to Higher Education," Governor Kathy Hochul, January 9, 2024, www.governor.ny.gov/news/governor-hochul-announces-initiatives-increase-access-higher-education; Jessica Blake, "Wisconsin Legislature Approves Guaranteed Admissions Policy," *Inside Higher Ed*, February 15, 2024, www.insidehighered.com/news/quick-takes/2024/02/15/wisconsin-legislature-approves-guaranteed-admissions.

52. Knox, "Political Standoff over Affirmative Action."

53. Nick Anderson, "Not Done with Your College Application? No Problem. You're In," *Washington Post*, November 6, 2023, www.washingtonpost.com/education/2023/11/06/common-app-direct-admissions-colleges.

54. Eric Hoover, "Here's How Yale Is Changing Its Admissions Practices for a New Era," *Chronicle of Higher Education*, September 7, 2023, www.chronicle.com/article/sffa-yale-reach-agreement-to-dismiss-lawsuit.

55. "Weighing the Future of Harvard Admissions," *Harvard Gazette*, October 3, 2023, https://news.harvard.edu/gazette/story/2023/10/weighing-the-future-of-harvard-admissions.

56. "Princeton Sets 70% Financial Aid and 22% Pell Enrollment Goals," Princeton University, March 26, 2024, www.princeton.edu/news/2024/03/26/princeton-sets-70-financial-aid-and-22-pell-enrollment-goals.

57. Eric Hoover, "A Time to Tear Down, a Time to Build Up," *Chronicle of Higher Education*, October 4, 2023, www.chronicle.com/article/a-time-to-tear-down-a-time-to-build-up.

58. Sara Weissman, "Transfers on the Rise: A New Report Shows the Number of Students Transferring Grew Last Fall, Especially Among Disadvantaged Groups, a Tentatively Hopeful Sign to Higher Ed Experts," *Inside Higher Ed*, February 28, 2024, www.insidehighered.com/news/students/academics/2024/02/28/new-report-shows-transfers-rising-among-disadvantaged-groups.

59. Santa Ono, "Univ. of Michigan President on Achieving Diversity Without Affirmative Action," *PBS NewsHour*, June 29, 2023, www.pbs.org/newshour/show/univ-of-michigan-president-on-achieving-diversity-without-affirmative-action.

60. Knox, "Political Standoff over Affirmative Action" (paraphrasing Cardona).

61. Justin Driver, "Think Affirmative Action Is Dead? Think Again," *New York Times*, October 26, 2022, www.nytimes.com/2022/10/26/opinion/supreme-court-case-for-affirmative-action.html.

62. David Card, "Expert Report, *Students for Fair Admissions v. Harvard*," December 15, 2017, 103, https://affirmativeactiondebate.org/wp-content/uploads/2021/06/card-principal-reportredacted.pdf.

63. "Brief of Amherst, et al., Amici Curiae Supporting Respondents, *Students for Fair Admissions v. Harvard*," Amherst College, 13–14, www.amherst.edu/system/files/media/20-1199%2520and%252021-707_Brief%2520of%2520Amici%2520Curiae%2520Amherst%2520et%2520al%2520Colleges%2520and%2520Bucknell%2520et%2520al%2520Universities.pdf; Stephanie Saul, "Ruling May Mean a Sharp Drop in Black and Latino Students," *New York Times*, June 29, 2023, www.nytimes.com/2023/06/29/us/politics/affirmative-action-college-students-black-latino.html.

64. *Students for Fair Admissions v. Harvard* 600 U.S. at 318, 363, 383 (Sotomayor, dissenting).

65. The Class of 2027's Black share was 18 percent, according to a new methodology Harvard adopted in 2024. Because Harvard saw an uptick in the share of students who declined to report their race, school officials calculated racial shares for the Class of 2028 based only on those who did report their race, a departure from past practice. To be consistent, they recalculated the numbers for the Class of 2027. But even accounting for this difference, Harvard managed to create far more diversity than it predicted during the litigation. See Richard D. Kahlenberg, "The Results Are In: Harvard Doesn't Need Racial Preferences to Be Diverse," *Harvard Crimson*,

Notes to Chapter 11

September 12, 2024, https://www.thecrimson.com/article/2024/9/12/kahlenberg-harvard-admissions
-data-success/.

66. Elyse C. Goncalves and Matan H. Josephy, "Harvard Reports Drop in Black Enrollment," *Harvard Crimson*, September 11, 2024, https://www.thecrimson.com/article/2024/9/11/harvard
-black-enrollment-drops/.

67. Kahlenberg, "Expert Report, *Student for Fair Admissions v. University of North Carolina*," Appendix, Table C2, Status Quo and Simulation 1.

68. Susan Svrluga, "Black Enrollment Drops at UNC After Ruling; Other Schools Vary," *Washington Post*, September 5, 2024, https://www.washingtonpost.com/education/2024/09/05
/diverse-college-enrollment-down-post-affirmative-action-ruling/.

69. Richard D. Kahlenberg, "In Harvard's Admissions Decisions, Signs of Progress but Some Data Missing," *Harvard Crimson*, April 2, 2024, www.thecrimson.com/article/2024/4/2
/kahlenberg-harvard-admissions-numbers-progress.

70. The share of first-generation college students was 17 percent among students admitted for the fall of 2017. See Kahlenberg, "Expert Report, *Students for Fair Admissions v. University of North Carolina*," 28. In the Class of 2028, admitted in the fall of 2024, the figure remained at 17 percent. University of North Carolina at Chapel Hill, "Meet Carolina's Newest Class," https://admissions
.unc.edu/explore/our-newest-class/.

71. Kahlenberg, "The Results Are In."

72. Liam Knox, "An Early Look at Diversity Post-Affirmative Action," *Inside Higher Ed*, September 6, 2024, https://www.insidehighered.com/news/admissions/traditional-age/2024/09/06
/early-look-racial-diversity-post-affirmative-action; and Svrluga, "Black Enrollment."

73. James Murphy, "Tracking the Impact of the SFFA Decision on College Admissions," EdReform Now, September 9, 2024; and Melissa Korn, "The Colleges Falling Behind on Black Student Enrollment: A year after a landmark Supreme Court decision, some schools held their share of minority students steady. Others lost ground," *Wall Street Journal*, September 9, 2024 (re: Bates), https://www
.wsj.com/us-news/education/the-colleges-falling-behind-on-black-student-enrollment-f3728f99.

74. Knox, "An Early Look"; Murphy, "Tracking the Impact."

75. Sally Kornbluth, "Undergraduate Admissions Transcript," Massachusetts Institute of Technology, August 21, 2024, https://president.mit.edu/writing-speeches/undergraduate-admissions
-transcript.

76. Anemona Hartocollis, "Yale, Princeton and Duke Are Questioned over Decline in Asian Students," *New York Times*, September 17, 2024, https://www.nytimes.com/2024/09/17/us/yale
-princeton-duke-asian-students-affirmative-action.html.

77. Svrluga, "Black Enrollment."

78. Knox, "An Early Look."

79. Anemona Hartocollis, "Harvard's Black Student Enrollment Dips After Affirmative Action Ends: Defying expectations, a Supreme Court decision curtailing race-based admissions still had a relatively small impact at some highly selective schools like Harvard, even as other schools saw big changes," *New York Times*, September 11, 2024, https://www.nytimes.com/2024/09/11/us/harvard
-affirmative-action-diversity-admissions.html.

80. Dartmouth College, "Dartmouth Undergraduate Class of 2028 Sustains Diversity," https://
home.dartmouth.edu/news/2024/09/class-2028.

81. Svrluga, "Black Enrollment."

82. Eric Hoover, "A Fraught New Era of Scrutinizing Admissions Metrics Has Begun," *Chronicle of Higher Education*, September 17, 2024, https://www.chronicle.com/article/a-fraught-new
-era-of-scrutinizing-admissions-metrics-has-begun.

83. Zachary Schermele, "Public Trust in Higher Ed Has Plummeted: Yes, Again," *Chronicle of Higher Education*, July 11, 2023, www.chronicle.com/article/public-trust-in-higher-ed-has-plum
meted-yes-again (citing Gallup polling).

Notes to Chapter 11

84. Paul Tough, "Saying No to College," *New York Times Magazine*, September 10, 2023, www .nytimes.com/2023/09/05/magazine/college-worth-price.html.

85. Douglas Belkin, "Donors, Alumni Helped Take Down an Ivy League President: Is This a Moment or a Movement?," *Wall Street Journal*, December 17, 2023, www.wsj.com/us-news /education/donors-alumni-helped-take-down-an-ivy-league-president-is-this-a-moment-or-a -movement-a7b98273.

86. Carnevale, interview with author.

87. Nick Anderson, "Will Top Schools Continue 'Legacy' Admission Preferences? Many Say Yes," *Washington Post*, September 29, 2023, www.washingtonpost.com/education/2023/09/29 /colleges-keep-legacy-admissions (citing Dartmouth, Yale, Cornell, Duke, Brown, Vanderbilt, Emory, and the University of Pennsylvania).

88. Phillip Levine and Sarah Reber, "Can Colleges Afford Class-Based Affirmative Action?," Brookings Institution, December 11, 2023, Table 1, www.brookings.edu/articles/can-colleges -afford-class-based-affirmative-action (model providing a two-hundred-point SAT point boost); Aatish Bhatia and Emily Badger, "We Tried to Create a Diverse College Class Without Affirma- tive Action," *New York Times*, March 8, 2024, www.nytimes.com/interactive/2024/03/09/upshot /affirmative-action-alternatives.html (Model 4, conducted by Sean Reardon). See also Alon, *Race, Class, and Affirmative Action*, 254–256 (Figure 11), 268–269 (Table A8.2); and Anthony Carnevale, Zachary Mabel, and Kathryn Peltier Campbell, "Race-Conscious Affirmative Action: What's Next?," Georgetown University Center on Education and the Workforce, March 2023, 12, 59 (Model 3), https://cew.georgetown.edu/wp-content/uploads/cew-race_conscious_affirmative_action-fr.pdf.

89. George F. Will, "Thankful for Soon Being Able to Say 'Good Riddance, 2023,'" *Washing- ton Post*, November 23, 2023, www.washingtonpost.com/opinions/2023/11/22/thanksgiving -relief-year-almost-over; Melissa Korn, Andrea Fuller, and Jennifer S. Forsyth, "Colleges Spend Like There's No Tomorrow: 'These Places Are Just Devouring Money,'" *Wall Street Journal*, August 10, 2023, www.wsj.com/articles/state-university-tuition-increase-spending-41a58100.

90. Paul Tough, "What College Admissions Offices Really Want," *New York Times Magazine*, September 10, 2019, www.nytimes.com/interactive/2019/09/10/magazine/college-admissions -paul-tough.html; Tamara F. Lawson and Heather K. Gerken, "Law Schools Should Abandon Merit- Based Scholarships," *Chronicle of Higher Education*, April 13, 2023, www.chronicle.com/article /law-schools-should-abandon-merit-based-scholarships.

91. Carnevale, interview with author.

92. Jack Feuer, "The Faces of Change," *UCLA Newsroom*, January 1, 2011, https://newsroom .ucla.edu/magazine/african-american-enrollment (describing extensive efforts, including from the philanthropic community, after UCLA's Black representation declined to 2 percent in 2006); Jason Lewis, "UCLA Black Alumni Association Has Greatly Increased the University's African Ameri- can Population," *Los Angeles Standard*, May 20, 2017, https://lastandardnewspaper.com/index.php /education/592-ucla-black-alumni-association-has-greatly-increased-the-university-s-african -american-population.html.

93. Carnevale, interview with author.

94. Scott Jaschik, "Poll: Public Opposes Affirmative Action," *Inside Higher Ed*, July 7, 2016, www .insidehighered.com/news/2016/07/08/poll-finds-public-opposition-considering-race-and -ethnicity-college-admissions (citing Gallup/*Inside Higher Ed* poll that 61 percent of Americans support counting "family economic circumstances," while 63 percent oppose the use of "race or ethnicity").

95. Kahlenberg and Potter, "Better Affirmative Action," 11, 26–61 (which includes state-by-state discussion).

96. Potter, "Transitioning to Race-Neutral Admissions," 78, 82–83, 85; Kahlenberg, "Middle Ground on Race and College."

97. Dannenberg, "Getting Rid of Legacy Preferences."

351

Notes to Chapter 11

98. Katherine Knott, "'The Gloves Have Come Off': Lawmakers Ramp Up Scrutiny of Higher Ed," *Inside Higher Ed*, December 19, 2023, www.insidehighered.com/news/government/politics -elections/2023/12/19/congress-ramps-scrutiny-higher-education; "ASPIRE ACT Summary," *Ed Reform Now*, accessed July 4, 2024, https://edreformnow.org/wp-content/uploads/2020/07/AS PIRE-Summary-Question-and-Answer_final.pdf; Dannenberg, "Getting Rid of Legacy Preferences"; Kahlenberg, "What Biden Should Do About Affirmative Action."

99. "NAACP President Commends U.S. Dept. of Education Investigation into Harvard University Legacy Admissions," NAACP, July 25, 2023, https://naacp.org/articles/naacp-president -commends-us-dept-education-investigation-harvard-university-legacy.

100. Knox, "Legislating to End Legacy Preferences," *Inside Higher Ed*, August 14, 2023, www .insidehighered.com/news/admissions/traditional-age/2023/08/14/breathing-new-life-legacy -admissions-legislation; Teresa Watanabe, "California Effort to Crack Down on Legacy and Donor Admissions Could Hit USC, Stanford," *Los Angeles Times*, February 29, 2024, www .latimes.com/california/story/2024-02-29/california-move-to-crack-down-on-legacy-and -donor-admissions-could-hit-usc-stanford.

101. Colbi Edmonds, "Virginia Bans Legacy Admissions in Public Universities and Colleges," *New York Times*, March 10, 2024, www.nytimes.com/2024/03/10/us/virginia-legacy-admissions -public-colleges-universities.html.

102. Jack Hogan, "Md. House Votes to End Legacy Admissions at Colleges and Universities," *Maryland Daily Record*, February 15, 2024, https://thedailyrecord.com/2024/02/15/md -house-votes-to-end-legacy-admissions-at-colleges-and-universities; Hallie Miller and Olivia Sanchez, "Maryland Becomes the Third State to Completely Ban Legacy Preferences in Admissions," *Hechinger Report*, May 1, 2024, https://hechingerreport.org/maryland-to-become-the -third-state-to-completely-ban-legacy-preference-in-admissions.

103. Liam Knox, "Illinois Becomes Fourth State to Pass Legacy Ban," *Inside Higher Ed*, August 14, 2024, https://www.insidehighered.com/news/quick-takes/2024/08/14/illinois-bans-legacy-pref erences-public-institutions; and Jaweed Kaleem, "California Lawmakers Pass Bill Banning Legacy and Donor College Admissions," *Los Angeles Times*, August 31, 2024, https://www.latimes.com /california/story/2024-08-31/california-moves-to-ban-legacy-and-donor-college-admissions.

104. Rikki Schlott, "Bipartisan Congress Wants to Defund Colleges over Legacy Admissions: It's About Time," *New York Post*, January 11, 2024, https://nypost.com/2024/01/11/news /bipartisan-congress-aims-to-defund-colleges-over-legacy-admissions.

EPILOGUE

1. Lind, "Charity vs. Solidarity."

2. David Leonhardt, "Ron DeSantis and the 'Scaffle' Vote," *New York Times*, May 25, 2023, www.nytimes.com/2023/05/25/briefing/ron-desantis.html; Lee Drutman, "Political Divisions in 2016 and Beyond: Tensions Between and Within the Two Parties," Democracy Fund Voter Study Group, June 2017, www.voterstudygroup.org/publication/political-divisions-in-2016-and-beyond.

3. Matthew Desmond, "Capitalism," in Hannah-Jones et al., *1619 Project*, 166–167.

4. Aaron Zitner, "Voters See American Dream Slipping Out of Reach, WSJ/NORC Poll Shows," *Wall Street Journal*, November 24, 2023, www.wsj.com/us-news/american-dream-out-of -reach-poll-3b774892.

5. Kahlenberg, "Achieving Better Diversity."

6. Julian Mark and Taylor Telford, "Conservatives Are Suing Law Firms over Diversity Efforts: It's Working," *Washington Post*, December 9, 2023, www.washingtonpost.com/business /2023/12/09/conservatives-sue-law-firms-dei.

7. Julian Mark and Taylor Telford, "Federal Judge Orders Minority Business Agency Opened to All Races," *Washington Post*, March 6, 2024, www.washingtonpost.com/business/2024/03/06 /minority-business-programs-racial-disadvantage-unconstitutional.

Notes to Epilogue

8. Matthew Watkins, "Texas Senators Mull Eliminating Top 10 Percent Rule," *Texas Tribune*, April 5, 2017, www.texastribune.org/2017/04/05/texas-senators-mull-eliminating-top-10-percent -rule.

9. Richard D. Kahlenberg, "Building a Multiracial, Cross-Party Populist Coalition for Zoning Reform: What New York Can Learn from California." Century Foundation, November 15, 2023, https://tcf.org/content/report/building-a-multiracial-cross-party-populist-coalition-for-zoning -reform-what-new-york-can-learn-from-california (describing political coalitions in California, Oregon, Massachusetts, and Texas).

10. Chetty et al., "Mobility Report Cards."

11. Kahlenberg, "How to Fix College Admissions Now."

Index

Index

Index

Index

Index

Index

Index

Index

Index

Index

Index

Index

Index

Index

Richard D. Kahlenberg is director of the American Identity Project at the Progressive Policy Institute and teaches at George Washington University. Known as "the nation's chief proponent of class-based affirmative action in higher education admissions," his work has been published in the *New York Times, Washington Post, Wall Street Journal, New Republic,* and *The Atlantic.* He is the author or editor of eighteen other books, most recently *Excluded: How Snob Zoning, NIMBYism, and Class Bias Build the Walls We Don't See.* He lives in Rockville, Maryland.

PublicAffairs is a publishing house founded in 1997. It is a tribute to the standards, values, and flair of three persons who have served as mentors to countless reporters, writers, editors, and book people of all kinds, including me.

I. F. Stone, proprietor of *I. F. Stone's Weekly*, combined a commitment to the First Amendment with entrepreneurial zeal and reporting skill and became one of the great independent journalists in American history. At the age of eighty, Izzy published *The Trial of Socrates*, which was a national bestseller. He wrote the book after he taught himself ancient Greek.

Benjamin C. Bradlee was for nearly thirty years the charismatic editorial leader of *The Washington Post*. It was Ben who gave the *Post* the range and courage to pursue such historic issues as Watergate. He supported his reporters with a tenacity that made them fearless and it is no accident that so many became authors of influential, best-selling books.

Robert L. Bernstein, the chief executive of Random House for more than a quarter century, guided one of the nation's premier publishing houses. Bob was personally responsible for many books of political dissent and argument that challenged tyranny around the globe. He is also the founder and longtime chair of Human Rights Watch, one of the most respected human rights organizations in the world.

·   ·   ·

For fifty years, the banner of Public Affairs Press was carried by its owner Morris B. Schnapper, who published Gandhi, Nasser, Toynbee, Truman, and about 1,500 other authors. In 1983, Schnapper was described by *The Washington Post* as "a redoubtable gadfly." His legacy will endure in the books to come.

Peter Osnos, *Founder*